FAMILIES
UNDER STRESS

Adjustment to the Crises of
War Separation and Reunion

FAMILIES UNDER STRESS

Adjustment to the Crises of War Separation and Reunion

By

REUBEN HILL

Professor of Sociology and Research Professor in
Family Life in The Institute for Research in the Social Sciences
University of North Carolina

WITH CHAPTERS IN COLLABORATION WITH
ELISE BOULDING

Assisted by
LOWELL DUNIGAN AND
RACHEL ANN ELDER

GREENWOOD PRESS, PUBLISHERS
WESTPORT, CONNECTICUT

Reprinted in 1971 by Greenwood Press, Inc.,
51 Riverside Avenue, Westport, Conn. 06880

Library of Congress catalog card number 73-90529
ISBN 0-8371-3108-1

Printed in the United States of America

10 9 8 7 6 5 4 3 2

CONTENTS

v

CONTENTS

APPENDIX A: SELECTED BIBLIOGRAPHY   365

APPENDIX B: METHODOLOGICAL NOTE   368

APPENDIX C: SCHEDULE FORMS USED IN THIS STUDY   399

   I. *Family Adjustments in Wartime (Wife)*   399

   II. *Family Adjustments in Wartime (Husband)*   409

   III. *Adjustments to Reunion (Wife)*   413

   IV. *Adjustments to Reunion (Husband)*   414

   V. *Family Adjustments in Wartime (Interviewer)*   416

INDEX   435

PREFACE

MAN'S scientific quest began, curiously enough, with an interest in the stars of the heavens, objects farthest removed from himself. Astrology had become astronomy long before man began studying himself. Family study, it must be recorded, developed in the late evening of mankind's development. No more personal quest has yet been attempted.

Family study has followed the pattern of science in general. Students first focused on ancient family life or on far away exotic families. They were concerned with family origins and with the evolution of family forms. Even relatively recent histories of domestic institutions close with scant reference to the present American family. Only in the last twenty years have students found rewarding the analysis of contemporary family living.

It is perhaps no accident that the way has been opened to study the contemporary family during a period of transition in family life. Individual families, feeling the pangs of inadequacy in the face of changing tides and times, have been more willing to coöperate with students who promise solutions, if allowed to share the family secrets. The sanctity of the home is shared increasingly with the census enumerator, the social worker, the Gallup-poll interviewer, and the family research worker. If it were not for this willingness of most families to coöperate, family studies could not yet be made.

One aspect of the changing family scene is the loss of many once meaningful duties and functions connected with *making* a living. Working together in the fields, fighting shoulder to shoulder for survival, family members were bound together in a web of economic and social interdependence unknown to present-day families who *buy* their living on the market and tend to maximize the independence of each member from every other family member.

vii

Since the historic patterns of family living and child rearing, derived from an agrarian way of life now largely passed, are no longer
adequate or even tolerable for families today, every family is, to a
greater or less extent, harassed, anxious or guilt-burdened, beset
with perplexities, and periodically buffeted by crises. The old order
changes but the new order is not yet established, and the family is
caught betwixt and between.

The modern family lives in a greater state of tension precisely
because it is the great burden carrier of the social order. In a society
of rapid social change, problems outnumber solutions, and the
resulting uncertainties are absorbed by the members of society, who
are for the most part also members of families. Because the family
is the bottleneck through which all troubles pass, no other association so reflects the strains and stresses of life. With few exceptions
persons in work-a-day America return to rehearse their daily frustrations within the family, and hope to get the necessary understanding and resilience to return the morrow to the fray.

Thus, the good family today is not only the focal point of frustrations and tensions but also the source for resolving frustrations and
releasing tensions. A good family has become one in which a person
can be his worst without risking permanent ostracism. No longer effective as a producer of domestic goods the modern family elaborates
other functions concerned more intimately with the production and
preservation of personality. Through its capacity for sympathy, understanding, and unlimited loyal support, the family rehabilitates
personalities bruised in the course of competitive daily living. In that
capacity the family is literally love in action.

To understand the processes of stress which test and try families,
studies have been launched which chronicle the reactions of families
to sudden impoverishment, to bereavement, to desertion, to infidelity, to wartime separation and reunion, and to the daily exigencies of living. They underline the fundamental family task of
maintaining the mental health of the population. As stated by
Lawrence K. Frank for the first National Conference on Family

Life to be held in the White House, "Only the family can guard the emerging personality and protect the mental health of individuals through the quality of its interpersonal relationships, the provision of reassurance and comforting, the releases and encouragement each needs to keep on striving for orderly living and fulfillment of his or her aspirations."

For too long the family has been called upon to take up the slack in a poorly integrated social order. If fiscal policies are bungled producing inflation, the family purse strings are tightened; if depressions bring sudden impoverishment, family savings and the family's capacity to restrict consumption to subsistence levels are drawn upon; if real estate and building interests fail to provide housing, families must adapt themselves to filtered down, obsolete dwellings or double up into shoehorned quarters with other families. For too long the family has been ignored in social planning, and the strains are telling. Family disorganization reflected in the four D's of divorce—disease, desertion, dependency, and delinquency —have aroused a lethargic public to the discussion and talking stages. A national policy for family life is being called for.

But research in the family is needed first to provide the premises of fact upon which any national and state policies must be built. Challenging questions face us. Under what conditions do families best perform their vital personality-building functions? What kinds of families find even the daily exigencies precipitating factors for trouble? What varieties of families thrive in the face of crises and trouble? How are stable families produced which absorb the blows of social change without breaking under strain? What are the histories of families which combine integration around unique family values and loyalty to those values with adaptability in the face of crises and high mobility?

Answers to these questions require both exploratory and definitive studies. *Families Under Stress* is one of a series of such explorations currently under way.

In closing this preface we wish to acknowledge the helpful as-

sistance we have received from hundreds of family minded people
unnamed in this report. The generous legwork and counsel supplied by the many field workers and child welfare workers of the
Iowa Department of Social Welfare in locating the families for
study, the services of the Iowa Selective Service in drawing the
sample, and the stimulating consultation with the staff of the National Council on Family Relations are remembered with deep
gratitude. Our own families—the Bouldings, the Dunigans, the
Elders, and the Hills—deserve high tribute for having repeatedly
postponed family satisfactions in order that the research continue.
For critical suggestions on research strategy, for technical statistical
services, and for administrative support the project is especially
indebted to Dean Harold V. Gaskill, Dr. W. G. Murray, and Dr.
Ray E. Wakely of the Iowa State Industrial Science Research
Institute and Professors Paul Homeyer and Leonid Hurwicz of the
Iowa State Statistical Laboratory. Beyond these stellar supports we
owe much to our fellow sociologists and family researchers who
generously read the completed manuscript under pressure of a
punishing deadline and aided immeasurably in the task of checking
for errors of analysis, logic, and readability: Dr. Ernest W. Burgess,
Dr. Ruth S. Cavan, Dr. F. Stuart Chapin, Dr. Evelyn Duvall, Dr.
Sylvanus Duvall, Dr. Neal Gross, and Dr. Earl Koos. Finally we
wish to express gratitude to the hundreds of Iowa families who
willingly shared the sanctity of their homes and pooled their experiences in wartime that all families might know how family
collectivities react under stress. We have done what we could to
keep faith with these families by so designing our research that our
findings would have meaning for all families facing trouble. In
the chapters which follow we hope our interpretations will give
added insight and understanding concerning the urgent task of
producing the kinds of dynamically unified families that can thrive
in an unstable world.
August, 1949

R. H., E. B., L. D., and R. A. E.

PART ONE

~~~~~~

Sharing the Sanctity of the Home

CHAPTER I

THE FAMILY AS A CLOSED SYSTEM

"THE latch is out" heralds a standing invitation to drop by and visit. When the latch is in any man entering is an interloper and liable to criminal action. The sanctity of the home is buttressed by law as well as by custom. A man's home is his castle, not to be violated without a legal warrant. Drawn shades, locked doors, fences, and walled-in courts remind the observer that the family is a closed system.

Family customs, rituals, and routines regulate much of the behavior of family members. Family skeletons, family secrets, and taboos operate to produce the unique sources of tension and insecurity which negatively motivate family members. Family meals and celebrations, reunions and wakes, all bespeak the structure and processes of life *within* the family milieu. When family status is threatened from outside, there is a rallying of forces to meet the challenge, bringing sometimes a realignment of roles, but oftener reinforcing the original pattern. The phrase, "closing of ranks," epitomizes the family as a closed system, facing dismemberment through death or separation or imprisonment, but always preserving its contours to the world. It is this shell of exclusion which the student of the family must pierce to get his data. Manifestly, he has not gained admittance to the family by his physical entrance into the dwelling. The family as a closed system admits him only when it shares the sanctity of its home with the investigator.

The early students of the family faced no such baffling problems. Their macroscopic sweep carried them far afield from actual flesh-and-blood families into the universals and timelessness of family life

3

in all countries and in all times. As Burgess, Eliot, Waller, Folsom, and Angell, to mention only a few, turned the interest of family sociologists microscopically on the family as a unity of interacting personalities, these problems arose. It is as if the first bacteriologist examining his specimens under the microscope had found them all blushing at him. If in turn the bacteriologist had blushed and turned away, we would have the phenomenon of the neophite family researcher interviewing his first family. Both interviewer and interviewee reflect the taboos against violating the sanctity of the home. Said one interviewer after several interviews, "If anyone were to come to my home and ask me those questions, I would order him from the place." The notion of the inviolability of the family has been so much a part of our family mores that research workers must be specifically trained and prepared for the task, as the artist is trained to view the nude body without guilt feelings, or the medical student is trained to observe the unclad form as a collection of systems of respiration, circulation, digestion, etc. Given a trained interviewer convinced of the value of the research, the same detachment is possible in family study.

Like the first medical workers who were forced to steal cadavers from the town cemeteries in the middle of the night, the students of the family have run risks of social and legal sanctions in carrying out their work. Their task has become that of persuading families to *share* the sanctity of their home for scientific purposes. It is not one of breaking down the family as a closed system, but one of using the closed nature of the family to advantage.

ADVANTAGES OF THE CLOSED SYSTEM

Because each family is a closed system, the data collected will be more likely to have integrity and reliability than data collected from more adventitious and porous associations. Consider the relative integrity, for example, of the data collected by interview from the inhabitants of a college boarding house with its touch-and-go relationships and its amorphous lack of structure with the data obtained from a well-integrated, closed family. The shell of exclusion protects and maintains the integrity and ordered nature of the data on family living.[1] Once admitted by the family as a confident, the interviewer can have considerable confidence in his informants. Once in, the interviewer is more likely to find ordered data, structural bases for understanding and prediction than in non-family associations he might study. In a sense each family is a universe of data in itself, and for that reason many of the early studies dealt intensively with very few cases and their results have had widespread application.[2] They have studied each family as a separate system of interaction, *explaining family events by family events.* Because relations within the group are closer, deeper, more inclusive of the whole person, and more persistent than the relations of members with non-members, the family often behaves as if it were an organism. Burgess once said that he "was about to call it a super-personality." It was precisely the discovery of this phenomenon of the family as a partially closed causal system which has driven sociologists to focus on the intra-family action patterns in present-day research.

INFORMATION NEEDED ABOUT INTRA-FAMILY LIVING

A pragmatic objective of family research for these latter-day workers has become *to release resources of the family to design its own pattern of living and to solve its own inter-personal problems.* To attain that objective much more information is needed about the

---

[1] We hasten to point out that some unintegrated families are as porous as the boarding-house example cited. See pp. 190–193 for a discussion of the families of low integration and low adaptability.

[2] Angell's pioneer study which recognized the family as a closed system focused on the histories of fifty families before and during the depression (*1*), Komarovsky pursued the elusive question of what happens to family authority in the face of unemployment of the father in fifty-eight families (*25*); Koos studied sixty-two low-income families for three years as they faced 109 successive troubles (*27*), and has recently followed forty-eight middle-class families through a similar series of troubles (*28*). Waller's pioneer study of divorce and readjustment was based on thirty-eight families (*33*). In comparison the present study of war separation and reunion with its 135 families bulks large and its original goal of 822 families appears huge.

effects of family members upon one another and the relative effectiveness of the roles they play. The dynamics of family interaction are more subtle than the breaking of crockery in a conflict-ridden family would indicate. The family life cycle itself is generated by a number of interacting processes which we can separately name and discuss but cannot dissociate in actual living. We are desperately in need of knowledge about the patterns and media of communication which may be the key to problem solving and democratic decision making. Our realization that the family is designed for intimacy brings with it recognition of its reciprocal, the smothering sense of confinement. The latent counterpart of deep affection is known to be disgust and alienation. Recent evidence that two generations within the same house get along better through a pattern of mutual avoidance[3] underlines the possibility that family members may harbor resentment as well as gratitude as they contemplate what it means to belong to a family. The discovery that unsolved conflicts become tensions challenges us to a study of family tensions. We need much more knowledge about the sources of family tensions which, like the equivalent unpleasant feeling states of the individual, put the damper on activity and self fulfillment.

Obviously, no study can fulfill all the above requirements, particularly within the limitations of skill, understanding, and funds imposed by current levels of training and size of research budgets. The present study of families under stress is in line with some of the above needs. *Families Under Stress* had its inception shortly after selective service had begun to call bonafide fathers of children born prior to Pearl Harbor into military service. For almost two years the policy of selective service had been to defer family men with dependents. Although families had dreaded and anticipated the day when the policy would be changed, it was still a shock to many when fathers were called into service.

[3] See the report by David Goldman for New York families in 1947, *New York Times*, October 6, 1947, p. 23.

If there is any ingenuity in the design of this study, it is that we have identified an external threat common to every family as a basis for comparing reactions. The threat was carried out and the crisis of dismemberment or separation was forced on each family. The study has something in common with the stimulus-response type of experiment in the laboratory, although it is manifestly much more complex. The adjustment to the amputation of the father from the family constituted an index of all the adjustments the family had made before and the readjustment at reunion time constituted another measurement of the family's capacity to meet a crisis. It was hoped that careful analysis of the histories of the 135 families in the study would reveal some of the answers to the questions posed in the Preface. Phrased as objectives, the hopes of *Families Under Stress* have been:

1. To sample family adjustment in general by the study of adjustment to two crises: war separation and reunion.
2. To test the findings of other studies of the family in crisis in a new context.
3. To record the variety of modes of adjustment to a heretofore unstudied set of family crises.
4. To discover the types of family organization and processes of adjustment which make families most invulnerable/vulnerable to separation/reunion crises.

The focus of the study is necessarily internal. Residual categories that receive scant attention are extra-family influences, such as, inter-family operations, social forces of urbanization, secularization, and war itself. It would be highly improper to characterize *Families Under Stress* as a study of the effects of war on family life. More precisely it is a search for the characteristics and processes which set off successful from unsuccessful families in the face of two war-born crises. An analysis of what is meant by crisis and its role in American family life is meat for the next chapter.

THE SOCIOLOGY OF FAMILY CRISES
AND FAMILY ADJUSTMENT

IF it were not for the closed nature of the family the stereotyped question, "Hya, Joe, how's the family?" would bring a recital of troubles and woes. Of course, no one really means how's the family? They are just saying hello or, at most, are asking if the baby has recovered from "pink eye." Actually, it is neither good taste to ask, nor to talk as yet, about how the family is really getting along, important though that may be to human understanding. The family sociologist renders a real service in studying the incidence and causes of these ubiquitous but little discussed evidences of family distemper.

Robert S. Lynd writing in the preface to Koos' classic monograph, *Families in Trouble* (27), introduces us to the American family in this wise, "The reverse of the American dream is woven of trouble . . . the vulnerable underside of our vaunted individualism and opportunity, of our lack of social structure that heaps people together in cities and leaves them seeking vitality in massed rows of human anonymity at the movies."

Problems, troubles, worries, and insecurities beset American families from wedding day to dissolution day. "I don't remember when I didn't have to worry," commented one family head in the Koos study. A revealing comic strip caricatures the typical family head as a "worry-wart."

Family crises, however, involve more than the unraveling of life through worry; they refer to the bigger jolts which not even worry anticipated. The daily exigencies of life are challenging, but they do

8

not become crises unless they pyramid without warning. "Death and taxes" we always have with us, but if death, taxes, unemployment, and infidelity hit at once, most families are stricken with panic. In fact, crises have been defined in terms of their effects upon families, as "those situations which create a sense of sharpened insecurity or which block the usual patterns of action and call for new ones."

Crises strain the resources which families possess, exhaust the repertoire of ready-made answers the family may have built up, and force family members to shape answers out of whole cloth. To some families impoverishment isn't a crisis because they have been there before and know what to do; moreover, they don't interpret it as a crisis.

At least three variables are at work to determine whether a given event becomes a crisis for any given family: (1) the hardships of the situation or event itself, (2) the resources of the family, its role structure, flexibility, and previous history with crisis, and (3) the definition the family makes of the event; that is, whether family members treat the event *as if it were* or *as if it were not* a threat to their status, their goals, and objectives.

TYPES OF FAMILY CRISES

A classification of family crises may help to sort out the particular crises to be studied in *Families Under Stress* from others already studied or still to be investigated.

First, crises differ in their sources—some are extra-family and some are intra-family in origin. Crises which arise as a result of depression or of war, both of which are beyond the family's control, present different problems from the crises arising out of the inter-personal relations within the family. The loss of life's savings due to bank failure during a depression will induce a crisis for most families. But consider the crises created by the loss of life's savings through the improvidence of the father or some other member of the family, which had in turn been precipitated by a serious rift in the affectional relations within the family. It isn't the loss of life's savings in this instance but the inter-personal relations which constitute the matrix of trouble.

Another type of classification involves the combination of dismemberment (loss of family member) or accession (addition of unprepared for member) and demoralization (loss of morale and family unity):

A Classification of Family Breakdowns[1]

Dismemberment Only	Accession Only	Demoralization Only	Demoralization plus Dismemberment or Accession
Loss of child	Unwanted pregnancy	Non-support	Illegitimacy
Widowhood	Deserter returns	Progressive	Runaway situations
Orphanhood	Stepmother, step-	dissension	Desertion
Hospitalization	father additions	Infidelity	Divorce
War separation	Some war reunions		Imprisonment
			Suicide or homicide

Most crises sooner or later come to involve de-*morale*-ization since the family's role patterns are always sharply disturbed. Dismemberment creates a situation where the amputated one's roles must be reallocated, and a period of confusion and uncertainty ensues while the members of the family cast learn their new lines. Adding a member later, such as is involved in the remarriage of a widower or widow, although not yet studied, undoubtedly strains the resources of a family which "closed ranks" too well.

Ernest W. Burgess has recently (7) classified family crises which threaten to disrupt the family into a threefold set of categories: (1) change in status, (2) conflict among its members in the conception of their roles, and (3) loss of family members by departure, by desertion, by divorce, or by death.

A sudden upturn in economic and social status may constitute a crisis quite as disruptive as that of economic loss or social disgrace. The price of the American dream of upward mobility may be family

---

[1] Adapted and amplified from the work of T. D. Eliot (20).

disorganization and breakdown. Too little is known of the conditions under which the family survives or goes to pieces when there is a rapid change from poverty to riches or from obscurity to fame (7).

Many of the difficulties which build into crises involve the different conception of their roles by family members. Conflicts between parents and children should be understood and studied in terms of differences in conceptions of roles. Koos (28) finds the adolescent-parent relationships to be a focal point of crisis situations in the middle-class family. In upward-mobile families, the proper roles for wife and mother shift from one socioeconomic group to another, and the husband may wish for a hostess to replace his work-a-day *Hausfrau* whose roles fitted so well in their early married years.

Burgess' third variety of crisis situation is identical with the classification identified earlier, namely, dismemberment; this involves threat to the family organization, that is, to its form and structure. The average urban conjugal family cut off from kin has no reserve team of father or mother substitutes to call upon when a member is hurt or rendered ineligible to function. The game has to be played with a revised constellation, and involves an entirely new set of signals and positions.

Using the classifications we have just described, the crises of war separation and subsequent reunion of this study are: (1) extra-family in origin rather than intra-family, (2) crises of dismemberment with a minimum of demoralization (reunion consisting of the reciprocal of dismemberment), and (3) crises involving change in status, conflict of its members in the conception of their roles, and loss of family members. A more detailed account of these two crisis situations is given in Chapter IV.

CRISIS AND ADJUSTMENT

Thinking at the family level is third dimensional in a sense, and we have only recently attempted it. The first dimension involves the individual, the crisis situation, and the individual's adjustment to that situation. The second dimension involves the pair (it may be an engaged pair, a married pair, a business partnership, or just roommates), a crisis situation involving the pair, and the pair's adjustment to that situation. The third dimension involves the larger grouping of the family made up of parents, children, and any kin living within the closed system of the family unit; it involves a crisis situation defined by the family as a crisis; and it involves the family's adjustment to that situation *as a family!* Holding all the participants in focus as a unit is no mean task. Finding the vocabulary to describe their activities is hard. Communicating the results to readers unacquainted with third dimensional thinking is even more difficult.

An illustration of the problem of vocabulary is seen as we attempt to transpose terms appropriate for describing individual adjustment of the first dimension into appropriate third dimensional family terms. Jonathan Daniels, an insightful author who wrote a feature article on this research for *McCall's Magazine* (*12*) was thinking in first dimensional terms when he said the successful families in the study were characterized by the two qualities of *character* and *intelligence*. Now, these two omnibus terms imply presence or absence of *personal* attributes or traits, but they do have precise equivalents in *family* life. The family equivalent of character for the individual is probably our term *integrity,* seen in the coherent unity and sense of economic and emotional interdependence of some families. The family equivalents of intelligence in the individual are probably our terms *adaptability* and *flexibility*. As Angell pointed out in his study of families facing a sharp decrease in income (*1*): "Adaptability is another complex consideration. We are concerned here, not with the adaptability of the family members as individuals, but with the adaptability of the unit in meeting obstacles in *its* way. It is possible for the individuals to be quite rational and open-minded in making their own private decisions, but for the family as a whole to be sluggish in adjusting to economic changes, because of a lack of any established habits of collective discussion and decision."

At the family level individual traits become patterns, personality organization becomes family resources to solve problems, varieties of family organization, and so on. Where the laity inquires about a person's physical, mental, and emotional health, the family expert inquires about the health of the *intra-family relationships*. Speaking familywise, we might test the hypothesis that to keep the relationships healthy there must be frank and above-board discussion of issues, accommodation, consensus, sometimes avoidance, and a minimum subordination of the self for the family good seen in respect for the rights and recognition of the needs of other members.

Koos has described well the process of adjustment to crisis in family terms in a recent report for the National Conference on Family Life (26):

> Since the family consists of a number of members interacting with each other, it follows that there must be socially prescribed parts (roles) each member plays in the family's life. The individual functions as a member of the family largely in terms of the expectations other members place upon him; the family succeeds, as a family, pretty much in terms of the adequate role performance of its members.
>
> One major effect of crises is to cause changes in these role patterns. As the role performances change—as the individuals concerned do not live up to the expectations of the other members of the family (or in some cases surpass these expectations), the usual patterns of action are distorted or abolished, and the family finds it necessary to work out new patterns.
>
> Another major effect is to impede or facilitate the functioning of the family in its affectional and emotion-satisfying performances.

THE COURSE OF ADJUSTMENT

The course of family adjustment in the face of crisis varies from family to family and from crisis to crisis but the common denominator may be charted in the truncated form of a roller coaster. Upon meeting a crisis the family members are numbed collectively by the blow. They may meet friends at first as if the blow hadn't happened. Then as the facts are assimilated there follows a downward slump in organization, roles are played with less enthusiasm, resentments are smothered or expressed, conflicts are expressed or converted into tensions which make for strained relations, and as the nadir of disorganization is reached things begin improving, new routines arrived at by trial and error or by thoughtful planning and sacrificing are put into effect, and some minimum agreements about the future are reached. The component parts to the roller-coaster profile of adjustment to crisis are: crisis → disorganization → recovery → reorganization.

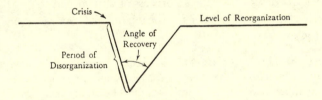

Refinements of this basic pattern are to be found in Koos' Families in Trouble (27) and in Chapter IV.

EFFECTS OF CRISIS ON THE FAMILY

An analysis of what happens as the family breaks old habits and organizes new routines during the downhill and uphill part of the roller-coaster figure above, shows some interesting changes in family organization. The frequency and pattern of sexual relations change, ceasing altogether for some couples (25). In crises involving interpersonal recriminations, where the crisis is regarded as the fault of any one member, the position of that member is greatly devaluated (27). Personality changes in members reflect the anxiety and feelings of insecurity engendered by the crisis, and in a sense each responsible member experiences a roller-coaster pattern of personal shock, disorganization, recovery, readjustment. Particularly is this evident in bereavement, where the adjustments of family members follow a course of disbelief → numbness → mourning → trial-and-error adjustments → renewal of routines → recovery (*19, 21*).

Changes in parent-child relations are frequently reported in adjustment to crisis. In well-integrated families Angell (*1*) found few changes in relative position of parents and children as a result of the crisis of impoverishment, but did find changes in less well-integrated families, particularly in the more adaptable families. In the Komarovsky and in the Koos study younger children shifted position rarely (*25, 27*), but the parent-adolescent relationship in crisis "was a highly volatile one and subject to great displacement."

Inter-family activities vary as a result of crisis (*1, 27*). Some families withdraw from all activities until the "shame" is over, become more than ever closed systems. Others become quite unbuttoned in their open-door policy during the troubled period.

The evidence concerning the long-time effects of crisis on families is conflicting. If they were well organized before the crisis of impoverishment, Cavan (*11*) found that her families tended to remain well organized; moreover, it seemed that previous successful experiences with crisis was predictive of recovery in a new crisis. Angell (*1*) found well-integrated, adaptable families invulnerable to crisis; that is, they took it in stride without marked changes in their organization or role structure. Koos, focusing on poor families defeated by crisis, found evidence of permanent demoralization, a blunting of the family's sensitivity, and a tendency to be more vulnerable in future exposures. "Once having been defeated by a crisis, the family appears not to be able to marshall its forces sufficiently to face the next event; there is, in other words, a permanent defeat each time (*26*)."

If the conflicting evidences were to be reconciled, the synthesis would follow these lines: Successful experience with crisis tests and strengthens a family, but defeat in crisis is punitive on family structure and morale.[2] These findings have provocative implications for a national policy for family life.

FINDINGS PERTINENT TO THE CRISES OF WAR SEPARATION AND REUNION

In closing this chapter on the sociology of family crises and family adjustment, we propose to examine the research literature further for those special findings which are pertinent to the specific crises of war separation and reunion under study. From these findings hypotheses will be formulated which can be tested in the new context of separation and reunion situations. In closing we will present additional hypotheses which grow out of an exploratory analysis of the unique aspects of the separation and reunion situations which were not taken into account in studies of other crises.

The literature on dismemberment is scanty as far as reference to family adjustment *as families* is concerned. Most of our hypotheses will, therefore, be drawn from the studies of marriage adjustment and of the crises of demoralization and changes of status. The findings from these studies fall into three general categories: (1) those referring to the attributes of personal, marital, and family organization and role structure which are most frequently associated with success in facing crises; (2) those referring to the processes of adjustment which are most frequently associated with recovery from crisis; and (3) references to the short and long-term effects of crisis on the families studied.

From the two classic studies of marriage adjustment (*8, 32*), several findings may be pertinent to family adjustment in the face of war-born separation and subsequent reunion. Certainly a good marital adjustment between man and wife is the foundation of family adjustment. A first hypothesis would be then, "Good marital adjust-

---

[2] For a more detailed discussion of these materials in which it is shown that family disorganization mediates reorganization quite as frequently as it mediates dissolution, see Reuben Hill, "The American Family: Problem or Solution," *The American Journal of Sociology* (September, 1947), pp. 125–130.

ment is predictive of good adjustment to separation." Similarly, "Good marital adjustment is predictive of good adjustment to reunion." Other findings related to marital adjustment which were deemed pertinent to this study were:

1. History of happiness in childhood of spouses
2. Readiness for marriage at marriage
   a. length of acquaintance before marriage
   b. years of school completed by spouses
   c. age at marriage of spouses
3. Attachment to parents and in-laws
4. Personality adequacy of spouses
5. Satisfaction with the marriage, prized equally by both
6. Settling issues by mutual give and take
7. Children desired in the marriage
8. Marriage is in-faith, not inter-faith or non-faith

From the studies of families in the depression—Koos' study (27) of troubles in low-income families was published too late to incorporate his findings into our schedules—several findings and concepts proved worthy of test in the context of war separation and reunion. It is assumed for purposes of testing that factors characteristic of families which survived depression-born crises would prove predictive of success in war-born crises of separation and reunion. Of the studies, Angell's (1), Cavan's (11), and Komarovsky's (25) were especially productive of findings; those incorporated and tested were:

1. Previous success in meeting family crises
2. Non-materialistic goals predominate
3. Flexibility and willingness to shift traditional roles of husband and wife or of father and mother, if necessary
4. Acceptance of responsibility by all family members in performing family duties

5. Willingness to sacrifice personal interest to attain family objectives
6. Pride in the family tree and in the ancestral traditions
7. Presence of strong patterns of emotional interdependence and unity
8. High participation as a family in joint activities
9. Presence of equalitarian patterns of family control and decision making
10. Strong affectional ties between father-mother, father-children, mother-children, and children-children

These ten items incorporate most of the points involved in *family adequacy* stressed by Koos (27) and by Cavan (*11*). The twin concepts used by Angell (*1*) *family integration* and *family adaptability* are also represented in these findings. By the former Angell meant "the bonds of coherence and unity running through family life, of which common interests, affection and a sense of economic interdependence are perhaps the most prominent." Adaptability, on the other hand, referred to the family's flexibility as a unit in meeting obstacles and difficulties, to the family's readiness to adjust to changed situations, and to its habits of collective discussion and control. In the findings above, family integration would refer to items 5, 6, 7, 8, and 10. Family adaptability would refer to items 1, 2, 3, 4, and 9. A scale, worked out by Ruth Cavan as a basis for rating families on adaptability and integration and adapted by us for this study, enables us to test with some precision the association between family adjustment to separation and to reunion with the resources of family adaptability and integration.

GOING BEYOND THE PREVIOUS STUDIES

In addition to the hypotheses suggested by the findings of previous studies, we explored several hunches we thought might explain good and poor adjustment to separation and reunion.

1. Successful carrying over of personal roles from pare[nt] into marriage
2. Marriage based on companionship and common interests
3. Financial security based on adequate income and savings at induction
4. Middle- and upper-middle-class social status, based on area of community lived in, quality of housing, source of income, and occupational status
5. Number of children at induction, whether wanted, loved, rejected
6. Years married
7. Years of experience as parents
8. Residential mobility before induction
9. Balance of power and social roles of husband and wife
   a. Dominance of marriage
   b. Handling of family purse
   c. Handling of issues and differences
10. Hardships of separation period
    a. Living arrangements
    b. Employment of wife outside the home
    c. Decrease in income after induction
    d. Indebtedness during separation period
    e. Difficulties in disciplining and controlling children
    f. Loneliness of wife
11. Experiences during separation
    a. Social participation of wife outside home
    b. Outlets for affectional needs
    c. Understanding concerning relationships with opposite sex during separation
12. Modes of communication during period of separation
    a. Number of letters exchanged
    b. Content of letters, adequacy of communication
    c. Number of and activities during furloughs and visits to camp

13. Hardships of reunion
    a. Length of time separated
    b. Irritations reported by father in home situation at return
    c. Lack of preparation of wife and children for return of father
    d. Failure of wife to resume traditional wife-mother roles
14. Effects of military service
    a. Rank in service
    b. Combat experience
    c. Reason for discharge
    d. Illusions of home and family built during service

These fourteen general areas of investigation revolve about the attributes of marriage and family organization, the nature of the situations facing the family at induction, the specific hardships of the separation and reunion periods, the contingency factors of family life while separated, and the somewhat peripheral effects of military service. These may all be tested for association with the family's adjustment to separation and to reunion scores to ascertain what combination of family resources and social situations predict best adjustment in the face of crisis.

An independent analysis of the data using the case study method of analysis will plumb the ups and downs of the adjustment process itself. See Chapter IV and Chapter VII for details.

Summary

Using the present study of family adjustment to the crises of war-born separation and reunion as our focus, these generalizations may be made from our review of previous studies of family crises and adjustment.

1. The crises of war separation and reunion studies are largely extra-family in origin, crises of dismemberment with a minimum of demoralization, and involve changes in status and conflict among members in the conception of their roles.

2. The adjustment of the crises under study must be looked upon as third dimensional, involving family patterns and resources, and intra-family relationships.

3. The course of adjustment to crisis should be tested to see how closely it approximates the roller-coaster pattern of crisis → disorganization → reorganization → recovery.

4. The effects of most crises on families are pervasive, entering into every phase of family life, as would be expected in a closed system; but the effects of separation and reunion remain to be tested.

5. The most suggestive findings concerning the factors which make for successful adjustment to family crises came from the marital adjustment and depression studies. Beyond these findings other areas of probable significance were identified by the author to be explored. Joined together to be tested in the special context of the separation and reunion crisis, they lend themselves to classification as follows:

   a. History of happiness of spouses
   b. Readiness for marriage at marriage
   c. Personality adequacy of spouses
   d. Family adequacy: marital adjustment, family integration, family adaptability, and family maturity
   e. Distribution of power in family and social roles of members
   f. Financial security and social status
   g. Contingency factors of the separation period
      (1) hardships of separation
      (2) communication devices
      (3) modes of releasing tension while separated
      (4) effects of military experience
   h. Contingency factors of the reunion period

PART TWO

~~~~~~

Breaking and Reuniting Families

CHAPTER III

THE FAMILIES STUDIED: THEIR MAKE-UP
AND SURROUNDINGS

SELECTING the families for study involves the basic question of research procedure which in turn requires the ability to make sharp relative judgments.[1] The research procedure determines how close the investigator gets to real flesh-and-blood families, the basis for persuading them to share their experiences, and the precision with which those experiences are recorded and handled in analysis. Once selected the procedure itself often delimits the problem, confines the analysis, and determines how far one can go in making generalizations.

Two tasks were clear: We wished to test the findings of other studies in a new context, and we wished to delve adequately into the new context itself, namely, the crisis of war separation and reunion. The one task was definitive and the second explorative. For the first task fairly precise questionnaires using as often as possible standardized scales and inventories were indicated. A statistical analysis of those materials would be feasible. For the second task a prolonged interview with open-end questions seemed important if we were to record the variety and depth of human experience with the as-yet-unstudied separation and reunion crises. Questionnaires were built and a detailed interviewer's schedule constructed, submitted to experts in the field for criticism and revision, and pretested on thirty families with the coöperation of the Story County Red Cross. When

[1] The details of research methodology are placed, as the tool shed should be, in the back, see the appendix on method, Application of the Scientific Method to Family Crises, pp. 368–398.

it was apparent the schedules could be filled out accurately by a wide variety of families and interviewers, the study was ready to be launched.

The schedules contain, roughly, the information needed to answer the questions discussed in Chapter II, pp. 16–20, and may be examined in the appendix, pp. 399–434. From the wife, in a two-hour interview, the interviewer was given a picture of life without the husband, living arrangements before and after induction, the financial history of the family, the adjustments of the wife and children to separation. The devices of communication, of visits, furloughs, and letters were recorded and the content of letters as well as the activities during the visits and furloughs were discussed. As background, the wife took the interviewer back in time to discuss her own childhood, her relationships with her parents, her courtship and early marriage experiences with her husband. A discussion of the circumstances of the reunion, the reactions of the wife and the children to the husband during the first weeks and months after reunion, and her estimate of the effects of military life on his effectiveness as a family man concluded the interview. The interviewer was expected at the conclusion of the interview to rate the family on adaptability and integration, using scales developed by Cavan.

The questionnaire filled out by the wife asked for basic identifying information, such as, age, schooling, number of children, and so on, and contained the following tests and inventories: the Burgess-Cottrell marital adjustment test, the modified Thurstone psychoneurotic inventory, a test for adjustment to separation, and a test for adjusment to reunion constructed by the author.

The questionnaire was mailed to the father if he was still in service. If he was back from service, the father was interviewed, particularly concerning the reunion period, his reactions to his family, to his job, and his attitude toward the wife and children while he was in service and after returning. He also filled out the questionnaire at the time of the interview. This contained questions paralleling those of the wife in all respects, except for the test for separation. He was also questioned on the extent to which the family was a morale builder while he was in service, and the things about family life he missed most while in service.

SELECTING THE FAMILIES

One school of statistical thought insists that generalizations concerning any propositions may not be extended beyond the families studied unless those families are in turn representative of a larger population. Iowa was chosen as the locale for the study, because the research was sponsored and financed by the Iowa State College in coöperation with the Iowa Department of Social Welfare. How might a representative sample of Iowa's families, temporarily broken by war, be drawn? Selective service officials in Washington and in Des Moines consulted with us in designing and drawing the sample. Of the several alternatives considered, the simplest and the most representative of our population (about which relatively little was known, incidentally) was a 4 percent random sample drawn by order number from the files of the 100-odd local boards in the state of Iowa. The State Selective Service Headquarters supervised the drawing of such a sample as of October 1, 1945.

A list of 3325 families and their most recent addresses was furnished. Multiplying by twenty-five we can see that roughly 82,000 pre-Pearl Harbor fathers from Iowa were in service in October 1945. The sample was further subdivided, taking every fourth case, so that our final sample was a 1 percent random sample of the Iowa families with a father in service, or 820 families.

The interviewing phase of the project was shared with the state and county departments of social welfare without whose help and counsel the project would never have moved off dead center. Field workers in public assistance and child welfare workers have shared the task of locating the families, making appointments, and even occasionally interviewing the wife and husband. Most of the interviewing was done by the two Iowa State supervisors, Reuben Hill and Elise Boulding, who had also conducted the pretest of the schedules.[2]

Four major sources of shrinkage cut the number of 820 families in the original sample drawn by selective service to the more modest figure of 135 families whose experiences make up the warp and woof of the study:

1. Funds for travel and living expenses for interviewers were exhausted when roughly half the state was covered accounting for some 444 families who were never approached for interview.
2. Sixty-three families had already migrated outside of the state of Iowa by the time the interviewers reached their homes for interview. We know that one of the adjustments to war separation must be migration.
3. Another forty-one families approached refused to coöperate with the study for various reasons.[3] As far as we could tell, the proportion of disorganized and unhappy homes which coöperated was quite as high as the well-organized homes. Often the chronically unhappy were looking for a chance to spill their troubles to a stranger, and we provided a means of ventilation.
4. Some 137 completed family histories were rejected because of lack of confidence in the interviewer, due to the discrepancy between her interviews and those made in a follow-up study of many of the same families by another interviewer. This was the most disheartening source of shrinkage in the study, for which we weren't prepared at all. The interviewer, to remain nameless in this report, was a seasoned worker whose interviews were most readable and plausible. Reasonably accurate in her first interviews, this worker faltered under the combined pressure of meeting a self-imposed quota of so many interviews a day and a sense of guilt

[2] See the appendix on method for an account of the interviewing headaches encountered and our counsel for other students using this method of obtaining research data, pp. 384–387.

[3] See the appendix on method for a discussion of the reasons for refusal, and a more detailed discussion of shrinkage of cases, pp. 387–390.

which built up because she felt she was violating the sanctity of the homes she was visiting. The sense of guilt eroded her integrity in interviewing and recording her interviews so badly that she would leave homes without asking all the questions, if the interviewee became restive. She would fill in from hearsay and from guess.

TABLE 1. Flow Chart Showing Effects of Shrinkage from Original Sample of 820 Families to Completed Study of 135 Families

820 families in original sample October 1945	→ 376	→ 313	→ 272	→ 135 families left in study August 1947
Reasons for Elimination				
1. Ran out of funds before covering counties in which these families lived.	444			
2. Attempted interview but found families had migrated outside Iowa.		63		
3. Attempted interview but families refused to coöperate with the study.			41	
4. Completed interviews, but results rejected because of lack of confidence in interviewer.				137

The interviewer did not confess her indiscretions until confronted with the conflicting results of the follow-up interviews. The personality conflict engendered by the interviewing and her sense of guilt at what she had done brought this worker to the verge of complete collapse. Her memory of the completely reliable cases was judged to be so poor and untrustworthy that all the interviews she had completed were rejected. A careful reading of all 137 family histories revealed very little evidence of dishonest recording. Apparently inaccuracies and even fictitious interviews are extremely difficult to identify because of the fundamental assumption made at the start; namely, variety in family behavior is expected, and almost anything is possible. Only through follow-up and reinterviewing is it possible to check on this phenomenon of dishonest recording.

A flow chart showing the source of shrinkage in summary form is presented in Table 1.

The representativeness of the 135 completed family histories is hard to prove since there is so little information about the 82,000 Iowa families they are supposed to represent. The 135 families are located in 25 of the 99 counties of Iowa, and disproportionately concentrated in the urban counties of Polk, Black Hawk, and Wapello (see map of Iowa). Only 3 percent of the 135 families had an RFD

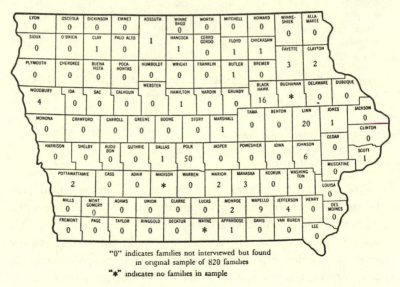

"0" indicates families not interviewed but found in original sample of 820 families

"*" indicates no families in sample

Distribution of 135 Families Within Iowa by County in Which Living at Time of Interview, January to June, 1946

address as compared with 26 percent for the state as a whole. Within the small towns and cities the families were found disproportionately in the poorer sections of the community. This distribution may only indicate the groups in Iowa most vulnerable to selective service. Farmers, professional, and managerial personnel were more likely to be in the deferred classification. Nevertheless, it would be folly to attempt to make generalizations from the study for all of Iowa's 82,000 families whose family heads saw service. In some respects our findings may have validity for all families under stress; in other respects they may well represent only Iowa families who faced war separation, and in some respects the findings are valid only for the 135 families in the study. We wish we could tell how broadly our generalizations apply in each case, but we share this inadequacy with every other study of family life yet attempted.

THE FAMILIES STUDIED

In achieving an understanding of the impact of the war-born crises of separation and reunion on 135 Iowa families, it may be helpful to visualize the milieu in which they are living, the social geography, their positions in the social structure, their patterns of living, and their general social characteristics.

THE ENVIRONMENT

The state of Iowa in which our families are found is a study in contrasts. Rigorous winters follow suffocating summers. Iowa's climate is better suited for the growing of corn than for family living at any stage of the family life cycle. Iowans retire to California and Florida in greater numbers than the inhabitants of most states. The brilliance of prairie sunsets contrasts with the drabness of small-town slums. Scattered among twenty-five counties (see map of Iowa), the families were drawn from rich farming sections, from Missouri river towns, from southern coal mining communities, and from the thriving small cities of Waterloo, Cedar Rapids, Ottumwa, and Des

Moines. The addresses of our families make a homesick sound like
a brakeman on a local train reciting home-town names nearer and
nearer to American destinations: Red Oak, Moravia, Strawberry
Point, Charles City, Storm Lake, West Branch, Mason City, Goose
Lake, Mound Valley, and Aspenwall, What Cheer, Center Point,
and Morning Sun, Correctionville, Eagle Grove, and Clarion.

Their very names make the sound of an American neighborhood:
names like Tyson, Moats, Stout, and Bean, Buckalew, and Krieger-
meir, Graham, Junkins, Bolt, Barlow, Wunkes, and Purdy, Rose-
berry, Cafferty, Kirkbush, Sorensen, Smith, and Proskovec, Gold-
stein, Putnam, Arp, Brady, Van Sickle, and Patterson. They are first
and second generation, and occasionally third generation, families
whose antecedents migrated to Iowa from New England and from
Europe and from the South. The East contributed leadership to
Iowa and an ordered community life; the South, a desire for social
liberty. The combination of these qualities in a productive land has
led to the development of a middle-class society, solidly anchored in
secure, conservative, self-satisfied middle-class families.[4] The essential rural character of the Middle West has developed independent,
semipatriarchal families, and this is no less true of our Iowa families
as we shall see in the latter sections of this analysis.

The church affiliations of these families spell the diversity of religious backgrounds of Iowans who settled this prairie country in
successive waves of variously motivated migrations: Roman Catholic
(14 percent), Methodist (13 percent), Presbyterian (10 percent),
Lutheran (7 percent), Church of Christ (6 percent), and, in more
modest numbers, Baptist, Church of the Brethren, Evangelical, Naz-
arene, Congregationalist, Peoples Church, Universalist, Latter-Day
Saints, Dutch Reformed, Church of God, and Episcopal. Eight percent listed themselves as "just Protestant" and in 28 percent of the
families either husband or wife claimed "no affiliation" to any

---

[4] For a more detailed analysis of family life in the Middle West, see Ruth Cavan,
"Regional Family Patterns: The Middle Western Family," *The American Journal of
Sociology* (May, 1948), pp. 430–432.

church. Even for those with no church affiliations, the religious environment is still important. It would be a mistake to assume, because of the variety of church affiliations represented, a similar heterogeneity in conceptions of the "good life." Work, thrift, and security are values most highly prized. There is little evidence of leisure, or of enjoying the fruits of their labors. Life is earnest, humorless, and serious. These are all attributes of the middle-class protestant ethic shared to a considerable extent by families from all denominations.

RECREATION AND HOUSING

Community facilities for recreation are especially poor in the small towns. Extra-family activities are in inverse proportion to the size of the community, although the activities in the larger communities are predominantly of the spectator variety.

Intra-family living is complicated by inadequate housing, even among families of better than average income. No other topic was as certain to open up resentment in the first interview. The amount of doubling-up is inadequately demonstrated by the numbers living with in-laws, but it gives some indication of the cramped quarters in which our families live. Fifty-five families alone of the 135 studied had always lived separately from in-laws. With space at such a premium, the kitchen often serves as living room, dining room, laundry, and general storeroom. Bedrooms do triple duty; in fact, in only forty-two families does the mother sleep separately from the children.

In understanding the sources of tension in families, the role of cramped living space must be taken into account. The shoehorning of families into inadequate quarters where wishes are bound to collide compounds the vulnerability of families to crisis.

SOCIOECONOMIC STATUS

Social position is closely related to the question of socio-physical environment. Increasingly we are finding our society proliferated by social class divisions reflecting source of income, size of income, part of community lived in, source and amount of education, occupation, and family tree. Using a scale for social status standardized for a Midwestern community, by Kenneth Eels (*17*) of the Committee on Human Development, University of Chicago, we attempted to place our families in social class categories as shown in Table 2.

TABLE 2.   Social Status in the Community of 135
Iowa Families

Social Class	Number	Percent
Upper	7	5.2
Upper-middle	8	5.9
Middle-middle	49	36.3
Lower-middle	46	34.1
Lower	25	18.5
Total	135	100.0

Social status is compounded of many different elements within any given community. In a sense it is folly to measure social standing for 135 families which have been drawn from almost fifty different communities, because social class position is ascribed, involving a community definition for each of our families. The scale standardized by Eels (*17*) probably contains most of the elements Iowans also employ in rating families in a community. We recognize, however, that our use of the scale does not allow for the phenomenon of acceptance or rejection in any given community of any given family for reasons not included in the scale. The results are, therefore, presented for illustrative purposes only and without claim for their precision within any given community. Having made these reservations, we see that our families are predominantly in the middle classes with a more generous representation from lower- than upper-class groups.

Koos (*28*), in his study of middle-class families in Rochester, New York, concluded that they were both better organized than the lower-class families he had studied in New York City (*27*) and more sensitive to trouble. But he found that since they were better organized,

they were more likely to survive difficulties without becoming em-
bittered. They had the necessary margin of income, health, and living space to work out solutions. It will be interesting to check his
findings for Iowa.

TABLE 3. Years of Schooling Completed by Husband and Wife Compared
with Married U. S. Population, 25–34 Years of Age (April 1947)

Years of School	Husband		U. S. Male (Pop. 25–34 yrs.) Percent	Wife		U. S. Female (Pop. 25–34 yrs.) Percent
	Num-ber	Per-cent		Num-ber	Per-cent	
Grade School						
Under 7 years	2	1.6	10.5	1	0.7	9.2
7 and 8 years	18	14.7	19.4	6	4.5	19.5
High School						
1 to 3 years	41	33.6	23.2	39	29.3	21.9
4 years	43	35.2	30.6	69	51.9	37.2
College						
1 year or more	18	14.7	16.3	17	12.8	12.2
No information	13	—	—	2	—	—
Total	135	100.0	100.0	135	100.0	100.0
Median years com-pleted	12.0		11.6	12.3		11.9

Of the many indices of social class tested by Kinsey (23) in his
study of human sex behavior, the index which served him best in
setting the population off into homogeneous behaviorial groupings
was *years of schooling* completed. As far as amount of schooling
went, the 135 families in the Iowa study with their 270 family heads
were distributed pretty much like the married population of the
same general age in the United States as a whole in April, 1947 (see
Table 3).

Compared with the married population of the U. S. as a whole,
the family heads of the Iowa study are better educated, averaging

more years of schooling. They less frequently dropped out of school before reaching high school or before graduating. The mode for these family heads is high-school graduation. Mothers appear to have been endowed with more schooling than fathers in both populations, which should speak well for their ability to share in family decisions in the face of crisis. Certainly families with adequately educated

TABLE 4.   Monthly Income at Induction

	Number	Percent
$ 50– 99.99	4	3.0
100–149.99	34	16.9
150–199	33	24.4
200–249	36	26.8
250–299	9	6.7
300–349	6	4.5
350 and over	15	11.0
No information	9	6.7
	135	100.0

mothers should be better equipped to take the crisis of war separation than those staffed with less endowed female family heads. These generalizations remain to be tested.

Income at induction, shown in Table 4, illustrates the status of our families in another important area.

This table of income distribution is somewhat misleading since each and every family in this population has children to support. When income distribution is linked with number of consumers in the family, a truer picture of economic status appears (see Table 5).

In assessing the reactions of these 135 families to the war-born crises of separation and reunion, it will be interesting to observe the relative responsiveness of families with low incomes and many mouths to feed and the families in the bracket with as much as $151 available for each person in the family. Our families are like other American families in that the amount of money they earn appears inversely related to the number of children they bear. Most of the high incomes go to professional men who postponed parenthood until they were through their professional training and established in practice.

Undoubtedly their middle-class bias was showing when the interviewers linked per-consumer income with social status and occupa-

TABLE 5. Income per Family by Number of Children

Monthly Income	Income per Consumer Unit (Average)	Number of Children					Av. Number of Children	Total
		1	2	3	4	5 and over		
$ 50– 99	$ 17.65	1	2	0	1	0	2.25	4
100–150	29.34	10	6	6	0	1	2.26	23
150–199	39.06	7	19	1	1	5	2.48	33
200–249	54.74	8	19	6	3	0	2.11	36
250–299	70.69	1	7	1	0	0	1.89	9
300–349	82.69	3	2	1	0	0	1.67	6
350 and over	151.00	2	10	3	0	0	1.93	15
No information	——	3	2	2	2	0	—	9
Total		35	67	20	7	6	2.20	135

tion in recording their impressions of family life among these 135 families. In going over the interviewers' notes we see that their general overall impressions were that life was predominantly hand-to-mouth, with little margin, little evidence of leisure or of enjoying the fruits of labor. On the other hand, few people complained of the burdens children brought, and many commented on them as sources of satisfaction, suggestive proof that children are not added to families for economic reasons but for affectional and personal satisfactions.

VARIETY OF BACKGROUNDS AND EXPERIENCES

It is hard to realize that these sets of parents, now eleven years married with more than two children each, evolved from young couples who were once the despair of their respective parents. The study enabled us to visualize them on their first dates together, and get some picture of the patterns of dating and of courtship in Iowa communities.

Nearly a fourth of these couples met through blind dates or pick-ups, or at public dances and skating rinks. The hazards of young people meeting and marrying compatibly are very nearly as great in Iowa as anywhere else. Few controls operated to cause these couples to question whether they should be marrying one another. Other couples met under less risky circumstances, through friends (18 percent), and the next largest group through school or church affairs (16 percent). The balance (about one-third) claimed they met through parents, relatives, or grew up knowing one another.

If the first meeting was haphazard, the reasons for marriage are more hopeful. Nearly three-quarters of the couples claimed their primary reason for marriage was companionship and common interests. Another 16 percent stated they married on impulse, to escape from parents, just to be in the married set, love at first sight, or without much thought. A negligible 3 percent married from felt social pressure of the shotgun marriage variety.

In courtship about half the couples admitted occasional spats and quarrels, and 10 percent revealed they "scrapped" almost constantly. The balance claimed they got along very well without conflict before marriage, although many had had continuous conflict since marriage. About half the couples claimed they followed the same pattern of conflict after marriage as before, while roughly a fourth claimed they fought more after marriage.

The reports of conflict before and after marriage do not prove that these are unstable marriages. When tested on the Burgess-Cottrell marital adjustment scale, the 135 families scored well above average: 26 percent of the families had "good" marital adjustment (scores 65 and over), 61 percent had "fair" adjustment (scores 35 to 65), and only 13 percent scored less than 35 which would register "poor" adjustment.

There are, however, families which still fester intact about bitterness. These latter are often so unhappy it is perplexing to understand why they remain together at all. One lawyer speaks to his wife only through the children. She has kept his books faithfully and well; he trusts her with his income, but it has been a dozen years since she has been in his bed. One family would be termed polyandrous, and in that atmosphere is rearing a precocious child who sees all, hears all, and ponders all. The wife has been waiting for two years for her husband to buy out his partner in the radio repair business or for the partner to buy out her husband, while she lives with both. She plans to stay with the business in any event—it's very profitable.

Another factor conditioning our families was that the majority of the spouses had married during the depression years when postponement of marriage for economic reasons was common. It often took courage to marry in the face of such odds. Many of these families were just getting on their feet financially when the father was drafted into service. Troubles of all sorts are nothing new to these

Unsolved Problems at Induction	Number of Families Reporting
Jealousy	32
Handling money	31
Sickness and need for medical care	26
Mounting expenses	24
In-laws	22
Drinking	20
Housing	19
Child discipline	17
Recreation	15
Troubles on the job	14
Number of children	11
Sex satisfactions	10
Clashing temperaments	9
Wife working	5
Religion	5
Use of contraceptives	1
Personal habits	1
Demonstration of affection	1
No problems at induction	14

families who were married in the depths of the depression. The case records show that our families, like those studied by Koos (*27, 28*) in New York State, had many sources of continuous worry and conflict. In answer to the question, "What unsolved problems faced you when your husband was inducted?" the following answers were received.

THE FAMILY ROLE STRUCTURE: ITS VARIETY AND COMMONALITY

Once a man and woman are married, the division of labor and division of power within the marriage have to be worked through. In terms of sheer dominance-submission our families judged themselves to be more father-dominated than mother-dominated, but the largest grouping considered husband and wife equally powerful (see Table 6).

TABLE 6.   Relative Dominance of Husband and Wife

	Number	Percent
Husband much stronger	12	8.9
Husband somewhat stronger	45	33.3
Husband and wife equal	65	48.2
Wife somewhat stronger	11	8.2
Wife much stronger	2	1.5
Total	135	100.0

MOTHER ROLES

The division of labor between husband and wife was predominantly the traditional father-provider and wife-homemaker combination. Even so, seventy of the 135 mothers had worked for pay on at least one job, and some on several jobs since marrying. In the event of crisis these wives are prepared to share the economic burden of earning, although 20 percent of the husbands register opposition to the wife's working under any circumstances. By careful analysis of the wife's social role in the marriage, the interviewers devised a tabulation as follows:

69%   wife and mother (stays at home, cooks, cares for children, doesn't work for pay, traditional role)

27%   partner (shares economic burden by earning, shares planning, and goal setting of family, and shares housekeeping with father)

2%   hostess (entertainer, manager of servants, ornament)

3%   non-functioning wife (invalid, or infantile, requiring protection)

Of the many mothers in our Iowa study, Jonathan Daniels chose for his *McCall's* story (*12*) Trudy Baker[5] as the most typical of our urban mothers of modest circumstances. Her position in the family is described in Daniels' words:

Trudy seems as naturally American as Iowa's tall corn. . . . She is 28, dark and pretty. In the cluttered, crowded imitation-brick house on Oak Park Avenue, her own six children and generally other children of relatives and friends surround her. When she was 15, she was married to Jack Baker who was lucky enough in those depression days to have a job as driver of a delivery truck. They were married just in time to take together the common American crisis of hard times. Jack lost his job. Beyond the aid of in-laws, there was the WPA. They'd planned two children. By 1946 there were six children. A seventh child had lived only a few days.

Trudy is smiling and sure, satisfied and serene in the swarm of children, friends and assorted relatives. . . . The interior decoration of the Baker home seems almost spontaneously compounded of worn linoleum, well-used furniture, toys and tools, coats and rubbers, model airplanes, dilapidated dolls, dull and gawdy junk, and some of the nicest, happiest people, big and little, in the world. . . . Jack would like to give his family a better house. The beds are pretty close together, on the crowded second floor. No Baker, big or little, sleeps alone and probably would not regard such sleeping spaciousness as a privilege if it were attained. Jack thinks about the possibility of owning a big cross-country van but the way to its acquisition would be long continental trips away from home which Trudy would not like. He is content at home. The children as

[5] The names, occupations and identifying data have been disguised to preserve the anonymity of cooperators in the study.

Trudy says, follow him about like "little dogs." He and Trudy do not go out much but relatives and friends, children and dogs swarm in. They are partners in marriage. Indeed parents and children seem partners in the family.

"Daddy goes out and works for us," says Bill 12, "but Mommy has to work just as hard at home."

Trudy laughs. It is the slow laugh not of a lazy woman in an untidy house but of a wise one in an almost absurdly nappy home full of noise, clutter, confidence and affection.

Mother roles are hard to characterize because they are in flux. In most of our families, mothers do what needs to be done, adapt to the whims and fancies of husband and children, and assert themselves when they feel so minded. We can safely speculate that mothers make a somewhat greater proportion of the adjustments than do fathers and children.

CHILDREN ROLES

Although their roles were decidedly subordinate to those of the parents, the children of our study were conscious of their importance in the household. They often shared in the interviews, entertained the interviewers, and competed with the interviewers for the mother's attention. To be noticed, to leave the impact of their presence, was a need of the younger fry. In almost no instance were any of the children models of propriety, quiet, meek, shy, or overly polite. These children come into society as part of a generation which has rights to be heard as well as seen. Still, there was little evidence of parents paying more than lip service to family councils, and only infrequently were children part of the family's finance planning.

We found with Koos (27) that the subordinate roles of the young were relative to age, sex, sibling position, economic contribution to the family, and the family's position in the community. Of the 289 children in the study 111 were under five years of age, and played much more dependent roles in the family than the older children. Dawdling was frequently a younger child's prerogative, but the older children were already caught up in the seriousness of living. With the departure of the father for service many of the older youngsters played at being foster father, or "man of the house," and eagerly took responsibilities they would not have assumed had the father remained home. The Bakers tell us something about children's roles:

David Baker, 6, has an almost standard Baker family equipment—two stitches in the back of his scalp. He was setting up bottles and old cans on the top of an abandoned automobile chassis for the other boys Bill 12, Frank 8, and a normal Baker complement of juvenile friends, to knock off with rocks. He did not get down behind the chassis fast enough when Frank was throwing. Davey seems to be the cheerful recipient of most of the constant Baker wounds which Trudy treats with care and then handles with assumed casualness. He lost his front teeth with the help of a lick from Frank and a kick from two-year-old Bobbie. . . . With his father's help, Bill makes model airplanes which are part of the home decorations. . . . Edith is the smartest one in school. Frank is the bashful one—which is not very bashful. Davey despite the lack of front teeth, is said to be the ladies' man. Joyce, at four, with ribbons in her hair is an outrageous flirt. There is some of the gleam in her eyes which shines in her mother's.

"And Bobby at two is a toughie who skedaddles to Trudy in time of trouble. He cries desperately all the way through the eating of a first piece of candy in bellowing demand for a second one . . . .

One of the knottiest problems, to be discussed in more detail later, is the differential conception of the child's role by father and mother and even by grandparents who may be living in the family. As the child is admitted to the family as a person and the mother is elevated to the position of partner with the husband, new and sometimes baffling roles are introduced for family members.

FATHER ROLES

Our interest in the father roles in our families is magnified because it was precisely these roles which were left begging to be played when the father was called into service. What services did he perform? In what ways was he indispensable? The father roles were inadequately reported in the first interviews of this study, but fortunately a follow-up study of thirty-two Polk County families was made by Elder (*18*) in roughly a fourth of the original families which focused specifically on the father roles. Elder found the father to be much more of a functioning father than is commonly thought. She found only one case of an absentee father who was only a "meal ticket," a non-functioning father, if you will. Moreover, two-thirds of the fathers said they enjoyed being a father as much as their wives enjoyed being mothers, and only 15 percent felt that motherhood was more enjoyable.

When their activities were examined it was found that only two fathers had never played with their children and the other fathers listed from one to nine father-child play activities, such as, games, reading funnies, playing with toys, telling stories, teasing and joking, listening to the radio, romping, etc. Homemaking activities which involved activity *with* the child on family tasks were listed by half the fathers; among these were yard and garden work, cleaning and doing dishes, laundrying, cooking, etc. Most of the fathers had children in school, and only a third reported they didn't help their children with school work. Indeed, the father appeared to help more frequently with school work than the mother.

One of the most frequent notions abroad is that fathers don't participate in child care. This notion was verified among about half of the fathers. But a third of the fathers participate in actual physical care of the child—bathing, feeding, and dressing—and the balance had done so when the children were younger.

About half the fathers reported their children had visited them at their employment and had some idea of what they did for a living. The father role as earner was thus more clearly conceptualized by the children than we had suspected.

Fathers were inclined to view their home activities as more accurately father-mother-child activities rather than solely father-child activities. They stated that the wife was included in household routines, recreation, church going, school work, going for visits, and fixing the house.

As far as the children were concerned, the fathers were divided about fifty-fifty as to whether they had brought husband and wife closer together or whether they had both "tied us together and tied us down." About 60 percent felt that fatherhood had made them more responsible.

In concluding this summary of the father's roles in the family and the services he renders, it is apparent that he is manifestly much more than a meal ticket. He is a source of companionship, confidant and friend to mother and children. He provides security against crises, through his confidence and skill in problem solving. He supplies intimate masculine response to all members and is particularly necessary to keep the mother normal and happy. These are services difficult to replace in our society as it is organized today.

CHANGING SOCIAL ROLES OF PARENTHOOD

Elder applied Duvall's (14) schema for the identification of traditionalism and developmentalism in mother roles to the analysis of father roles played among the fathers in the study. To further identify these two competing systems of fatherhood, Elder constructed the father types shown in Table 7.

Fathers were asked to respond to three questions designed to obtain expressions of traditional or developmental conceptions of a "good father," a "good mother," and a "good child" based on the Duvall technique:

What are three things that a good father does?
What are three things that a good mother does?
What are three things that a good child does?

Analysis of the answers to these questions showed that nineteen of the thirty-two fathers interviewed had predominantly traditional

TABLE 7. Constructed Father Types

Developmental Father	Traditional Father
Father and child are both individuals; therefore, Father seeks to understand the child and himself;	Father is a strong individual, always right, and child is his ward; therefore, Father knows what child should be, so does not seek to understand child as an individual;
therefore, Father concerns himself with all activities and needs of the child;	therefore, Father is interested only in activities which he determines are his responsibility for the child's "good";
therefore, Father places emphasis on the growth of child and of himself;	therefore Father places emphasis on giving things to and doing things for the child;
therefore, Father is interested in child's determining and attaining the child's own goals;	therefore, Father is interested in child's accepting and attaining goals established by father;
therefore, Father finds satisfaction in child's becoming a mature individual and in the child's contribution to father's growth as an individual;	therefore, Father finds satisfaction in child's owing father a debt which can be repaid by the child's obedience and by bringing honor to the father by achieving goals established by the father;
therefore, Father feels that parenthood is a privilege which he has chosen to assume.	therefore, Father feels that parenthood is a duty which the church, the family, and/or society expect him to discharge, or which is forced on him as a biological function.

conceptions of fatherhood and that thirteen of them had predominantly developmental conceptions.

Two fathers gave completely traditional responses, as follows:

Father No. 589: A "good father" makes a good living, maintains his family to the best of his ability, and likes to have his family have the best he can offer. A "good mother" takes pride in her house, pride in its appearance, and enjoys keeping a nice home. A "good child" is polite, minds, and knows enough not to act a fool.

Father No. 531: A "good father" is obligated to care for his children, gives them what they need, and supports his family. A "good mother" cares for the children, is obligated to care for them, and provides a home for the family. A "good child" inherits his parents' traits, obeys, and is what his parents try to make him.

Although there were no fathers who gave all developmental responses, two predominantly developmental fathers' responses follow:

Father No. 561: A "good father" is interested in what his child does, helps his child to be interested in what the father does, and wants to help the child attain his own goals. A "good mother" is interested in the child, shares activities with the father and the child, and places care of the child above anything else. A "good child" is lively, not smart aleck if intelligent, and is full of the devilment so that he wants to be in everything.

Father No. 563: A "good father" and a "good mother" are the same. They talk things over with the children as equals, see that the children go to school, and see that the children associate with other children. The "good child" is healthy, and responds affectionately to attention from parents.

These examples express something of the extremes of conceptions held by different fathers. Curiously enough there was a marked tendency for the father to conceptualize his own father role in developmental terms better than he could visualize his wife's mother role or his child's child role in developmental terms. A permissive, understanding father role would frequently be found in a man whose conception of a "good mother" was of the traditional sort involving physical care of the child, housekeeper, and orderly routines. Because of the emphasis on the child in parent guidance literature and in research, fathers might be expected to be more developmental in their conception of childhood than of fatherhood, but this was not borne out in Elder's study of Iowa fathers (*18*). Fathers are confused, as are mothers and children, as they appraise the alternative roles proposed by a society in conflict within itself. A colorful explanation of the reasons for these conflicts is given by Duvall (*14*):

The family, as the primary unit of our society, reflects and adjusts to industrialization, urbanization, and the secularization of life. In its transition from the traditional institution type of family to the person-centered unit of companionship that it is becoming, conceptions of the roles of the parent and the child are shifting. These changes do not appear all at once and with equal force throughout the total society, but are evidenced first in little islands of the new that break off from the mass of tradition and become established in subgroups within the culture. These developmental islands are characterized by such concepts as respect for the person (both child and adult), satisfaction in personal interaction, pride in growth and development, and a permissive, growth-promoting type of guidance as opposed to the more traditional attempts to "make" children conform to patterns of being neat and clean, obedient and respectful, polite and socially acceptable. . . . This theory of the shift in conceptions of role as part of the adjustment to social change would bear further investigation.

SUMMARY

The research procedure used in selecting and interviewing families for this study was only partially successful in insuring the representativeness of the sample for the entire state of Iowa. Shrinkage from a sample of 820 families to a completed study of 135 families requires modesty when generalizations are made for the entire state.

The compelling impression concerning the environment and backgrounds of the families studied is one of diversity, heterogeneity, and contrasts. The Midwest is indeed a multiverse rather than a universe of families. Churchwise, over twenty denominations were listed. By socioeconomic status the families appear predominantly middle class with the accent on middle-middle and lower-middle; income distribution follows similar lines, and per-consumer income blueprints the uneconomic aspect of family life. Family size decreases as per-consumer income increases among our families. The 270 family heads in the study are predominantly high-school graduates, and mothers have slightly better education than fathers. Married in the depression years, their income, occupational make-up, housing, family size, and philosophical outlook spell families operating with little margin in mental health or wealth. Work, thrift, and security are Iowa values most highly prized but most vulnerable in a society ridden by wars and depressions.

Family histories reveal a variety of experiences in meeting and forming the marriage. Yet the families are stable enough to have persisted for eleven years and to have produced over two children per family. In terms of marital adjustment, over a fourth would be termed "good" in adjustment, 61 percent "fair," and only 13 percent "poor," according to the Burgess-Cottrell tests for marital adjustment.

A variety of family roles for father, mother, and children appeared in these families. The mode was an equalitarian family where the mother was a homemaker, the father a provider, and the children sources of satisfaction and response. But there were striking variations and combinations of roles possible. Many mothers worked outside the home for pay before and after the induction of the father. Many fathers were active homemakers in their own right, if a study of thirty-two of the fathers by Elder in Polk County is generalized for all fathers. They shared in child care activities, play activities, household routines, and helped with school work in a substantial proportion of cases.

A majority of the fathers and mothers are probably traditional in their conceptions of parenthood, but a tangible minority are conceptualizing and practicing a set of parental roles which have been termed *developmental* because of the emphasis they place on the *development* and *growth* of the person (both adult and child). Elder's study (*18*) showed fathers in the study to be more developmental in their conceptions of the father role than of the mother or of the child role, and showed that Iowa families are themselves in transition with respect to what a "good father," a "good mother," and a "good child" really are.

CHAPTER IV

CRISIS SITUATIONS EXPERIENCED BY
ALL FAMILIES[1]

THE Iowa families studied have been shown to be much like American families generally in their multiversity. They are heterogeneous in make-up and varied in the roles played by family members. In this chapter we hope to depict the range and variety of the strains and stresses to which our families were subjected during the war years.

All families have experienced the dislocation of home life as a result of war separation and most of them have also completed the intermittently joyful and sorrowful processes of readjusting to life with one another in reunion. Our task in this chapter is to determine precisely how comparable are these crises of separation and reunion for all families.

When we say that each of the 135 families in this study was faced with the same crisis we leave much unsaid. In order to understand fully the meaning of war separation for individual families, it is necessary to examine the family situations upon which this event impinged. We are indebted for our frame of reference for this analysis to James H. S. Bossard (6) who has ably outlined the situational approach to the study of family problems.

Bossard defines the family situation as "a unit of stimuli operating

[1] This chapter was written by Elise Boulding from our case study materials. It provides an understanding of the variety of crises and reactions to crisis which the statistical analysis misses. Depth of family living and processes of adjustment are also caught by this method, supplementing nicely the generalizations reached from the statics of statistical analysis.

within the confines of the family circle, and organized in relation to the person or object which serves as the focal point in the case being considered." The focal point in this case, of course, is the departure of the husband-father for military service. Bossard further suggests that there are three aspects of a family situation: the structure or organization of the family, the social interaction of the group, and the cultural content of the situation.

In applying the situational framework to our study the structure will be described in terms of the roles and duties that will have to be reorganized to meet the coming crisis. The social interaction will be described in terms of the family's anticipatory behavior in regard to the crisis. The cultural content will be given, for our purposes, a rather limited interpretation and circumscribed primarily to include the hardships engendered by the crisis.[2]

We find as we analyze the family situations in our study that the event of induction does not produce a crisis in every case. We have defined a crisis earlier as any sharp or decisive change for which old patterns are inadequate. Phrased in situational terms, a crisis is a situation in which the usual behavior patterns are found to be unrewarding and new ones are called for immediately. Theoretically we know that three variables are present in a situation which determine whether or not a crisis is created: (1) the hardships of the event, (2) the resources of the family to meet the event, and (3) the family's definition of the event.

There was tremendous variation from family to family in the number and extent of hardships endured. Some families suffered only the obvious minimum hardships of the absence of the husband-father from the home and other families suffered a pile-up of all

[2] Bossard used cultural content to expound the traditional patterns and cultural heritage of family life. Assuming that it is justified to alter a theoretical framework if it is more useful in its altered form, we are including the traditional patterns under family structure so that the classification of cultural content (more accurately, simply content) can be used to describe the external realities of the situation which the family as an organization must meet and to which it must react.

kinds of troubles, not all directly related to the husbands' departure but increased in their intensity by his absence. When we use the term hardship or trouble, we mean those aspects of a crisis-precipitating event which ordinarily demand a response in terms of resources which the event itself has temporarily paralyzed or made unavailable; those aspects will not be considered to be hardships by the family involved if it has other nontraditional resources with which to meet the event which have not been affected by the event itself.

We can profitably examine the range of hardships resulting from the father's induction. Consider, for example, the situation of a sheltered, dependent woman unused to responsibility who had to handle alone within a few weeks after her husband's departure the birth of a second child and the death of her husband's mother who had been very close to the family. To further complicate matters, the elder child responded to this pyramiding of catastrophes by developing an acute fixation on the mother and wouldn't let her out of sight. In pleasant contrast is the situation of a devout Catholic family which was able to turn to accessible grandparents who played successfully all the roles of the absent husband. Family life continued for this family with hardly a break in the usual routines.

The resources which families were able to muster to meet the situation varied too. In one family the wife's capacity of adaptability and self-sufficiency was supplemented by her parents who helped with the children and provided financial aid whenever necessary. At the other extreme we have a family in which the wife, who had never had any responsibility before the separation, found herself without in-laws or friends to turn to, and because of her inability to take her husband's place in the home the family lived a completely demoralized existence until he returned.

Likewise, the definitions or meanings which the families made of the event of separation exhibited wide differences. On the one hand is the family where husband, wife, and children before induction were inseparable, did all their family planning together, and took all their recreation as a group. For them the absence of the husband left an aching void which could be filled only by his return. On the other hand we see a family which for years suffered neglect from a drinking, philandering husband, in which there was never any assurance how much of a pay check would arrive home. For them the fact of the father's absence was a relief and the security of the allotment checks was doubly appreciated.

We see, then, that for some families the induction of the husband came as an overwhelming blow from which they did not recover until his return. For others it was a sorrowful event to which they quickly adjusted. Still others were indifferent or even happy to be released from the authority of the father. In order to understand better just what happened when induction hit these families, we will begin by examining the roles played within the families.

The Structure of the Families

The patriarchal type leads by a small majority over other types in the group, claiming fifty-five families. In this traditional type of family structure the father is the ultimate authority in the home. In the complete patriarchy the father makes all the decisions—how much money shall be spent on food, clothes, recreation, where the family shall live, where they shall go on holidays, and how the children shall be punished. The function of the wife is solely to administer her husband's decrees. The wife in such a family is very helpless in the husband's absence unless she has latent, repressed abilities or relatives to fall back on. Less than eight or nine of the families in the patriarchal group are of this extreme type, however. In the rest of the cases the wife has more or less autonomy in dealing with the children or is allowed in on the decision-making process of the husband with the understanding that although she may make suggestions, his decision is final. In one or two cases the husband is only a patriarch because the wife insists that he be one; that is, she really wants to be bossed and puts him in a position of authority that he assumes somewhat unwillingly.

In the *matriarchal family* father brings home the pay check and his responsibilities end there. Mother makes all the decisions regarding finances, recreation, etc., and considers the children entirely in her department. Father's chief function is to provide the money to carry out her decisions, to romp with the children, and generally to coöperate around the house as his wife deems necessary. There are eighteen families that fall into this general classification, and about ten of these fall into the absolutist group—a much higher proportion than in the patriarchal group. The rest are modified matriarchies, the husband sharing in the decision-making process with the understanding that the wife will make the final decision. Here again we find several husbands forcing their wives into the matriarchal position because they prefer to be in a dependent position and have decisions made for them. "I do my share when I bring the pay check home. The rest is up to my wife," exemplifies this attitude. These wives are well equipped to meet crises but are sometimes incapacitated by extreme emotional dependence on the husband.

Adult-centered (two-headed) families run a close second to the patriarchal, numbering fifty-one. In this type all decisions of importance affecting the family are arrived at jointly, although minor decisions may be delegated by common consent to one or the other of the pair. In thirty-three of these fifty-one families, the guidance and disciplining of the child is shared equally by both parents and in fifteen it falls more heavily on the mother or father as the case may be. The wives in this group on the whole adjust well, but not as well as the matriarchal group because they miss the process of "talking things over."

The democratic families number only ten. This type is the best equipped to meet any kind of crisis because the whole family sits around the council table and the resources of each individual are put to their best use. Decisions and responsibilities are shared alike by all, so redistribution of jobs becomes easy if one family member is absent.

Size of family figures are given in Chapter V. We will just review briefly here the fact that thirty-five families had one child, sixty-seven had two, and thirty-three had three or more children. The larger families had more problems. A more important resource for the family than children was adult relatives. Thirty-one families had parents or siblings living in the same community, and eight of these had a relative living right in the home. When the father left the home, these relatives were able to absorb some of the extra burdens and enabled this group of families to make a better-than-average adjustment.

Affectional ties figured in the picture. Half of the families in the study had an equalitarian affectional relationship; that is, the members of a family were all equally close to one another. Of the remaining, fourteen of the husbands and wives were in conflict, sixteen of the couples were closer to one another than to the children, twenty-seven of the fathers were closer to their children than to their wives, and forty of the mothers were closer to their children than to their husbands.

REACTIONS TO THE IMPENDING CRISIS

When the families were brought face-to-face with the fact that their men were to be drafted, their reactions varied widely. Twenty-two were unprepared for this event and suffered shock, or had worried in a fretful way about the possibility of induction without doing anything to prepare for it. Another sixteen enlisted with the wife's consent and only four enlisted without the wife's consent. Fifteen looked forward to the separation as a release from an intolerable marital situation or welcomed the opportunity to think out marital problems and decide whether the marriage was worth continuing. For some families the emotional upheaval was the most upsetting part of the separation, and eleven families faced their emotional crisis in advance, cried it out, and were ready to go through with the separation when the time came. A calm, rational attitude was characteristic of seven families: "There's a job to be done, and we'll see it through." Foreseeing a drop in the family income, four wives started working before their husbands were actually drafted in order to have a sum laid by for emergencies, and two husbands changed their jobs in an unsuccessful attempt to get deferrment. Six families gave up their homes and moved in with the in-laws, either for reasons of economy or to make the burden of household chores lighter for the wife. Moving to an apartment from a larger home was undertaken for the same reasons by four families. Three families reversed this procedure and bought or built homes. A gradual drifting apart over a long period of time had taken place with four couples, and the impending separation brought them closer together, made them more aware of the values of family living.[3]

Content of the Crisis Situation

HARDSHIPS AND DEFINITIONS OF HARDSHIPS

The external realities of a situation as seen by other people and the conception of that same situation by the person who is participating in it, may be two very different things. Thomas and Znaniecki, in the *Polish Peasant,* have pointed out the importance of the definition of the situation in determining its effect on the person who is experiencing it. The materials gathered in this study illustrate this point extremely well. Time and time again we find families faced with circumstances that would be termed hardships by any observer, and, yet, because the circumstances are regarded differently by the

[3] A wider range of responses might have been charted had the schedules been set up to catch these anticipatory reactions. As it is, the material is only available where the wife volunteered it of her own accord, so there is no information for fifty of the cases.

family, they may not only fail to produce hardship reactions but they may serve as a stimulus to better adjustment. On the other hand, a family may be faced with a situation that would not seem to other people to involve any hardships, and yet the family itself considers that it had trouble. Because our study offers such a unique opportunity for validating this concept of the definition of the situation, a distinction will be made, as we discuss each, between the trouble itself and the family's conception of it. This will be done by using two or three cases to illustrate each hardship; the first case will be one in which the family faces what would be considered by the general public to be a hardship, and feels itself that the situation is a hardship; and the second case will reveal a situation where trouble, as defined by the outside world, is present but is not defined as such by the family. Where an example is available of a family which considers that it has a hardship which outsiders would not define as such, this will be given also.

MISSING THE HUSBAND AS A COMPANION, FATHER, HANDY MAN, AND PROTECTOR

Theoretically, all the families suffered the same hardship in the mere fact of being deprived of their men; that is, they were all deprived of companion, father, handy man, protector, and whatever other things the man of the house was to them. However, as we saw earlier, the men played widely different roles in their respective families, and each family missed its man in terms of his own special role in the home. In most families, the man was all of the four things mentioned above, and more, and these folks, like the B's, missed him hourly and longed for his return:

The B's were an extremely happy, coöperative, equalitarian family who tried to make the best of a bad situation when it became evident that B was to be drafted. The B's were still romantic about each other after nine years of marriage and letters were no substitute for the frequent demonstrations of affection they were used to. The older child never got used to his father's absence, moped, and did poorly in school, and Mrs. B missed his disciplining hand with the children very much. The responsibility of keeping the home running smoothly and making decisions about family activities, expenditures, etc., seemed very heavy to her also, and she longed for the day when Mr. B could take over again.

Let us turn now to the families that missed their man in a more specific way.

The C family, for example, missed Mr. C chiefly as a companion. The C family was an equalitarian partnership which had wanted to do its part when war broke out. Mr. C tried to enlist but was turned down, so the draft a year later came as an unexpected shock. Mrs. C had always taken a good deal of responsibility in the home, but was also very dependent on her husband emotionally—he gave her the love and security that her childhood in an orphanage had lacked. She managed the physical routines of the house well but poured out her soul in letters and lived for the day when he would return, as did the children.

In other families he was missed only as the children's father, the wife feeling completely adequate in every way except as disciplinarian.

Mrs. J, a charming and intelligent woman, had for years submitted to a tyrannic patriarchal husband as was the custom in the Italian group of which they were a part, and found herself free to plan her own days for the first time since their marriage. Her enjoyment of the separation would have been complete if it had not been for the fact that she was so accustomed to having her husband rule the children that she did not know how to manage them alone, and always missed him when a disciplinary situation arose.

In some cases the children were still close to their father when the parents were already estranged. One wife refrained from divorcing her husband while he was overseas only because her daughter, who loved her father dearly, begged her not to.

Some women who had felt that husbands could be dispensed with discovered to their dismay that a home was a complicated physical plant, among other things, and that a man was mighty helpful in keeping it going.

In the D matriarchy, Mrs. D had long ignored her home and concentrated on a career which was to her all-important, while her husband with the help of her grandmother attended to many domestic details and helped make their house a home for their two children. She welcomed his departure, feeling that she could get along better without him, and was considering a divorce. She felt very differently about it after the furnace went on the blink on the coldest day of winter, the gas stove broke down and filled the house with gas, and the sewer pipes got out of order. She found that running the home was practically a full-time job and longed for the days when her husband used to look after things for her.

Twenty-three of the families did not miss their husbands at all, were glad to be free. The reason for this total inversion of the expected attitudes was chiefly, as one could guess, poor marital adjustment. However, there were also cases where the wife was so self-sufficient and emotionally self-contained and the children already so dependent on the wife, that the departure of the husband really seemed to make no difference to the family. He would, nevertheless, be welcomed back when he returned. The A family is an example of failure to miss the husband because of poor marital adjustment.

Mr. A was a very prosperous lawyer who was able to provide well for his wife and three children, but the marriage relationship had turned from one of love to a cold business partnership. Mr. A would not divorce his wife because of the damage to his reputation that would ensue, but delighted to practice refined mental torture on her. She bore this because there was no other way of providing for the children, and her husband's departure for the service meant a blessed respite from his cruelty.

The majority of today's hardy womanhood would hardly sympathize with the hardship claimed by timid women who missed their husbands as physical protectors; they were literally afraid to be alone in their own homes. One brought a sister to live with her, the other already had a mother in the home, and added a 200-pound girl friend as extra protection whenever she went down town.

FINANCES

Money trouble, which might have been expected to affect a large number of families, was more a source of challenge than a hardship. Considerable adjustment was necessary, however, in twenty-nine families. Actually, some families had a larger income while Uncle Sam was sending them allotment checks than they ever had before, and in most cases where the income was reduced the wife took pride in managing on the smaller sum. In some cases, however, the drop in income was sufficiently severe that the wife had a real struggle to make ends meet, as in the Z family.

The Z's were a coöperative matriarchy with a comfortable income and two children. When Mr. Z was drafted, their income was cut by two-thirds and Mrs. Z tried to work to supplement it. She had no one to help her with the children, however, and found that she couldn't care for them and the home adequately and work too. She gave up her job and spent the rest of the separation turning every penny twice in an effort to manage on their inadequate income. She actually did avoid going into debt, although it meant going without many of the things they were used to and living under considerable strain.

Eight of the twenty-nine families who had money trouble did not define it as a hardship, chiefly because they had been through that difficulty before, in the depression, and knew how to handle it. To them the allotment check represented at least security, if not riches. The BD's, for example, took an income cut easily in their stride.

Mrs. BD was a slight, hardworking woman in an equalitarian family who had helped pull her husband and two children through the long lean years of the depression. She had expected her husband to be deferred because of his health, so the induction caught them unprepared, with unpaid debts and a smaller income. When she got over the initial shock of his departure, she just started scrimping a little harder and saved her worries for more important things like having a baby in Mr. BD's absence in a tiny house in an isolated area where no help was available. Scrimping was second nature anyhow, she said, with no special hardship.

A few families were fairly secure financially but had money trouble because the wife wasn't used to handling money and didn't plan her expenditures well. No observer would think that the S family had any cause for complaint.

Mr. S was a kindly patriarch. Mrs. S had been a lonely and neglected child who found her first real happiness in marriage, and depended on her husband for everything, never handling money or making any household decisions. She was overwhelmed with the responsibility of deciding how the money should be spent in addition to all her new responsibilities in regard to the home and her two children. However, she was living with her husband's parents, had few of the usual household expenses, and had a sufficiently good relationship with her in-laws that they were able to help her in many ways. In spite of this assistance and an adequate income, she never learned to manage her money well.

CHILD DISCIPLINE

"Making the children mind" was a problem in sixty-nine cases. It might generally be considered that child discipline in the father's absence would always be a hardship, but this was not the case. In a number of families the wife had already carried most of the responsibility for the children, as in the case of the doctor's family where the father only saw his children on Sundays; and in other cases there was a male relative in the home or nearby who became a father substitute. The C family was not so fortunate.

In the patriarchal C family, Mrs. C had never trusted her own judgment. She had never managed her two children well because she had never been sure of herself, and she always depended on backing from her husband in dealing with them. Now she found herself powerless to make them mind. Her sister was living with her and helped with the children but that only added to the trouble. Whenever Mrs. C tried to assert her authority, her daughter would threaten her with "I'll tell daddy on you!"

In rare cases the children actually were behavior problems but their mothers did not admit it, even to themselves, because they wanted to feel themselves completely adequate to the situation. The F family is a case in point.

Mrs. F was all mother and no wife, considered herself and her daughter the complete family unit, and had for some years left her husband "out in the cold." She had always felt that she could run the home just as well, if not a little better, without a husband around to clutter up the place. His departure was no great sorrow to her, but her daughter did not share her attitude and moped constantly for daddy. She brooded alone for hours and became unresponsive and uncoöperative, in spite of mother's insistence that they got along fine.

It is well known that all mothers at times have mixed feelings about their "little darlings." In one interesting case little Johnny took his daddy's role in the home in a way that gave him the fond admiration of the community but drove his mother wild. The hardship in this case was not obvious to the observer but very real to the mother.

The DS couple had gradually built up a coöperative, equalitarian relationship after an estrangement early in their married life. Mr. DS wanted to enlist and do his part, but for a year his wife wouldn't let him. When she finally gave in, he had a little talk with their eleven-year-old son before he left, in which he told him to be the man of the house while daddy was away and take good care of mother. The son became transformed overnight from a carefree boy who played with the gang all the time and was never home, to a serious-minded little gentleman who stayed home and helped mother in the house. This was what the community admired, but what drove mother wild was that he considered part of his duty to be making a minute check on all mother's activities. She had to account to him for every moment spent away from the house and was scolded when she went out too much. He told her how to do things in the home and was generally bossy in the way that only self-important children can be bossy. She was helpless to assert herself, particularly as the son wrote long letters keeping his father minutely informed about mother as well as about himself.

PROLONGED MALADJUSTMENT OF CHILDREN

The children were surprisingly little disturbed by the departure of their fathers. There was usually an initial upset followed by a fairly quick recovery. In only twenty-one families did we find children who remained more or less maladjusted during the entire separation period. The mothers of the children are unanimous in defining this maladjustment as a hardship, which is understandable considering that most of these maladjustments expressed themselves as behavior problems. One of the hardest-hit children was Sally H, an only child.

The H family was a contented, equalitarian one that wisely faced the possibility of induction a whole year before it happened, prepared for it by planning to move in with the in-laws and have Mrs. H go to work. The plans made little impression on Sally, though. All she knew was that the tight little family group within which all her world and her joys lay was suddenly disrupted. Father had gone off to war and might be killed. Mother went out to work every day because there wasn't enough money and it helped to keep her mind occupied. They moved from the nice little apartment that had always been home to a big house in a strange neighborhood and there was no one home all day to take care of her except grandmother. All of a sudden the very bottom had dropped out of her happy, secure existence, and she was badly frightened. She began to feel that nobody loved her, and as the comfortless situation continued she lost all confidence in her mother, becoming convinced that she and the whole family hated her and wanted to get rid of her. Evenings spent by Mrs. H with Sally did nothing to dispel her fears, and it was not until father returned and the old three-way companionship was reëstablished that she regained her zest for life.

A case less fraught with emotional tension but, nevertheless, hard on the mother was in the G family.

The G family was a matriarchy only because Mr. G wanted his wife to mother him and run things; she had raised seven brothers and sisters and was tired of family responsibility. Mr. G was always willing to romp with the children, but never to assume authority with them. Mrs. G gave good care to their two children, however; and welcomed the separation as a respite from her too dependent husband. Billy, the four-year-old, didn't say much about missing his father and acted pretty normal until one day he drove a rusty nail through his foot while he was playing. The ensuing infection kept Billy off his feet for a few days but when the wound healed Billy reverted to crawling instead of walking. Despite all his mother's pleas and artful wiles, the boy remained on all fours until the day daddy came home. On that day he walked again, and there was no more trouble of that kind!

LIVING WITH IN-LAWS

A change of residence sometimes had to be made when the family was left without its furnace man. Twenty-six of the families went to live with grandparents or had grandparents move in with them. The reasons for these moves were numerous. In one or two cases the husband insisted on it before he left, so that he could feel that the family was looked after. Sometimes it was a question of saving money, sometimes of easing the wife's burdens by letting the grandparents take over some of the husband's responsibilities. Sometimes it was just plain loneliness that drove the wife out of her own home. The more the move was dictated by necessity, the more it was apt to be regarded as a hardship; twenty-six families did combine with grandparents, and fourteen of them regarded it as a hardship. Mrs. I was one of these.

The I family had done well financially and had a lovely, well-ordered home. Mr. I was the leader in the family but the couple were coöperative and affectionate. They enjoyed their home and had established a pattern of family living which suited them very well. Mrs. I had always been sheltered, however, first by her parents and then by her husband, and when she was faced with the prospect of having a second baby after her husband left for the service, she did not feel up to managing it alone and asked her parents to come and live with her. The parents assumed their old protective attitude and tried to take over the rearing of the older child, but Mrs. I had learned different ways of doing things from her husband. The child became spoiled and insecure as a result of too many bosses and there were many conflicts about how things should be done.

Other families got along with the grandparents very well and were grateful for the help and security they were able to give. Perhaps no other family enjoyed the situation as much as the F's.

The F's were a flexible, democratic family who took everything in their stride. When faced with the prospect of induction, they accepted Mr. F's departure in terms of "a job to be done" and moved in with Mrs. F's family for the duration. It seemed like the most natural thing in the world for Mrs. F to pack up and go home with her only daughter to mother. She slipped right back into her old place as the favorite child, the grandchild got a good deal of fond attention, and the family enjoyed the separation as a sort of prolonged vacation, although daddy was missed.

In one or two cases where observers would not have anticipated hardships as a result of living with grandparents, the wife felt a severe hardship. In the case below, Mrs. CT had lived with her parents ever since her marriage and a new hardship would not be expected as a result of the departure of her husband from the service.

In the CT family, the husband was an irresponsible patriarch who made all the decisions but left the work and worry to his wife. He had never made a separate home for his wife and two children, living with them at the home of her parents when he chose, working elsewhere and making unfulfilled promises of sending for them at other times. He enlisted without consulting his wife, and her struggle to maintain her self-respect and her confidence in him against the onslaught of her increasingly critical parents created a very unpleasant situation in the home. Conflicts which had long been repressed as Mrs. CT waited and hoped for a home of her own now suddenly broke out. Since she was now handling the money for the first time since her marriage she also felt more independent than ever before, and less willing to put up with the insulting pity of her parents.

HOUSING INADEQUACIES

Housing troubles, precipitated by the induction of the husband, in terms of overcrowding, inadequate facilities or sheer inability to locate a place to live, were felt by only seven of the families, and only three of these considered it a hardship. The J family were hit hard by this problem.

Mr. J was an ex-army man who liked to give orders, but made a happy home for his love-starved, dependent wife and only daughter. They had been on the move when the war began, looking for a place to settle down, and accepted the husband's call to service philosophically enough but were caught without a place to live. Mrs. J and her child moved from bleak boarding house to bleak boarding house for months in an effort to find a place where they could settle down until the end of the war, and were despairing of ever finding a more permanent residence when her husband's mother invited them to share her home until Mr. J came back. Now the earlier experience is only a distant nightmare.

A situation that few wives used to the privacy of their own homes would care to put up with was forced upon Mrs. M, but she and two or three others in similar situations thought nothing of it.

The M's were a highly individualistic but coöperative family, used to getting along without their man for fairly long periods at a time because of his long-distance trucking job. Between the time of notification by the draft board and Mr. M's actual departure, the family had done their crying, dried their tears, and moved into a larger house together with her parents and a sister with husband and two children. The M's also had two children. The house was not nearly large enough for such a tribe, and privacy was impossible. Mrs. M, instead of complaining, was grateful that they had a home at all in the face of their reduced financial circumstances and cheerfully and patiently spent the next couple of years sorting out children, possessions, and tempers.

MANAGING THE HOME

The physical management of the home was a hardship for forty-three of the families. This problem, like child discipline, was in a sense common to all the families, but again a number of women had carried the full responsibility for the home previous to the separation, either by common consent or because the husband was lazy or irresponsible. Also, a number of families had husband-substitutes in the shape of grandparents or other relatives, who helped with odd jobs, budgeting and planning for the family. Of the forty-three families who had no such help or who had trouble in spite of help or previous experience, thirty-five defined their problem as a hardship. The KL's were among these.

The KL's were Bohemians and followed traditional patterns of family living. The husband was rigidly patriarchal and his wife was very dependent on him in everything. She couldn't believe that he would have to go into service until he actually left, so she was unprepared and wept a great deal. She had just returned recently from the hospital with a second baby, and just didn't feel able to take on her new responsibilities. They also lived in an isolated area where help was hard to get. Never during the whole separation period did she make an independent decision. She either wrote to her husband, or, if there wasn't time for that, she asked her parents who lived in a nearby town what to do. She barely kept the daily routine moving, and the parents handled any exigencies.

The M's in their crowded home, mentioned above, had a more difficult situation but were better equipped to meet it. Mrs. M considered her job as manager of their home as a challenge rather than a hardship. It was her job to clean and keep orderly the overcrowded quarters. It was she who called in the plumber, did the shopping and cooking, supervised all the children while her sister worked, and kept everyone from getting in each other's hair. She succeeded to an astonishing degree, too!

In other cases the wife thought she was having a pretty hard time of it when the community thought she was well cushioned from hardships. Mrs. K was one of these fretters.

The K family was happy but turbulent, equalitarian but with plenty of bickering, especially over how the only son should be handled. Another source of quarrels was that Mr. K thought, with some justification, that his wife was a poor manager. After he left for the service, Mrs. K went to live with his parents, and in spite of their sympathetic help she was as disorganized and impractical as ever. The mother-in-law was glad to take care of the housework and cooking because whenever Mrs. K tried, the house never looked right and the meals were never on time. Just caring for her new baby seemed more than she could handle, and she managed to run through all the family savings in spite of help from the in-laws.

ILLNESS OF A CHILD

When the man of the family is gone, illness of the mother can create a very difficult problem, and all fifteen of the families who faced this difficulty felt that it had been a hardship. The women on the whole were a hardy group, and there seems to have been no feigning of illness in order to avoid assuming unpleasant responsibilities. The situation in the A family was nearly desperate.

The A's had traditional patriarchal patterns of family living, but the general standard of role-fulfillment was low because husband and wife were in poor health and keeping their five children fed and clothed seemed to be almost more than they could manage. Mrs. A was tubercular, and feared that she would not be strong enough to look after the family alone if her husband was drafted. Her fears were realized, because she was soon so weak and ill that she could scarcely move around the house. She could not cook, so the children lived on bread and milk, and had not a brother come to live with Mrs. A and taken care of the food shopping and some chores, the family would not have managed to keep going. As it was, they barely managed to survive until the husband returned, and the latter would certainly have been eligible for a dependency discharge had the wife applied to the Red Cross for aid.

A number of wives worried constantly while their husbands were away. They worried about their husbands' safety, and even more about their own responsibilities and the welfare of their children. Several women suffered from insomnia and two from nervous breakdowns as a result of extreme nervous tension, while a fourth who was already a migraine sufferer found that her attacks increased in intensity and frequency. The women who had nervous breakdowns were the only ones who were incapacitated as family heads. In both these cases the families just barely existed until the husbands returned, and one husband received a dependency discharge.

ILLNESS OF A CHILD

Serious illness of a child hit seven families, and, as might be expected, all seven considered this a hardship. None of the families had quite such a dose of illness as the T's, however.

The T's were a highly flexible, coöperative family that had survived all sorts of ups and downs with their five children and managed to have a good time doing it. Mrs. T missed her husband very much when he left for the service but made the best of it. She usually had her hands full when all the children were well, and was even busier after she came home from the hospital, a couple of months after Mr. T's departure, with her sixth baby. Soon after this, however, all five children fell ill one after the other, two of them with pneumonia, and for a time they were all in bed at once. Mrs. T had not yet recovered from childbirth, the allotment check was not large, and their home was small and inadequate, with only two beds for five children. Sheer grit and determination, plus some help from a parental family used to such crises, helped Mrs. T to pull her family through.

HAVING A BABY

Having a baby while the father was away was the hardship that most clearly revealed the mettle of these war wives. Most of them admitted that it had been tough (ten out of twelve) but they nearly all came through with flying colors. It should be remembered that all these wives already had from one to five children at home. We have just mentioned Mrs. T, who came home from the hospital with her sixth only to have the other five fall ill all at once, and who somehow managed to nurse them back to health before she had regained her own strength. Nearly every family seemed to suffer from additional complications when the childbirth period was at hand. Mrs. G, whose family is described on pp. 63–64, barely made it to the hospital. Just as she was ready to leave to have her third child, her mother-in-law informed her over the telephone that she couldn't come to care for the other children, as she had earlier promised to do. Mrs. G had to sit down to the telephone while the taxi was waiting at the door and make a whole new series of arrangements regarding the children. Not only was she able to keep her presence of mind and make the new arrangements, but she was even able to forgive her mother-in-law for letting her down at the last moment.

WIFE WORKING

Thirty-one of the wives went to work after their husbands left, and only eleven of them considered this a hardship. Those who considered it a hardship were doing it for financial reasons alone, although many who started working for financial reason ended by thoroughly enjoying their work. A great deal was demanded of these women, because they had the same problems all the other women in the study did of being father and mother both to the children, making decisions for the family, and so on, in addition to giving a major portion of each day to an entirely different and often exacting set of tasks. On the whole, those women managed best who had relatives who could help care for the children, but several women who had children of school age managed to give them everything they needed and work too. Part-time jobs were the answer for a few. Mrs. CT was one of the eleven who agreed with the general public that working was a hardship in a husbandless family. (The CT family is described on p. 65.) In an effort to be even more independent of her parents and save for a separate home, she tried working. She had always been a worrier, however, and spent the days on the job fretting about how her mother was handling the children. She could not bear to give up any part of her own role as a parent and finally preferred staying home with the children to working and saving for a separate home. This merely shifted the emphasis from the hardship of working to the hardship of being cooped up with her parents.

Most of the women enjoyed working. If they didn't do it for financial reasons, they usually did it in order to "keep busy," to occupy their minds, to keep from missing their husbands. To many of them it gave a feeling of independence and self-sufficiency they had never had before. This was true of Mrs. U.

In the U family, Mr. U was the affectionate and indulgent patriarch who liked to make his wife feel important by asking her opinion on family matters. His induction caught them unprepared, and left her feeling lost, or, as she put it, "only half alive." Money was short, and she was faced with the necessity of earning additional income. She had never worked before, having lived the sheltered life of the daughter of self-respecting Italian immigrants. She left the baby with grandmother, and, with much fear and trembling, got herself a job in a bank. To her amazement, they liked her work very much. She soon discovered that she was perfectly capable of handling money and making decisions herself, and took great pride in being able to save a nice sum of money to be used when Mr. U got back.

HUSBAND REPORTED MISSING

Only one family had to go through this agony, the V's. This was a cooperative patriarchy in which induction was accepted as a necessary evil and the family prepared to make the best of it. For six months after the notification that Mr. V was missing, mother and child lived in a nightmare of fear. They said little to one another because the family was not one to display emotions or be loquacious, and they performed the family routines in a mechanical manner. Another few dreary but more hopeful months set in when Mr. V was discovered to be a prisoner of war, and only his sudden return, weak but whole, brought this family back to life.

LACK OF SOCIAL LIFE

No social life was reported as a hardship by only one wife. The tendency of most wives was to increase their social contacts, especially with other war wives, but Mrs. W had to cut out social life entirely.

Mr. W was a patriarch, kind to his shy and somewhat shrinking wife who had been rejected by her own parents. Induction took the family by surprise as they were starting to build a home, so they had to live in a temporary structure until he returned. Their income was cut in half, so Mrs. W felt that all her efforts were needed to keep the family above water and rejected all social life. She devoted herself more fully to her child but missed the social contacts sorely and felt that deprivation as much as her financial difficulties.

NO HARDSHIPS

Eleven families felt that they had had no hardships during the separation period. None of these families missed their men enough to be worth mentioning, although some of them had had a good marital adjustment before he left and wanted him back. In these cases the wives were unusually self-sufficient or unusually close to their parental families. In other words, the wife either ran the home quite capably alone and was adequate to all the children's needs, or she went home to mother and resumed her premarital status in the home, except that attention was now divided between her and her children. The F family, described on p. 62, typifies the latter situation. The Z's, in contrast, are an excellent example of a family that not only felt no hardships, but found the going easier without Mr. Z.

The Z's were a leaderless, disunited Negro family. Mr. Z preferred hanging around the YMCA and Scouting headquarters, doing things that gave him a certain amount of recognition in both colored and white communities, to going out to work to support his family. At the time of his induction he was taking no part in the family life at all. Mrs. Z was supporting the family by doing house cleaning by the hour; she handled all the family finances, looked after the children, kept her own house in reasonable order, and quarreled constantly with her husband in an effort to get him to take some responsibility whenever he was home. When he left, she felt that a great weight had been lifted from her shoulders. The allotment checks meant that she did not have to be the chief wage earner, and the house ran much more smoothly because, as she told the interviewer, "There wasn't any use nagging my husband to do the chores, because he wasn't around, so the children and I did them without any fussing!" Possibly another result of her not being able to nag at him was that he took more interest in the family while in service than he ever had before, and they reëstablished a companionship by mail that they had not known for many years.

SUMMARY OF SEPARATION CRISES

We have seen that the induction of the husband and the father into the armed forces meant very different things to different families, and that it was by no means a crippling crisis for all of them. Keeping in mind the three variables which determine whether or not an occurrence becomes a crisis—the hardships of the event, the resources of the family to meet the event, and the family's definition of the event—we have examined a number of family situations characterized by one or more hardships. The hardships included absence of the husband as companion, father, handy man, and protector, finances, child discipline, and prolonged maladjustment of a child, living with in-laws, housing, managing the home, illness of the wife, illness of children, having a baby, wife working, lack of social life, and, in one case, having the husband reported missing. Some families ran the gamut of these hardships; others felt few of them. The resources were examined in terms of the previous role structure of the family, the wife's experience in family management and her latent abilities, and the availability of relatives outside the immediate family circle. The family was observed in action as it prepared to meet the crisis in ways ranging from ineffective worrying and hoping the induction wouldn't happen, to combining households with a relative and the wife going to work to supplement an anticipated decrease in income. Finally, the enormous range of variation in the definitions of the situations was delineated. There were families who had their full share of troubles and felt that the going was tough but made the best of it. There were other families who would be considered by the community to have just as many troubles, but because of past experiences or a deviant husband-wife relationship these families didn't feel that they were suffering any hardships. Still other families had what the community would regard as pretty easy going, and yet special circumstances made these families regard themselves as in trouble. In the last analysis, the family's definition of the event would seem to be the determining factor in deciding whether or not the separation was a crisis. If the family felt that it was having difficulty, no matter how easy the situation might seem to others, that family acted in a disorganized and ineffective manner or suffered extreme emotional upset, which is typical crisis behavior. If the family continued to function smoothly and was not in the least disturbed by the adjustments it had to make, then no matter how many hardships knocked at the door, it experienced no crisis.

TYPICAL ADJUSTMENT PATTERNS

Making a profile of the process of adjustment to a crisis was suggested by Koos in his *Families in Trouble* (27), and was found useful in giving a summary picture of what happened during separation to each family in this study. (See our previous discussion, p. 15.)

Before attempting the silhouettes for individual families, the adjustment patterns were broken down into five periods and a summary was written for each family covering these five periods. The first period was the pre-crisis family situation, and was described in terms of role structure and adaptability and flexibility of the family. The second was anticipatory reactions to the crisis, or how the family did or did not prepare for it. Third was the immediate reaction to the departure of the husband and father, in terms of emotional upset and type of activity after he left. Fourth was the long-run reaction and readjustment process, with the wife taking over or failing to take over her new responsibilities. Fifth was the final readjustment made by the family to the husband's absence, with a picture of the new role structure. A profile was then drawn to represent each summary, as illustrated below, and the families were classified according to the profiles. Four classifications were made as follows:

good, rapid adjustment to separation; good, slow adjustment; fair adjustment and poor adjustment.

GOOD, RAPID ADJUSTMENT TO SEPARATION

The typical profile for the good, rapid adjustment to separation is pictured here. The number 1 represents the level of marital adjust-

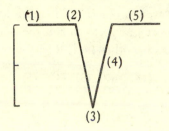

ment before the separation. Two represents anticipatory disturbance and preparation; 3, the immediate emotional impact of the departure of the husband; 4, the long-term reactions and adjustment process; and 5, the level of adjustment after reorganization is complete.

Actually, there are two typical profiles for good adjustment to separation, as there are two typical profiles for each of the four classifications. One is the profile given above, where there was good marital adjustment before the separation, and the second in which

there was poor marital adjustment before the separation and good adjustment to separation, possibly resulting from the husband's absence. A third profile is a straight line, indicating a very flexible family that was not in the least disturbed or disorganized by the separation. In the first type the greatest number of husbands enlisted with the consent of their wives and the greatest number made some type of preparation for the separation, chiefly in terms of moving in with parents, "crying it out" in advance and rationalizing the need for the husband's absence through emotions of patriotism, and so on. Immediate reactions to his departure were predominantly feelings of numbness and unreality, more tears, and, above all, loneliness. Long-term reactions were a continued longing for the husband but with considerable effort put forth to run the house as well as possible and be father and mother both to the children. There was a

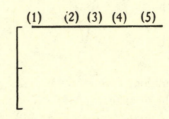

(1)　　(2) (3) (4) (5)

conscious effort to keep busy so the husband wouldn't be missed so much, and the wife often felt that she was under some strain. When adjustment and reorganization had been achieved, the wife in the majority of cases was handling the family responsibilities alone but continued to miss her husband and derived emotional satisfaction from writing and receiving letters. The husband was still felt as a vital part of the family and might have continued to share in the decision-making process.

In the second type, where there was poor marital adjustment before separation, there was little preparation for the separation and it was regarded as "a good thing" all around. In spite of this, however, the immediate reaction to the departure was a feeling of loneliness. Long-term reactions were more revealing, indicating enjoyment of the new freedom. These wives took considerable pleasure in running their homes to suit themselves now that the husbands were away and they managed their responsibilities well. The final readjustment found the ranks closed against the husband. The wife and children were having a satisfactory home life without him, things were running smoothly, and the wife, at least, dreaded her husband's return.

GOOD, SLOW ADJUSTMENT TO SEPARATION

The typical profile for the good, slow adjustment to separation where the initial marital adjustment was good is shown here.

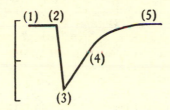

Notice the more gradual slope of the upcurve. A number of these families were caught unprepared by induction, although there were also enlistments with the wife's consent. As in the rapid adjustment group, the immediate reactions were numbness, tears, and loneliness. Long-term reactions were continued loneliness and great effort to manage new responsibilities, with some discouragement when things didn't go too well, and considerable sense of strain. The final readjustment was similar to that of the group that adjusted more rapidly. Responsibilities were successfully redistributed, but the husband was still felt to be part of the family and his return was longed for. The readjustment was a greater effort for this group than for the first group.

The next profile is for the families that made a good, slow adjustment to separation but had a poor reunion.

Like its counterpart in the rapid adjustment group, this series of families tended to regard the separation as a good thing, but felt lonely when the separation actually struck. More readjustments had to be made before they could fully enjoy their freedom, but relatives

stepped in to care for the children and half the group was able to go
to work. In the final readjustment these wives discovered they were
more independent than they had ever been before and closed ranks

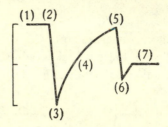

completely with the children against the husband, feeling self-sufficient and not desiring his return.

FAIR ADJUSTMENT TO SEPARATION

The families with good previous marital adjustment who made
only a fair adjustment to the separation are shown in the accompanying profile. These families were, in the main, unprepared and

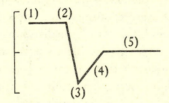

shocked by the separation and suffered considerable emotional upset
when the departure took place. The wives did not seem to be able to
take over effectively the extra responsibilities left by their husbands.
They managed to keep going and the families were able to present
a more or less normal "front" to the community, but the adjustment
process was a severe strain on the family resources and there were a
number of cases of personal maladjustment among the children as
a result of the father's absence. For these families there was no sense

of having finally made a reorganization of the family for the "duration." They worked out a *modus vivendi* but there was no closing of ranks at all and the group was just waiting for their husbands to return. A number of the children continued maladjusted throughout the separation.

Those families who had a poor marital adjustment but made a fair adjustment to separation have the accompanying profile. The

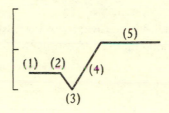

separation was looked forward to but, as in the earlier poor marital adjustment groups, the actual departure stimulated feelings of loneliness. The wives in this group either felt little responsibility for their families and stepped out pretty freely, or were very poor managers and suffered greatly from worry and nervous strain. The families kept going, but there was never any satisfactory reorganization of roles even where the ranks were closed against the husband.

POOR ADJUSTMENT TO SEPARATION

The next profile characterizes poor adjustment to separation with good previous marital adjustment. There is no characteristic re-

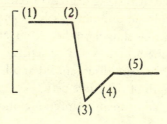

sponse to the impending crisis in this group—the range is from complete unpreparedness to thorough preparedness. These families were, nevertheless, more or less paralyzed by the departure of the husband and unable to readjust the roles in the home. There was continued emotional disturbance, and two wives suffered complete nervous breakdowns. The families could not reorganize themselves and only survived the separation period with outside help, or, where demoralization was complete, by having the husband returned to them through a dependency discharge.

Only one family fell in the category of poor adjustment to separation and poor previous marital adjustment. This family was com-

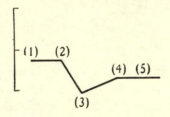

pletely unprepared for the separation and missed the husband very much, particularly as the wife was very ill. She got worse and was unable to continue her own role in the home, let alone her husband's, and the family just barely existed with the help of a relative until the husband was discharged.

USE OF PROFILES

Although the profile is at best a brief summary of the adjustment process, it can be used in varying degrees of refinement of detail. For example, in this study no attempt has been made to measure the slope between 2 and 3, as shown on the accompanying profile. It has been assumed that the actual events of separation disorganized all families rapidly if they were disorganized at all, although there is a difference in the length of the curve between 2 and 3, depending on the level of marital adjustment before separation. A more refined

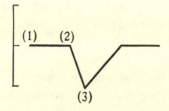

use of the profile might indicate the speed of disorganization by the slope of the curve and the degree of disorganization by the height of the turning point. On the upward curve, 4 on the accompanying profile, we have distinguished between steep and gradual slopes and

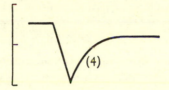

have indicated the degree of reorganization by the height of the leveling-off line, but actually the slope is not always a steady upward one as represented. There may be ups and downs in the reorganization process, so that a profile would look like the one shown here.

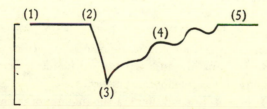

For present purposes the less detailed profile is adequate, but it should be exploited more fully than has been done here.

Definition of Good Adjustment to Separation

On what basis were families classified as having made good, fair, and poor adjustments to separation? Two sets of data were used:

the one for our statistical analysis to be discussed in the next chapter, and the other for the present case study analysis.

For purposes of statistical analysis a scale that could be scored was necessary. We, therefore, constructed a scale for adjustments to separation and a scale for adjustment to reunion based largely on personal and family outcomes and personal and family attitudes which the wife (and husband in reunion) could fill out at the time of the interview (see pp. 399–413 for a copy of the scale). Good adjustment to separation involved closing of ranks, shifting of responsibilities and activities of the father to other members, continuing the family routines, maintaining husband-wife and father-child relationships by correspondence and visits, utilizing the resources of friends, relatives, and neighbors, and carrying on plans for the reunion.

Good adjustment to reunion involved opening the ranks to let the father back in, realigning the power and authority, reworking the division of labor and responsibilities, sharing the home and family activities with the father, renewing the husband-wife intimacies and confidences, catching up on one another's friends, resuming the father-child ties, bringing balance between husband-wife and mother-child and father-child relationships, picking up the plans made during separation, reworking and finally putting them into action.

In our case study analysis we have been able to assess other aspects of adjustment to separation and reunion and have achieved a broader and more discriminating and yet more dynamic definition of adjustment than was possible in our statistical scale.

Good adjustment to separation may be thought of in two different ways. One type of adjustment is in terms of the whole family unit, including the husband. Another type of adjustment is in terms of the family unit that is left behind, excluding the husband. The criteria for the two types of adjustment are exactly the same, except where the relationship of the husband to the family is concerned. The first criterion would involve the effectiveness of the process of role redistribution. The important questions are: Does the family continue to do the same things for its remaining members that it has always done? Does the household run smoothly? Are the chores done? Do decisions continue to be made about finances, for the children, and so on? It does not particularly matter *how* the roles are redistributed. It may be a very well-adjusted family in which the wife carries alone the full responsibilities for her own role and her husband's, acting as father to the children and doing his chores in the home, while the children's role in the home is unchanged. In another well-adjusted family the children may take over all the father's chores and one of the children may take over the mother or father role to a younger sibling. In still a third, the wife and children may remain in their previous roles and a relative may step in to take over the husband's responsibilities. The speed of role reorganization has nothing to do with the degree of adjustment. Some families redistribute responsibilities immediately, and family life goes on without a break. Other families become temporarily disorganized and take a little while to get on their feet again, but, once they do, they adjust just as effectively as the ones who did not suffer temporary disorganization.

A second criterion is the absence of nervous tension and emotional upset *to an incapacitating degree* in any member of the remaining family unit. Even if the family has managed an adequate role redistribution, if the new roles are played at the cost of extreme emotion and nervous tension, or with constant overt conflict, the family is no longer fulfilling the same functions for its members. It has provided physical security at the expense of emotional security.

The criteria for adjustment diverge when the role of the husband is considered. When good adjustment is measured in terms of the complete family unit, then an added criterion would be that the husband plays a role in the family that is mutually satisfactory and emotionally satisfying to husband, wife, and children. The type of role may differ widely from family to family. In one family the husband may continue to play his old role from a distance, the wife turning to him by correspondence for all but the daily unimportant decisions. In another family the father may assume a completely new father-husband role by correspondence, participating in family life through his letters in a way which he never did when he was at home. In a third family the husband may relinquish all but his companionship role in the family, so that affectional ties between him and the wife and children are continued and perhaps even deepened through the exchange of letters. So long as this role-by-correspondence is emotionally satisfying to all concerned, the family may be well adjusted.

Some families fulfill the first two criteria of good adjustment, but at the expense of the third. They have closed ranks against the husband and excluded him completely from the group. In most cases the marital adjustment before separation was poor, and the good adjustment of the remaining unit is possible because of his absence. This is unquestionably not good adjustment of the *family* as such, but it is good adjustment of that part of the family with which we are here most concerned; thus these families are rated as well adjusted to separation. When we discuss adjustment to reunion, the weaknesses of this type of adjustment to separation will be apparent.

The families who were rated as having made only a fair adjustment to separation were those who managed an adequate, but not completely satisfactory, role redistribution, or those who managed new roles at great emotional expense. The families rated as having made poor adjustments were those who were unable to reorganize to meet the demands of the new situations, or who suffered extreme emotional maladjustment or nervous breakdown. The degree of adjustment, then, has been judged by effectiveness of role reorganization, by degree of accompanying nervous strain and emotional maladjustment, and, in general, by whether the family continues to satisfy the needs of its members. Two types of adjustment have been noted: those made in terms of continued participation of the husband in the family unit, and those made by excluding the husband from the family unit.

Adjustment to Reunion

The reunion was defined as a crisis by surprisingly few families in the study. It was certainly a new situation calling for new action patterns, because the return of a husband after one to three years of absence calls for very different behavior than the return of a husband from a day's work. There were also hardships, but, as in the separation crisis, the deciding factor seemed to be the family's definition of the event, and most families felt that the husband's return was a very joyful event.

Most of the husbands who had returned to their families when the study was made had not been home for very long, which meant that the families were in a sort of a "reunion glow" and not as likely to be aware of hardships as they would be later. Nevertheless, there were troubles. In ten of the families the wife had become permanently more independent as a result of the husband's absence, and this created a role conflict when the husband returned, causing trouble between them. In twenty families the children had grown so close to the mother or another relative in the father's absence that they resented the return of the father, or accepted him as companion but refused to accept him as a disciplinarian—so there was conflict between father and children.

For the husband, there were special hardships which had repercussions for the whole family. After the lack of responsibility in army life, eleven of the men found it hard to settle down to family life. This they rarely admitted, but their restlessness and moodiness at home and their impatience with the children was ample indication to the wives that these husbands were finding the adjustment a bit difficult.

Lack of adequate housing was a hardship for eight families. In these cases prewar homes had been given up so the families could double up with relatives or live in smaller apartments while the husband was away, and when the husband returned they were unable to find anything to rent or buy which compared with their prewar housing and was within their means. Although housing troubles hit this group hardest, many families had grave disappointments in regard to housing because so many husbands and wives had planned together in their letters about the dream house they would build after the war, only to find that they could not possibly afford to build after the reunion because of rising building costs.

Seven men had not been able to find jobs that they liked. One or two were beginning to be seriously worried about their employment opportunities, but most of them felt that something would turn up sooner or later and did not regard their unemployment too seriously. Six of the men were ill and were not yet able to take up their full family responsibilities. Several of these families were desperate because the veteran's compensation they were getting was not enough to support the family.

Old conflicts which had been present before the separation began cropping up in nine families, and ended in a decision to divorce in five families. None of the divorces were due to conflicts that arose during the separation, but all dated back to prewar difficulties.

The hardships caused by the separation-reunion situation rarely caused crisis situations, partly because, as mentioned before, the return of the husband was considered a joyful event, and partly because the same resources which the family had used to meet the separation hardships were available to meet the reunion hardships; the husband himself was an additional resource, and certain adaptive skills might also have been developed during the separation.

Typical Separation-Reunion Adjustment Patterns

GOOD ADJUSTMENT TO SEPARATION; GOOD ADJUSTMENT TO REUNION

The families will be kept in their adjustment-to-separation classifications as the adjustment-to-reunion patterns are outlined. The first

profile represents good adjustment to separation and good adjustment to reunion. The first five points on the diagram were explained
on p. 75. Six represents the positive, joyful reaction to the impending reunion, as opposed to the negative, fearful reaction indicated

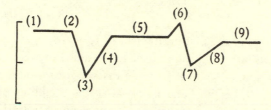

by 2. Seven is the disorganization of joy, as opposed to the disorganization of sorrow represented by 3. Eight represents the gradual readjustment to normal family living and 9 represents the final reorganization, which may be a return to prewar patterns or different
patterns, but which is in all events a reorganization which is satisfying to the whole family. An alternative profile contains an arrow,
indicating the point at which the husband's arrival is anticipated.

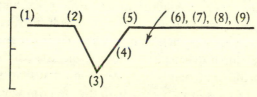

The families with this profile did not experience upheaval of any
kind as a result of the husband's return. The families were glad to
have him back but were undemonstrative, and he slipped back into
his old role in the home without any fuss at all. A rare profile in this
group is one which indicates that an otherwise well-adjusted family
was temporarily numbed and disorganized by the husband's return
but quickly adjusted again. This was most likely to happen where
the husband and wife were unused to separation of any kind and
did not have techniques for bridging the gap of absence.

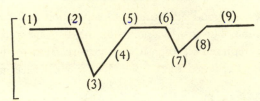

The families of the first profile looked forward eagerly to the husband's return to his old roles in the home and experienced joyful, if disrupting, reunions which in some cases were regarded as second honeymoons. Like the honeymoon after the wedding, there were sometimes extended trips together, vacations away from the routines of home life, and even where the family didn't journey away from home, the atmosphere was euphoric and characterized by elation. Depending on the nature of the affectional ties within the family, the honeymoon would be shared only by husband and wife or would include the whole family together. After the honeymoon was over, the majority of families tended to pick up somewhere near where they had left off when the husband departed for the service, although there were minor adjustments to be made, and some disillusioning rearrangements to reality of humdrum routines necessary. The most frequent adjustment recorded was the problem of getting the children to accept the father's role as a family authority. Since all but three husbands had been home less than six months, some families were still struggling with this problem when the interview took place.

The honeymoon glow was especially apparent in recently returned families where many of the disillusionments which preceded real reorganization had yet to take place. Even when the families insisted that things were already just as they used to be, it was apparent that there were adjustments that had not yet been faced which just hadn't worked their way to the surface yet, because the husband was still "company" within the home. Some families moved more rapidly than others in recognizing the effects which separation had made on the family ties and made a conscious attempt to redistribute the responsibilities in the family so that the husband would have his say again and be recognized as a source of authority by the children. Other spouses showed that they had developed an increased appreciation of the meaning of the wife-and-mother and the husband-and-father roles during the separation, and came to the reunion with the firm resolve to participate more fully in the family than they had before the induction.

GOOD ADJUSTMENT TO SEPARATION; POOR REUNION

Two distinct profiles are formed here from merging individual family silhouettes. The first is one in which the families experienced a good separation adjustment and in the initial stages of reunion had the illusion of happy family relations but as the psychic honeymoon

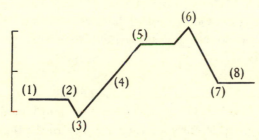

wore off and the routines, the old differences, and the frustrations of family living began showing through the ectoplasm of hazy unreality which had heretofore hidden them, the family became maladjusted.

The second profile is made up of family adjustments as follows: Beginning with a poor marital adjustment before induction, the family made a good separation adjustment with the husband absent, only to be immediately disorganized by his return.

Both sets of families had poor marital adjustment before the separation. They reacted toward the anticipated reunion either with hope that things would be better than before, or with fear that they would be the same or worse than before. The families that had an initially happy reunion soon became as badly disorganized as those which reunited under tension. Both sets of families shared covert tensions

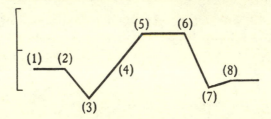

and troubles before the war separation occurred. These families were more sensitive to new troubles, too. Husbands thought that their wives were too independent, and were at odds on that count. They were less likely to conceal their restlessness at being tied down to family life again. Oddly enough, however, the children in this set of families had no difficulty in accepting their fathers, as they did in better adjusted groups.

FAIR ADJUSTMENT TO SEPARATION; GOOD REUNION

The individual family silhouettes merged into four distinct profiles in this group of fairly adjusted families. In the first profile we

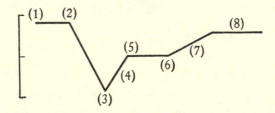

have a set of families with good marital adjustment before the separation which makes only fair adjustments to separation, anticipates a return to the prewar patterns of family life, and experiences a happy family reunion with a fairly easy return to former roles.

The second profile represents families with good initial marital adjustment which did only so-so during separation but experienced a real "honeymoon type reunion," with children included, followed by

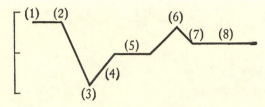

a gradual settling down to the realities of family life, with friendly give and take and few conflicts.

Profile number three charts the adjustments of families with good previous marital adjustment, in which a slight disorganization followed immediately after the father's return, chiefly because the chil-

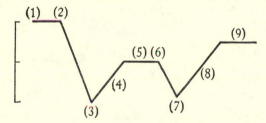

dren were jealous of having to share mother with father and were unwilling to accept his discipline. The children are gradually won over within these families by patience, playing on the floor with them and "bribing" them with toys. Once they were settled into an accepted place, these fathers thrived on family life.

Profile number four describes families in which the reunion glow may not be over, in which there are some doubts that the reunion adjustment is permanent. Starting initially with only fair marital adjustment, the family makes only fair adjustment to separation, but hopes for better relations in reunion. A honeymoon type of reunion brought back emotions of courtship days, and there was evidence of

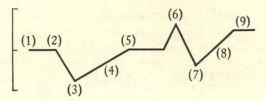

increased awareness of family responsibilities on the part of both wife and husband. These augur for more coöperative roles in the home for both of them.

FAIR ADJUSTMENT TO SEPARATION; POOR REUNION

Two profiles are prevalent in this group of families. The first represents families that had only fair or poor marital adjustment before the separation, and anticipated a return to the same somewhat unsatisfactory kind of family life after the reunion, a life not fully

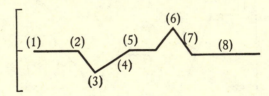

pleasant, but yet preferred by both husband and wife to continued separation. Since there had been real loneliness experienced in the husband's absence, the reunion actually reached the intensity of a honeymoon experience, but old conflicts soon began cropping up and new, unanticipated difficulties complicated the reality phases of the reunion. The children were jealous of the attentions received by the stranger-father, and the husband himself felt that the wife had become too independent. These conditions introduced a state of tension that pulled the family down below its previous level of maladjustment.

The second profile describes families which had a very bad marital adjustment before the separation. In families of this category neither husband nor wife desired a reunion, although occasionally one mate wanted to give the marriage another chance. Sometimes a reunion was attempted but old conflicts flared so high that divorce was the

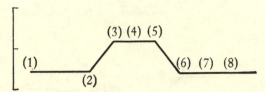

only thing the couple agreed upon. Other families did not even attempt a reunion but simply went ahead with plans for divorce.

POOR ADJUSTMENT TO SEPARATION; GOOD REUNION

The families in this type of adjustment category are highly integrated but highly inflexible families which were utterly unable to adjust to separation and virtually suspended effective family living until the father returned to assume responsibility for the family. It

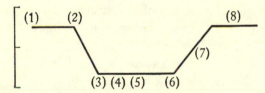

was expected that family life would be resumed as before immediately upon his return, and to a surprising extent that is the story of what happened. Many families who made the poorest adjustment to the separation seemed to have the fewest adjustments to make to the reunion. This is not a generalization which holds for the entire sample. The profile for the families in this category is shown here.

POOR ADJUSTMENT TO SEPARATION; POOR REUNION

There is only one family in the sample classified by the case study analyst as poor adjustment to separation and poor reunion. Its silhouette is a graphic portrayal of trouble and stress.

This family, because of a combination of illness and ineffective husband and wife, were just barely managing to survive as a unit before induction. They sank well below the level of meeting the family needs during the husband's absence, and just barely returned

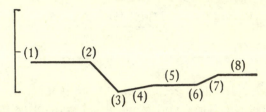

to minimum adequacy with his return. Family members did not expect to do much more than struggle on as they had before the separation. When the husband returned, the family had to face the added complication of service-induced poor health. The children also had difficulty in accepting the father because they had become so accustomed to an uncle who had lived in the home as a type of father substitute while their father was away. The family had just come to the attention of a social worker at the time of the interview.

DEFINITION OF GOOD ADJUSTMENT TO REUNION

We have already discussed the definition of good adjustment which was used in constructing the scale for the statistical study. In that scale both husband and wife were instruments in judging the adequacy of their own reunion adjustments through the device of checking statements which applied to their family experience (for details see Methodological Note, Appendix B, pp. 375-377).

The case history accounts of reunion adjustment offer additional data on which to base a judgment of reunion adequacy. In some ways the same criteria which apply to separation adjustment apply equally well to reunion. In discussing separation adjustments, we said that two types of adjustment could be classified as "good": one was the case in which the family adjusted well but included the absent husband in their thinking and planning; and the second was an adjustment in which the family adjusted well by excluding the husband, which we have termed a good closed ranks adjustment. In both these adjustment types the general criterion of adjustment used was whether or not the family continued to fill the basic needs of family members in a satisfying manner. The tests involved ascertaining the effectiveness of role reorganization after the separation and the lack of incapacitating emotional maladjustment and nervous strain among family members.

When we turn to reunion, we find only one of these separation adjustment types just discussed predictive of good adjustment to reunion. Many of the families which adjusted nicely to the husband's absence by closing ranks against him were not anxious for him to return. Even if they were willing for him to return, they had no techniques to bridge the gap created by his absence, because there had been little or no communication during the separation and even letter-to-letter relationships had practically ceased. On the other hand, the families that made a good adjustment to separation by continuing to include the husband in the family unit through letters, visits, and a general awareness of his place in the home can be predicted to make a good adjustment to reunion.

The same criteria that differentiated among families with respect to separation adjustment may be used profitably in measuring reunion adequacy. Effective role reorganization remains very important. The family must redistribute responsibilities and privileges so that the father will have either his old roles in the home again or will have a set of new roles which are both satisfying to him personally and don't reflect adversely on his status within the family. In the shake-up, family members must have complementary roles. It is perfectly possible, for example, for the wife to continue to handle, after the husband's return and even with his glad consent, the control of the finances which he deeded her when he left. Some men found their accounts better kept, their bank balance higher, and their resources better stewarded under the wife's management than had been the case under their own direction. Again, the wife may have become more or less independent in decision making than she was before, and the husband willing to assume more or less responsibility. A few wives could hardly wait to give up their new-found independence and felt that they never wanted to make another decision again without the crutch of a husband. As we analyzed these many combinations of roles, we saw that it was not the combination which was important but the facts that the roles of husband and wife and children dovetailed together. As long as the roles were complementary and acceptable to parents and children, it did not matter whether they were the old preseparation roles or new patterns developed during the husband's absence, or new patterns which came out of the scramble after he returned, they worked equally well.

The ability to effect this reorganization of roles without undue nervous strain and emotional maladjustment has also been regarded as important to good adjustment to reunion. The wife in a patriarchal family who has enjoyed her independence, for example, may overtly return to her old role because she knows that this is what her husband desires, but she may suffer painful frustration knowing she no longer functions effectively in the subservient role. Again, both husband and wife in a family of status in an upper-middle-class neighborhood may attempt to return to earlier "gracious living" roles because they value outward family solidarity although they have grown apart during the separation. The strains and tensions which arise in playing uncongenial roles are noted in assaying adequacy of adjustment to reunion by the analyst. It should be pointed out that *some* strain is invariably involved in readjusting to the presence of a long-absent member of the family. Very few families were able to pick up where they had left off before the husband's departure without conscious effort. These families tended to be more or less undemonstrative in their home life, well integrated but not intimate with one another, people who worked well together because they felt that it was the thing to do, but not because of strongly felt emotional bonds. Where the affectional ties were strong and family life was lived more intensely, there was apt to be more strain in the readjustment process, perhaps because person-centeredness in families and strong emotional attachments go together. The strains felt in such families were a necessary part of the adjustment process but did not prevent a final adjustment from taking place which was mutually satisfying to all members of the family.

We have defined good adjustment to reunion, in sum, as the attainment of a working dynamic equilibrium in which reorganization of roles into complementary patterns has been satisfactorily completed, duties and responsibilities have been reallocated, and the emotional strains and stresses of readjustment have not left serious scars on family relations. In families that are well adjusted following reunion, the basic needs of all members of affection, security, and growth are again being met in a satisfying fashion.

As a means of summarizing the great variety of types of adjustment to separation and reunion perceived through the analysis of the narrative records by the case study method, we have constructed two tables containing the range and distribution of profiles of adjustment to separation and reunion—Table 8, Distribution of Profiles of Adjustment to Separation of 116 Families Cross-Classified by Types of Adjustment to Separation (p. 98), and Table 9, Distribution of Profiles of Adjustment to Reunion of 116 Families Cross-Classified by Types of Separation Adjustment (p. 99).

TABLE 8. Distribution of Profiles of Adjustment to Separation Cross-Classified by Types of Adjustment to Separation
(116 Iowa Families)

Types of Adjustment to Separation	Profiles Depicting Course of Adjustment to Separation					Number of Families with Unique Profiles	Total
Good, Rapid Adjustment to Separation Number of Families	34	8	6	6	2	8	64
Good, Slow Adjustment to Separation Number of Families	17	2	2	5		1	25
Fair Adjustment to Separation Number of Families	16	2	2			1	21
Poor Adjustment to Separation Number of Families	4	2				0	6 / 116

TABLE 9. Distribution of Profiles of Adjustment to Reunion Cross-Classified by Types of Adjustment to Separation

(116 Iowa Families)

Types of Adjustment to Separation	Profiles Depicting Course of Adjustment to Reunion	Number of Families with Unique Profiles	Total
Good, Rapid Adjustment to Separation			64
Number of Families	31 7 3 4 4 2 6 3	4	
Good, Slow Adjustment to Separation			25
Number of Families	17 0 2 0 1 1 2 2	0	
Fair Adjustment to Separation			21
Number of Families	13 3 2 1 1	1	
Poor Adjustment to Separation			6
Number of Families	4 1 1	0	116

~~~~~~

PART THREE

Families Which Thrive and Families Which
Crack Under Stress

CHAPTER V

STATISTICAL FINDINGS: FACTORS MOST
ASSOCIATED WITH GOOD ADJUSTMENT

BY now it is apparent that the task of setting off families which thrived during separation and in reunion from those who lost heart when the going was rough, is a complex assignment. It was an over-simplification to compare the experiences of our families under crisis to reactions of individuals to prescribed stimuli under the controlled conditions of the psychological laboratory.

The preceding chapters have detailed for us the many variables operating when a group of families face two situations in common, like war-forced separation and peace-arranged reunion. Since each family is to a large extent a closed system, the impact of the situation on its structure will not be exactly the same as the impact of a similar situation on another family's structure. Secondly, the situation represented by separation of father from family varies in the hardships it entails family by family, and the resources families bring to meet the situation differ greatly. Third, the definition the family makes of the situation, that is, treating it *as if it were* or *as if it were not* a threat to their cherished goals, differs from family to family. With all of these elements varying, we can truly say that the uniform quality of the stimulus itself is an illusion, and its variation needs to be taken into account. A fourth source of variation is the variable of the family itself, its adequacy to meet crises, its past history with trouble, and its integrity and adaptability, to mention only a few of the several score attributes of organization which determine capacity to survive in a dynamic society, many of which have been discussed in Chapter II. Finally, the fifth item, which is treated in this chapter as the dependent variable, is family adjustment, a slippery and difficult segment of behavior to capture, define, and measure. Two measures of family adjustment are taken for most of the families—adjustment to separation (for all 135 families), and adjustment to reunion (for 114 families whose fathers had returned at the time the interviews were taken). The variety of adjustments to separation and reunion have been described in Chapter IV and will be reviewed again in more detail in Chapter VII as the depth-delving skills of case study analysis are brought to bear on our materials. In the present chapter this variety of adjustment to crisis is minimized by reducing every family's agonies and accomplishments during the separation period to a simple score, ranging from *one* for very poor adjustment to *five* for superlative adjustment. The adjustments during the reunion period are likewise reduced to a comparable one-to-five score for each family.

We have some misgivings about what we have done in attempting, through scales and tests, to reduce the variety of family behavior in a complex situation to a numerical score. We secured the best of help from other family experts in constructing the scales. We pretested them and attempted to validate them by testing them on families in Ohio which were well known to Dr. John Cuber of Ohio State University, and comparing the results by our scales with his intimate judgment of the same cases.[1] Yet we know the limitations which should be placed on what we have done. No scale can adequately capture as yet the subtleties of family behavior within the closed family system of interacting personalities. If the reader will generously postpone his objections to our method, he may judge for himself whether the results justify the steps that have been taken.

In a sense all the careful plans which went into selecting the families, constructing the questionnaires and building the interview

---

[1] The method of constructing, validating, and checking these scales is discussed at some length in the appendix, pp. 370–375.

forms, interviewing the families and tabulating the results, all these steps lead directly to the central question: How is it that some families adjust well and others poorly to crises they experience in common? The scientific question is always "how?" The journalist is more modest. He contents himself with description of *what* happened. Chapter IV is such a chapter—journalistic, descriptive of what happened to people during a period of trouble and crisis, the variety of situations they faced, the hardships they endured, the heights and depths of human experience as troubles are met and transmuted into family strengths to meet the next trouble. The multiversity of family behavior is most apparent in sweeping panoramic descriptions. The scientist asks for something more difficult to obtain, the causal connections between the colorful events which the journalist has described. It is not so much *what* happened to families as *how* some families managed to do well and some poorly during the same period that we are seeking.

To accomplish this end we are placing in juxtaposition three sets of data and analyzing their interrelationships. We are joining (1) data concerning the situations families faced, with (2) data concerning the family organization and family characteristics themselves, with (3) data reflecting how well families adjusted to these situations. We hope that we may capture in this process of analysis the structural connections between crisis situations, family characteristics, and family adjustment.

Causation must not be interpreted too narrowly. The depression, for example, may not be properly termed a basic cause of crisis; the loss of a job or the loss of part of the family's income is only the *precipitating factor*. For example, given unemployment in a family, its success in riding out the depression-born crisis by reorganization of the family's consumption patterns and finding new sources of income, may be due to a complex of internal factors which may have made the family relatively invulnerable to the depression in the first place and adjustively inclined to face and solve problems in the second place. No single factor operated, but several, in interaction, account for the family's sensitivity to crisis and its capacity to adjust to trouble. The ingenious chart devised by Koos (26) expresses well the interrelationship of causes as an event traverses the closed system of the family and becomes a crisis or doesn't, as the case may be. His list of causes of family inadequacy can be readily translated into the variables we will be dealing with as we survey the interrelationships of family organization and family adjustment in the face of crisis. To use Koos' words: "There is (sometimes) an initial cause which tends to create tensions in other areas of family life, which in turn become conflicts themselves." The whole may be represented in the accompanying diagram.

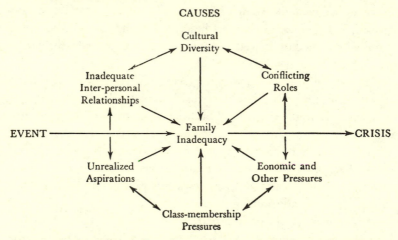

For example, cultural disparity may cause a lack of sexual satisfaction because of the differing ideas and standards of sex behavior, which in turn may lead to suspicion of the mate and lack of coöperation as breadwinner or homemaker, which in turn may create conflicting roles in the family and draw individual members into new positions of responsibility in the family at the expense of other members, all of which so weaken the affectional relationships and integration of the family as to render it unable to meet even the simple departure from its ordinary life patterns; the result, when an out-of-the-ordinary event occurs, is a crisis (26).

The Koos chart, if carried another step into the adjustment of the family crisis, would undoubtedly reveal again the interplay of many forces reflecting family adequacy in determining the adjustment itself. Causation is as multifactorial in adjustment as in the definition of, or sensitivity to, crisis, as depicted so colorfully by Koos.

Having pointed out that family behavior may only be explained adequately as a consequence of many factors operating together, we, nevertheless, are tempted to peer at it slide by slide, taking one factor at a time to aid us in the difficult mental process of conceptualizing the interrelatedness of things. In so doing we are inferring, to use one example, that because families which adjusted best to separation are more frequently democratic than autocratic in their decision making that there is some structural connection between the two sets of behaviors. The shortcoming of our thinking is that there are also many families which are quite autocratic and still adjust quite well to separation, which in a way spoils our generalization. As long as we keep the reservation in mind that statistical generalizations have limited applicability and that the associations we are observing are only first approximations, a warm-up to more precise testing, we may proceed.

To help us in perceiving the adjustment success of categories of families, we have constructed average adjustment to separation scores and average adjustment to reunion scores for the subdivisions of families studied. To take social class as an example, you will remember from Chapter III that the 135 families were divided on the basis of social status characteristics into five major social classes, upper, upper-middle, middle-middle, lower-middle, and lower classes. For purposes of illustration we will merge them into three classes: upper, middle, and lower. The upper-class families number seven, with scores of adjustment to separation of 3.6, 4.0, 4.5, 4.0, 3.4, 3.5, and 4.1. An average adjustment to separation score is obtained by adding these seven scores and dividing by seven, giving an average of 3.89. This average adjustment score may be compared with the average score for the 103 middle-class families of 3.78, and of the 25 lower-class families of 3.56 (see Chart I). Looking at such a set of comparative scores, with adjustment to separation becoming poorer as one moves from high class standing to low standing, it looks as if there might be some connection between class standing in the community and adjustment to separation in wartime.

A second measure to check the magnitude of association is necessary to compute the likelihood that this is just a chance arrangement of adjustment scores. For a table involving status characteristics which are not numbered, we can use chi-square analysis. In this instance the chi-square is sufficiently large to prove that our first supposition of an association between social status and adjustment to separation was not illusory. We can also arrange families statuswise by numbers using Kenneth Eels' scale for social status, mentioned in Chapter III. Each family is given a score which enables us to make use of the familiar coefficient of correlation r to express the magnitude of association present. In this instance, the coefficient r is 0.18 and that is large enough that the chance that it is really zero is about four out of a hundred. In statistical language this would be a significant association. We will indicate the likelihood of the relationship being due to chance by the terms *nonsignificant* if above the 5 percent level, *significant* if at the 5 percent level, and *highly significant* if at or below the 1 percent level.[2] Whenever possible, we

[2] We hasten to point out that *statistically significant* associations may have little *practical significance,* especially when the magnitude of association is very small. For purposes of prediction, the family researcher needs large coefficients of correlation; statistical significance is not enough. Actually, statistical significance merely reflects the stability of the association in question, answering only the first question of *reliability* not the crucial question of *degree of control*. In summary, as we use statistical significance in this book:

An association is,

　nonsignificant when the magnitude obtained occurs in 6 percent or more of many random samples; as an example, note that in the summary table p. 138, r = 0.16 between adjustment to reunion and flexibility in the shifting of roles, but at only the 9 percent level.

　significant when the magnitude obtained occurs in 5 percent of many random samples; as an example, note that in the summary table p. 138, r = 0.19 between

CHART I. Social Class Status in the Community and Adjustment to Separation and Reunion

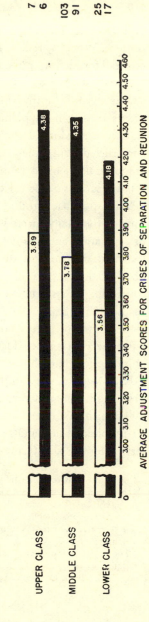
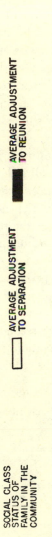

AVERAGE ADJUSTMENT SCORES FOR CRISES OF SEPARATION AND REUNION

will use the coefficient of correlation r to reflect the association present. Where variables may not be scored, chi-square will serve as our tool for identifying non-chance relationships.[3]

As a first approximation to the connections between family characteristic and family adjustment, the average adjustment score passes muster if supplemented by correlation analysis and tests of significance. Most of the charts shown in the body of the text are constructed using these average adjustment to separation and average adjustment to reunion scores as our means of depicting the relative success of the various categories of families studied.

With this background we will proceed with a factor-by-factor tour of the many faceted problem of family adjustment in the face of separation and reunion hardships. The tour will follow roughly the natural history of the families studied, starting with the childhood of the parents, the nature of the couple's initial meeting and courtship, their readiness for marriage at marriage, the roles played in the marriage itself—division of labor, and distribution of power —the degree of family adequacy, financial security, and concluding with the contingency factors of the separation period and the reunion period, hardships experienced, and modes of adjustment used.

Each stage in the family history will be discussed in three parts: first, the findings which confirm our hypotheses; second, the findings which cast questions on or disprove our hypotheses; and third, a summarized presentation of the magnitude of the relationships observed, for the statistically-minded reader.

---

adjustment to reunion and degree of affection among family members and yet is significant at the 5 percent level.

highly significant when the magnitude obtained occurs in 1 percent or less of many random samples; as an example, note that in the summary table p. 128, $r = -0.22$ between adjustment to separation and number of children in the family.

[3] For a detailed discussion of chi-square analysis and of the significance of a correlation coefficient, see T. C. McCormick, *Elementary Social Statistics* (New York: McGraw-Hill Book Company, 1941), pp. 203–209, 257–258.

CHILDHOOD EXPERIENCES OF THE SPOUSES

Current psychiatric thinking and certain previous studies (*8, 32*) insist that marriage aptitude and the capacity to be good parents are developed in childhood. Obviously what is good for marriage adjustment should have some bearing on family adjustment in the face of separation and reunion. Our study confirms this hypothesis in part, in that the happiness score of the wife in childhood, adolescence, and early marriage appears significantly related to good adjustment to separation. Another measure reflecting the wife's childhood experience is the Thurstone Neurotic Inventory, modified by Burgess for his marriage adjustment studies. The inventory probes the self-confidence of the wife, the presence or absence of fears and haunting worries, and summarizes her emotional health through a score reflecting the number of neurotic answers she checks (see the appendix for a copy of this scale, pp. 404–405). On the assumption that the fears and worries of the wife are brought from childhood to the marriage, it is interesting indeed to observe a negative but significant relationship between the Neurotic Inventory Score and the family's Adjustment to Separation Score (see Chart II).

On none of the other indices of childhood experiences, namely, happiness of wife's parents, happiness of husband's parents, number of siblings of wife, or closeness of wife and husband to their parents, was there any appreciable relationship apparent with good adjustment in separation or reunion.[4] In conclusion, it is doubtful if childhood experiences as measured in this study are of great significance in determining adjustment patterns in the face of separation and reunion crises.

[4] Two other sets of materials were solicited from childhood but were not used. The interviewer's impressions of the wife's personality make-up proved too cumbersome to tabulate and test in this context, and the intensity of relations with siblings also proved difficult to transcribe to IBM cards for analysis. The study is the poorer for these deficiencies.

CHART II. Wife's Psychoneurotic Inventory Score and Adjustment to Separation and Reunion

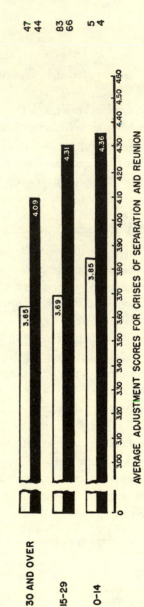

AVERAGE ADJUSTMENT SCORES FOR CRISES OF SEPARATION AND REUNION

Factors in Childhood Experience	Statistical Summary Adj. to Separation		Adj. to Reunion	
	r	Level of Sig.	r	Level of Sig.
Wife's happiness score in childhood	0.17	.05	0.06	0.26
Wife's neurotic inventory score	−0.18	.04	−0.08	0.24
Happiness score of husband's parents	—	—	0.11	0.18
Number of siblings (wife)	0.04	.28	0.05	0.27

COURTSHIP EXPERIENCES

No materials from the courtship experiences proved significant in connection with later separation and reunion adjustment. Circumstance of first meeting, whether pickups, blind dates, old friends, or meeting at church gatherings, did not seem important. It was expected that conflict patterns in courtship would carry over into marriage and family behavior, but the edge on adjustment went to parents who quarreled occasionally or frequently in courtship, an interesting finding if statistically reliable, which it wasn't in this sample. Courtship roles are, however, reflected in the marital roles played with respect to decision making and to the division of labor with respect to family duties, which we will investigate later in the chapter.

READINESS FOR MARRIAGE AT MARRIAGE

Only the crudest of evidences of preparation for marriage are available to test the association between readiness for marriage at marriage and family adjustment. If there is any justification for this crudity, it is in the lack of scales for measuring marriage readiness of settled family people eleven years after marriage. Moreover, the laws of the state are lax in this area of marriage readiness. Currently we ask fewer questions of applicants for marriage licenses than we ask applicants for automobile operators' licenses.

Only one of the measures of readiness used proved related to later separation and reunion adjustment, namely, the major reasons for getting married (see Chart III). Those who married on impulse or as an escape or because of social pressures, adjusted less well to reunion than couples whose marriages were based on companionship and common interests. Deviations from this generalization must be made for separation where the adjustment of the few couples whose marriage was based on social pressures was better than any other group, suggesting possibly that separation for them may have constituted a temporary release from a marriage held together primarily by external controls.

Age at marriage of wife, and of husband, proved unrelated, as did years of schooling of wife, in getting along later in separation and reunion. Length of acquaintance before marriage, which has been considered important for good marriage adjustment (8), was only slightly related to good adjustment in separation, but not significantly so in this study.

One crude measure of readiness for marriage is conventionality with respect to mate choice. Our only measure of that phenomenon is in the matter of marrying within the same broad divisions of religious affiliations—Catholic, Jewish, and Protestant. When marriages were classified according to the combination represented, whether in-faith, inter-faith, or without church affiliation, interesting results were obtained. In-faith adjusted no better in separation or reunion than the non-faith or the inter-faith marriages. This negative finding is as suggestive as a positive confirmation of the hypothesis that in-faith marriages are decidedly superior. The much heralded maleffects of mixed marriages are not borne out in adjustment to separation or reunion.

Further study needs to be made to confirm the importance of preparation for marriage in order to successfully withstand family crises. The present evidence is neither convincing, nor sufficient to make generalizations that will stick.

CHART III. Major Reasons for Getting Married and Adjustment to Separation and Reunion

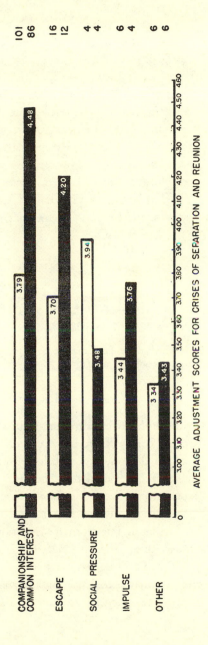

AVERAGE ADJUSTMENT SCORES FOR CRISES OF SEPARATION AND REUNION

Background factors, taken singly, have not proved successful in setting off families which adjust well to separation hardships from those who adjusted poorly. Their importance in producing personalities which are adequate for marriage and family living may have been minimized, however, by our statistical methods of inference. As we approach the present tense in our study, namely, what is happening in the marriage, the roles played by the husband and wife in decision making, in demonstrating affection, in the allocation of responsibilities and sharing of duties, we may see in sharper focus the effects of background items of happiness in childhood, courtship patterns, and preparation for marriage, on family adjustment scores in the face of trouble.

Statistical Summary

Factors in Readiness for Marriage	Adj. to Separation			Adj. to Reunion		
	χ^2	r	Level. of Sig.	χ^2	r	Level. of Sig.
Major reasons for getting married	40.1	—	0.01	48.0	—	0.01
Inter-faith vs. in-faith marriage	14.2	—	0.90	8.6	—	0.90
Years schooling (wife)		0.01	0.90		0.05	0.85

SOCIAL AND PERSONAL ROLES IN MARRIAGE

In our Midwestern communities at the present time family roles are not firmly fixed, but are undergoing modifications to meet the changed demands on families. Social roles have always been more stable than personal roles, because they have grown out of the past experience of the group. For example, the role of breadwinner in the American family is a culturally determined role ordinarily assigned the husband. The woman's traditional roles are those of homemaker and mother. The personal role is one which is determined by the individual and personal experiences of childhood, modified often by the personal experiences in the marriage relation. The husband, if acting like a dependent child in his relationships with his wife and family, is exercising a personal role (27). Personal roles have always varied more from family to family than social roles.

Role playing is inadequately captured as yet in our statistical tables because we do not yet have measures with which to assess the dynamic character of the family roles. Analysis of the case materials in a later chapter will make possible generalizations we are not prepared to make statistically in this discussion. It is our considered conviction that through the analysis of roles played within a family will come the greatest understanding of the meaning of family adaptability, integration, stability, and permissiveness for the personality growth of members.

From previous studies (8, 29) we would have expected that the equalitarian roles making for democratic relationships would have best prepared our families for the crisis studied. Mather (29) studied family types on the basis of control and concluded that the family council type showed a tendency to exhibit "desirable" family attributes in the highest degrees, and the "undesirable" family attributes in the lowest; the joint dominance type came second; the father dominance third, and the mother dominance a rather poor fourth. There is some agreement among writers (1, 5, 8, 11) that type of control in the family may be related to family success. Dunigan (13) found type of control related to dynamic stability in families in Iowa (see also pp. 135–138).

We will test the hypothesis that certain types of family roles are better than others for adjustment to crisis in this section. Our first test reflects the personal role of "caring most" about the marriage. When asked, "Who cares most about the marriage?" the families in which "both care equally" were significantly better off in reunion, but not quite significantly better off in separation, than those families where "wife cares most" or where "husband cares most." The question may probe more adequately the "pairedness" of the relationship and the mutuality present than the personal roles played by husband and wife. Again, it is interesting to note that reunion adjustments require more mutuality than successful separation adjustments. This will be analyzed in more detail in the case study analysis.

Out of the adjustments of the early years of marriage husband and wife build roles which are more or less comfortable for them to play, and which tend to make for predictability and harmony in the family. These roles reflect the distribution of power within the family which enables us to characterize the family as essentially patriarchal, matriarchal, or equalitarian. Four sets of data were collected to serve this purpose.

1. Dominance-submission in husband-wife relation; that is, "Who is most frequently the boss?"
    ..... husband much stronger, assertive, dominant, leading, responsibility assuming
    ..... husband somewhat stronger
    ..... husband and wife equal
    ..... husband somewhat weaker
    ..... husband much weaker, non-assertive, passive, dependent
2. Social role played by wife in marriage; that is, "What is the wife's function as a complement to the husband?"
    ..... wife and mother (stay-at-home, housewife, housekeeper, traditional role)
    ..... partner (shares economic burden of earning, works outside home and/or pools earning and/or is person in own right)
    ..... hostess-companion (exists to please and entertain husband, clothes horse, ornament, wears clothing and jewelry as means of conspicuous consumption)
    ..... other, invalid, sister role, non-functioning wife, etc.
3. Method of handling the family purse; that is, "Who controls the purse strings?"
    ..... husband handles all
    ..... wife has allowance
    ..... joint checking account, husband handles most of bills
    ..... joint checking account, wife handles most of bills
    ..... wife handles all money
    ..... other

4. Method of settling disagreements; that is, when they arise, they usually result in?
   .....husband giving in most of time
   .....wife giving in most of time
   .....arguing it out until some sort of agreement is reached
   .....can't agree

When analyzed singly only the fourth question, methods of settling disagreements, segregated well-adjusted families from poorly
adjusted families sharply enough to satisfy the statisticians. The
more democratic pattern of frank open arguments in marriage until
agreement is reached makes for significantly better relations in separation and reunion than the pattern of husband or wife giving in
without argument. The eleven couples who can't agree at all had the
lowest adjustment scores in separation and reunion, as would be expected.

Taking a leaf from Komarovsky (25) and Mather (29), we attempted to classify our families on the basis of the several evidences
of expressions of control above. We first sought three pure types of
family control—patriarchal, matriarchal, and equalitarian—but soon
found that the majority of families were mixed and not pure types.
We ended with the following pure and mixed types of family control.

> Type I. Patriarchal (Pure) 18 Families
>   Dominance-submission (husband much or somewhat stronger)
>   Role of wife (wife and mother)
>   Purse (husband handles all or wife has allowance)
>   Disagreements (wife gives in most of time)
> Type II. Husband-Dominant (Mixed) 68 Families
>   Evidence from all four areas points toward husband dominance,
>   but some contrary evidence too.
> Type III. Equalitarian (Pure) 18 Families
>   Dominance-submission (husband and wife equal)
>   Role of wife (partner)
>   Purse (joint checking account, either handles)
>   Disagreements (argue till agreements reached)

Type IV. Husband-Wife Equal (Mixed) 12 Families
Evidence from all four areas points toward husband-wife equality, but some contrary evidence too.

Type V. Matriarchal (Pure) 2 Families
Dominance-submission (husband much or somewhat weaker)
Role of wife (partner)
Purse (wife handles all money)
Disagreements (husband gives in)

Type VI. Wife Dominant (Mixed) 16 Families
Evidence from all four areas points toward wife dominance, but some contrary evidence too.

Chart IV portrays the adjustment scores of the six types of families defined above. The evidence is quite insufficient to confirm the hypothesis that equalitarian families succeed better in the face of crisis than less well-balanced families, powerwise. The matriarchal families are patently too few in number to warrant conclusions being drawn from their behavior. They constitute the only type which deviated sharply from the average scores in both separation and re-union.

When the marital adjustment scores of the six types of families were computed, there was a significant difference in favor of the more equalitarian families, followed by the patriarchal and husband-dominated, and trailed by the matriarchal and wife-dominated families.

Cross-classified by the earlier materials reflecting who cared most for the marriage, it was found that the equalitarian families (85 percent) had the highest proportion in which "both cares equally" for the marriage. The emotional investment of the husband in the marriage was highest in the wife-dominated and matriarchal families as reflected in the statement, "husband cares most." The wife's emotional investment, contrariwise, was highest in the husband-dominant (but not pure patriarchal) families, in which 31 percent of the responses were of the "wife cares most" variety, 55 percent of the "both care equally," and only 13 percent of the "husband cares

CHART IV. Types of Family Control and Adjustment to Separation and Reunion

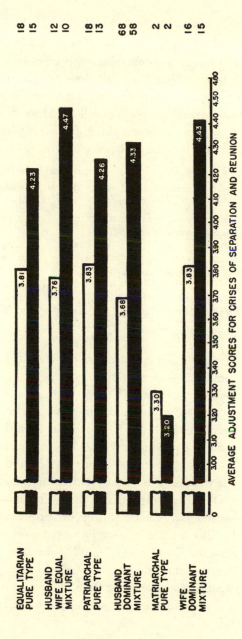

AVERAGE ADJUSTMENT SCORES FOR CRISES OF SEPARATION AND REUNION

TYPES OF FAMILY CONTROL	□ AVERAGE ADJUSTMENT TO SEPARATION	■ AVERAGE ADJUSTMENT TO REUNION	NUMBER OF FAMILIES
EQUALITARIAN PURE TYPE	3.81	4.23	18 / 15
HUSBAND WIFE EQUAL MIXTURE	3.76	4.47	12 / 10
PATRIARCHAL PURE TYPE	3.83	4.26	18 / 13
HUSBAND DOMINANT MIXTURE	3.68	4.33	68 / 58
MATRIARCHAL PURE TYPE	3.30 / 3.20		2 / 2
WIFE DOMINANT MIXTURE	3.83	4.43	16 / 15

most." Further analysis of the principle of least interest might prove rewarding in connection with types of family power organization.

Our statistical analysis does not identify the family characteristic of equalitarianism as important for high separation and reunion adjustment scores. We will see if its superiority is revealed in the *process* of decision making, further analysis of which may be undertaken in the case study section of the book.

Statistical Summary

Factors Involving Social and Personal Roles in Marriage	Adj. to Separation χ^2	Level of Sig.	Adj. to Reunion χ^2	Level of Sig.
Who prizes marriage most	18.7	0.30	33.35	0.01
Modes of settling disagreements	23.94	0.10	29.60	0.01
Social role of wife	16.88	0.20	9.50	0.50
Dominance-submission pattern	16.25	0.50	11.03	0.70
Handling the family purse	16.32	0.70	19.16	0.30
Types of family control	21.48	0.60	20.79	0.30

SOCIAL STATUS, TRANSIENCY, INCOME, AND OCCUPATION

In only two instances are the identifying marks of social class, income, occupation, transiency, type of house living in, type of residential area living in, and so on, of any signal importance in predicting success or failure in adjusting to separation or reunion. The social status illustration, used earlier in the chapter (see Chart I), of social class position within the community is barely significant in setting off separation adjustees who did well from those who did less well. In reunion the relationship is non-significant.

Occupation of husband also differentiates good adjustment in separation and reunion from poor adjustment (see Chart V). Farmers' families are best adjusted to separation and second best adjusted to reunion. Day laborers' families do most poorly in the face of both crises, confirming findings (27) from Koos' families who possessed few occupational skills. Both groups are numerically small, however, and generalizations should not be made beyond this sample.

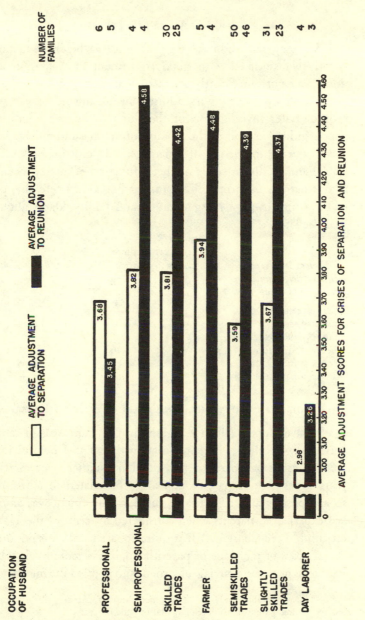

CHART V. Occupation of Husband and Adjustment to Separation and Reunion

Transiency, reflected in changes of residence before induction, was negatively associated with good adjustment to separation and reunion, but not significantly so. Income at induction was expected to be associated positively with adjustment but this hypothesis was not proved. Later investigation of the shifts in income after the husband's induction, and of the amount of savings and indebtedness incurred during the period of separation, all point in the same direction: Family adjustment is neither a function of money income, nor of fluctuations in income. The answer lies somewhere else, possibly in the realm of family organization and family adaptability, as we shall see later.

	Statistical Summary					
Factors Involving	Adj. to Separation			Adj. to Reunion		
Social Status, Transiency,			Level of			Level of
Income, and Occupation	x^2	r	Sig.	x^2	r	Sig.
Social status in community score		0.18	0.04		0.09	0.23
Changes of residence before induction		−0.12	0.16		−0.03	0.26
Income at induction		0.08	0.24		0.08	0.26
Occupation of husband	45.3	—	0.05	43.5	—	0.01

FAMILISM: FAMILY SIZE AND YEARS OF FAMILY EXPERIENCE

We have tapped evidence of familism in four areas of family experience with almost no confirmation that it is a helpful factor in meeting crises of separation and reunion. Neither years married nor years experience as parents appear to be related to adjustment in separation or reunion. Actually, the best adjustment was among the less experienced parents when considered in terms of the age of oldest child.[5] (See Chart VI.) It is quite apparent that it is not the number of years of marriage or parenthood, but is more likely what one has brought to the marriage, learned, and applied during these years,

[5] In her remarkable study of developmentalism in parents, Duvall (14) found less experienced parents most developmental in outlook.

CHART VI. Years Experience as Parents and Adjustment to Separation and Reunion

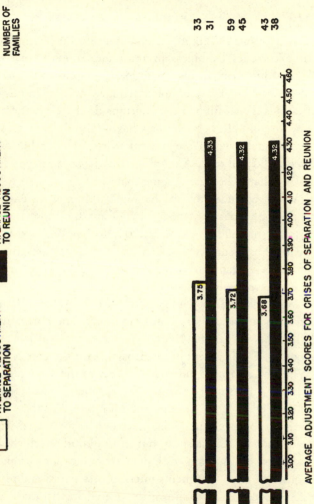

YEARS
EXPERIENCE
AS PARENTS

☐ AVERAGE ADJUSTMENT
   TO SEPARATION

■ AVERAGE ADJUSTMENT
   TO REUNION

NUMBER OF
FAMILIES

IO AND OVER   3.75   4.33   33
                                       31

6.0 – 9.9   3.72   4.32   59
                                       45

2.0 – 5.9   3.68   4.32   43
                                       38

0   3.00 3.10 3.20 3.30 3.40 3.50 3.60 3.70 3.80 3.90 4.00 4.10 4.20 4.30 4.40 4.50 4.60

AVERAGE ADJUSTMENT SCORES FOR CRISES OF SEPARATION AND REUNION

which counts. Nimkoff, in commenting on Terman's finding that time corrodes happiness in marriage, supports our interpretation, ". . . adjustment in marriage does not seem to improve very much after the first few years of marriage. . . . An implication of these findings is that human relationships do not carry themselves, do not improve simply because they have existed for a certain length of time. Habits which are hurtful to the relationship can develop as well as helpful ones. A marriage that has been happy for a time may turn unhappy because of some change of circumstance."[6]

When attitudes toward having children were elicited, the more familistic response, namely, the desire for more than the average number of children, is more likely to be associated with poor than good adjustment to crisis. Contrary to expectations, the better adjustment to separation and reunion scores were associated with the desire to have small families.

When the size of family is taken into account, the effects on adjustment to separation scores are significantly negative (see Chart VII). The larger the family when the husband left for service, the poorer the adjustment to his departure on the part of his loved ones. When he returned, the relationship was the same although not significant—the smaller the family, the better the adjustment to reunion. There is no denying the importance of these findings. Children are burdensome. They may not be associated with divorce as frequently as childlessness, but in the families which remain intact, numbers of children introduce complications which appear to worsen family adjustments to crises of separation and reunion.[7]

All evidences of familism discovered in the study are either unrelated to good adjustment or are unfavorably associated with adjustment. This brings us to an impasse. If familistic items are un-

[6] Meyer F. Nimkoff, *Marriage and the Family* (Boston: Houghton Mifflin Company, 1947), p. 634.
[7] Bossard (5) illustrates the reasonableness of this finding as part of his Law of Family Interaction. The number of relationships increases by order of triangular numbers as persons are added to the family.

CHART VII. Number of Children and Adjustment to Separation and Reunion

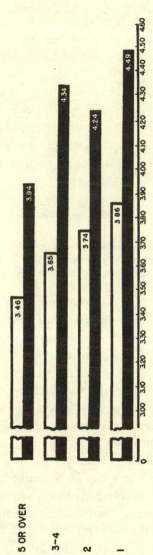

NUMBER OF
CHILDREN
IN FAMILY

☐ AVERAGE ADJUSTMENT
TO SEPARATION

■ AVERAGE ADJUSTMENT
TO REUNION

NUMBER OF
FAMILIES

5 OR OVER   3.46   3.94   6 / 5

3-4   3.65   4.34   29 / 25

2   3.74   4.24   62 / 50

1   3.86   4.49   38 / 34

AVERAGE ADJUSTMENT SCORES FOR CRISES OF SEPARATION AND REUNION

favorable or irrelevant, if income with which Americans have hoped to buy the good life is also of no avail, if democratic forms of married living are not clearly superior, and if preparation for marriage and sheer time in keeping company promises little, wherein then lies the explanation of family adjustment in the face of crisis? We have still to consider the phenomena of attained husband-wife marital adjustment, family integration, family patterns of adaptability and flexibility, family affectional patterns, and the many situational factors in the separation and reunion period itself. To these we turn for more significant light on why some families did well and others poorly when facing wartime crises.

Statistical Summary

Factors Reflecting Familism	Adj. to Separation		Adj. to Reunion	
	r	Level of Sig.	r	Level of Sig.
Years married	−0.08	0.26	−0.04	0.26
Years experience as parents	−0.08	0.27	0.001	0.90
Number of children desired	−0.14	0.12	−0.05	0.26
Number of children in family	−0.22	0.01	−0.10	0.23

ADEQUACY OF FAMILY ORGANIZATION

From the ingenious studies of families in the depression, the literature of which was selectively reviewed in Chapter II, came the discovery of the importance of adequate family organization to meet the crises of existence. Testing their findings in the specific context of war-born crises of separation and reunion, we confirm the generalizations in almost every instance. Family integration, family adaptability, and marital adjustment constitute the most important statistically identifiable factors making for successful adjustment to crisis in this study.

Once it has been attained, a good marital adjustment constitutes admirable preparation for crisis. Our families were scored by the Burgess-Cottrell Marital Adjustment Scale (8) from the perspective of the wife and, if home, of the husband too. The scale scores a family high where the attitudes and acts of husband and wife are in

CHART VIII. Marital Adjustment (Wife's Score) and Adjustment to Separation and Reunion

WIFE'S MARITAL ADJUSTMENT SCORE

☐ AVERAGE ADJUSTMENT TO SEPARATION

■ AVERAGE ADJUSTMENT TO REUNION

NUMBER OF FAMILIES

70 AND OVER GOOD — 35, 31

40–69 FAIR — 84, 71

0–39 POOR — 16, 12

70 AND OVER GOOD: 3.83, 4.50

40–69 FAIR: 3.77, 4.37

0–39 POOR: 3.41, 3.58

AVERAGE ADJUSTMENT SCORES FOR CRISES OF SEPARATION AND REUNION

agreement on the chief issues of marriage, such as, handling finances and dealing with in-laws; where they have come to an adjustment on interests, objectives, and values; where they are in harmony on demonstrations of affection and the sharing of confidences; where they have few or no complaints about their marriage and settle their differences by mutual give and take (as may be seen in Chart VIII). These high scoring families also made excellent adjustments to separation and to reunion.

Taking the other side of the penny, evidences of poor marital adjustment prior to induction of the husband into the armed services, we have some interesting findings. To check the results from the marital adjustment scale, we read carefully the case records of each family to record every instance where divorce was seriously considered before induction. There were three questions in which the information was elicited, two in the questionnaire and one in the interview form. The families were classified into two classes: those who had considered divorce prior to induction, and those who had not. They were then further subdivided into the family status at the time of final interview. Table 10 lists the average adjustment to separation scores of the twelve varieties of families involved. The results are convincing evidence that neither the war nor the strains of separation and reunion can properly be blamed for family breakups. The rate of breakup registered in Table 10 is over a very short time span, October, 1945 to June, 1946, and is much lower than that of the population as a whole, because these are child-burdened families of some duration. Nevertheless, contrary to popular thinking, few families separated, deserted, or divorced, or even contemplated divorce during the separation periods, which had not seriously discussed and contemplated divorce before the crisis of war separation occurred. The seeds of family disorganization which blossom in wartime are sown much earlier in the marriage.

Family integration, first identified by Angell (*1*) and scaled by Cavan (*10*) for statistical treatment, involves the unifying phenomena seen in the sense of economic and emotional interdependence: the strong affectional ties between husband and wife, father and children, mother and children, and among the children; a certain pride in the family traditions, and high participation as a family in

TABLE 10. Marital Status of 135 Iowa Families at Time of Interviews (January–July, 1946); Number Who Had Considered Divorce Prior to Induction; Average Adjustment to Separation Scores of Families by Family Status

Family Status	All Cases Number	Av. Adj. to Separation Score	Number Who Had Considered Divorce Prior to Induction Number	Av. Adj. to Separation Score
Reunited families not now considering divorce or separation	97	3.9	12	3.7
Reunited families but considering divorce or separation	10	3.4	10	3.4
Divorced since induction	4	2.2	4	2.2
Separated or deserted since induction	1	3.2	0	—
Husband reënlisted or still in service	20	3.6	2	3.6
Husband killed in service	3	3.4	1	3.6
Total	135	3.75	29	3.38

joint activities. Dunigan (13) has tested the scale for validity and for reliability in another recent study with reassuring results (see appendix pp. 379–381 for a table showing the item analysis of the scale for integration and the scale for adaptability).

Taking degree of affection of all members for each other out of the scale as a key component of family integration and correlating it with adjustment to separation and reunion scores, we found affection significantly related to reunion adjustment results, but just short

of being significant in separation. American families place a tremendous burden on affection to keep the family intact, and fiction
is replete with assertions that love alone is enough to survive family
crises. The present study would not support such romantic notions.
Only when joined with the other factors making up family integration is affection a dominant factor. It undoubtedly adds the ingredi-
ent which unifies and suffuses the relationships with savor and satisfaction. Taken as a whole, family integration is highly significant in
predicting success both in separation and reunion, but as can be seen
in Chart IX, its relationship is higher with reunion adjustments than
separation adjustments. The most highly integrated families did best
in reunion and second best in separation.

Bossard and Boll (6) offered a classification of families according
to their intra-family relationships which we have tested against the
backdrop of separation and reunion crises. The classification of families followed the instructions of Bossard and Boll for the affectional
relationships from excess of affection seen in the overindulgent home
along a continuum of normal affection, inconsistency of affection,
discrimination of affection, and lack of affection to frank rejection
(see Chart X). The differences in adjustment to separation and reunion are large enough for the various homes to be statistically significant.

Family adaptability was also identified by Angell (*1*) and scaled
by Cavan (*10*) for statistical treatment. Involved in the scale of
adaptability is the flexibility and willingness of family members to
shift social roles if necessary, the acceptance of responsibility by all
family members in performing family tasks, the presence of habits
of collective discussion and control, and a repertoire of crisis meeting
devices built out of previous successful experiences with trouble.
Adaptability refers to the family's readiness to adjust as a unit to
changed situations. Angell's critics, in reviewing his study of family
life during the depression, concluded that adaptability was of much

CHART IX. Family Integration and Adjustment to Separation and Reunion

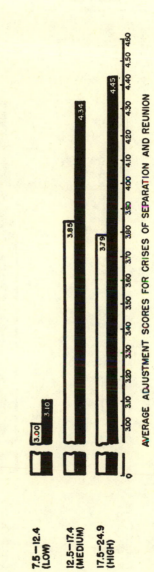

AVERAGE ADJUSTMENT SCORES FOR CRISES OF SEPARATION AND REUNION

INTEGRATION
SCORES OF
FAMILY

□ AVERAGE ADJUSTMENT
TO SEPARATION

■ AVERAGE ADJUSTMENT
TO REUNION

NUMBER OF
FAMILIES

7.5—12.4
(LOW)   3.00 3.10   11 8

12.5—17.4
(MEDIUM)   3.85 4.34   42 31

17.5—24.9
(HIGH)   3.79 4.45   82 75

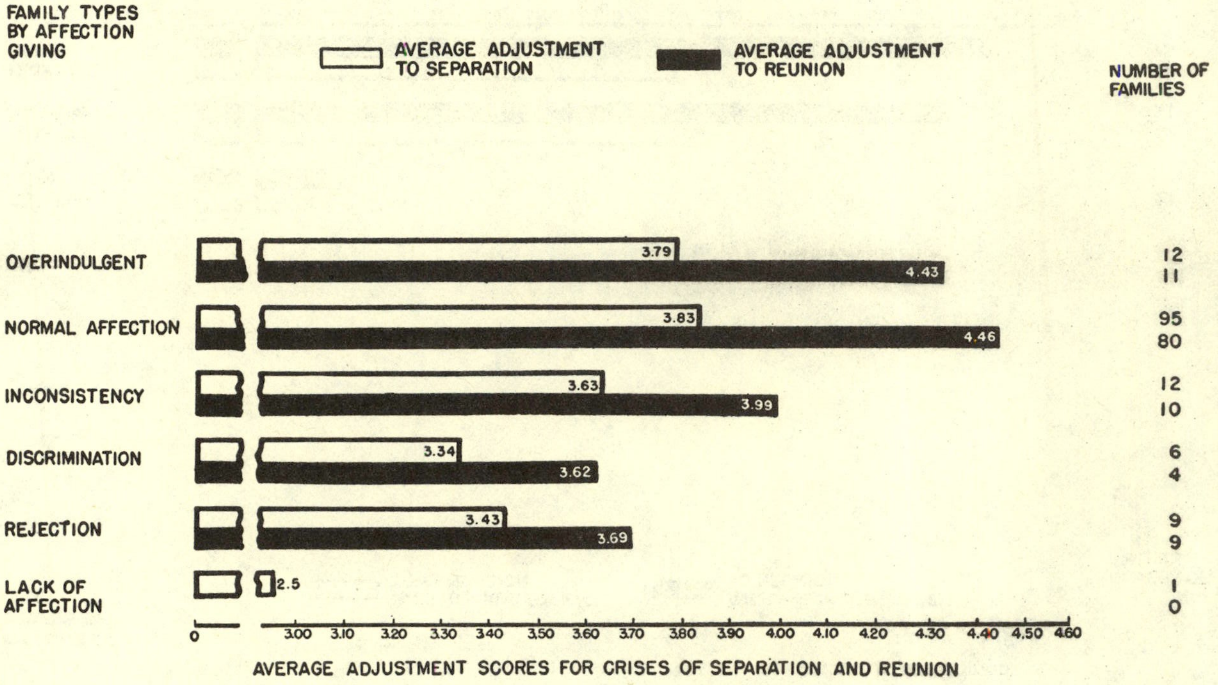

CHART X. Family Types by Affection Giving and Adjustment to Separation and Reunion

more importance than integration in successfully adjusting to the crisis of sudden impoverishment (*10*).

Flexibility of family roles is a key component in the scale of family adaptability, but taken singly there was insufficient relationship between separation and reunion adjustments to satisfy the demands for statistical significance. *Family adaptability* as an omnibus of several components was highly significant in both the reunion and separation adjustment situations. But a glance at Chart XI will reveal that adaptability counts more for separation adjustments than for reunion adjustments, and that the most adaptable families are not the most successful in adjusting to the two crises in question. This will bear further analysis.

Lowell Dunigan (*13*) of Iowa State College has recently constructed a Scale for Dynamic Stability which combines the equilibrium contributions of good *marital adjustment*, and the unifying bonds of *family integration* with the dynamic adjustability of *family adaptability*. He has validated the scale and tested it for reliability following standard procedures and is interested in applying it to larger populations than the 135 families in the present Iowa study. For our purposes the scale's strength lies in its three-way measurement of processes making for adjustive invulnerability in the face of crisis. High dynamic stability in a family would give a gyroscopic quality which would equip it peculiarly to meet the exigencies of life in a changing industrial society where rootlessness and anonymity wreck havoc on rigid, unbalanced, poorly ballasted family organizations. Dunigan found his Scale for Dynamic Stability quite sensitive in its ability to differentiate between families which did well and families which did poorly in separation and reunion (see Chart XII).

Adequacy of family organization has supplied us with a better fitting key to what makes for success in crisis meeting than any of the other hypotheses we have investigated in this factor-by-factor tour of separation and reunion adjustment. We may achieve a

CHART XI. Family Adaptability and Adjustment to Separation and Reunion

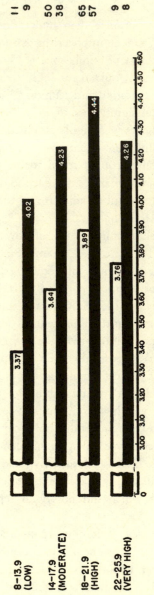

AVERAGE ADJUSTMENT SCORES FOR CRISES OF SEPARATION AND REUNION

ADAPTABILITY
SCORE OF
FAMILY

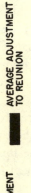 AVERAGE ADJUSTMENT TO SEPARATION

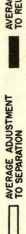 AVERAGE ADJUSTMENT TO REUNION

NUMBER OF
FAMILIES

8-13.9
(LOW)
11
9

14-17.9
(MODERATE)
50
38

18-21.9
(HIGH)
65
57

22-25.9
(VERY HIGH)
9
8

CHART XII. Dynamic Stability and Adjustment to Separation and Reunion

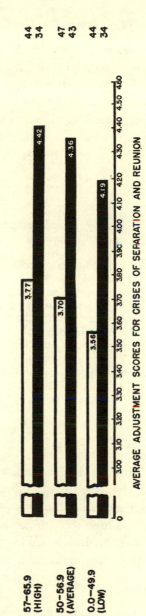

AVERAGE ADJUSTMENT SCORES FOR CRISES OF SEPARATION AND REUNION

DYNAMIC
STABILITY
SCORES

□ AVERAGE ADJUSTMENT
  TO SEPARATION

■ AVERAGE ADJUSTMENT
  TO REUNION

NUMBER OF
FAMILIES

57–65.9
(HIGH)   3.77   4.42   44
                                           34

50–56.9
(AVERAGE)   3.70   4.36   47
                                           43

0.0–49.9
(LOW)   3.56   4.19   44
                                           34

greater purchase on the tough problem of family analysis and diagnosis by joining the important measures of family adequacy, such as marital adjustment, family integration, and family adaptability into one scale for dynamic stability. In another chapter further attempts at combining these significant measures will be attempted by the process of cross-classification, and by the better known processes of multiple and partial correlation.

Statistical Summary

	Adj. to Separation			Adj. to Reunion		
Adequacy of Family Organization	x^2	*r*	Level of Sig.	x^2	*r*	Level of Sig.
Marital Adjustment Score (wife)		0.31	0.01		0.44	0.01
Marital Adjustment Score (husband)		—	—		0.46	0.01
Family Integration Score		0.27	0.01		0.43	0.01
Family Adaptability Score		0.26	0.01		0.20	0.01
Degree of Affection Among Family Members Score		0.12	0.15		0.19	0.05
Family Types of Affection Giving	51.3	—	0.01	24.6	—	0.02
Flexibility in Shifting Roles Score		0.11	0.18		0.16	0.09
Dynamic Stability Score		0.40	0.01		0.37	0.01

EXPERIENCES AND HARDSHIPS OF SEPARATION

Separation varied in its impact on families according to the hardships which it entailed, and according to what it meant to families as they experienced it. The preceding chapter has supplied the details of separation, the anticipatory reactions as well as the short-time and long-time reactions of mother and children. Reunion adjustments were vitally affected by the way the family responded to the separation crisis; indeed, the most highly associated single factor with reunion adjustment is the separation adjustment score. Early in the study we had a hunch that many families with high scores on adjustment to separation would have closed ranks too well, making later reunion difficult. This hasn't proved to be the case at all. Adjustment to separation is highly correlated with adjustment to reunion. Those who managed well without a husband and father were precisely those who managed well when he returned.

Hardships of separation when viewed singly affected separation and reunion adjustments very little, but we constructed a Hardship in Separation Score which appears significantly related to later adjustments to separation. Hardships identified were as follows: (1) change of residence forced by separation; (2) change of residence to in-laws, or to doubled-up quarters because of money limitations; (3) income decreased by more than 20 percent; (4) child(ren) under three years of age; (5) no furloughs during separation; and (6) wife working, for money reasons not for enjoyment. A simple score of one was given for each hardship, except children which was given double weight, giving a possible total score of seven. If income was increased by separation by more than 20 percent, the score was reduced by one. The eight families which had experienced slight improvement or no hardships at all had the highest average adjustment to separation score (see Chart XIII) and the adjustment scores were successively poorer as the Hardship in Separation Score became greater.

Hardships not caught by the Hardship in Separation Score were inadequate sleeping space and difficulties in managing the children with the father gone. Child discipline became a major problem during separation, many families reporting that the children were harder to control. Family relations were happiest, we found, in those homes where reasoning and talking, isolation, and withholding priviliges were the dominant disciplinary methods or where no marked discipline was apparent. Least successful in separation and reunion adjustment were those families in which spanking was the dominant method. None of these findings were statistically significant.

Time separation was another hardship not included in the hardship score, but there seemed to be no relationship either between

CHART XIII. Hardships in Separation and Adjustment to Separation

HARDSHIP IN SEPARATION SITUATION SCORE	AVERAGE ADJUSTMENT TO SEPARATION	AVERAGE ADJUSTMENT TO REUNION	NUMBER OF FAMILIES
SLIGHT IMPROVEMENT OR NO HARDSHIP 0—0.9		3.95	8
MINIMUM HARDSHIP 1.0—2.9		3.78	49
MEDIUM HARDSHIP 3.0—4.9		3.72	63
MAXIMUM HARDSHIP 5.0—6.9		3.53	20

AVERAGE ADJUSTMENT SCORES FOR CRISES OF SEPARATION AND REUNION

3.00 3.10 3.20 3.30 3.40 3.50 3.60 3.70 3.80 3.90 4.00 4.10 4.20 4.30 4.40 4.50 4.60

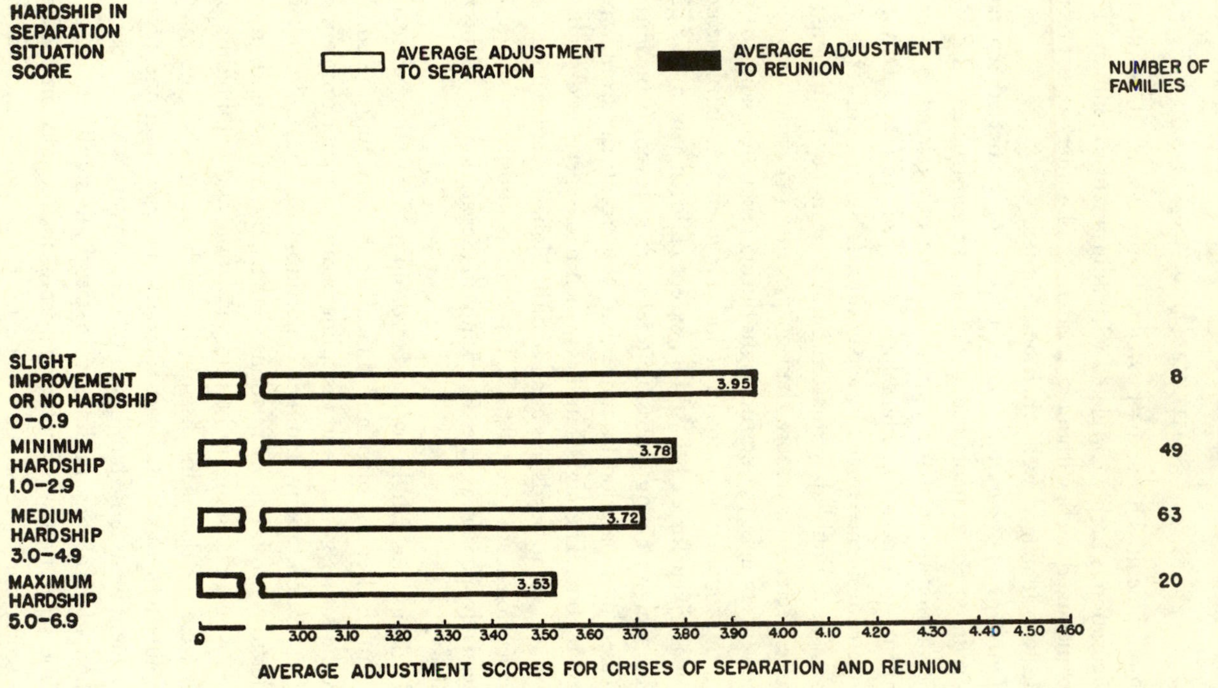

adjustment to separation or adjustment to reunion and the number of months that father had been separated from his family.

Communication devices for maintaining a sense of family unity were exceedingly important in some families. Adjustment to separation was distinctly improved by the number of letters written, the number of topics covered (less so), and the adequacy of the communication. These evidences of keeping in touch with one another also appeared associated with good reunion adjustments, the father being thereby better prepared for his family when he returned. The content of the letters is often the key to adjustment, however, rather than the numbers written, although both appear statistically significant in their bearing on adjustment (see Chart XIV). If the wife could pour out her affection and troubles into her letters, she obtained a release from her household worries and tensions, and, if in turn his letters were loving and affectionate, she obtained great satisfaction from them. No communications, however, could patch up the split between a nagging home and an escaping husband. "Let me fight one war at a time," one of the husbands wrote home.

Furloughs and visits broke up the period of separation and enabled the father to be a family man again for a few days. The total days spent with the family appears significantly related to good adjustment during separation, although the parting was often extremely painful and disruptive of early separation adjustments. Furloughs played fast and loose with the children's emotions, some families reported. In other families fathers became reacquainted with their children's development and they with a father in uniform. As proof of its importance in maintaining communications, those families with no furloughs adjusted least well of all.

Our findings with respect to communication confirm our initial hunches that crises of separation and reunion may be cushioned and even used to strengthen the relationship if the processes of communication are adequate and the avenues kept open. The author has commented elsewhere (22) on the necessity of maintaining contacts be-

CHART XIV. Adequacy of Communication During Separation and Adjustment to Separation and Reunion

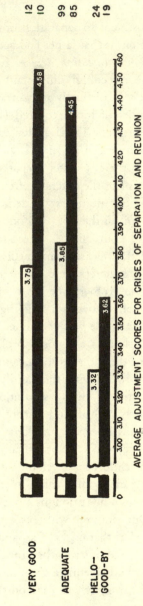

tween the father and his family, both to bolster family morale and to keep at a minimum the idealization which builds up when family members let their imaginations whitewash the humanness of family living. Even so, there is a temptation to build a letter-to-letter relationship to replace the face-to-face relationships of homely family living, all of which complicates the adjustments of reunion. Nevertheless, little evidence of such fantasy was found in our interviews with wives and husbands after reunion.

Separation provided the necessity of attaining some understanding concerning relationships with the opposite sex while separated. Twice as many families had *no understanding* as had a definite understanding concerning these relationships, and they adjusted almost as well to separation and reunion as those who spelled out their relationships in black and white. The worst adjustment to separation and to reunion was among those who agreed on freedom for both, next worse was among those who assumed a double standard of morality, in which one was free to step out while the other was required to be faithful; next is the set of families who prescribed that there were to be "no contacts with opposite sex" whatsoever. Best adjusted were those who permitted friendly contacts in a mixed crowd but no intimacies; next were couples who agreed on fidelity to one another (see Chart XV). These differences are large enough to be listed as statistically significant in separation adjustments but not for reunion adjustments.

Wives left behind developed symptoms of strain and tension which have already been described in some detail in Chapter IV. The number of symptoms seems unrelated to the phenomenon of adjustment to separation or to reunion, but the ways of releasing those tensions do. For example, the needs of affection and intimate response once met by the husband caused the wife great initial loneliness and insomnia as she sought affectional substitutes for him.

Those mothers who sought "other men" as substitutes for the husband adjusted least well to separation; those who had "no outlets" at all also did poorly, whereas those who displaced their affection on "other women" and on their own children did significantly well. It was simply not true that wives needed to keep "in training" by dating men in order to adjust well to separation.

Somewhat related to separation adjustment, although not significantly so, was the number and variety of social activities of the wife expressed in her social participation score, which in a sense might be regarded as a social outlet for her war-born tensions.[8] Another outlet closely related to it was gainful employment outside the home. Part-time work was more hazardous for separation and reunion adjustment than full-time work which was almost as important for good adjustment to crisis as staying home with the children. The differences are not significant, nor is the evidence convincing that working mothers made poorer adjustments to crisis than mothers playing the more traditional stay-at-home roles (see Chart XVI).

SELF-SUFFICIENCY AND SELF-RELIANCE OF WIVES

Separation had the effect of making many mothers more self-sufficient and self-reliant, and fathers home on furlough noted these changes and some worried about them. Decision making is a habit which feeds on itself. Which set of wives would adjust best to separation and reunion—the sturdy self-reliant types or the clinging vine I-want-to-be-dependent types? The evidence is somewhat conflicting when each evidence of self-reliance is viewed singly. Wives who managed well without their husbands adjusted significantly better to separation and reunion than more dependent wives who did poorly without their husbands. On the other hand, wives who "longed to be dependent again" did significantly better in adjusting to separation than wives who did not yearn for a dependent role

---

[8] Social participation proved most helpful of all outlets in relieving loneliness of Chicago war wives. See Evelyn M. Duvall, "Loneliness and the Serviceman's Wife," *Marriage and Family Living* (August, 1945), pp. 77-82.

CHART XV. Types of Understanding Concerning Contacts with Opposite Sex and Adjustment to Separation and Reunion

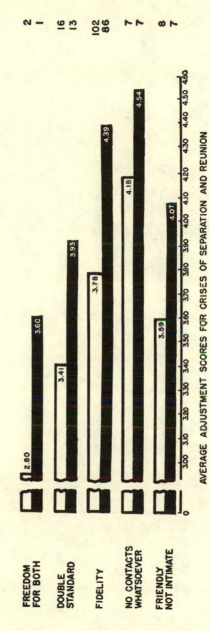

UNDERSTANDING
CONCERNING
OPPOSITE SEX
WHILE SEPARATED

☐ AVERAGE ADJUSTMENT
   TO SEPARATION

■ AVERAGE ADJUSTMENT
   TO REUNION

NUMBER OF
FAMILIES

FREEDOM
FOR BOTH   2.80   3.60   2
                                        1

DOUBLE
STANDARD   3.41   3.93   16
                                        13

FIDELITY   3.78   4.39   102
                                        86

NO CONTACTS
WHATSOEVER   4.18   4.54   7
                                        7

FRIENDLY
NOT INTIMATE   3.59   4.07   8
                                        7

0   3.00 3.10 3.20 3.30 3.40 3.50 3.60 3.70 3.80 3.90 4.00 4.10 4.20 4.30 4.40 4.50 4.60

AVERAGE ADJUSTMENT SCORES FOR CRISES OF SEPARATION AND REUNION

CHART XVI. Wife Working Outside Home and Adjustment to Separation and Reunion

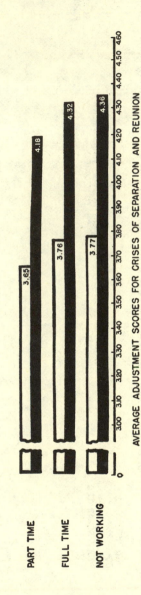

WIFE WORKING
OUTSIDE HOME

☐ AVERAGE ADJUSTMENT
TO SEPARATION

■ AVERAGE ADJUSTMENT
TO REUNION

NUMBER OF
FAMILIES

PART TIME   3.65   4.18   19
                                         17

FULL TIME   3.76   4.32   39
                                         34

NOT WORKING   3.77   4.36   77
                                         63

0   300 3.10 3.20 3.30 3.40 3.50 3.60 3.70 3.80 390 400 4.10 4.20 4.30 4.40 4.50 4.60

AVERAGE ADJUSTMENT SCORES FOR CRISES OF SEPARATION AND REUNION

again. Wives who felt they had become more self-sufficient adjusted somewhat less well to separation and reunion, but not significantly so, than wives who didn't.

In order to combine all these evidences of growing self-reliance into one complex, we gave each family a score based on the presence of self-sufficiency items in responses of the mother during the separation period, and called it Wife's Self-Sufficiency Score. Items which were given a weight of *one* were: managed well without a husband, feel more self-sufficient, make own decisions now, do not long to be dependent again, can now earn own living, am working for pay. A weight of *two* was given if on the last question the wife gave as her reason for working that it was not only for money, for something to do "to keep her mind occupied," as many put it, but that she *enjoyed working*. The results are shown in Chart XVII which reveal a tendency for adjustment to separation to improve as self-sufficiency scores increase up *to* a score of *three* and then to decrease. The relationship is significant but curvilinear. The less self-reliant wives do somewhat better than the more self-dependent mothers, reflecting a negative relationship between self-sufficiency and good adjustment to reunion, but there is the same curvilinear pattern in reunion that was seen in separation. There is a provocative hypothesis to be tested in this finding that neither dependency nor extreme self-sufficiency makes for best adjustment in the face of dismemberment crises.

EFFECTS OF MILITARY EXPERIENCE

The effects of military service on the family adjustments of the returning father are not made clear by our figures. There is not the close connection between characteristic and behavior seen in the other aspects of separation period; at best the relationship is peripheral. If the father found his family serving his morale while he was in the service, through the many pleasant memories, tokens, and gifts he received, his reunion adjustments were better than average.

CHART XVII. Wife's Self-Sufficiency Score and Adjustment to Separation and Reunion

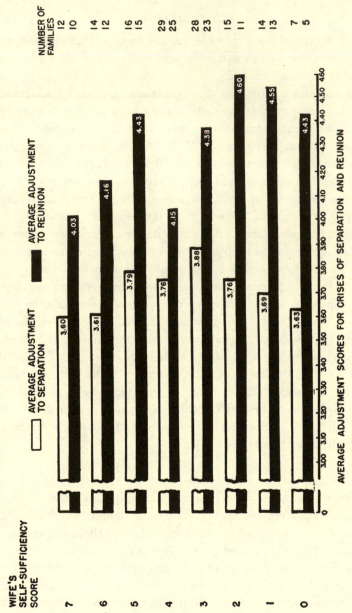

WIFE'S
SELF-SUFFICIENCY
SCORE

☐ AVERAGE ADJUSTMENT
TO SEPARATION

■ AVERAGE ADJUSTMENT
TO REUNION

NUMBER OF
FAMILIES

Score	Separation	Reunion	Number of Families
7	3.60	4.03	12 / 10
6	3.61	4.16	14 / 12
5	3.79	4.43	16 / 15
4	3.76	4.15	29 / 25
3	3.88	4.38	28 / 23
2	3.76	4.60	15 / 11
1	3.69	4.55	14 / 13
0	3.63	4.43	7 / 5

AVERAGE ADJUSTMENT SCORES FOR CRISES OF SEPARATION AND REUNION

If the family, in turn, regarded his service experiences as beneficial in fitting him to enjoy his family more, his reunion adjustments were slightly better. If the father saw combat duty, the family adjustments were slightly poorer than in families where the father experienced no such hazards. If he was a non-commissioned officer in service, his family's reunion adjustments were better than the families of other personnel. If he was given a discharge on points, his family adjustments were somewhat better than if he was discharged because of age, children, or for medical reasons.

Military experience neither permanently misfitted men for family life nor prepared them in any fashion to better understand domestic conflict. From the case materials rich evidence of learning to appreciate one's family, remembering Sunday afternoon picnics and good times, yearning for home and children, characterized the thinking of countless fathers. Yet when they returned, home was usually not the opposite of everything hateful they had experienced in service, and some registered a sense of disillusionment. Family life in the States did not live up to their idealizations.

Military experience and the attitudes of fathers and families toward it does not appear to be significant in determining reunion adjustment in the same measure as adequate communication, adaptable family organization, and workable husband-wife relationships.

In summary, the factors in the separation period which appeared significant in affecting adjustment to separation and reunion are: (1) the hardships of separation totaled into a Hardships in Separation Score; (2) devices of communication, letters, furloughs, and adequacy of communication judged from the content of letters; (3) permissive patterns of understanding and finding outlets for frustrations within the conventional codes, and moderate self-sufficiency-dependency patterns in the wife.

Statistical Summary

Experiences and Hardships of Separation	Adj. to Separation			Adj. to Reunion		
	χ^2	r	Level of Sig.	χ^2	r	Level of Sig.
Adjustment to Separation Score	—	—	—		0.50	0.01
Hardships in Separation Score		−0.19	0.03		—	—
History of living with in-laws	4.99		0.80	1.34		0.98
Extent of crowding in sleeping space	13.98		0.50	16.26		0.10
Difficulties in handling children	9.31		0.10	6.17		0.20
Methods of discipline used	48.87		0.02	37.35		0.20
Percentage change in income due to induction of husband		−0.04	0.80		0.06	0.60
Net savings or indebtedness from induction to interview		0.05	0.75		−0.09	0.30
Months separated from family in service		0.05	0.70		−0.09	0.35
Number of letters written per month		0.21	0.04		0.20	0.04
Adequacy of communication (content of letters)	39.29		0.01	36.33		0.01
Days of furlough or visits during service		0.22	0.02		0.23	0.02
Ways of spending furloughs	25.48	—	0.10	13.97		0.50
Understanding concerning contacts with opposite sex during separation	47.60	—	0.01	23.21	—	0.10
Types of affectional outlet during separation (wife)	44.48		0.05	15.53		0.80
Wife's Social Participation Score during separation		0.11	0.18		−0.001	0.99
Extent of wife working outside home	15.37		0.10	5.92		0.50

Statistical Summary (*Continued*)

Experiences and Hardships of Separation	Adj. to Separation			Adj. to Reunion		
	x^2	r	Level of Sig.	x^2	r	Level of Sig.
Number of symptoms of emotional imbalance due to separation		−0.06	0.60		−0.06	0.60
Wife longs to be dependent again	33.01		0.01	3.25		0.80
Wife has become more self-sufficient	13.25		0.20	7.06		0.50
Wife managing without a husband	52.27		0.01	26.72		0.10
Wife's Self-Sufficiency Score[a]	$Rho = $ −0.205		0.05	$Rho = $ −0.23		0.02
Family as morale builder scored by husband	—	—	—	—	0.22	0.04
Family's reaction to husband's service experience as affected home adjustment	—	—	—	17.46		0.50
Extent of combat duty	—	—	—	4.32		0.70
Reasons for discharge from service	—	—	—	16.24		0.50
Rank attained in service	—	—	—	8.98		0.50

[a] When the relationship between self-sufficiency of wife and adjustment to separation was recognized as curvilinear and the "index of correlation" *rho* computed, the influence of self-sufficiency was shown to be significant at the 5 percent level, $Rho = 0.205$, $P = 0.05$.

EXPERIENCES AND HARDSHIPS OF REUNION

There was a tendency for adjustment to become somewhat poorer the longer the husband was home, verifying a hunch that the early months of reunion are like honeymoon periods, but not reliable evidences of marital compatibility or adjustment. The best adjustment was found among families who planned to meet the father upon his return and the worst were among those families where the father returned unannounced and surprised his family. None of these differences was significant, however.

In order to capture the cumulative effect of reunion experiences, a Hardships in Reunion Score was computed for each family. From the case records families were studied to see how many of the hardships of reunion described in Chapter III were experienced in each family. Scores of one were given families that had been separated for more than twenty-four months, where the wife and children were not prepared for the return of the father, and where the mother was regarded by the father in interview as still playing *both father and mother roles* to the children. A score of two was given families in which the wife continued to work because she enjoyed it, in spite of the husband's disapproval, and to families where the husband reported more than two sources of irritation in the home situation (described in some detail in Chapter III, such as, wife too independent, children undisciplined, routines less well organized, children irritating, etc.). Families varied in the hardships they experienced in reunion from "no hardships" with a score of zero to five hardships with a score of seven. When hardships experienced were joined with adjustments to reunion, a highly significant relationship appeared. Chart XVIII shows adjustment improves as number of hardships decreases, as would be expected.

Statistical Summary

Experiences and Hardships of Reunion	x^2	Adjustment to Reunion	
		r	Level of Significance
Months home from service		0.11	0.24
Circumstances of reunion	27.41		0.20
Hardships in Reunion Score		−0.65	0.01

DIFFERENCES IN FACTORS MAKING FOR SUCCESS IN SEPARATION AND REUNION

Strikingly different though the two crisis situations are when viewed from the standpoint of the processes of family organization involved (see Chapter IV), this study has showed that factors mak-

CHART XVIII. Hardships in Reunion and Adjustment to Reunion

HARDSHIP
IN REUNION
SITUATION SCORE

☐ AVERAGE ADJUSTMENT
   TO SEPARATION

■ AVERAGE ADJUSTMENT
   TO REUNION

NUMBER OF
FAMILIES

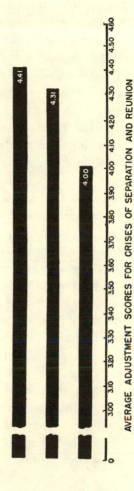

MINIMUM
HARDSHIP
0—1.9   4.41   5

MEDIUM
HARDSHIP
2.0—3.9   4.31   44

MAXIMUM
HARDSHIP
4.0—5.9   4.00   14

0   300 3.10 320 330 340 350 360 370 380 390 400 4.10 420 430 4.40 4.50 460

AVERAGE ADJUSTMENT SCORES FOR CRISES OF SEPARATION AND REUNION

ing for adjustment in separation are also important in determining adequacy of reunion adjustment. Moreover, there is close correspondence between success in meeting the crisis of separation and later success in completing the process of reunion (see p. 138). Cavan anticipated this result in her study of families facing sudden impoverishment, when she found the most important factor in meeting that crisis was previous successful experience in meeting other crises (*11*).

The factors which are most important for reunion and less important for separation adjustment are invariably factors involving mutuality of interests and satisfactions, good marriage pair adjustments, and pair and family integration. For example, good marital adjustment, modes of settling disagreements, who cares most about the marriage, and family integration are much more closely related to good reunion adjustment than to successful separation experiences. If one were to hazard a generalization to cover all of these factors, it would be that reunion adjustments involve subordination of the interests of individual family members to the family interest, where the accent is on maximum identification with the family. That the Wife's Self-Sufficiency Score was so negatively related to good reunion adjustment supports our point.

The factors which support separation adjustment without affecting reunion adjustment, on the other hand, are predominately factors which underline the wife's personality adequacy or the family's general adaptability. Perhaps more than we had supposed, family adjustment to separation was a function of the wife's ability to "take it." In reunion the presence of both spouses enabled them to meet, and even to be challenged, by the hardships of their position. In separation the wife carried that burden for the most part herself. It is understandable therefore, that high happiness score in childhood and adolescence and low neurotic score are associated with good adjustment to separation, but are not nearly so important in reunion adjustments. Where hardships are implied by reason of the position in the social structure, or by reason of the number of children or the amount of previous family transiency and mobility, the adjustments to separation are affected more adversely than the adjustments to reunion. Burdened with children, handicapped by fewer friends because of previous mobility, and endowed with fewer facilities reflected in social status position in the community, the wife and family do less well than reunited families under the same circumstances do in reunion.

Again, the greater importance of family adaptability in separation as against reunion requires an explanation. The family is not prepared for separation, having probably never experienced family life without the father, and flexibility of role playing proves important, as do patterns of collective discussion. On the other hand, the family knows what to expect in reunion, having lived with a father, and the key factor in reunion is, therefore, not *adaptability* but *integration* in determining family success in reunion. This is an hypothesis, not a finding, and should be tested in some future study of separation and reunion.

Finally, there were situational factors peculiar to the separation period which bore more directly on separation adjustment than reunion adjustment. Take the types of understanding concerning contacts with the opposite sex and the types of affectional outlet used by the wife which differentiated well-adjusted families in separation from poorly adjusted, but failed to affect reunion adjustments of the same families. This may also have accounted for the greater importance of the classification of families by affection giving, since the routing of affection was so clearly a matter of importance in the separation period, with its rude rechanneling of affection output within the family.

A summary statement would remind us that adjustment to separation and adjustment to reunion were affected similarly by most of the factors studied, that reunion adjustment is, indeed, a function of prior successful adjustment to separation. Where the factors affecting the two situations differed was in the importance for separation of wife's personality adequacy, affectional control, and family adaptability; and for reunion the greater import of workable pair relationships, family integration, and devotion to family interest at the expense of self-sufficiency and self-interest.

CHAPTER VI

STATISTICAL FINDINGS CONTINUED:
STATISTICAL FAMILY TYPES

A RECURRING comment in the discussion of statistical findings in the last chapter was the statement, "when viewed singly no factor appeared important." The limitations of the simple factor-by-factor analysis were amply demonstrated as we attempted to draw conclusions which would help all families. At several points attempts were made to preserve the wholeness of families by scoring families on a number of attributes at a time, as in the Marital Adjustment Scale, the Adaptability Scale, the Integration Scale, the Hardships in Separation Score, the Hardships in Reunion Score, the Wife's Self-Sufficiency Score and the schema for categorizing Types of Family Control. Dunigan's Dynamic Stability Scale (*13*) represented an attempt to combine three of these scales into one, for purposes of increasing our purchase on the baffling question, "What kinds of families do well and what kinds do poorly in the face of crisis?" In this chapter we will continue to explore methods of combining materials to identify more clearly the types of families we are seeking. Two methods suggest themselves: cross-classification and correlation, multiple and partial.

Cross-Classification Matrices

A simple method of capturing patterns of behavior is to cross-classify families on the more important factors affecting behavior and then note what effects are produced. For example, when income at induction is cross-classified by number of children in the family,

TABLE 11. Factors Most Associated with Good Adjustment in Separation and Reunion

	Adjustment to Separation			Adjustment to Reunion		
	C	r	Level of Sig.	C	r	Level of Sig.
Childhood Experience						
Wife's Happiness Score		0.17	0.05			ns
Wife's Neurotic Inventory Score		−0.18	0.04			ns
Readiness for Marriage						
Major reasons for marriage	0.48		0.01	0.54		0.01
Social and Personal Roles in Marriage						
Who prizes marriage most			ns	0.48		0.01
Modes of settling disagreements			ns	0.45		0.01
Social Status, Transiency, Occupation, and Income						
Social Status in Community Score		0.18	0.04			ns
Occupation of husband	0.50		0.04	0.52		0.01
Familism						
Number of children in family		−0.22	0.01			ns
Adequacy of Family Organization						
Marital Adjustment score (Wife)	0.31		0.01	0.44		0.01
Marital Adjustment Score (Husband)	—		—	0.46		0.01
Family Integration Score	0.27		0.01	0.43		0.01
Family Adaptability Score	0.26		0.01	0.20		0.01
Degree of Affection Among Family Members Score			ns	0.19		0.05
Dynamic Stability Score	0.40		0.01	0.37		0.01

TABLE II. Factors Most Associated with Good Adjustment in Separation and Reunion (*Continued*)

	Adjustment to Separation			Adjustment to Reunion		
	C	r	Level of Sig.	C	r	Level of Sig.
Family types by affection giving	0.52		0.01	0.42		0.02
Experiences and Hardships of Separation						
Adjustment to Separation Score	—	—			0.50	0.01
Hardships in Separation Score		−0.19	0.03	—		—
Methods of child discipline used	0.51		0.02			ns
Number of letters written per month (wife)		0.21	0.04		0.20	0.04
Adequacy of communication	0.47		0.01	0.49		0.01
Days of furlough or visits		0.22	0.02		0.23	0.01
Understanding concerning contacts with opposite sex during separation	0.51		0.01	0.41		0.10
Types of affectional outlet	0.49		0.05			ns
Wife managing without husband	0.53		0.01	0.43		0.10
Longs to be dependent again	0.44		0.01			ns
Wife's Self-Sufficiency Score	Rho= −0.205		0.05	Rho= −0.23		0.02
Family as morale builder scored by husband	—	—			0.22	0.04
Hardships in Reunion Score					−0.65	0.01

the negative relationship between the number of children and adjustment to separation and reunion becomes less pronounced. Innumerable combinations of this sort could conceivably be tested.

A summary chart depicting the most important factors we might use is a necessary beginning as we consider what matrices we wish to construct (see Table 11). Only factors which were thought to be sufficiently related either to separation adjustment or to reunion adjustment to be regarded as statistically significant are listed. To give a common denominator for factors involving classifications of families rather than scores, the coefficient of mean-square contingency C was computed which parallels in crude fashion the simple coefficient of correlation r for the quantitative variables. No significance should be attached to the fact that the C in most every case is larger than the r.[1]

Examination of Table 11 reveals that the largest cluster of significant factors are to be found in the areas of Adequacy of Family Organization and Experiences and Hardships of Separation. The first cluster refers to the crisis-meeting resources of the family and the second to the variety of situations faced and patterns of adjustment followed in the period of crisis. We are tempted, for our first cross-classification matrix, to observe what happens when we cross-classify three influential factors from the areas of Adequacy of Family Organization; namely, family adaptability, family integration, and marital adjustment. We will subdivide our 135 families into thirds; first on their integration scores; and further subdivide those three piles by their adaptability scores; then finally subdivide those nine piles by their marital adjustment scores into twenty-seven piles.[2]

If there are no strong forces at work influencing the families in question, we should have twenty-seven piles with five families each. That this is not the case is apparent when we complete the task (see Table 12). The cases cluster in the upper right-hand corner of the

---

[1] For a discussion of the coefficient of mean-square contingency C see T. C. McCormick, *Elementary Social Statistics* (New York: McGraw-Hill Book Company, 1941), pp. 203–208.

[2] The statistical procedure used was to compute the 33.33 and 66.66 percentiles for the distributions of each factor, thereby designating the trisecting points for each variable.

table where high marital adjustment, high adaptability, and high integration are found,[3] in the center where medium marital adjustment, medium adaptability, and medium integration are found, and in even more marked fashion in the left-hand corner where low marital adjustment, low adaptability, and low integration prepon derate. High intercorrelation among these three factors is evident, the precise extent of which will be shown statistically later in this chapter. Dunigan (*13*) noted this intercorrelation in his study and used it to support his thesis that the three factors in question were contributing toward the same end, the measurement of family adjustment, but measuring somewhat different aspects of family adjustment which are inextricably intertwined in actual behavior.

A second gain of the cross-classification matrix shown in Table 12 is to visualize how adjustment to separation scores and adjustment to reunion scores are affected by this division of families into twenty-seven arbitrarily designated statistical family types. Because the number of families in many of the cells is so small, it is quite hazardous to make generalizations. We will, nevertheless, attempt to make five:

1. There are no families with low marital adjustment–high adaptability–high integration scores, and conversely no families with high marital adjustment–low adaptability–low integration scores.
2. Contrary to our theoretical expectations, the effects of good marital adjustment on the average adjustment to separation scores and the average adjustment to reunion scores are not consistently favorable. In only one grouping of families, the High Integration–Medium Adaptability group, do the scores for separation and for reunion adjustment increase with improved marital adjustment. In one group, Medium

[3] At the suggestion of the editor we add this note of orientation which should make Table 12 more readable. Each of the twenty-seven cells contains families with scores ranging within the intervals indicated by the captions at the head of the columns and at the extreme left of the rows. For example, in the upper right-hand cell are twelve families with an average adjustment to separation score of 3.72 whose marital adjustment scores ranged from 67.7 to 89.9, whose adaptability scores were between 19.4 and 25.0 and whose integration scores ranged between 19.1 and 25.0.

Integration–High Adaptability, the relationship is reversed for separation and inconclusive for reunion. In most of the groups the separation and reunion scores appeared to be less dependent on marital adjustment than was true in the total sample of 135 families.

3. The theoretical expectations concerning the effects of adaptability on separation adjustment are maintained for most of the twenty-seven family types; the most inconsistency is found in the nine High Integration types. With respect to adjustment to reunion, the adaptability effects are not consistently favorable except for the Low Integration types.

4. The theoretical expectations concerning the effects of integration on separation and reunion adjustment hold only for the Low Adaptability types. In the Medium Adaptability types the scores vary more with marital adjustment than with integration and within the High Adaptability types the expected relationship between integration and separation and reunion is reversed.

5. The best statistical family types with respect to separation and reunion adjustment in this matrix are found in the Medium Integration–High Adaptability grouping. High individual statistical family types are found, however, all over the matrix, and will be studied more intensively to discover why they vary from the expected. Why should the Low Integration–Low Adaptability–Medium Marital Adjustment family type have adjustment to separation scores higher than any other type, and adjustment to reunion scores identical with the average of the sample? Or even more puzzling, why should the High Integration–High Adaptability–High Marital Adjustment family type have adjustment to separation and adjustment to reunion scores which are not higher than the average of the entire sample? These deviations from the expected will bear further study.

These are not generalizations we enjoy making. We hope they will have a healthy effect, in so far as they destroy the easy illusion of close, straight-line relationships between influential factors and the crisis-meeting phenomenon of family adjustment. When a population of 135 families is broken up into groups based on their scores in family integration, adaptability, and marital adjustment, as we have done in Table 12, there is little guarantee that the poorly adjusting have thereby been segregated from the well adjusting. A be-

TABLE 12. Distribution of Families and Their Average Adjustment to Separation and Adjustment to Reunion Scores Cross-Classified by Adaptability, Integration, and Marital Adjustment Scores

Integration Scores		Adaptability Scores												Grand Total
		8–16.4				16.5–19.3				19.4–25.0				
		0–54.1	Marital Adjustment 54.2–67.6	67.7–89.9	Total	0–54.1	Marital Adjustment 54.2–67.6	67.7–89.9	Total	0–54.1	Marital Adjustment 54.2–67.6	67.7–89.9	Total	
19.1–25.0	Number	1	2	4	7	2	7	7	16	0	1	12	13	36
	Av. Adj. to Separation	3.90	3.55	3.84	3.77	3.50	3.60	3.81	3.68	0.00	4.10	3.72	3.75	3.72
	Number	1	2	3	6	1	6	7	14	0	1	12	13	33
	Av. Adj. to Reunion	4.80	4.75	4.50	4.63	4.10	4.45	4.53	4.46	0.00	4.40	4.24	4.25	4.41
16.8–19.0	Number	2	3	2	7	9	12	9	30	4	8	10	22	59
	Av. Adj. to Separation	3.55	3.93	3.70	3.76	3.82	3.80	3.83	3.86	4.18	3.91	3.84	3.90	3.86
	Number	1	3	2	6	5	8	8	21	4	7	9	20	47
	Av. Adj. to Reunion	4.20	4.40	4.25	4.32	4.57	4.40	4.65	4.53	4.48	4.44	4.52	4.48	4.49
7.5–16.7	Number	21	6	0	27	3	5	2	10	1	2	0	3	40
	Av. Adj. to Separation	3.37	4.03	0.00	3.52	3.00	3.92	3.85	3.63	4.10	4.00	0.00	3.59	3.59
	Number	19	3	0	22	2	5	2	9	1	2	0	3	34
	Av. Adj. to Reunion	3.75	4.26	0.00	3.82	4.20	4.42	4.25	4.41	4.9	4.70	0.00	4.80	4.06
Total	Number	24	11	6	41	14	24	18	56	5	11	22	38	135
	Av. Adj. to Separation	3.41	3.92	3.79	3.60	3.60	3.76	3.82	3.77	4.16	3.88	3.77	3.86	3.74
	Number	21	8	5	34	8	19	17	44	5	10	21	36	114
	Av. Adj. to Reunion	3.82	4.45	4.40	4.05	4.42	4.42	4.55	4.48	4.56	4.46	4.36	4.42	4.33

TABLE 13. Distribution of Families and Their Behavior Profiles when Cross-Classified into Nine Adaptability-Integration Categories

Integration Scores		Adaptability Scores			Total
		Low, (8-16.4)	Medium, (16.5-19.3)	High (19.4-25.0)	
High (19.1-25.0)		High Integration-Low Adaptability	High Integration-Medium Adaptability	High Integration-High Adaptability	
	Number of Families	7	16	13	36
	Av. Marital Adjustment Score	67.94	64.4	75.02	
	Av. Wife's Self-Sufficiency Score	2.1	2.94	3.8	
	Av. Adjustment to Hardships of Separation Score	3.71	3.66	3.65	
	Av. Adjustment to Separation Score	3.77	3.68	3.75	
	Av. Adjustment to Hardships of Reunion Score	4.63	4.41	4.22	
	Av. Adjustment to Reunion Score	4.63	4.46	4.25	
	Types of Family Control — Father-Dominated	85%	75%	46%	
	Equalitarian	0	19	38	
	Mother-Dominated	15	6	15	
Medium (16.8-19.0)		Medium Integration-Low Adaptability	Medium Integration-Medium Adaptability	Medium Integration-High Adaptability	
	Number of Families	7	30	22	59
	Av. Marital Adjustment Score	60.3	60.1	64.66	
	Av. Self-Sufficiency Score	3.1	3.33	4.09	
	Av. Adjustment to Hardships of Separation Score	3.67	3.75	3.81	
	Av. Adjustment to Separation Score	3.75	3.86	3.90	
	Av. Adjustment to Hardships of Reunion Score	4.34	4.50	4.42	

TABLE 13. Distribution of Families and Their Behavior Profiles when Cross-Classified into Nine Adaptability-Integration Categories (*Continued*)

Integration Scores		Adaptability Scores			Total
		Low, (8–16.4)	Medium, (16.5–19.3)	High (19.4–25.0)	
		Medium Integration-Low Adaptability	Medium Integration-Medium Adaptability	Medium Integration-High Adaptability	
Medium (16.8–19.0) (Continued)	Av. Adjustment to Reunion Score	4.32	4.53	4.48	
	Types of Family Control Father-Dominated	85%	80%	54%	
	Equalitarian	15	13	36	
	Mother-Dominated	0	17	9	40
		Low Integration-Low Adaptability	Low Integration-Medium Adaptability	Low Integration-High Adaptability	
Low (7.5–16.7)	Number of Families	27	10	3	
	Av. Marital Adjustment Score	42.4	58.9	58.13	
	Av. Wife's Self-Sufficiency Score	4.39	4.40	2.7	
	Av. Adjustment to Hardships of Separation Score	3.51	3.54	4.0	
	Av. Adjustment to Separation Score	3.52	3.63	4.0	
	Av. Adjustment to Hardships of Reunion Score	3.86	4.38	4.6	
	Av. Adjustment to Reunion Score	3.82	4.41	4.7	
	Types of Family Control Father-Dominated	65%	50%	33%	
	Equalitarian	15	30	66	
	Mother-Dominated	19	20	0	
Total		41	56	38	135

havior profile of each of these nine major groupings may reveal just how much variation there is among them. To that task we now turn.

BEHAVIOR PROFILES OF NINE STATISTICAL FAMILY TYPES

Much of the evidence presented to this point emphasizes the extreme variability of family behavior in the face of separation and reunion situations. Such uniformity as has been obtained has resulted from excluding exceptions from view. This is likely whenever researchers deal mainly with measures of central tendency and measures of goodness of fit, with little attention to evidences of dispersion. In the last chapter we did just about that—pointed up the uniformities, soft-pedaled the inconsistencies. In this chapter, our approach is at a second level of analysis—grouping and regrouping materials with the hope of capturing patterns of relationships while preserving the wholeness of families in analysis wherever possible. Necessarily our attention also turns to the exceptions.

The first cross-classification matrix, Table 12, illustrated the matter of variability well. To see the interrelationships of as many variables as possible while holding the important factors of integration and adaptability constant, Table 13, was constructed. The result is a shorthand statement of the make-up of each of nine key family types: (1) High Integration–High Adaptability, (2) High Integration–Medium Adaptability, (3) High Integration–Low Adaptability, (4) Medium Integration–High Adaptability, (5) Medium Integration–Medium Adaptability, (6) Medium Integration–Low Adaptability, (7) Low Integration–High Adaptability, (8) Low Integration–Medium Adaptability, and (9) Low Integration–Low Adaptability.

All of the scores except two listed in the behavior profile are average scores of factors already defined in our earlier discussion.[4] The range for each family type is unfortunately quite large, as we

---

[4] The two new scores are the Adjustment to Separation Score *corrected for hardships experienced in separation,* and the Adjustment to Reunion Score *corrected for hardships experienced in reunion.* They are listed in the profile as the Adjustments to Hardships of Separation Score and the Adjustment to Hardships of Reunion

STATISTICAL FINDINGS CONTINUED 167

will see. The distribution of families by types of family control is self-explanatory.

What can we learn from these nine family types and their behavior profiles?

1. Wife's self-sufficiency increases when adaptability is held constant as family integration decreases. Whereas there is a curvilinear relationship between adjustment to separation and wife's self-sufficiency, the relationship between family integration and wife's self-sufficiency appears distinctly negative.
2. Wife's self-sufficiency increases as adaptability increases for both High Integration and Medium Integration groupings, but remains static for the Low Integration group. This is a positive relationship which makes it appear that a very important element in adaptability is self-sufficiency of wife, when integration is held constant.
3. Marital adjustment is closely related to both integration and to adaptability in that the marital adjustment scores increase as one moves from low integration to high integration and from low adaptability to high adaptability.
4. Hardships to which families were forced to adjust in separation and reunion were greatest for the three family types that were low in adaptability. This is seen in the correction upward of adjustment to separation and adjustment to reunion scores when hardships are taken into account. Two of the High Adaptability and two Medium Adaptability family types by contrast experienced few or no hardships in reunion and their scores have been deflated from the original raw scores.
5. The highest proportion of equalitarian families are found among the three High Adaptability family types, and the LI-MA family type, all except one of which also has high Wife's Self-Sufficiency Scores. It begins to appear that adaptability, wife's self-sufficiency, and equalitarian type of family control may all be components of an important complex.
6. By contrast the highest proportions of father-dominated families are found in families of low adaptability and high or medium integration,

Score. Each family's separation or reunion score was deflated or inflated by the amount their particular hardships category exceeded or fell short of the mean adjustment to separation or reunion score of the sample. To our knowledge this is the first time the hardships of a crisis have been taken into account in computing the adjustment to crisis score or rating. Unfortunately the idea occurred to us too late to be able to incorporate it into our previous analysis.

which in turn are characterized by lower Wife's Self-Sufficiency Scores. Since patriarchalism is the traditional form of family control, it would be expected to be associated with low adaptability and with less maternal self-sufficiency. Other studies (*1, 3*) have mentioned patriarchal control sometimes appearing associated with marked family integration.

7. The range of actual scores within family types is so large that any generalizations we have made based on averages of these scores need to be treated more as hypotheses for future testing than as definitive findings. In no case, however, does any family type approximate the range of the entire sample, and in a few instances one could arrive at the same generalizations from an examination of the ranges of scores of given family types as were arrived at from an analysis of their means.

To bring Table 13 closer to the reader, we propose to discuss each statistical family type and illustrate it from an actual family which conforms most closely in its behavior profile to the scores for the statistical family type itself. The illustrative material will be the un-edited case summaries written to give a thumbnail sketch of the family at the time of the interview. In some instances these summaries may cause the reader to question the adequacy of the statistical typology in classifying the cases. Statistical types need to be checked against the case records for this very reason. We have not edited the summaries with the hope that if there are inconsistencies they will appear.

Statistical types are empirical types drawn from the sample, as opposed to ideal or constructed types which are arrived at more or less intuitively after prolonged introspection. Both the totality and structure of the particular population and the theoretical considerations of the variables at work are taken into account in constructing ideal types.[5]

[5] Constructive typology as a method has been ably delineated for us in American sociological literature by Howard Becker (*3*), and applied to the family by Ernest W. Burgess and students (*9*); Winch (*35*) has summarized the distinctions between statistical typology, which he calls empirical, from constructive typology, which he calls heuristic. We have been impelled to use both methods and compare

The statistical family types whose profiles of behavior are summarized in Table 13 are by no means homogeneous types with respect to either classifying factor. A given family is classified as falling in the High Integration–High Adaptability family types if its integration score was more than 19.0 and if its adaptability score was more than 19.3. There were thirteen such families with scores varying from 19.4 to 24.0 on adaptability and from 19.1 to 23.5 on integration. Yet there are families classified as part of the Medium Integration–Medium Adaptability type which may have scores close to 19.0 and 19.3 on integration and adaptability, respectively, which may be more like the High Integration–High Adaptability family type members in many other respects than they are like the members of their own classification type. The typology we have used of trisecting a population on the basis of scores is quite arbitrary and does not take into account the clustering of families as suggested by Winch (35), nor does it provide for the examination of a case in its totality as is arranged for in the classification of families into constructed types. Having pointed out these limitations in our method, we proceed to describe our empirical statistical family types:

HIGH INTEGRATION–HIGH ADAPTABILITY FAMILY TYPE (HI-HA)

There are thirteen families falling into this cell of Table 13. If a combination of high integration and high adaptability were desirable for adjustment to the crises of family life, these families should average the highest scores and be most invulnerable to crisis. Actually the evidence is conflicting: The husband-wife relationships are the healthiest of all the family types as measured by the Burgess-Cottrell Marital Adjustment Scale, the upper tenth

---

findings. In the case study analysis Mrs. Boulding has used a form of constructive typology in defining and classifying adaptable and integrated families, whereas in this chapter Reuben Hill has used an empirical typology for his classifications. The results from the analyses will be compared in the next chapter.

of the entire sample in that respect. Moreover, this adjustment is not at the expense of the wife's personal development because the Wife's Self-Sufficiency Score among these thirteen families is also high. Finally, the adjustment is not a result of slavish traditional deference to a male head, because no other family type has fewer male-dominated families or more equalitarian, many-headed families.

Yet, the record shows this set of families adjusted no better to separation and adjusted no better to reunion than the average of the entire sample of 135 families. They experienced more than the average number of hardships in both separation and reunion, but even with these hardships taken into account their adjustment scores in both crises are below those expected for this combination of integration and adaptability.

Of the thirteen families the one family whose profile scores most closely approximates those of the family type (itself an average) is Case No. 561, the case of John and Evelyn Foster and their six children. A quick glance at the scores proves this point: Marital Adjustment Scores, 74.2; Wife's Self-Sufficiency Score, 4; Type of Family Control, Equalitarian, mixed type; Adjustment to Hardships of Separation Score, 3.74; Adjustment to Hardships of Reunion Score, 4.50. On only one count, the last score mentioned, do the scores differ markedly from the average of the family type; that is, the Fosters adjusted better to reunion than the other twelve families they are to represent here.

Evelyn, a housepainter's daughter in a family of eight children, at fifteen had just left school to care for an invalid mother when she met John Foster, a 19-year-old fireman's son who had a trucking job, at the home of a relative. They went together for a year and then married, having six children in ten years. They had planned on two children and John's income as a truck driver was small, but when six came they accepted them cheerfully and Evelyn buckled down to the job of making their income stretch. Twelve years later she was still a very charming lively person who never seemed to get weighed down by her responsibilities. The home was not too tidy or attractive but there was love in it and Evelyn, in skimping on household details, was probably choosing the only way to give something of herself as a person to her children. The family group was of indefinite size—there were usually one or more young relatives living in the home, and Evelyn cheerfully washed, cooked and made clothes for all of them. John also accepted his large family with equanimity, enjoyed working around the home, and took almost all his recreation within the home with Evelyn and the kids. John and Evelyn are still very much in love, make a good team, and both have a lively sense of humor. They find all their social needs filled right within their own family circle. The children are a happy, healthy-looking swarm of activity, affectionate and demonstrative, and each had his share of household chores from an early age, participating also in family councils and all important decisions.

Evelyn had pretty tough sledding in John's absence and missed him sorely both as companion and helper in the home. She had the sixth baby after he left for the service and had a great deal of illness among the other five while he was gone. At one time all five were in bed at once, two with pneumonia. Evelyn herself was not well after the baby was born, and developed a nervousness which was not normal to her. She feels now that if she had been well she would not have suffered particularly from nervous tension because of his absence, because she is the easygoing type. The two oldest boys missed their father the most, were nervous and had frequent upset stomachs, but they were also the ones who had been closest to him before he went into service. The younger boy and the two girls had always been more dependent on their mother so they did not miss him so much although they often spoke of him. Evelyn wrote daily of all the family activities, never tired of letter-writing, and John displayed a constant interest in the family in his letters, at the same time revealing that he was also enjoying his army experience.

John, adaptable to whatever new environment he was in, brought home a new language and some new habits when he returned home on furlough which made him seem strange to his family at first, but he immediately fell back into his old place in the family circle. As for the children—"They just followed him around like so many little dogs!" says Evelyn. She wasn't worrying about the reunion and knew that if they had troubles again they would lick them as they had in the past. They both came from families used to trouble and were accustomed to helping one another out. Evelyn's favorite saying is, "Where there's a will, there's a way!"

When John got back it was as if he had never been away. He started on his old chores and helped make the decisions from the very first day. The older children also accepted him immediately, but the fourth child was a little shy of him at first and the baby did not know how to behave to him at all. John did not force himself on them but played with them as much as they would let him and won them over in a very short time. They are still apt to turn to mother for help, however. The fifth child conceived a passionate attachment to daddy at once and was jealous when he gave attention to the other children. Evelyn feels she may have spoiled her somewhat. She is gradually getting over it but the problem still exists. John is happy to be back home and there is a gay, light-hearted atmosphere in the home, a warmth of affection between family members, which is very pleasant to observe. At the same time John was very happy in the service too and would have been glad to stay there if he had not had the children. (He had had very interesting work and good training in the service.) He assured the interviewer that this did not mean that he felt burdened by the children or unhappy to have less congenial work than he was doing in the service. He seems to be the type of man who can be happy under almost any circumstances and he is obviously proud of his family, as they are all proud of him.

In this particular instance the statistical family type is clearly exemplary of the roles we would expect to find in a family possessing high integration and high adaptability. Family-centeredness in activity and affection was most apparent, arguing for high integration. Success in meeting past crises of sickness, income inadequacies, children arriving at close intervals, and the flexibility of role patterns with John helping out in the home, and the children sharing jobs, bespeak great adaptability. The family's adjustment to separation was poorer than expected, but average for this statistical family type, possibly in this case because of the tremendous interdependence of family members, which poorly prepares them for the crisis of dismemberment. That they have adjusted so well to reunion further supports this explanation. The children and Evelyn all reflected the extra burdens thrown on them during the absence of the father, experiencing more sickness, upset stomachs, and nervousness.[6]

HIGH INTEGRATION–MEDIUM ADAPTABILITY FAMILY TYPE (HI-MA)

There are sixteen families falling into this category in Table 13. High integration maintained at slight expense to adaptability produces a slightly different picture from HI-HA family type just described. The Wife's Self-Sufficiency Score declines, the proportion of father-dominated families increases, and marital adjustment varies from very poor to excellent (scores of 22–80) with a lower-than-average score. Adjustment to separation is not improved, but adjustment to reunion is decidedly improved over the HI-HA family type. The hardships of separation were greater for the family type described here, yet the Adjustment to Separation Score was the same.

There are undoubtedly many families in our communities whose integration record exceeds their excellence in adaptability as a family. We have taken the Jackson family with farm parental backgrounds to illustrate this family type of High Integration–Medium Adaptability. Their scores conform closely to the averages for this statistical family type: Marital Adjustment Score, 68.2; Wife's Self-Sufficiency Score, 3; Type of Family Control, Husband-Dominant, mixed type; Adjustment to Hardships of Separation Score, 3.70; Adjustment to Hardships of Reunion Score, 4.70. Again in this case the adjustment to reunion exceeds the average of the statistical type, although a careful study of the case summary which follows may cast some doubt on the adequacy of reunion adjustment, in spite of the high score listed for them.

June and Harry Jackson were both from large farm families and grew up together in the same neighborhood. Harry went away to business col-

---

[6] For an interesting discussion of the interrelationships of family difficulties and the illnesses which afflict family members read, Henry B. Richardson, *Patients Have Families* (New York: Commonwealth Fund, 1945).

lege and when he came back began meeting June again at church affairs. They started going steady when she was 19 and he 22, planned and saved for their marriage three years later. In spite of all their planning they had a very difficult time financially for the first few years, and began having children before they were able to afford it. This put some strain on the marriage but they were sufficiently in love to stick it out. June had come from a home where the parents were very strict although kind and well-meaning, and she was determined to give her two children more freedom than she had had and to make as happy a home as possible for the family. She had a natural tendency towards irritability and impatience which she let out on the family from time to time but she was very ashamed of this and tried hard to overcome it. Harry was affectionate and kind, and they worked together closely in the home. They had a good deal of family pride and June would work her fingers to the bone to sew clothes for the kids so they could look nice when the family had little or no money. She got to be an old hand at making something out of nothing. The family always did everything together, and June and Harry would never dream of going anywhere without the children.

June missed Harry when he went into service but got along fairly well in his absence, became somewhat more independent, and didn't have to worry about him because he never went overseas. The older child wasn't much affected by his absence although he missed his companionship and often spoke of him, but the younger grieved deeply for him, became very nervous and clung closely to his grandfather and June. She found it hard to make the children mind without Harry around. She gave up their house in town and took a small house in her old home town near her parents so that she could have their help if she needed it. Harry and June planned a lot for the future in their letters, and his favorite dream was about building a home for the family.

During furloughs the family was even closer than they had been before, and always content to spend their time at home, alone together. June isn't worrying about the reunion except that she knows it will be difficult to find a home again in the city.

Harry was the same as ever when he came back, as June had expected, and they were very happy to be together again. However, they have not been able to find a home in the city where Harry's new job is, so the family has only been together on weekends when he can come out to the little town where June and the children have a house. This means that Harry hasn't been able to help around the house or do things with the children, although they both long for the time when he can do this. They are both more independent than they were, and this might be a problem when they do get together again. Right now they are unhappy and upset about not being able to be together, and there is some conflict about whether they should put money into a car so Harry can visit them oftener or into a house which Harry feels they can't afford at present prices. This is a difficult problem but they have faced harder ones before and will probably work out a satisfactory solution eventually.

Except for the fact that June and Harry Jackson are of farm family backgrounds attempting to work out a way of life in the city which will be congenial to them, there is little in the record expressing integration and adaptability which clearly differentiates the Jacksons as representatives of the HI-MA family type from the Fosters of the HI-HA category. High adaptability is more difficult to maintain when family forms designed for life in the country are transported to urban environments, and some of the difficulties of the Jacksons stem from that maladjustment. Here may be one of the deficiencies of the empirical typology—the inability to make clear-cut distinctions in the dynamic make-up of families when relying solely on position in a statistical distribution for categorizing families.

HIGH INTEGRATION–LOW ADAPTABILITY FAMILY TYPE (HI-LA)

There are only seven families categorized as of high integration and low adaptability. From another study (1) we would expect these families to be relatively more rigid and hidebound in their organization which in turn makes it difficult for them to make ready adaptations to new situations. The proportion of father-dominated families is highest in this family type, and the scores for wife's self-sufficiency are lowest of all the family types. There are no equalitarian families in this group.

Adjustment to the hardships of separation is about average, roughly the same as for the sample of 135 families. Marital adjustment and adjustment to the hardships of reunion are high, reflecting the relatively great importance of integration in determining high performance in these areas. In some respects this is the most homogeneous of the high integration family types. The range is smaller for most factors than is found among the other two family types heretofore considered.

To illustrate family life for these seven families, we have selected Case No. 591. Bob and Helen Mallory and their four children are members of a father-centered family whose behavior profile closely approximates the average of all the HI-LA families. Marital Adjustment Score, 66.6. Wife's Self-Sufficiency Score, 2. Adjustment to Hardships of Separation Score, 3.60; Adjustment to the Hardships of Reunion Score, 4.80. The Mallorys' scores, like the Jacksons' and the Fosters', conform well to the average scores of their respective types on all items except the adjustment to reunion, which is higher than expected. The lack of adaptability does not appear to affect the Mallorys' reunion experiences sharply.

Helen, a brickmason's daughter, was 17 when Bob Mallory, an eighteen-year-old farm boy came to town to try grocery store clerking, moved to her street. They double-dated with her sister and his brother for seven months, then had a double wedding. Helen was one of eight children and used to doing her share of the work at home, had also worked in a factory, been a sales clerk, a receptionist, and was altogether a very self-reliant person. When four children came along in rapid succession she was able to handle them without too much difficulty, although it put a strain on her physically and on the whole family financially. Bob was a good provider, but was not much help around the house. In fact, he felt strongly certain kinds of jobs were woman's work and would only reluctantly help with home duties. They were very much in love, however, and had lots of good times together. Helen liked Bob to be the head of the house, because she felt that he could think things through better than she could. He usually consulted her before making any decisions, but she sometimes wished that he would consult her more. She was definitely the adaptable one of the two. When questioned about having his wife work outside the home for pay to augment the income he indicated he would rather starve first.

Helen and Bob and the children all seemed fond of one another, and the oldest boy was especially close to the father. Helen was not very successful at disciplining her brood but good-naturedly let things go with a good-natured whack across a particularly obstreperous bottom. Sometimes the household would get to be too much for her, but her health and temper improved considerably when they decided not to have any more children. Sex relations became more fun for her then too. This was just before Bob went into service. The family had its little problems; Bob and Helen were both quite attractive and each tended to be a little jealous for the attentions the other received, but there was no real cause for jealousy. They didn't always agree on how to spend money, and the oldest boy had worms for some years—could never be completely cured and was a worry to Helen. Underlying family unity was strong, however, and the family was a happy one.

Helen and the two oldest boys were deeply affected by Bob's absence, but the third youngster soon forgot his father and the baby was born after he left. Helen found it hard to have to be mother and father too, hardest of all to have a baby with Bob away. The oldest boy was very lonely, became nervous and temperamental, also much more independent. They all longed to have the father back and lived for his vivid, interesting letters, kept him posted on everything that happened at home.

When Bob came back on his first furlough Helen found that they didn't know how to behave to each other. They had never been apart for even a night in their whole married life and didn't know how to bridge the gap of absence. The strangeness only lasted a day or two, however, and then the family picked up where it had left off before Bob went away. Helen is nevertheless afraid that he might seem strange again when he returns, although his letters reveal that he is the same old Bob.

The reunion was not as difficult as expected. Bob slipped back into family life without any trouble, unchanged except that he seemed to appreciate his home more, and was more considerate of Helen. He consulted her more, especially about money matters, and helped more around the house. Helen, needless to say, liked the changes very much, and all the family were delighted to be together again.

The Mallory family exemplifies high integration at two points: (1) in the affection which is shown for all members of the family, especially between Bob and Helen and between Bob and the oldest child; and (2) in the number of things the family did together. The focus of family life was so clearly around Bob and his interests that it was an integration poorly adjustive to a crisis of separation. Helen, able and self-reliant, with many skills, accepted a subservient role in family decisions and failed to use her vocational abilities to greatest advantage when they were needed, because it would displease Bob. Her personal adaptability was badly cramped in that context.

MEDIUM INTEGRATION–HIGH ADAPTABILITY FAMILY TYPE (MI-HA)

Here is a family type with an excellent record in separation and reunion. The twenty-two families characterized by medium integration and high adaptability have experienced hardships both in separation and reunion, yet their adjustment scores are the highest of the entire sample. Although their marital adjustment scores are in the middle third of the sample, there is evidence of compensatory achievement in other areas. Wife's self-sufficiency scores are high, and the proportion of equalitarian families is second only to the HI-HA type. The advocates of democratic family life where the wife is encouraged to develop as a person, is encouraged in self-reliance, and where the children are an integral part of the decision-making process in the home, would be happy with the attainments of this group of twenty-two families. Again, high adaptability, high wife self-sufficiency, and a high proportion of equalitarian families appear together, and this time they are linked with excellent adjustment to separation and reunion scores. We learn again that for best results one doesn't want highest scores in combination—but rather moderate concentrations of integration and marital adjustment.

The family with scores which most closely approximate the averages of the entire twenty-two families in this prize category is not a subject for sermons on Mother's Day. From our familistic heritage we retain a preference for high integration over high adaptability in our society. This family is far from a model of integration, yet it has adapted well to life in an Iowa community during wartime. It is not an idyllic family either in its genesis or in its present outlook on life. Virgil and Mina Pisha Rich and their two children, both of whom are in school, are a maturing family dominated sufficiently by Virgil to be listed as husband-dominant, mixed type. They live in the respectable, but not most swanky, section in a railroad town in northern Iowa. Their scores reflect attainments which qualify them as representative of the Medium Integration–High Adaptability family type: Marital Adjustment Score, 67.7; Wife's Self-Sufficiency Score, 5.0; Adjustment to Hardships of Separation Score, 3.94; Adjustment to Hardships of Reunion Score, 3.80. The Riches have a less happy adjustment to reunion than the average of the sample; an analysis of their unedited case history will reveal some of the reasons.

Virgil and Mina met in high school when he was 17 and Mina was 13. Today as the interviewer entered the home he found the eight-year-old daughter combing her mother's hair and saw pictures on the wall which showed how mature the family had become. In a few short years teenagers who were scrappy incompatibles had founded a family which had all the marks of respectability in this northern Iowa railroad town, and were soberly planning for a respectable future for their two children.

Virgil was a popular basketball player of a fine Marshalltown family whose insistence on going steady with Mina brought them quarrels, breakups and reconciliations during their first three years of acquaintance. Mina came from a divorced home, was cautious not to get involved or "get burned" as she put it, in any marital relationships. She did not agree to get married until she discovered she was pregnant when she was 17. Their courtship quarrels were frequently over who would decide what they did. Both wanted to be boss. In marriage, they didn't quarrel so much, have been more likely to sit down and talk things over, and particularly after the baby came they felt settled as a family.

Mina contrasts marriage with life before marriage to the advantage of the married state, "I was surprised how kind Virgil was, and how considerate. I was happier in marriage than ever before. I found I could stand on my own feet with Virgil to bolster me up, he's more often right, I can admit that now." Both love their children and have plans for them which include college, something Mina always wanted, but was never able to afford, besides she got married, or "or was it instead," she wasn't sure. Virgil wants more children, Mina is willing to call it quits.

After having held odd jobs as sales clerk and salesman on commission, Virgil accepted a position as postal clerk shortly before getting married and has been thriving ever since on the security of the government position. Both want more than anything else home, security and happiness, and neither wish to risk much to get them. A civil service position has some merit in that connection.

Both were shocked by Virgil's induction into the service, but it didn't floor them. Mina misses her husband, finds herself compensating by living more with her children. She has returned to work part time to help her mother who runs a restaurant. His mother cares for the children in the daytime. Mina explains she will gladly quit when Virgil returns, but Virgil's letters indicate he is afraid she won't.

Their letters are adequate, full of plans for the future, of getting a home of their own. Finances are adequate. The children are flourishing, and the wife saw no problems ahead at the time of the separation interview. Although he is in Manila, Virgil's presence is felt in the home because of his letters, gifts, snapshots, and their own talk about him in the home. Virgil writes he is a changed man, "Service has made me more appreciative of my wife, more proud of my boy and girl. It has given me time to plan our future more clearly, and it has also made me think of a lot of things and places that my wife and I could have seen together before but never gave it much thought . . . I will probably be somewhat a changed person at first after I am discharged from the Service, but will probably gradually get to be my old self once again."

Furloughs gave proof the family was prepared to return to old roles, with the father assuming his position in the family without a hitch. He doesn't think there will be any danger of becoming a "fifth wheel."

The reunion did not live up to its expectations, especially from the wife's standpoint. She found Virgil a stranger, and felt that she couldn't start where they left off at all, and that they have terrific arguments about the children. Her affection for her husband has diminished markedly. Virgil does not reflect this feeling, but is less attached to Mina than when he was in the service. The children accept him and he is glad to be back on his old job again.

The Riches illustrate expediency in family life combined with intermittent affection and consideration for each other. Beginning with a stormy courtship marked by incompatibility, marrying out of felt social pressure, seeking security and respectability rather than excitement and pleasure, meeting separation by shifts in role of wife to father and mother too, this is an interesting family sequence of expedient adaptability.

MEDIUM INTEGRATION–MEDIUM ADAPTABILITY FAMILY TYPE (MI-MA)

In this central cell are found more families than in any other category. Thirty families are located at this fulcrum in the adaptability–integration balance wheel. Their record is very nearly as exciting as the MI-HA group just discussed. Three sharp differences may be noted: reversal of types of family control, with the patriarchal families constituting 80 percent of the families; a marked decrease in marital adjustment; and a shift in wife's self-sufficiency. Adjustment to separation is very high and the highest scores of adjustment to reunion of the entire sample are recorded in this family type. It may well prove that for crisis-meeting purposes one doesn't look for combinations of high integation and high adaptability, but that they combine more effectively in moderate amounts. This is a provocative hypothesis which will bear testing in later research.

The family selected to represent this central family type is in the traditional American pattern. The husband is clearly boss and the sole provider, and the wife subservient and the homemaker. In a constructive typology this case would probably be classified as highly integrated of low adaptability, but the statistical scores on our adaptability and integration scales force us to place this family in the central cell. The scores of this family conform closely with the average of the entire thirty families: Marital Adjustment score, 58.2; Wife's Self-Sufficiency Score, 2; Adjustment to Hardships of Separation Score, 3.67; Adjustment to Hardships of Reunion Score, 4.50. The family in question is the Thomas and Claire Sckanky family, Case No. 584, a one-child grouping which survived both separation and reunion with a good record.

Claire Sckanky was reared as an only child by her aunt, uncle and grandmother after losing both her parents early in life. She was twenty when she met Tom, a 19-year-old watchmaker's son who was being apprenticed to his father's business. They met on a blind date and Claire was impressed by Tom's gay way; his boldness was so different from the few boys she had met in her sheltered foster home. They fell in love, went steady for fourteen months and married.

Tom comes from a long line of watchmakers—the skill has been handed down from father to son—and he has a strong sense of tradition and family pride. The women in his family have never worked gainfully and he exacted the promise from Claire that she would never work, which she was willing enough to grant. Claire moved quickly and easily from one sheltered environment to another. She was doted on by her relatives and developed a dependency which responded quickly to attention and affection. Both Tom and Claire found their roles dovetailing before marriage and in the marriage itself they proved complementary. Claire has become a model homemaker, getting a great deal of satisfaction out of buying beautiful furniture and making the home as attractive as possible. In so doing she has run Tom heavily into debt, but he has accepted the burden somewhat more graciously than most husbands. They enjoy going out together, doing the same things. Claire is inclined to be irritable and pessimistic, but Tom is absorbent, doesn't get angry when Claire "blows her stack" so they have got along very well.

Shortly before Tom was drafted they had a baby which has been enjoyed by both of them. The only problems they listed at the time of Tom's induction after three years of marriage were the debts incurred by the furniture, the car and the baby.

Claire was very nervous during Tom's absence, missed him greatly and found it difficult to make decisions without him. She tried at first to consult him by mail, going through agonies of impatience while waiting for replies on decisions. She worked during his absence (with his permission) in order to pay off their debts, with the understanding that she would stop as soon as he returned. But she didn't enjoy the work and worried constantly about the child who was in the care of her aunt and grandmother. She felt she was neglecting her home and that little Bobbie was being badly spoiled by her relatives. Tom worried about this and tried to give advice about the baby in his letters. Bobbie didn't remember his father and therefore didn't miss him. He constituted a tying factor in the day-to-day letters between Tom and Claire. Both shared their feelings about Bobbie, life in the service, and their longings for one another in their letters.

During every furlough there was usually a period of one day when Tom and Claire felt strange to each other, then both were able to relax and enjoy their old companionship. Bobbie was always included in their activities and he never had any shyness toward Tom after the first furlough. Claire worried about Tom being nervous when he returned, and wondered if they wouldn't have more trouble readjusting than other couples that had been married for a longer period.

Once Tom returned he found little difficulty in reëstablishing himself with his family. He slipped back into his dominant patriarchal role, into the enjoyment of close intimacies with his wife. The one area of difficulty was with Bobbie whom he found willful, stubborn, undisciplined, and completely out of hand. Neither Claire nor Tom could get Bobbie to obey them. This irritated Tom and whatever strains he felt in the readjustment he took out in irritability with the child rather than with his wife. Tom now resents the frequent visits from the doting aunt and grandmother, whom he blames for spoiling Bobbie. To date there has been no tendency for the marital relation to carry the burden of these antagonisms, and both Tom and Claire feel they have survived the separation and the reunion without a scar.

One of the impressive items in this family of medium integration–medium adaptability which may hold for the entire family type of thirty families is the feasibility of a family adjusting to crisis under the patriarchal system of family control, in which the wife is relatively low in self-sufficiency. Given a lively sense of interdependence and affectional unity, the father-dominated family makes its own characteristic adjustment to crisis.

MEDIUM INTEGRATION–LOW ADAPTABILITY FAMILY TYPE (MI-LA)

Most of the families with low adaptability scores also have low integration scores, which leaves only seven families in this incongruous family type. Most of the families are father-dominated and marital adjustment is just moderate. Wife's self-sufficiency is lower than any other medium integration type. Although these seven families experienced marked hardships in separation, their record for reunion shows few or no hardships. The adjustment score in the face of both crises is slightly better than average.

The family chosen to represent this type becomes better adjusted to family life as the years proceed. They are the Jim and Alice McCarthys, Case No. 552, another one-child family. Father-dominated, like the family type under study, the scores achieved were: Marital Adjustment, 62.0; Wife's Self-Sufficiency, 4; Adjustment to Hardships of Separation, 3.94; Adjustment to Hardships of Reunion 4.80. Their adjustment to reunion is markedly better than that of the family type they represent.

Alice was the daughter of a Des Moines theatre owner and was raised with her brother by an uncle and aunt after her mother's death. At twenty-five, while she was working on a government job, she met twenty-seven-year-old Jim McCarthy, a dentist's son who was in the finance business. After going together for four years they married. Alice had been happy in her uncle's home but may have felt some insecurity due to the remarriage of her father, who had two children by his second wife. She was nevertheless friendly with her stepmother and sisters and fairly close to her father. Her insecurity showed only in the fact that she was a constant worrier, irritable and easily frightened, and leaned a good deal on Jim. Fortunately, Jim could give her both warm affection and a high degree of financial security, and also bolstered her ego by consulting her on all family matters and telling her that she was the boss in the home. He liked a strict division of labor, though, and would never do anything that he considered to be "woman's work" or let Alice work outside the home. This was all right with Alice and they were good companions, although perhaps even more intimate with their only daughter than with each other. Alice particularly gave a great deal of attention to the child, was over solicitous about her welfare, and would have done well to have had a second child. Alice was grateful to Jim for the financial security and the love he gave her, and there were few conflicts between them. Their only real disagreement was that Jim liked to go out a lot to late parties and leave family worries behind, while Alice always worried about how things were at home when she was out and always wanted to leave parties early. The solution was usually a compromise. They had never faced any real crises.

When Jim went into service, Alice gave up their house and moved into an apartment so she would have fewer household cares, and she worried considerably about how she would manage alone. She found herself managing very well, which surprised her as much as it did Jim. She had hated to give up their home, however, and was never satisfied with apartment living. Apart from that the separation was not a hardship for her; in fact, she positively enjoyed it, because for the first time in her life she got to travel. Jim was in the Navy and docked in the U. S. often, on both East and West coasts, so Alice had several exciting trips to meet him. They both felt that her increased home responsibilities and the travel had broadened and matured her. Since she saw Jim fairly often and had many long-distance phone calls when she couldn't go to meet him, she never felt the separation very keenly. Although they both wrote regularly, they felt that the phone calls meant more to them than the letters. The little girl was more upset by her father's absence than Alice was, and cried whenever letters came from him, but on the whole adjusted fairly well and became more dependent on her mother in everything.

Furloughs and visits to camp were always happy occasions in which the daughter was usually included, but were also something of a strain on the family because each visit was so short. In anticipating the reunion, Alice wondered if Jim would be satisfied to settle down to family life again, whether he would be changed, although the furloughs hadn't indicated this.

When Jim did return he was pleased to discover what a good manager Alice had turned out to be, and allowed her to continue with more household responsibility than she had had before he left. He also left the disciplining of the daughter entirely in her hands. They continued to discuss all problems together, however, and Alice didn't feel that Jim had changed any as a result of the war experience. The only difference was that now they were closer to each other, felt more settled, and appreciated family life more. The child was very happy to have him home and enjoyed doing the things with him that they used to do together—horseback riding, and so on. They were good pals again. Jim still liked to go out more than Alice, but she gave in and went out with him whenever he wanted to. They both felt that they had made such a good adjustment because they had never gotten to feel entirely separated and had seen each other often while Jim was in service.

LOW INTEGRATION–HIGH ADAPTABILITY FAMILY TYPE (LI-HA)

That there are only three instances of low integration and high adaptability points to the rarity of this phenomenon among families. In dealing with constructed types Angell (*1*) found it hard to conceive of any families of this type. There are so few cases it is folly to generalize about them; yet it is interesting to note that they have high adjustment to separation and high adjustment to reunion scores. Marital adjustment scores hold up well considering the low element of integration present, but wife's self-sufficiency does not hold up as it does in all other high adaptability family types.

The family chosen to represent this rare family type is quite anarchistic in make-up, rather than truly democratic or equalitarian. Lacking integration, highly adaptable families are held together for expediency or for the freedom and independence mutually agreed upon for family members. The Jack and Dorothy Wallaces, Case No. 441, are such a family. There is no clear-out dominance in this "working-partner" marriage. The scores conform fairly closely to the average for the three families taken together: Marital Adjustment, 57.6; Wife's Self-Sufficiency, 4, Adjustment to Hardships of Separation, 4.0; Adjustment to Hardships of Reunion, 4.50.

Seventeen-year-old Dorothy Ricci and eighteen-year-old Jack Wallace met through a mutual friend and dated every night for nine months. They were good companions and married on that basis, both continuing in their old jobs. Dorothy remained a "working partner" for seven years, during which time there was a certain amount of quarreling and feeling of insecurity—neither was sure just what his role was in the marriage. Dorothy was the oldest child of a large family, as was Jack too, and they were both pretty independent people. Both had also been starved for affection at home, however, and found their relationship emotionally satisfying. With time each came to recognize the other's need for independence, and they learned how to come to agreement over things without leaving scars in a wounded pride. After the eighth year of marriage the children started coming, and the marriage relationship received new focus and stability. They both buckled down to the business of raising two children, although Dorothy remained psychologically on a working-partner basis and kept her independence. Their mutual concern for the welfare of the children reduced quarreling practically to the zero point;

Jack was very coöperative in the home and he and Dorothy worked well together. Jack was closer to the first child, Dorothy to the second, but they were really all good pals together and the children were pretty good about helping out at home.

Dorothy missed Jack but got along fairly well in his absence, keeping busy with the children, her friends, and having a new baby. The oldest child, a boy, missed his father a lot and reacted by becoming very independent and disobedient. His younger sister had been too young to remember her father very well and didn't feel much change in the situation, stuck close to mother as usual. Dorothy was not especially bothered by having to be mother and father too because she was used to responsibility, but she did have some trouble disciplining the boy. Although he tried to act independent and self-assured, inside he was insecure, just a little kid without his daddy. The biggest problem, though, was the birth of the third baby. Dorothy had to manage the home alone through her pregnancy, and this was especially difficult through the last two months when she was confined to her bed. Young Jack really assumed a man's responsibilities then and helped his mother a lot. His sister was sent off to relatives until after the baby was born. Dorothy and Jack senior maintained their close relationship pretty well through their letters, writing about all the little daily events, discussing plans for when he got back.

Whenever Jack came home on furlough they slipped right back into the old family routines. There were always happy times although it was harder than ever to say goodby. Dorothy didn't anticipate any reunion difficulties, although she did wonder if the children's noise wouldn't bother Jack. Now that Jack is back everyone is happy again, and Dorothy is gradually turning over to him his old responsibilities in the home. She hasn't tried to put too much on him at once, though, because he is suffering from battle fatigue. His temper is a little uncertain at times but Dorothy does her best to make everything run smoothly and knows that the family will be back in the old groove as soon as he is quite well again.

LOW INTEGRATION–MEDIUM ADAPTABILITY FAMILY TYPE (LI-MA)

Of a total of fifty-six medium adaptability families, ten were low in integration, the family type in which we are interested at this moment. This family type is characterized by high wife's self sufficiency scores, lower-than-average marital adjustment scores, and is divided more than any other family type on the variety of family control which is used. There are two families in which the wife dominates the decision making, five where the husband is dominant, and three in which controls are vested in a family council or dispersed among all family members. The families in this Low Integration–Medium Adaptability category experienced few hardships in separation, and yet adjusted less well than the average of the sample. The adjustments to reunion were slightly better than average. Like the LI-HA type, this family type is not convincing conceptually, since it is hard to visualize through statistical scores alone just how families with low integration and medium adaptability have enough binding quality to them to meet and resolve crises.

The Freemans (Case No. 427) are such a family—young, married for six years, two children, but divided by their children and relatives. Their scores closely approximate those of the family type they are to represent: Marital Adjustment, 47.2; Self-Sufficiency of Wife, 4.0; Adjustment to Hardships of Separation, 3.6; Adjustment to Hardships of Reunion, 3.70. The Freemans' reunion adjustments record is poorer than the family type as a whole; otherwise it is an apt selection to illustrate this statistical family type.

Martha and Lawrence Freeman met at a skating rink in Knoxville when she was fifteen and he was twenty-one. Martha had been reared strictly by an aged father and a dominating college-educated mother, both of whom were determined she would go to college and be a credit to her family. At fifteen, she was almost completely out of communication with her parents who had discouraged her dating, and had forbidden Lawrence continuing his attentions. Lawrence was an easygoing farm boy who didn't take her family's dictates too seriously, and he agreed to an elopement into Missouri to get married. Neither realized how inadequately Martha was prepared for the tasks of married life. She describes herself as uninformed, unexperienced, and rebellious, impulsive in her decision making and often apt to do things to spite or show her parents she was bigger than they thought.

. Efforts to annul the marriage failed, but Martha's mother became an active influence to break up the pair, so they moved from Knoxville to

New York to start life afresh. It was only after moving to New York where they worked as waitress and bus boy together that the marriage stabilized around companionship. Martha was surprised that she wasn't homesick, and that Lawrence proved so adequate as a substitute for her parents. She felt she achieved complete emancipation from her parents during the four years she was in New York.

The first evidence of difficulty in their marriage, which had been welded together by the opposition of Martha's parents, came when the first baby proved more interesting to Lawrence than his wife. Larry is in 7th Heaven with babies and became a very good father. Martha turned to the child for affection too when Larry ceased to give her the attention she wished, but found herself thwarted by the child and quickly got the feeling of being tied down. She began regretting her marriage after the babies came, when she realized how much of her youth had been cut short by early marriage and motherhood. She feels she has missed a lot of fun and it's too late to get it now.

Occupationally Lawrence was promoted from bus boy to chef of a New York restaurant, and he seemed unconscious of his wife's irritability with the marriage. When he was inducted, he agreed to Martha returning to Knoxville to be near her relatives, but specified that they were to live apart from them.

The Freemans' reaction to the separation was severe. Returning to Iowa brought complications with relatives although they took an apartment to be away from their influence. The baby was just three months old when they returned and the combination of events produced a distinct psychosomatic reaction in Martha. She developed nervous skin eruptions, sleeplessness and nightmares as she worried about the baby, "mother" and about Larry. She found some release in girl friends and letters, but they deteriorated after a while. When she wrote Larry, her letters were casual and matter-of-fact, and she didn't use them to demonstrate her affection. Larry, in turn, usually asked about the babies, rarely asked about how she was doing. Martha didn't tell Larry when she borrowed money from her folks to pay bills, and she kept the facts from him about the babies being sick. "I said, what he don't know, he won't worry about."

When Larry returned on furloughs the oldest child became upset and remained so for days after he returned to camp. It was during the furlough that Martha saw so clearly Larry preferred the babies to her. She admits tearfully that she is jealous of the babies and the hold they have on Larry. She feels he's a good father and she won't leave him, because he's so good for the children. "I'll stick by him, even though I'd rather be free and unmarried," she stated in interview.

Martha felt she grew considerably during the separation period, that she has developed more self-confidence, but that she is more nervous.

The reunion was arranged for Larry's benefit with the children along. They have accepted him readily, and he glories in his returning father role. Martha states, "As soon as I can, I want to take a vacation away from both Larry and the babies, it will be good for me."

Vocational and housing problems are the worst bones of contention within the family, and the arguments spill over into the relationships with the in-laws. Martha wants to remain in Knoxville, but Larry feels there's too little opportunity for a chef to jusify it, and he is anxious to be free of Martha's parents. "Larry is quiet and easygoing, but stubborn and set in his ideas," Martha explains, and they will probably end up by going where he decides to go. He appears unaware of the jealousy Martha feels for the children, and of the need Martha expresses of more love and attention. Martha is still "just a kid," and he's satisfied with her accomplishments to date.

Martha's parting statement in her interview was, "My mother said, 'a person's better off unmarried' and I see her point!"

LOW INTEGRATION–LOW ADAPTABILITY FAMILY TYPE (LI-LA)

Twenty-seven families fell in this statistically lowest category of the chart. A separate analysis shows that these families are pre-ponderately (23/27) of lower-middle or lower-class social status. This may account for the fact that they experienced so many more hardships in separation than the sample as a whole. They listed more hardships than any other type in reunion. This statistical family type, lacking as it does the important adaptability and in-tegration components, would be listed as "inadequate" by Koos (27) to face the daily exigencies without converting them into crises. Indeed, along with these low adaptability and low integration scores go low marital adjustment scores (the lowest of the entire sample). To keep things interesting, this is the only family type among the nine which was low in adaptability yet high in Wife's

Self-Sufficiency Score. Every form of family control is represented, but there are more mother-dominated families found in this type than in any other in the sample. Equalitarian families are under-represented in this low-ranking family type.

The record of adjustment to separation is the poorest of all nine family types, and the adjustment to reunion scores are lowest of all nine categories. With strikingly few exceptions, to be discussed later, if a family scores low on integration and low on adaptability, it will also be low on marital adjustment and low in adjusting to the crises of separation and reunion.

The family selected to represent the LI-LA family type is the closest approximation to the average we could find. Dave and Jane Morgan (Case No. 441) and their two boys are held together by external pressures rather than internal cohesiveness. The Marital Adjustment Score is 32.0, Wife's Self-Sufficiency Score is 5, Adjustment to Hardships of Separation Score is 3.37, and the Adjustment to Hardships of Reunion Score is 3.80. The family is dominated by the wife, who is also responsible to this date for having kept the family together. The case summary is as follows.

Jane was one of two daughters in a drunkard's family which was supported by her school-teacher mother. While she was studying voice and dancing and supporting herself by working in Bishop's Cafeteria, at 17, she met twenty-year-old Dave Morgan, a farmer's only son who was going to business school in the same town. After six months' acquaintance they began serious dating and married after they had known each other for a year. Jane had come from a very unhappy home but the father's drunkenness brought the mother and the two sisters very close together. She was an intelligent and talented girl who gave up a prospective career in the hope of building a happy home life with Dave. Unfortunately Dave turned out to be a weak, unstable, and consistently unfaithful individual who just didn't have the makings of a good husband. Idealistic Jane was heartbroken over her mistake but for a long time was determined to make the best she could of their marriage and keep up a good front. Dave escaped from constant bickerings over his infidelities by taking a trucking job in another part of the state and for the last four years before his induction only came home weekends. Jane had to become the head of the house, although she would have preferred a more dependent role. There had always been money trouble because neither Jane nor Dave had any sense about financial matters—they just left the money around and used it as the fit took them, running constantly into debt. Dave, the spoiled child, always ran to papa for more when this happened, and papa always shelled out, so Dave had never really had to face up to his home responsibilities. The rearing of the two children had fallen entirely on Jane's shoulders, and although Dave was fond of them in his way they were bitter toward him for the unhappiness he caused their mother and would not accept his companionship. Since things were getting worse, not better, Jane was beginning to consider divorce and was glad for the war separation as a chance to think things over.

Although Jane was relieved to see Dave go, and had run the home alone for a long time, she surprised herself by missing him a great deal and particularly felt that she needed his help in disciplining the boys. Also the allotment just wasn't big enough, and she wouldn't have been able to manage if her mother and sister, who were still very close to her, hadn't supplemented her income with a regular monthly allowance. However, things went on much as usual because Dave had never been around home much anyway, and Jane began to feel freer to indulge in outside activities. She took up singing and dancing again, did a lot of things with the boys, and enjoyed herself more than she had in years. She seemed to have very mixed feelings about Dave's absence—one minute she was telling the interviewer how much she had missed him, and the next minute she would be talking about how happy she had been while he was gone. She tried working for a while but didn't enjoy it because she worried too much about how things were at home, so she gave it up. The boys didn't miss their father especially, although they were proud of the fact that he was in the service, but the younger one did seem to develop some insecurity. He couldn't bear to have mother leave the home for anything, and he wrote to his father, which his brother did not. He didn't understand his father's defections as his brother did, and so didn't feel antagonistic toward him. Jane and Dave only wrote to each other once or twice a month, didn't have much to say. Dave's letters were chiefly about how he wanted to return to the family and how he thought more of them now that he was away.

On Dave's first furlough he and Jane were just strangers to one another, but on the second furlough they had something of a reunion that left Jane feeling that the marriage might go on, although she was far from sure. She longed to be "just a wife and mother," with a husband she could cling to, and would not have hesitated to stick by the marriage if she could believe that her husband was to be trusted. Dave seemed to want to come back to the family and make a fresh start.

When Dave returned from service he did his best to fit into the family and make Jane and the boys happy. Jane said that the only difficulty was on her side—she wasn't sure of her own feelings, of whether she wanted to make a go of it—Dave has yet to win her confidence. She admitted that he had definitely improved and seemed to appreciate the family much more. He was taking a good deal of responsibility in the home, helped Jane with the housework and children, but wasn't planning to take a regular job for a year, at the end of which time his father's farm would be available for him to work. He might take odd jobs in the meantime. The younger boy had accepted his father completely and loved to do things with him. The older boy was still bitter, Jane thought, but hiding his feelings under a mask of indifference. Perhaps he could be won over in time. Jane's attitude was, "So far, so good, but what will he be like in a few months?" Dave seemed pathetically eager to please Jane while the interviewer was there, and told the interviewer frankly in a private interview that he didn't expect that Jane would ever love him again as she used to, but that he hoped that she would at least put up with him. Perhaps a real change of heart, but sponging on papa for a whole year doesn't look too good to Jane.

Using the concepts of the three dimensions of family living introduced in Chapter II, the Morgans appear to be poorly equipped at all three levels. As individuals none of the four members are adequate personalities. The pair relationships are poor, except between the father and the youngest child and between the mother and the children. At the family level the family is amorphous, like a jelly fish, unintegrated, unadaptable, and poorly prepared to meet the exigencies of life. Without support from the in-laws and the sense of external pressure to maintain an "intact" home, the family would dissolve. Many of the other twenty-six families in this low-ranking family type were similarly handicapped. That so many have survived separation and reunion to this point is a matter of wonderment to the analysts.

In reviewing the foregoing descriptions of nine statistical family types and their behavior profiles, the overwhelming impression is the variability of family patterns which manage to meet satisfactorily the crises of separation and reunion. It is not possible from our basic data in Table 13 to say flatly that families which are highly integrated, highly adaptable, highly adjusted maritally, with a democratic form of family control are the only types which are prepared to face hardships and survive them without serious scars. The exact combinations of these elements of family adequacy elude us in a purely statistical analysis, but we are pretty sure that the recipe doesn't call for high scores on all factors. We are somewhat surer that low scores on adaptability, integration, and marital adjustment, with or without hardships, will make for poor adjustment to separation and reunion crises.

Our arbitrarily determined statistical family types did not turn out to be badly conceived when tested against the case summaries of the families whose behavior profiles most closely approximate the average scores of the family type they were to represent. The congruence between the type and the case summary of the most representative family was violated seriously in only one out of nine instances (see Case No. 584, the Sckanky family). As a method of joining statistical scores and case materials, the method has proved its worth.

In retrospect we can say the use of cross-classification matrices have yielded suggestive leads and the analysis of statistical family types produced by this method has been rewarding. We turn now to another more rigorous statistical method, multiple and partial correlation, to measure the combined importance of key factors in influencing family adjustment to crisis, and to measure the individual influences of these same factors when the interfering influences of other factors are eliminated.

INSIGHTS FROM MULTIPLE AND PARTIAL CORRELATION ANALYSIS

In Chapter V the simple factor-by-factor analysis provided us with provocative first approximations of the relative importance of sixty-five factors in affecting family behavior in separation and reunion. In Table 11 the twenty-nine factors which were most significantly associated with good adjustment to separation and reunion are shown. The method of multiple and partial correlation enables us to select those we consider key factors and assess their combined and partial influences on family behavior.

Three criteria help us in the selection of these key factors: (1) The factors should be representative of all phases of family make-up and experience; that is as many of the main headings in Table 11 as could be obtained should be represented. (2) The factors should have demonstrated some significant or very nearly significant relationship to separation and reunion adjustment when tested singly. (3) The factors should be quantitative, so that they could be manipulated arithmetically.

The factors selected were as follows:

A. From *Childhood Experience of Spouses* we selected Factor 6, Wife's Happiness Score in Childhood.
B. From *Social Status, Transiency, Occupation, and Income* we selected the measure of relative financial security, Factor 2, Family Income at Induction.
C. From *Adequacy of Family Organization* we selected Factor 3, Marital Adjustment Score (Wife), Factor 4, Family Integration Score, and Factor 5, Family Adaptability Score.
D. From *Experiences and Hardships of Separation* we selected Factor 6, Social Participation Score of Wife During Separation, Factor 7, Total Days of Furloughs and Visits, and as a factor in reunion adjustments, Factor 8, Family Adjustment to Separation Score.

These eight factors are by no means the most highly associated factors with separation and reunion adjustment scores, but they are all thought to be influential factors by professional and lay thinkers, and they do fulfill the requirements set up by the above criteria.

Childhood happiness is regarded universally as having importance in later family adjustments. Income as it reflects financial security, likewise, is a common requisite for high family morale. The three indices of family organization—marital adjustment, family integration, and family adaptability—have already been shown to be important, and their relative influence will be reassessed by merging them with the other five factors we have selected. Again, the social participation of wife has appeared important in other wartime studies (*15*) of marriage and family adjustment as the best cure for loneliness, and is retested here in larger context. Military authorities felt furloughs and visits boosted morale, and it has been generally accepted that they enabled families to maintain communications better, so we used the Total Days of Furloughs and Visits as an item in reflecting amount of communication between father and his family. Finally, the surprising finding that good adjustment to separation was the best preview of the adjustment to reunion argued for testing it in the larger context of seven other factors as they too impinged on reunion adjustment.

In a sense, we are extending the principle of combining factors into a composite score, as was done in the creation of the Scale for Dynamic Stability by Dunigan (*13*), in this multiple correlation analysis of seven and eight factors as they affect separation and reunion adjustments. Our machines could take no more than the eight factors, so we limited ourselves to that number. There are, without doubt, several dozen other factors affecting the adjustments of every family faced with a crisis. If we have done our job well, we have selected eight of the central factors; if not, the analysis will tell us so, and another study will be in order to try another set of variables.

INTERRELATIONSHIPS AMONG FACTORS

In Koos' very interesting chart, reproduced on page 106, depicting the multiplicity of causes operating to determine whether a given event became a family crisis, the interrelationship of causes was most evident. Our situation in analyzing the interplay of factors which affect separation and reunion adjustment parallels the Koos analysis of crisis-proneness closely. With due apologies we use the same method of demonstrating, substituting for Koos' causes, our key factors which we have chosen for multiple and partial correlation analysis.

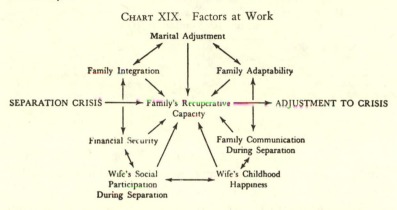

CHART XIX.   Factors at Work

The task of multiple correlation is to assess the combined effect of all these forces, which might be symbolized by the central core "Family's Recuperative Capacity," on the final result, "Adjustment to Crisis." The task of partial correlation is to assess, one by one, the unique contribution of each of the above factors when the effects of all except one of the forces, symbolized by the arrows pointing, are eliminated. By partialing out the other six forces, it is possible to measure the net relationship between adjustment to crisis and any single factor playing upon it. As an example, it has already been shown that marital adjustment affects a family's adjustment to separation, pp. 128–130. We find, however, that marital adjustment is also associated with family integration and family adaptability, as well as other factors and merges with them in producing the final result in the family's adjustment to separation. By partialing out the share contributed by family integration, by family adaptability, and the other four factors the influence of marital adjustment on adjustment to crisis is laid bare. The first step in that process is to note the extent of interrelationship among the seven factors in Table 14. The standard measure for all combinations is our familiar coefficient of correlation.

TABLE 14. Intercorrelations Among Seven Factors Selected for Multiple and Partial Correlation Analysis of Factors Making for Adjustment to Separation and Reunion in Iowa

	Marital Adjustment	Adaptability	Wife's Happiness	Integration	Furloughs and Visits	Social Participation	Income
Marital adjustment	—	0.54	0.42	0.58	0.10	0.07	0.13
Adaptability		—	0.22	0.47	0.14	−0.06	0.13
Wife's happiness			—	0.25	0.04	0.18	0 21
Integration				—	0.06	0.01	−0.12
Furloughs and visits					—	−0.03	0.14
Social participation						—	0.17

Chart XX may now be drawn to show the amount of interrelationship among factors. The heavier lines which we have drawn between marital adjustment and the three factors of adaptability, wife's happiness, and integration in Chart XX reflect the close interrelationships among these factors. The interrelation among wife's childhood happiness, income, and social participation of wife during separation marks another cluster of interdependencies. Financial security, represented by income of family, appears moderately related to many of the factors affecting the family's recuperative capacity, although it is negatively associated with family integration. As we come to think about causation and explanations of conduct at the family level, we will find ourselves asking increasingly the question, "How are these causal factors interrelated?" Table 14 and Chart XX provide this basic information for our elucidation as we enter the final phase of our statistical analysis, partial and multiple correlation.

UNIQUE CONTRIBUTIONS OF KEY FACTORS AS REFLECTED IN PARTIAL CORRELATION

In this final phase of our statistical analysis we have asked ourselves this question: When the influences of six key factors on ad-

CHART XX. Interrelationhips ("r") Among Eight Factors Selected for Partial Correlation Analysis from Factors Making for Adjustment to Separation and Reunion in Iowa

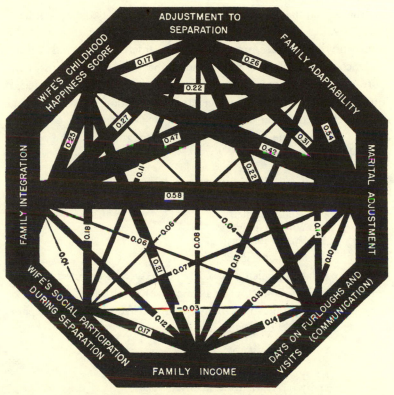

justment to separation are held constant statistically, what is the magnitude of the remaining association between the seventh factor and adjustment to separation? We pose the same question for each key factor in its relationship to adjustment to reunion. This is our opportunity to discover whether the simple factor-by-factor analysis summarized in Table 11, and discussed in detail in Chapter V, still holds when the more refined analysis of partial correlation is completed.

MARITAL ADJUSTMENT AND ADJUSTMENT TO SEPARATION: AN ILLUSTRA-
TION OF PARTIAL CORRELATION ANALYSIS

Perhaps the final results shown in Table 11 and Table 14 will have more meaning if an illustration is carried through with one of the factors in which we are most interested, namely, the Marital Adjustment Score. In Table 11 it will be noted that the Marital Adjustment Score and Adjustment to Separation are significantly correlated, r equals 0.31. When partial coefficients of correlation between Marital Adjustment Score and Adjustment to Separation were computed holding constant one factor at a time, the magnitude of the correlation held up pretty well.

Factor Held Constant	Partial Coefficient r
Days on furlough	0.30
Family income	0.31
Wife's happiness	0.28
Family integration	0.22
Family adaptability	0.18

When partial coefficients of correlation were computed holding constant two or three factors at a time, the magnitude of the correlation between Marital Adjustment Score and Adjustment to Separation declines sharply for certain combinations.

Factors Held Constant	
Family integration and days on furlough	0.21
Family integration and family income	0.20
Family integration and wife's happiness	0.20
Family adaptability and wife's happiness	0.16
Family adaptability, integration, and income	0.14
Family adaptability, integration, and wife's happiness	0.14

The original magnitude of association between Marital Adjustment Score and Adjustment to Separation reflected the close inter-relationship among all the factors listed under Adequacy of Family Organization. By itself marital adjustment is less important in de-

termining good adjustment to separation than we might have
thought, had we taken the simple correlation coefficient of 0.31 at
face value.

In the summary table (Table 15) we have held constant, not just

TABLE 15.   Partial Correlation Coefficients of Seven Factors and Adjustment
to Separation Scores

Factors Held Constant	Factor Not Held Constant	Partial Coefficient *r*
Marital adj., integration, adaptability, soc. part., income, wife's happiness	Days of furlough and visits	0.186
Marital adj., integration, soc. part., income, wife's happiness, furloughs	Family adaptability	0.164
Integration, adaptability, soc. part., income, wife's happiness, furloughs	Marital adjustment	0.130
Marital adj., integration, adaptability, income, wife's happiness, furloughs	Wife's social participation during separation	0.124
Marital adj., integration, adaptability, soc. part., wife's happiness, furloughs	Family income at induction	−0.038
Marital adj., adaptability, soc. part., income, wife's happiness. furloughs	Family integration	0.029
Marital adj., integration, soc. part., income, adaptability, furloughs	Wife's childhood happiness	0.0007

one factor, or two factors, or three factors, but we have held constant
statistically six of the seven factors in our list while measuring the
magnitude of the association between the seventh and Adjustment
to Separation Scores.

With their net relationship to adjustment to separation laid bare,
the seven factors under study take on a new appearance. We expected, from the interrelations between the four factors—marital adjustment, integration, adaptability, and wife's childhood happiness

—expressed earlier in Table 14 that some of these factors would lose weight when the partial correlations were computed; but it was difficult to say which would. It is apparent that family integration and wife's childhood happiness are of relatively minor importance in effecting adjustments to separation, whereas marital adjustment and family adaptability are relatively of more significance.

Family income at induction was not of striking importance before this analysis and is of even less moment when its true relationship to separation adjustments is computed.

Days of furlough and visits proves most important of our factors when taken singly, and would make a significant contribution to a prediction formula aimed at forecasting a family's adjustment to separation. Although furloughs were painful as well as helpful, they appear to affect adjustment to separation favorably, even when all other interfering influences are removed.

The wife's social participation score is as close as we get to a measure of the wife's self-reliance and self-sufficiency in this analysis, and it appears of relatively more importance in determining adjustment to separation than we had supposed from its earlier modest association in Chapter V.

We have the basis now for redrawing Chart XIX as far as the magnitude of forces symbolized by the arrows is concerned. The arrows pointing at Family Recuperative Capacity may now be drawn with heavier lines shown for some factors than for others (see new drawing, Chart XXI).

PARTIAL CORRELATION AND REUNION ADJUSTMENTS

In reunion, it will be remembered, we have another factor to add to the seven dealt with in the partial correlation analysis of factors affecting adjustment to separation. That factor is the powerful preceding experience with the separation crisis, reflected in the Adjustment to Separation Score. There are seven factors held constant as the influence of the eighth is measured in Table 16.

TABLE 16. Partial Correlation Coefficients of Eight Factors and Adjustment to Reunion Scores

Factors Held Constant	Factor Not Held Constant	Partial Coefficient r
Marital adj., integration, adaptability, soc. part., income, wife's happiness, days on furloughs	Adjustment to separation	0.425
Adj. to sep., marital adj., adaptability, soc. part., income, wife's happiness, furloughs	Family integration	0.200
Adj. to sep., marital adj., integration, adaptability, soc. part., income, furloughs	Wife's childhood happiness	−0.125
Adj. to sep., marital adj., adaptability, soc. part., wife's happiness, furloughs	Family income	−0.113
Adj. to sep., integration, adaptability, soc. part., income, wife's happiness, furloughs	Marital adjustment	0.109
Adj. to sep., integration, adaptability, soc. part., income, wife's happiness, marital adj.	Days on furlough and visits	0.102
Adj. to sep., marital adj., adaptability, income, wife's happiness, furloughs, integration	Wife's social participation during separation	−0.096
Adj. to sep., marital adj., integration, income, wife's happiness, soc. part., furloughs	Family adaptability	−0.050

A comparison of the two summary tables (Tables 15 and 16) provides an opportunity to test whatever hypotheses we might have erected about the similarities and differences between the forces at work in adjusting to the two crises of separation and reunion. In Chapter V we highlighted the many similarities and differences between the two crises. Reunion required mutuality of interests and satisfactions, good marriage-pair adjustments, and pair and family integration. Separation required adaptability and high personal adequacy of wife—a wife who could "take it." In general, the conclusions reached from the less refined analyses are not overthrown by the selective controlled analyses of this chapter.

That there are similarities is most evident in the high and stable association between adjustment to separation scores and adjustment to reunion scores when seven interfering sets of influences are held constant statistically. In addition, marital adjustment and the amount of communication during separation reflected in days on furloughs and visits both remain as positive influences in both crises. Family income is even more negatively associated with adjustment to reunion than it was to separation adjustments.

That there are differences is seen in the demise of family adaptability and the rise of family integration as individual families move from the shock of separation to the challenges of reunion. Again, we underline the changing importance of these two important components in dynamic stability, as the nature of the crisis changes.

We would be remiss in our duty as analysts if we didn't point out the change in importance of wife's childhood happiness as one moves from separation to reunion. From an irrelevant factor in affecting separation, it becomes a negative influence on reunion adjustment scores. The magnitude of association is small and not significant, but its direction is completely out of line with our expectations. Intensive case analysis may provide hypothetical explanations which can be tested in later studies. All statistical avenues have been used to trace down this variant relationship without success.

To make our findings graphic, we now join a chart for reunion, based on Table 16, with a chart for separation, based on Table 15. The two sets of findings are joined together in one presentation in Chart XXI. As long as we recognize that there are many other factors which are also operating but are not listed in the chart, we are justified in reducing our findings in this form.

CHART XXI. Forces at Work in Family Adjustment to Crises of Separation and Reunion—Relative Contributions of Each Factor Expressed by Its Partial Correlation Coefficient with Adjustment to Separation Scores on the One Hand and with Adjustment to Reunion Scores on the Other

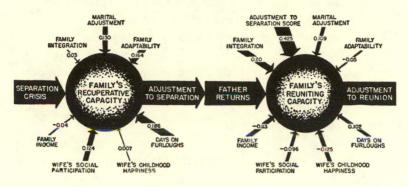

COMBINED CONTRIBUTIONS OF KEY FACTORS AS REFLECTED IN MULTIPLE CORRELATION

The most rigorous test of the strength of any factor is to submit it to the measures of partial correlation as we have just done for our several key factors. A select few held up under the test nicely, either for separation or for reunion, and marital adjustment proved important for both crises. Actually these factors are inextricably bound together in actual family behavior, and it is folly to consider them separately, except for understanding and insight of their separate influences. In this final section of our statistical analysis we propose to combine all seven factors in multiple correlation to assess the magnitude of association which they severally bring to bear on adjustment to separation. We will then combine all eight factors in multiple correlation to measure the force they bring to bear on adjustment to reunion.

MULTIPLE CORRELATION AND ADJUSTMENT TO SEPARATION

When all seven factors are joined, the multiple correlation coefficient R is 0.409. No single factor in the combination of seven approximates that figure singly. In Table 15 it can be noted that the three highest factors, days on furlough, family adaptability and marital adjustment, were all less than half as large. Dropping the least important factors, wife's happiness and family integration, reduces the multiple correlation coefficient only slightly, to 0.408.

Two factors reflecting family adequacy of organization, marital adjustment and family adaptability together contribute most to the R of 0.409 above. When they are joined (dropping out of consideration all other five factors) a multiple correlation coefficient of 0.354 is obtained. All three of these combinations are statistically significant.

At best, in the seven factors we have joined together, we only have a small proportion of the total number of factors operating to determine family adjustment to separation. The multiple coefficient of determination, R^2 is 0.168 which is an indication of the variation in separation adjustment scores we are able to explain with our seven factors. In percentage form we have left unexplained roughly 83 percent of the variation. There remains much to be done before we completely understand the factors making for success in separation adjustment.

MULTIPLE CORRELATION AND ADJUSTMENT TO REUNION

When all eight factors, which includes adjustment to separation as the eighth factor, are joined in correlation with the adjustment to reunion scores, the multiple correlation coefficient R is 0.603. From Table 16 it is apparent that adjustment to separation and family integration are major contributors. Dropping out the least important factors, family adaptability, social participation score of wife, and family income, reduces the multiple correlation coefficient to 0.584.

When the two most important factors, adjustment to separation and family integration, are joined (dropping all other six factors), a most respectable and highly significant multiple correlation coefficient of 0.565 is left. All of these associations are statistically significant.

Our control of the factors contributing to reunion adjustment is better, because the highest ranking factor, adjustment to separation undoubtedly reflects many forces we haven't yet measured and incorporates them into our prediction formula through its own score. Previous experience with crisis is a better gauge of a family's ability to survive trouble than are any of the attributes of family organization or evidences of personality adequacy we have used. It is noteworthy that when we join together these eight factors, we have a better purchase on reunion adjustment than we had on separation adjustment. The multiple coefficient of determination, R^2, is 0.374. In percentage form we have left unexplained roughly 62 percent of the variations in reunion adjustment. This is better than we are now able to do in the current scholastic prediction studies, and better than the students of current marital prediction have been able to do. There still remains, however, much to be done in explaining the behavior of families in the face of a reunion crisis.

Summary of Statistical Findings

For two chapters we have used statistical methods to sort, grade, and evaluate our data, gathered originally by questionnaire and by interview, concerning the forces making for adjustment to separation and to reunion of Iowa families in wartime. The statistical methods used have been nomothetic, pointing up generalizations from the behavior of *most* families, testing and retesting whether the findings are "happenchance" or whether they are reliable. The generalizations were made, for the most part, from observations of 135 families who experienced separation of the father from the family due to enlistment or induction into the armed services, and from records of 114 families who had already experienced reunion adjustments by the time of the interview.

Most of the first of the two chapters on statistical findings (Chap-

ter V) was devoted to a factor-by-factor analysis of separation and
reunion adjustment, relating first one and then another factor to
family behavior in crisis to see what associations obtained. All told,
sixty-five factors were tested statistically by methods of correlation or
chi-square analysis. Hypotheses from previous studies and hunches
of the authors were included which might be classified under the
headings: Childhood Experiences of Spouses; Courtship Experiences; Readiness for Marriage at Marriage; Social and Personal
Roles in Marriage; Social Status, Transiency, Occupation, and Income; Familism; Family Size and Years of Family Experience;
Adequacy of Family Organization; Experiences and Hardships of
Separation; and Experiences and Hardships of Reunion. A summary table, Table 11, is found at the beginning of Chapter VI which
lists the twenty-nine factors which were found to be most highly
associated with adjustment to separation and with adjustment to
reunion scores. A quick overview of the categories of family life
which contributed most significantly to family adjustment to crisis
can be seen in summary Table 17.

When viewed singly, the most influential factors in determining
separation adjustment were found to be aspects of the family's recuperative resources and of the hardships and experiences of the
separation situation. Good marital adjustment, family adaptability,
family integration, family dynamic stability were examples of the
first. Adequacy of communication, moderate self-sufficiency of wife
during the separation, severity of hardships in separation, and adequacy of affectional outlets during separation were illustrations of
the second. We found that the more distant the experience, or the
more peripheral the forces were to the day-by-day experiences of
family living, the smaller was the influence on later family adjustments to separation. For example, parents' happiness, courtship patterns, and readiness for marriage at marriage indicated by age at
marriage, years of schooling, and length of acquaintance, as well as
years married, years experience as parents, and similar marginal

items appeared to be of little or no importance in this study of factors making for success or failure in adjusting to wartime separation.

Adjustment to reunion was more affected by the factors which also affected adjustment to separation than by any factors which didn't appear important in the separation context. Moreover, there

TABLE 17. Distribution of Factors Tested and of Factors Found Significantly Associated with Good Adjustment to Separation and to Reunion

Categories of Family Life	Number of Factors Tested	Number of Factors Found Significant
From childhood experiences of spouses	4	2
From courtship experiences	3	0
From evidences of readiness for marriage at marriage	6	1
From social and personal roles in marriage and family	6	2
From social positional factors: social status, occupation, income, and transiency record	4	2
From evidences of familism: family size and years of family experience	4	1
From measures of adequacy of family organization	8	7
From experiences and hardships of separation period	27	13
From experiences and hardships of reunion	3	1
Grand total	65	29

is close correspondence between success in meeting the crisis of separation and later success in completing the process of reunion. The factors most important for reunion were also drawn disproportionately from the family's recuperative resources and the severity of separation and reunion hardships. Evidence of self-sufficiency of wife, high social participation of wife during separation, and high family income were negatively related to success in reunion. If one were to hazard a generalization to cover all of the factors found important in reunion, it would be that reunion adjustment involves more frequently than separation did, interdependence of the interests of individual family members to the *family* interest, where the accent is on maximum identification with the family.

The limitations of the simple factor-by-factor approach led us, in Chapter VI, to combine factors by cross-classification into statistical family types and compare the behavior of these family types through the use of the behavior profile. An appreciation of the variation and dispersion of behavior among the modal family types was obtained from this analysis. The folly of making generalizations for all families from the modal or average families was most apparent. A second finding of interest was that there was no close, straight-line relationship between many of the influential factors and the crisis-meeting phenomenon of family adjustment. For example, following such an assumption, the best adjustment might be expected from families of high adaptability–high integration–high marital adjustment; yet our findings indicate that combinations of medium integration and high adaptability or of medium integration and medium adaptability work out much better in adjusting to crises of separation and reunion. Impressive evidence was obtained from the analysis of nine statistical family types characterized by varying amounts of integration and adaptability that many types of family control lend themselves to crisis meeting, and that a variety of personality combinations appear workable within different family types. A fourth generalization which would cast doubt on all generalizations based solely on the nomothetic method was that the range of actual scores within statistical family types is so large that any generalizations based on the averages of these scores should be treated more as hypotheses for future testing than as definitive findings. We concluded that the use of cross-classification matrices for the construction of statistical family types proved most rewarding, both in the overall perspective they made possible, and in the suggestive leads for future research.

To complete our statistical analysis we turned to the method of multiple and partial correlation to measure the combined importance of key factors in influencing family adjustment to crisis, and to measure the individual influences of these same factors when the interfering influences of their fellow factors were eliminated. Each of the major areas contributing to family success in the previous chapter was considered, and the eight most representative of those areas and most associated with crisis meeting were selected for analysis. Chart XXI shows graphically the factors selected, the extent of interrelationship among them, and their partial association with adjustment to separation and with adjustment to reunion. Days of furlough and visits, family adaptability, marital adjustment, and wife's social participation during separation proved most important in determining adjustment to separation. Adjustment to separation, family integration, and negatively, wife's childhood happiness proved most important in determining adjustment to reunion. Again we underline the greater importance of family adaptability in separation and of family integration in reunion adjustments. Family income is negatively associated with crisis meeting in both crises.

When viewed singly with the influences of closely related factors partialed out, only one of our factors appeared very influential— adjustment to separation which we used as a basis for predicting adjustment to reunion. Actually these eight factors are inextricably bound together in family behavior. When the combined influences of all eight are measured in multiple correlation, it is apparent that we have identified factors of some importance, for separation adjustment and *especially* for reunion adjustment. The magnitude of these multiple correlation coefficients is modest enough, however, and we recognize that there remains much to be done in statistical and case study before we have captured even the majority of the influences that are at work in meeting and surviving the hardships of separation without scars, and in readjusting to family life again during the months which follow the father's return to the home.

CHAPTER VII

FAMILIES IN CRISIS VIEWED DYNAMI-
CALLY FROM CASE STUDY[1]

IN this chapter are incorporated the generalizations we have dis-
tilled from the detailed family histories collected from the mothers
and fathers in our sample of 135 families in Iowa. The mode of
analysis is the case study method which is peculiarly well adapted
to capture the process and inner workings of family life during a
period of crisis. Because of the tremendous variety of family behavior and conduct in the face of critical situations, it is difficult to
make generalizations which might have broad application. Our
measurements, likewise, are unprecise by scientific standards, but
we have confidence in the patterns, trends, and tendencies they have
uncovered.

The case study method, used here, blazes trails for the more definitive studies to follow. Most of the questions we have dealt with
in this chapter are frankly exploratory, opening up two new areas
of strain and stress which families meet frequently—the critical
situations of separation and reunion. Our findings will, therefore,
need to be repeatedly tested in follow-up studies before we will regard them as definitive, applying to all families in crisis.

As the study was launched we carried over from previous studies
of families in crisis and from studies of marriage adjustment a few
hypotheses which we wished to test in the new context of separation
and reunion. We knew, for example, that the superiority of certain

[1] This chapter was written by Mrs. Elise Boulding from an analysis of the narrative materials collected by interview from 135 families in Iowa. A description of
the division of labor worked out for treatment of the statistical and case narrative
materials is given in Appendix B, pp. 394–395.

family forms—patriarchal, matriarchal, adult-centered equalitarian, and democratic—needed to be tested under crisis. We wished to assay the importance of the consultative process as a preliminary to decision making. We wanted to know if certain values held by families are factors in crisis meeting, and if families which are highly integrated around common family objectives and common interests are less prone to crisis. These are just samples of the generalizations (presented in more detail in Chapter II), which the study proposed to test and which only an analysis of the narrative materials would answer.

The first reading of the cases ignored, for the moment, the specific hypotheses to be tested and concentrated on the patterns of behavior which appeared associated sequentially with good and poor adjustment to separation and reunion. The result was that a number of similar as well as a sizable set of quite different patterns emerged which, joined with the original hypotheses, have made a fruitful basis for analysis.

SIFTING AND WINNOWING FOR PRIMARY FACTORS

In the first reading of the case narratives, notes were made at random as questions and ideas came to mind. It soon became evident that some sort of summary or master index card would greatly simplify manipulation of the data because the histories were too bulky to be shuffled easily. After the second reading such a summary card was devised on which were recorded all of the basic data for analysis. Since the focus of this part of the study was to be on the continuing *process* of adjustment to crisis, the summaries were written in the form of the five steps Koos (27) has already outlined as basic to the family adjustment process.

CONTENT OF THE MASTER CARD

The top line of each card was devoted to an identifying phrase about the family which would help bring the case history quickly to the analyst's attention. Also included on the top line was a judgment of the class status of the family. A rating on marital adjustment as good, fair, or poor, came next—a thoroughly subjective judgment based on evidences concerning marital harmony or conflict in the narratives. Finally, the last two identifying items included on the top line were the number of children in the family and the number of months the husband had been back from service, if he were back.

The second major section of the master card contained a description of the fivefold course of adjustment: (1) the pre-crisis situation, (2) the reactions to the impending crisis, (3) the immediate reactions at the moment of crisis, (4) the short-term adjustments of recovery, and (5) the long-term readjustment or reorganization achievements.

The pre-crisis situation included ratings on integration and adaptability,[2] a description of the pattern of family control in vogue, and any information concerning the type of adjustment the family might have made to previous crises.

Steps 2 to 5 were recorded both in short, abbreviated phrases and graphically by means of a silhouette for each family. Details concerning the variety of silhouettes and the profiles which emerged for groups of families are given in Chapter IV.

After these data had been committed to summary cards, a period of prolonged introspection intervened before additional materials were recorded. In the mulling and shuffling process, there was a noticeable convergence of evidence to point to the importance of family organization, particularly as it is seen in the performance of

---

[2] The ratings on integration and adaptability were subjectively arrived at from definitions developed by Robert Angell, *The Family Encounters the Depression* (1) and families classified in a nine-cell table ranging from combinations of Unintegrated and Unadaptable through moderate combinations to Highly Integrated and Highly Adaptable. To test the reliability of the subjective ratings on adaptability and integration, every fifth case history was drawn from the files and given to a layman, Mrs. Gerhard Tintner, to rate them. Her ratings and those of Mrs. Boulding coincided in 21 of 26 cases. This was a stronger confirmation of the reliability of the judgements than had been anticipated.

roles by various family members. What were the jobs that had to be done to keep a family going? Who did these tasks before the separation occurred? When the husband left, how were the "family jobs" taken care of? These were key questions. If, upon analysis, certain patterns of roles in the family could be ascertained, it might be possible to identify some as more successful than others as the family reorganized to get along without the father, and to show that certain of these patterns might be most effective when the father returned.

Four distinct classifications of tasks performed by most families were identified:

1. Making the major decisions
2. Maintaining and managing the household
3. Performing distinctly parental, "child-rearing" responsibilities
4. Meeting the need of affection of family members

Patterns of Decision Making. The patterns of decision making or dominance, as they might equally well be called, were divided

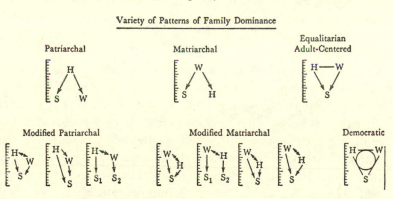

Variety of Patterns of Family Dominance

Patriarchal Matriarchal Equalitarian Adult-Centered

Modified Patriarchal Modified Matriarchal Democratic

into four main types: the patriarchal, the matriarchal, the equalitarian adult-centered, and the democratic. Definitions of these types are given in some detail, pp. 53–55. It was felt that if each pattern could be diagrammed—that is, taken out of the realm of word pictures into the realm of graphic portrayal—a more detailed picture of each case could be given. After considerable experimentation a device was constructed which obviated the necessity for words at all. The accompanying diagrams were used; one-way arrows indicate that authority is either forced from above on those below, or the one above is forced into a position of authority by those below, depending on the direction of the arrow. A two-way arrow indicates an authority willingly supported by those on whom it is imposed. The use of a circle instead of arrows for the democratic family indicates no imposition of authority, but a family counsel technique instead. The position of S (sibling) under H (husband) or W (wife) indicates which parent the child takes orders from.

Household Maintenance. This is an aspect of home management which deals with the degree to which husband and wife, and children if they are old enough (over eleven), have developed complementary roles for the routine and extra-routine care of the home. Does the wife play the role of the household drudge while the husband sits by the fire and reads a paper and the children run wild? Or does the husband help out either regularly, or in case of emergency, with household chores? If the roles are complementary, are husband and wife on an equal footing, or does the dovetailing conform to the leader-follower pattern? It did not seem possible to work out a descriptive diagram that was any more effective than a numerical system of rating, so husband and wife and children (if over eleven) were rated on a nine-point scale as to the degree of responsibility they took for family jobs. Rating only children over eleven was extremely arbitrary because some children take an interest in household chores from the time they are three, but that restriction of age was made on the schedules in gathering the information, so it was continued. Since there were very few children in these families over eleven years of age, the information regarding them proved to be of little significance and was discarded. The ratings were interpreted as follows:

H_3W_3: Both husband and wife take a great deal of responsibility for the maintenance of the home; have complementary roles, equal status.

H_2W_3: Wife very responsible, husband only moderately so; complementary roles, unequal status with wife the leader.

H_1W_3: Wife very responsible, husband very irresponsible; roles not complementary.

H_3W_2: Husband very responsible in home, wife moderately so; complementary roles, unequal status with husband the leader.

H_2W_2: Husband and wife take only moderate responsibility for upkeep of home; roles complementary, but lower standard of role-fulfillment.

H_1W_2: Husband irresponsible, wife only moderately responsible; roles not complementary.

H_3W_1: Husband very responsible, wife irresponsible, neglects home; roles not complementary.

H_2W_1: Husband moderately responsible, wife irresponsible; roles not complementary.

H_1W_1: Husband and wife both irresponsible, neglect home; roles not complementary.

PARENTAL RESPONSIBILITY

The assumption of parental responsibility was classified according to the way in which parents fulfilled their responsibilities both as disciplinarian-guide and as companion to their children. It is assumed that the "good" parent will not only care for the physical needs of the child and discipline his activity into socially acceptable channels, but also will be a companion in recreation to the child. A parent whose relationship with his child is purely disciplinary is no more inadequate than a parent who regards his child merely as a plaything. Here again no better method of condensing this information was found than rating it on a nine-point scale, as follows:

F$_3$M$_3$: Both father and mother are guide and companion to child.

F$_2$M$_3$: Father inconsistent in his role; mother guide and companion.

F$_1$M$_3$: Father purely disciplinarian or regards child only as plaything or ignores child; mother guide and companion.

F$_3$M$_2$: Father is guide and companion; mother inconsistent in her role.

F$_2$M$_2$: Father and mother are both inconsistent, alternate between playmate and disciplinary relationship.

F$_1$M$_2$: Father purely disciplinarian or regards child as plaything or ignores child; mother inconsistent.

F$_3$M$_1$: Father is guide and companion; mother either disciplines, ignores or regards child as plaything.

F$_2$M$_1$: Father inconsistent, alternates between playmate and disciplinarian relationship; mother either disciplines, ignores, or regards child as plaything.

F$_1$M$_1$: Father and mother both either purely disciplinarian, ignore child or regard solely as plaything.

Meeting the Needs of Affection. It was felt that a picture of the affectional configuration for each family would be useful even though it did not capture the *quality* of the affectional relationships. A diagram was devised which indicates roughly which family members are closest to which. Arrows are used to indicate the direction of the affection. Dotted lines are used to indicate a low degree of affection, heavy single lines indicate average to considerable closeness of affection, and heavy double lines indicate extremely close ties. Crossed lines indicate conflict between the members involved. A few of the possible combinations are shown in the accompanying diagram. Note that not all the lines are reciprocal—that is, one family member may feel closer to another family member than that person

feels to him. These diagrams have some advantages over the socio-
grams devised by Moreno for non-family groupings.[3]

With these additions for each family, the master card summarizing the pertinent data nears completion. It remained to cover in
comparable form the three major stages of family life dealt with

Variety of Affectional Patterns Among Families

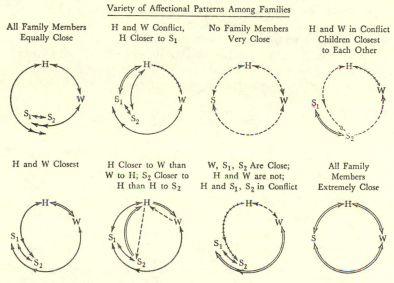

during the period of study. When the role configurations of the
families before induction were graphically recorded on the master
card, it became apparent that it would be possible to make the same
notations on the reorganized role configuration which followed the
final separation adjustment, and again on the role configuration produced by the adjustments to reunion. When this was done, there was
available at one glance a picture for each family of just what took
place in the role configurations at three stages: (1) pre-induction,
(2) after adjusting to life without a husband and father, and (3) in

[3] J. L. Moreno, *Who Shall Survive?* (New York: Nervous and Mental Disease
Publishing Company, 1934).

Sample Master Card[a]

#430.   Hardworking, adapt. H & W build fam. life thru lean yrs.
        MMC, Ga., 2sch. 2mo.

1. Equalitarian, very integrated, moderately flexible, good adjustment
to previous crisis. 2. Prepared for induction crisis by moving near W's
parents. 3. Loneliness, weeping. 4. Continued lonely, nervous, children hard to manage, but enjoyed making decisions. 5. Felt more independent, competent, enjoyed managing home alone but shared
plans for future with husband, continued emotional interdependence.
Reunion: Happy to have H back but no proper reunion, for H only
sees family week ends, can't find place to live together; they long to
return to family life, feel strain, argue.

I.   1. H——W   2. H_3 W_3 3. F_3 M_3 4.
          S_1 S_2

II.   1.   W   2. W_3 3. M_3 4.   Same
          S_1 S_2

III. 1. H——W   2. H_2 W_3 3. F_3 M_3 4.   Same
          S_1 S_2

[a] Note that the three stages of family life are indicated by Roman numerals, I,
II, and III. In this family the wife took over all the husband's responsibilities in the
home without much difficulty, so that the only role which the husband continued
to play while in service was an affectional role. In this family stage III is probably
not to be regarded as the final reorganization after the husband's return. At the
time of the interview, the children were still more deferent to the mother's authority
as they had been during the father's absence, and the father was not able to do
very much in the home because of his week-long absences. The affectional relations
remain the same, however, and a solution of the housing problem for this family
may bring about a return of the earlier role configuration.

reunion after adjustments had been made to the father's return. A
sample of a completed summary or master card is shown above.

CONSTRUCTING MEANINGFUL HYPOTHESES

    After the various types of family roles had been classified and the
master card was completed, we asked ourselves which role configura-

tions within each classification would be most predictive of good adjustment to separation and reunion. Theoretically our hypotheses would read as follows:

1. That family will adjust best to separation and reunion which before separation satisfies the following conditions: It is equalitarian adult-centered or democratic in its patterns of decision making—both husband and wife rate high on degree to which they assume responsibility for maintenance of the home; they are complementary in their respective roles; the husband and wife rate high on the fulfillment of their parental responsibilities, both acting out the dual roles of guide and companion to the children, and all family members participate equally in the affectional configuration.

2. Families which rate high as listed in hypothesis 1, would also be very adaptable and well integrated, and both integration and adaptability will prove important for separation adjustment. For reunion it was hypothecated that integration would be more important than adaptability in achieving a satisfactory adjustment.

3. The degree to which husbands and wives share experiences and express affection through letters would be an important factor in adjustment to separation and reunion.

4. The degree to which wives share problems and household decisions with husbands through correspondence would not be an important factor in adjustment to separation and reunion.

5. Where either set of grandparents or other relatives are able to participate in the family life during the husband's absence, adjustment to separation is aided.

6. Families will adjust well to separation and reunion which present the following evidences of family adequacy:
   a. Good marital adjustment
   b. Good adjustment to previous crises

    c. More than one child in the family

    d. Upper- or upper-middle-class status

A number of subsidiary hypotheses were formulated which we will elaborate later in the discussion. In order to prepare the data on the master cards for testing these hypotheses, tables were constructed relating the types of adjustment to separation and to reunion to the family make-up and organization and to the processes of adjustment and recovery which the family exhibited. The classification of type of adjustment to separation conformed closely to the silhouette of the family's course of adjustment drawn on the master cards to summarize the adjustment process. After looking over the silhouettes that had been drawn, four profiles seemed to emerge. The first was the good, rapid adjustment to separation, second was the good, slow adjustment, third was the fair adjustment, and fourth the poor adjustment. (See Table 8, page 98, for a picture of these profiles.)

When the tabulations of all the relevant data for the families of the first classification—good, rapid adjustment—had been completed, the table gave the impression that there were no factors, among those listed, of special significance for the adjustment to separation. The frequencies found under the factors that one would ordinarily consider as making for poor adjustment were as high as the frequencies found for factors that were hypothecated as predictive of good adjustment. This original classification did not differentiate between the families having good reunions and the families having poor ones. A careful rereading of the case histories induced us to link type of adjustment to reunion to adjustment to separation so as to sharpen our analysis. The cases under good, rapid adjustment to separation were now subdivided into three groups: the first was the families having a good reunion (ninety-one families); the second was the families having poor reunion (twenty-three families); and the third was the families having no reunion (twenty-one families). Definite patterns for the first two groups emerged at once, but the third group remained as mixed as the original classification had been and was, therefore, discarded for purposes of analysis. The pattern emerging for the good reunion group was one of high family adequacy and good marital adjustment, while the pattern for the poor reunion group was one of poor family adequacy and poor marital adjustment. Both groups adjusted well to separation—one group in spite of the husband's absence, the other group because of it.

FAMILY ADEQUACY AND SUCCESS IN MEETING CRISES

PATTERNS OF DECISION MAKING

The democratic or family counsel type of family pattern for decision making was definitely confirmed as a factor in good adjustment to separation and reunion. Every family of this type fell in either the good, rapid or the good, slow adjustment group, and no family of this type had a poor reunion. The total number of democratic families in the study was small, however (only ten out of 135), and this may have been partly due to the fact that many families had children still too small to have participated verbally in family activities and decisions. Where it was very plain that a family was democratic in intention—that is, in present attitudes toward their small children—they were rated as democratic even if the children were not of "voting age." Some families may have been democratic in intention, however, without having revealed this fact to the interviewer.

Although a slight majority[1] of the equalitarian adult-centered families (twenty-eight out of forty-three) made a good adjustment both to separation and reunion, a fair number of these families adjusted well either to separation *or* to reunion. It could be said that adult-centered families do not necessarily make a good adjustment to separation and reunion unless other factors of adequacy are also present. The modified matriarchy and modified patriarchy appeared much

---

[1] The totals used in this chapter refer only to those 114 cases out of the 135 in which reunion had already taken place at the time of the interview.

more strongly as patterns adequate to meeting crisis situations. Not only did these families, on the whole, make a good adjustment to separation (nineteen out of twenty-two), but they made a uniformly good adjustment to reunion, with not a single family falling in the poor reunion group. It may seem strange that the modified patriarchy and the modified matriarchy should adjust better than the equalitarian adult-centered families, but it may suggest that the *consultative process* in the family is more important than the seat of ultimate authority.

The matriarchal families, as might be expected, made for the most part a good, rapid adjustment to separation (nine out of twelve). Where the mother was already accustomed to making the major decisions there was not so much need for reorganization of family patterns when the father went into service. Reunion adjustments were almost as successful as the separation adjustments, indicating that affectional ties could bind a man strongly to his family whether or not he had a dominant position of authority in the home. The matriarchal families that had poor reunions had also had poor marital adjustment before the separation and were merely returning to their old ways.

The general pattern for the twenty-seven patriarchal families was a poor adjustment to separation and a good reunion. The wives in this group had always been very dependent on their husbands, and for the most part they remained dependent throughout the separation. Instead of rearranging family habits to make life more livable during the separation, these women just kept the family going until the husband could return and complete family life might again be resumed. There are a few interesting exceptions to this general rule, however. Some of the patriarchal families made a good adjustment to separation; the wives in these families had hidden capabilities that the separation crisis brought forth for the first time, and they enjoyed their new-found independence. The marital adjustment previous to separation had been poor in all these cases and the wife had felt dominated and oppressed. The reunion meant a return to servitude for these women because the husbands were unwilling to recognize their wives' newly discovered independence and abilities, and the adjustment was, therefore, usually even poorer than the marital adjustment had been before the separation.

In none of these families did it matter to the final adjustment whether the children were equally under the authority of the father and mother or more under the domination of one parent. However, there was a strong tendency in the good adjustment to separation group for the families with unequal dominance to make a rapid readjustment and for the families with equal dominance to make a slow readjustment. In a great majority of the families with unequal dominance the children were more under the authority of the mother than the father, and the shift to family life without a father would naturally be easier to make in these cases than in families where the children were accustomed to turning to the father for guidance on many occasions. The nature of the final readjustment of both groups was equally good, however. The democratic families also fell predominantly in the slow adjustment group, presumably because every member of a democratic family plays a vital part in the family life and when one member leaves it takes considerable reorganization before the various aspects of the role of the absent member can be absorbed by the remaining members.

The hypothesis that the equalitarian adult-centered and the democratic authority patterns make for the best adjustment to separation and reunion is then confirmed only in part. The study upholds the hypothesis with regard to the democratic families, but not with regard to the equalitarian adult-centered families, since the modified patriarchy and modified matriarchy made better adjustments than the equalitarian families. The equalitarian families, nevertheless, also made a better-than-average adjustment. In order to make a summary statement regarding these four types of families, it would be helpful to discover a pattern which they all have in common. The habit of *mutual consultation* seems to be such a pattern. In the democratic family every member of the group is included in the consultative process, and in the modified patriarchy and modified matriarchy as well as in the equalitarian family the husband and wife consult with one another. Since the democratic type is most predictive of good adjustment, and the other three types are fairly predictive of good adjustment, we might set forth a tentative conclusion as follows: A good adjustment to the crises of war separation and reunion is expected where family members consult with one another before making decisions which concern the entire group. A good adjustment is more certain when the ultimate authority is diffused among the family members, but the habits of consultation are more important than the focus of ultimate authority. When authority has been habitually concentrated in the parent remaining in the home, the adjustment to separation is rapid, and when the authority has previously been diffuse, the adjustment is slow but the final readjustment is equally effective in both cases.

Family Responsibility. A high degree of acceptance of responsibility for the maintenance of the home and physical care of family members on the part of both parents, combined with a coöperative relationship between parents, was more predictive of good adjustment to reunion than of adjustment to separation. The families rated H3W3 predominated in the good, rapid and good, slow adjustment to separation groups (sixty-one out of sixty-seven), but they are also to be spotted in the fair and poor adjustment groups. The five families which were rated H3W2—that is, the wife did not take quite as much responsibility in the home as the husband—fell in the good, rapid adjustment group and in the fair adjustment group, but avoided the poor adjustment group entirely. There is a tendency, then, but not a strong one, for these two types to make a good adjustment to separation. The adjustment to reunion is more uniformly good, with all but five of the H3W3 families having good reunion adjustments, and *all* of the H3W2 families having good reunion adjustments. The slight superiority of the H_3W_2 type families over the H_3W_3 is not significant, but the fact that the H_3W_2 type is at least as successful as the other is perhaps a confirmation of the finding in the previous section that the modified patriarchy makes a good adjustment to separation and reunion.

In the H_2W_3 pattern twelve out of fourteen families made a successful adjustment to separation. There were only four poor reunions out of the fourteen cases, but this is more than would have been expected by chance. The reason why this type did not make a better showing on the reunion adjustment seems to be that several families in the group were of the "irresponsible patriarchy" type of families in which the husband autocratically held the purse strings and made all the important decisions but left all the work of keeping up the home and rearing the children to the wife, treating her more as a domestic servant than a wife. These wives found it difficult after their taste of independence to return to their earlier subservient position with the husband's return. The roles were complementary in these cases, but compulsively not voluntarily so.

As might be expected, the thirteen cases of the H_1W_3 type made a 100 percent good adjustment to separation, but did not do so well in reunion. Six of the families had poor reunions. In these families there was little coöperation between husband and wife, and the husband was irresponsible in his attitude toward his family. This indicates a good adjustment to separation *because* of the father's absence —the type of separation and adjustment discussed on page 84. The H_1W_2 type made the poorest adjustment to both separation and reunion, reflecting more or less disorganized families in which neither member had the desire or ability to keep the family functioning effectively. The other types were randomly distributed throughout the type-of-adjustment groups, with the exception of type H_1W_1, which had no representatives in the study.

We have, then, a partial confirmation of the hypothesis that the families who rate high on the degree to which they assume responsibility for maintenance of the home and which rate high on the dove-tailing of roles will adjust best to separation and reunion. There is a more definite tendency for these families to have a good reunion than a good separation adjustment. Where the husband assumes slightly more responsibility in the home than the wife does and where a coöperative relationship exists between them, a successful re-union adjustment is, according to this study, even more certain.

Why do not the cases with the highest ratings produce a larger proportion of good adjustments both to separation and reunion? A glance at these cases indicates the possibility of a greater proportion of highly individualistic married pairs falling in this group than in the H3W2 group, with a pattern of at least slight dependence. In some cases these highly individualistic pairs found it difficult to get back into harness as a team after they had been making decisions separately during the separation period. We find again, then, as in our discussion of equalitarian families in which we discovered that equality of authority was not enough, that equal assumption of re-sponsibility is not enough. The process of coöperation and of com-plementing one another's roles is even more important.

Families which have the habit of coöperation adjust well to the separation and even better to the reunion, whether or not all mem-bers assume an equal degree of responsibility for the maintenance of the home. Our case would be stronger if the families rated H2W3 had made the same type of successful adjustment as did the families who rated H3W2. The reason for these families' reunion failure has been given, and it seems fairly clear that it is the classification that is at fault, and not the findings. The classification is not sufficiently re-fined, and if a new classification were developed which distinguished between complementing of a voluntary and compulsive nature, the findings might appear more consistent. A complementing of roles which is voluntary and congenial to both husband and wife, we feel sure, will be found some day to be highly predictive of successful separation and reunion adjustment.

Parental Responsibility. The rating of F3M3, which was the

highest rating a family could get on the discharge of parental responsibility of both parents, was moderately predictive of good separation
adjustment (forty-six families out of sixty-two with this rating made
a good adjustment to separation) and very predictive of good reunion adjustment (fifty-nine of the sixty-two families had good reunions). No other rating was predictive of good reunion, which indicates the importance of the companion-guide relationship between
father and children during a prolonged absence of the father. The
child in these cases was able to carry a realistic image of his father
in his mind throughout the separation and usually participated
somewhat in the all-important family correspondence. When the
father-child relationship was well established before the father left,
and continued and confirmed by correspondence, there was little difficulty in continuing the relationship when the father returned to the
family and there was much less "adjusting" to be done at reunion
time.

The rating F_1M_3, where the father had an irresponsible attitude
toward the children and the mother assumed the entire burden of
the companion-guide relationship, was associated with a good separation adjustment but produced more poor reunion adjustments
than expected (of thirteen families, eleven made good separation
adjustments and five poor reunions). This is not too surprising.
Since the mother was already in a sense acting as both father and
mother to the child before the separation, the father would hardly
be missed in his role as a parent after his departure. On his return, he
would have difficulty breaking into the close relationship between
mother and child, whose interdependence would be increased by
his absence. It should also be pointed out that the irresponsible parent was also frequently an irresponsible husband, and poor marital
adjustment characterized many of these families. The same situation
seemed to obtain to a lesser degree in the families where the rating
was F_2M_3. These families on the whole made a good adjustment to
separation and tended to have a poor reunion.

The families that were rated as F_2M_2, where both parents were inconsistent in their handling of the children, made a somewhat better-than-average adjustment to separation, but had definitely poor reunions. One would not expect them to make a better-than-average adjustment to separation, but a glance at the cases in this group reveals that a high percentage moved in with the wife's or husband's parents, and the good adjustment to separation was frequently in terms of sharing the burden of the care of the children with the grandparents, or giving that responsibility to the grandparents entirely. This type of adjustment to separation excluded the husband and did not lay the foundation for a good reunion.

None of the frequencies in the area of parental responsibility were striking. They showed a definite tendency for families to adjust well both to separation and reunion in which the parents undertook and shared equally their full parental responsibility. There was also a tendency for families to adjust well to separation and poorly to reunion if the mother was a more adequate parent than the father. If the father was more adequate as a parent than the mother, anything could happen—there were no significant tendencies. The various combinations of F_1 and F_2 and M_1 and M_2 were represented by too few cases to permit conclusions to be drawn from their types of adjustment, but the indication was that these types would adjust poorly to both separation and reunion. The lack of any highly significant figures for the factor of parental responsibility indicates that it may not be in itself a primary determinant of adjustment, but can be compensated for either in the direction of adequacy or by other factors.

Affectional Configuration. The equal participation of all members in the affectional life of the family—that is, a type of family in which all members love each other with more or less equal intensity —seems to make for both a good adjustment to separation and good adjustment to reunion. This was most significant in the group which made a good but slow adjustment to separation, indicating that for families where affectional bonds draw in all members equally the immediate adjustment of life without one member is more difficult, but that such families are well equipped to meet crises in the long run. Families with affectional "cliques" tended to have poor separations and reunions. It did not seem to matter what the combinations were, although some were more definitely predictive of poor reunions than others, as, for example, the mother-child cliques, or a conflict situation between husband and wife. The one exception was the group of families in which husband and wife were both closer to the children than to each other; these families had a definite tendency toward good reunion. In their concern for their children's welfare the husband and wife in these cases would have a strong common motive for maintaining family solidarity—so the exception seems a reasonable one.

Although the overall picture for the families in the study was one of good adjustment to separation and reunion for families in which all members participated equally in the affectional configuration and poor adjustment to separation and reunion for families in which affectional cliques existed, families with every type of clique did make every type of adjustment both to separation and reunion. A better picture of just what effects affectional cliques have on adjustment of families to crises might have been obtained if there had been more information on which to base the classification of the families by affectional types. The schedules were not designed to catch these affectional configurations and information was accordingly often inadequate. Perhaps a later study might make better use of these concepts.

Integration and Adaptability. The correlation between integration and adaptability on the one hand and adjustment to separation and reunion on the other hand did not turn out to be as clear-cut as expected. In general, however, it was clear that families with any combination of moderately adaptable to very adaptable and moderately integrated to very integrated tended to make a good adjustment to separation and to reunion. Of a total of seventy-seven families with these ratings, fifty-nine made a good adjustment to separation and seventy-three made a good adjustment to reunion. It was also true, however, that a larger-than-expected number of families with the rating "very adaptable and very integrated" made only a fair adjustment to separation. Contrary to the expectation noted in the formulation of hypotheses on p. 221, adaptability was discovered to be of more importance than integration in adjustment to crisis. Only four "very adaptable" families made a fair adjustment to separation and none made a poor adjustment, while twelve "very integrated" families did make a fair to poor reunion, and three "very integrated" families had a poor reunion. In other words, a larger proportion of unintegrated than unadaptable families were able to achieve a good adjustment to separation and reunion. Both integration and adaptability showed up as of more importance in reunion than in adjustment to separation. High ratings on these two factors were very predictive of good adjustment to reunion, with adaptability again more predictive than integration.

The findings on the relative importance of integration and adaptability are interesting. The concept of integration reflects the family ideal of an earlier day, and the concept of adaptability reflects the emerging family ideal of expediency and rootlessness of a dynamic tomorrow. The family needs both these attributes in order to survive, but the emerging emphasis in the family literature upon adaptability would seem to be a healthy one, in the light of the findings of this study.

Marital Adjustment. Good marital adjustment, as we have classified it from our case study materials, was distinctly related to good adjustment to reunion but less clearly related to good adjustment to separation. Of seventy-seven families rated as having good marital adjustment, only fifty-five made a good adjustment to separation but seventy made a good adjustment to reunion. A significant number of families who had made only a fair adjustment to separation had good marital adjustment. In addition, a number of families with

poor marital adjustment were rated as having made a good adjustment to separation in terms of the remaining family unit, by closing
ranks against the husband. In general, then, the families with good
marital adjustment made the best adjustment to separation, the families with poor marital adjustment made the next best adjustment
(by the closing-of-ranks technique), and the families with fair
marital adjustment made the poorest adjustment to separation, presumably not being able to get along *with* or *without* a husband.

In the reunion we find a similar pattern. The families with good
marital adjustment made the best reunion adjustment, and although
families with poor marital adjustment had a very low proportion of
good reunion adjustments, it was, nevertheless, higher than the good
reunion adjustments of the fair marital adjustment group. The materials of the study do not provide any explanation for this pattern,
but it might be interesting to investigate it further in a future study.

Good Adjustment to Previous Crises.   The factor of good adjustment to previous crises was moderately significant for the adjustment to separation and very significant for the reunion adjustment.
Forty-nine families had made a good adjustment to previous crises,
and although only thirty-eight of these made a good adjustment to
separation, forty-six made a good reunion adjustment. Ten of the
families made only a fair adjustment to separation. This can be explained only by the fact that the fair adjustment group suffered
the greatest number of hardships of any group and their family resources were strained most by the separation.

The importance of previous crisis-meeting experience is pointed
up by the interesting difference which emerges between the group
that made a good, slow adjustment to separation and the group that
made a good, rapid adjustment. The rapid adjustment group had by
far the greatest number of good adjustments to previous crises, and
the slow group had almost as large a proportion of poor adjustments
to previous crises as good ones. The slow group was apparently
hindered from making a rapid adjustment by previous experiences

of inadequacy but were, nevertheless, able to muster resources to make a good final adjustment.

Families that had fair and poor adjustment to previous crises had strong tendencies toward poor reunions but their adjustments to separation showed a random distribution. The families who made the poorest adjustment to separation, however, were, without exception, families which had failed to meet crises before and were generally low on family adequacy. Unexpectedly, however, these families made good reunion adjustments! The reason for this seems to be that they never "adjusted" to separation at all but lived more or less in a state of suspended animation until the husband returned, and then resumed their previous patterns of family living. One might conclude that had the husbands never returned these families would have become badly disorganized.

In summary, families with a history of good adjustment to previous crises made good adjustments to both separation and reunion unless subjected to unusually severe hardships. Families with a history of poor adjustment to previous crises, however, were not doomed to poor separation and reunion adjustments unless general family adequacy was also low.

Number of Children in Family. There was no relationship between the number of children in a family and the type of adjustment made either to separation or reunion.

Social Status. The two highest status groupings represented in the study, lower-upper and upper-middle class, were the only groups which made a distinctive type of adjustment to separation and reunion, and in both cases the adjustments were good. All four families of the lower-upper group adjusted well on both counts, and four out of five families of the upper-middle-class group adjusted well on both counts. However, families from all other classes also made good adjustments, and no class made significantly poorer adjustments than others, so better-than-average social status is not a necessary characteristic for good adjustment. We do not feel that the concept of social status is very satisfactory as we have used it here. If any conclusions were to be drawn from this material at all, it would be that above-average social status in the community indicates a family which is able to make a good adjustment to the crisis of war separation. But the concept of social class as we have used it is open to question and its measurement even more so. The subjective judgment made from the narrative materials was as unsatisfactory as the status scale which it supplemented. The concept will need to be refined before it will be of much value as an index of family adequacy.

FACTORS COMMON TO SEPARATION AND REUNION ADJUSTMENTS

We have seen repeatedly in the above discussions of factors in family adequacy that the same factor might not be equally important for both separation and reunion adjustment, or might be exclusively associated with one or the other adjustment. The factors are the same for both separation and reunion adjustments, however, when the separation adjustment is defined in terms of the entire family unit. The same factors which enable a family to continue functioning smoothly while one of its members is away, at the same time allowing the absent member as much participation in family life as possible through letters and other devices, will enable that same family to reabsorb the absentee into the family routine when he returns. Factors which enable a family to continue functioning smoothly while one member is away by closing its doors against the absent member will, on the other hand, certainly not enable that family to reabsorb the absent member, but will increase the difficulty of such a feat. For example, families in which the husband was irresponsible in the discharge of his duties in the home and as a parent, while the wife bore the main responsibility for taking care of the home and the children, were almost certain to adjust well to separation. The wife would not be carrying any heavier a load than she was already used to—and in addition a source of tension would be removed. The reintroduction of the tension into the home by the return of the husband would not usually be welcomed.

Most of the factors which were important both for separation and reunion adjustment were not as important for separation as they were for reunion adjustment. This would probably not be true of crises which did not involve dismemberment of the family. A family which functions very well even in difficult situations when the family circle is complete may be sufficiently dependent on one particular member so that when he is away that family cannot meet difficulties as *well,* although it might meet them *adequately.* The very factors which make it easiest to take the husband back into the home may be the ones that make the separation harder, as, for example, a high degree of integration and good marital adjustment. The husband may be so acutely missed that a good adjustment to separation is not made, although the ingredients for a good reunion are there. This was actually the case with some of the families who made the poorest adjustment to separation. This brings up the whole question: What is the best type of adjustment to separation? Perhaps it is better for a family not to get along too well without the husband so as to make it easier for him to fit into the picture when he returns. This problem will be considered in some detail in the next section of the chapter dealing with the processes of adjustment to separation and reunion.

SCALING AND CONCEPTUALIZING FAMILY ADEQUACY

Before closing our discussion of family adequacy, we will attempt to recapitulate our findings in two ways: one, by means of a family adequacy scale; and two, by means of a series of constructed family types conceptualizing the most striking elements discussed in this chapter. They constitute both a summary and a test of our findings, since we will be checking to see if items which individually showed a relationship to good adjustment to crisis are additively important, and whether they are integratively important.

The family adequacy scale is simply constructed, assigning a score of one to the presence within a family of each of the following attributes which have been shown to be associated with good adjust-

TABLE 18.   Distribution of 114 Families and Their Average Family Adequacy Scores by Type of Adjustment to Separation and Reunion

Type of Adjustment to Separation	Type of Adjustment to Reunion			
	Good Reunion		Poor Reunion	
	No. of Families	Average Family Adequacy Score	No. of Families	Average Family Adequacy Score
Good, rapid adjustment to separation	52	5.20	11	1.40
Good, slow adjustment to separation	21	4.62	4	2.50
Fair adjustment to separation	15	5.55	5	3.00
Poor adjustment to separation	5	3.80	1	3.00
Total	93	5.05	21	2.07

ment to separation and reunion: moderate or high integration; moderate or high adaptability; good adjustment to previous crises; one of the following types of family control—democratic, equalitarian adult-centered, modified matriarchy, or modified patriarchy; one of the following ratings on family responsibility—H_3W_3 or H_3W_2; a rating on parental responsibility of F_3M_3; equality of affection. Families were scored one for each of these evidences of family adequacy, total scores ranging from zero to seven.

As seen from the average scores for each type-of-adjustment group in Table 18, the good, rapid adjustment to separation, good reunion group has a fairly high family adequacy score, the good, slow adjustment to separation, good reunion group has a slightly lower score, and the poor adjustment to separation, good reunion group has the lowest score of all the groups that succeeded in the final reunion adjustment. The fair adjustment to separation group is a notable exception in this continuous decreasing of family adequacy as type of adjustment to separation adequacy declines, in that it has the highest average adequacy score of all the groups! Why didn't this group with such high family adequacy scores make the best adjustment to separation? A careful analysis of the records reveals that this fair adjustment to separation group of twenty-one families had the heaviest load of hardships of all the groups. A further investigation of the original narratives on these cases reveals that a majority have very high adequacy scores coupled with excessive hardships. The remaining families have poor family adequacy and an average number of hardships, thus fitting into the pattern we would have expected to find in this group. We can only conclude that the majority of these families would have broken down completely under their load of hardships if they had not had such high adequacy. If adjustment had been defined in terms of degree of hardship as well as ease and effectiveness of family reorganization, they would have been rated as having made an excellent adjustment to separation.

The family adequacy scores of the type-of-adjustment groups that had poor reunions display the opposite tendency from the good reunion groups: the good, rapid adjustment to separation group makes the lowest scores, the good, slow adjustment group makes the next to the lowest, and the fair and poor groups make the highest score. (The poor adjustment to separation group consists of only one case, however, so the score for that "group" is not significant.) None of these average scores is as high as the lowest average score of the groups having a good reunion, so the validity of the scale as a measure of ability to adjust to reunion seems to be upheld.

The fact that the lowest scores on family adequacy fall in the two groups making the best adjustment to separation can be explained by the fact that these families for the most part had very poor marital adjustment before the separation and were adjusting not as a complete family but as a new closed-ranks unit. Here again is this other type of adjustment that keeps cropping up, and it is a type of adjustment that naturally has a negative relationship to family adequacy. The families that made only a fair or poor adjustment to separation had higher adequacy scores but still had less than average adequacy, and in addition suffered a larger share of hardships than the other groups. Because of the absence of well-defined conflict situations in this group, there could not be as easy a closing of ranks as in the more disorganized families of lower adequacy, nor could the remaining unit function as well because of excessive hardships. The fact that these families could neither completely exclude nor completely include the husbands in the separation adjustment, because of their ambiguous level of family adequacy, meant they were prevented from making either of the two types of "good" adjustment to separation, and so fell between the stools into fair or poor adjustment.

In conclusion, then, families with high adequacy scores are able to make a good adjustment to both separation and reunion (making due allowance for hardship) in terms of the complete family group. Families with moderate adequacy do not make as good a separation adjustment but manage a good reunion adjustment. Families with below-average adequacy cannot make as good a separation adjustment either in terms of the complete family or the remaining unit, nor can they make a good reunion adjustment. Families with low adequacy can make a good adjustment to separation in terms of the remaining family unit on a closed-ranks basis, but cannot make a good reunion adjustment. Additively, our components of family adequacy prove discriminating in affecting adjustment to crisis.

A second way of summarizing the combinations of family adequacy distributed among our families is to construct an ordered series of family types which will integrate most of the elements of family adequacy and still provide a pigeonhole for most of the families in the study. Our first constructed series were experimental:

1. Democratic-Adjustively Integrated Families
   High or moderate integration
   High or moderate adaptability
   High marital adjustment
   Equalitarian and democratic control
   Family responsibilities (also parental) equally divided
   Equality of affectional focus
2. Modified Authoritarian-Moderately Adjusted and Integrated Families
   Moderate or low integration
   High or moderate adaptability
   High or moderate marital adjustment
   Modified patriarchy and matriarchy
   Family responsibility (also parental) not equally but complementarily divided; no sense of unfairness
   Equality or inequality of affectional focus
3. Authoritarian-Nonadjustively Integrated Families
   High integration
   Low adaptability
   Moderate or low marital adjustment
   Pure patriarchy and matriarchy
   Family responsibilities (also parental) one-sided in initiative and carrying of load
   Inequality of affectional focus
4. Unclassifiable Families

As an attempt was made to classify the cases into the first three types, it became evident that not enough types had been constructed to cover the range presented by the case materials. The following three types were then added:

1. Modified Authoritarian-Adjustively Integrated Families
    High or moderate integration
    High or moderate adaptability
    High marital adjustment
    Modified patriarchy and modified matriarchy
    Family responsibility (also parental) equally divided
    Equality of affectional focus
2. Authoritarian-Nonadjustively Unintegrated Families
    Low integration
    Low adaptability
    Low marital adjustment
    Pure patriarchy and matriarchy
    Family responsibility (also parental) one-sided in initiative and
        carrying of load
    Inequality of affectional focus
3. Anarchistic-Nonadjustively Unintegrated Families
    Same as authoritarian-nonadjustively integrated families, except
        for anarchistic pattern of authority instead of patriarchal or
        matriarchal

It will be seen that the modified authoritarian-adjustively integrated type is identical with the democratic-adjustively integrated
type, except for the pattern of dominance, and that the authoritarian-
nonadjustively unintegrated and anarchistic types are "disorganized"
versions of the authoritarian-nonadjustively integrated type. Ranking these types in their theoretical order of adequacy to crisis, we
have the following arrangement:

1. Democratic-Adjustively Integrated Families
2. Modified Authoritarian-Adjustively Integrated Families
3. Modified Authoritarian-Moderately Adjusted and Integrated
    Families
4. Authoritarian-Nonadjustively Integrated Families

5. Authoritarian-Nonadjustively Unintegrated Families
6. Anarchistic-Nonadjustively Unintegrated Families
7. Unclassifiable Families

The families were classified into these types from the master cards. In the first attempt at classification an effort was made to avoid putting any cards in the "unclassifiable" group. When a family seemed to have *most* of the characteristics of one of the six types, and unquestionably did not belong to any one of the other types, it was classified under the type to which it corresponded most closely. As a result, there were no "unclassifiables" left over at all. When a simple frequency table was constructed, however, indicating the kind of adjustment to separation and reunion made by each type, and the difference between the actual and the expected was computed, it was found that there was an almost completely random distribution throughout all six types on the adjustment to separation. This was not true of the adjustment to reunion, where significant differences between the types were found.

Obviously we couldn't be satisfied with findings that pointed to a significant relationship between family types and adjustment to reunion but not between family types and adjustment to separation. It was decided to attempt a more rigorous classification of the families, assigning each family to a given type only if it conformed to every trait listed for that type. This left us with forty-seven "unclassifiables" but also gave a relationship between family types and adjustment to separation more nearly like the relationship between family types and reunion adjustment. The choice clearly lay between stretching the classifications to the point that they would fit all the cases and learning nothing of importance, or keeping the classifications simon-pure and perceiving that some types were more adequate to crisis situations than others. Eventually, perhaps, the dilemma can be solved by discovering enough types to cover all the cases—we have probably carried the typology as far as it is warranted in this exploratory study. The results are shown in Table 19 and Table 20.

The democratic-adjustively integrated type has been confirmed in these two tables as a strong form of family organization making a good adjustment both to separation and to reunion.

The modified authoritarian-adjustively integrated family types showed a tendency in Table 19 to make only a fair adjustment to separation, but in Table 20 made a unanimously good adjustment to reunion, better even than the democratic-adjustively integrated fam-

TABLE 19. Types of Adjustment to Separation Achieved by Six Major Family Types (135 Iowa Families)

Family Type	Type of Adjustment to Separation						
	Good Rapid (Open Ranks)	Good Slow (Open Ranks)	Good (Closed Ranks)	Fair	Poor	Unclassifiables Approximating This Type	Total
	f	f	f	f	f	f	f
Democratic-adjustively integrated	19	10	1	7	2	17	56
Modified authoritarian-adjustively integrated	5	3	0	5	0	8	21
Modified authoritarian-moderately adjusted and integrated	6	6	1	3	2	7	25
Authoritarian-nonadjustively integrated	0	0	1	0	2	7	10
Authoritarian-nonadjustively unintegrated	1	1	5	2	0	4	13
Anarchistic-nonadjustively unintegrated	2	1	2	1	0	4	10
Total	33	21	10	18	6	47	135

ily type. The modified authoritarian-moderately adjusted and integrated type showed a tendency to make a good, slow adjustment to
separation but presented a completely random distribution on adjustment to reunion. Although it was only possible to classify three

TABLE 20.   Types of Adjustment to Reunion Achieved by Six Major Family
Types (114 Reunited Families)

| Family Type | Type of Adjustment to Reunion | | | |
	Good Reunion	Poor Reunion	Unclassi-fiables Ap-proximating This Type	Total
	f	f	f	f
Democratic-adjustively inte-grated	29	2	13	44
Modified authoritarian-adjus-tively integrated	12	0	6	18
Modified authoritarian-mod-erately adjusted and inte-grated	14	3	6	23
Authoritarian-nonadjustively integrated	1	1	6	8
Authoritarian-nonadjustively unintegrated	4	5	3	12
Anarchistic-nonadjustively unintegrated	3	3	3	9
Total	63	14	37	114

families as authoritarian-nonadjustively integrated, two of these
three fell in the poor adjustment to separation group. Only two of
the three cases had had reunions, and one made a good and one a
poor adjustment to reunion. The authoritarian-nonadjustively unintegrated type made a good closed-ranks type of adjustment to separation, and, as expected, a poor reunion. The anarchistic type also
made a good closed-ranks adjustment to separation and a poor reunion.

In general our expectations have been confirmed. The first three family types tended to make good adjustments to both crises and the second three types made poor adjustments to both crises. The picture is a little clearer in the case of the second three, or "inadequate," family types. Why the modified authoritarian-adjustively integrated families tended to make only a fair adjustment to separation when the only characteristic which differentiates them from the democratic families is the quality of modified authoritarianism which has elsewhere been shown to correlate with good adjustment to separation, is difficult to understand. The only explanation which comes to mind is that an exceptionally large number of the cases of undue hardship must have fallen into this type. It is not surprising that the modified authoritarian-moderately adjusted and integrated type showed a random distribution on the nature of adjustment to reunion, since it is an in-between family type with few distinctive characteristics.

When the components of family adequacy are integrated together into constructed family types, the resulting achievements in the face of crisis are most reassuring. These methods of typing families warrant continued exploration to keep abreast of the propensity of quantitatively-minded research workers to scale and score variables, as we did in Table 18. The scale is a simple method of adding, and sometimes weighting, elements in a complex, whereas the constructed type attempts to integrate the elements into wholes keeping always in view the unit of observation. There are advantages to both methods which justify using both where possible.

WHAT MODES OF ADJUSTMENT WORK BEST?

The findings on family adequacy gave a hint as to what kinds of families could make good adjustments to crises, but gave no indication of *how* they made the adjustment. We will now endeavor to ascertain what kinds of adjustment processes are most effective in meeting a crisis situation. The following hypotheses were formulated in regard to the process of adjustment:

1. The kind of family equilibrium at the time of separation will in part determine the type of adjustment made to separation and reunion.
2. The course of adjustment to the crises of separation and reunion will follow the roller-coaster pattern developed by Koos (27) to describe the course of adjustment to all types of family crises.
3. Immediate and secondary reactions to the separation and reunion crises will be different (discovered from the studies of crises of bereavement and impoverishment).
4. Those families which make a quick and immediate recovery after the crisis of separation and reunion will not make as good a final adjustment as those families which made a slower and more thorough recovery (also determined from studies on bereavement).
5. The following types of role reorganization during separation will make good adjustment to separation and reunion:
   a. Husband continues his affectional relationship with wife and children through sharing of experiences in letters.
   b. Wife makes decisions and manages home without advice from husband.
   c. Children carry more responsibility in the home. Significant for separation but not reunion.
   d. Grandparents or relatives are available and participate in family life.

FAMILY SITUATIONS

The concept of the family situation, as used by Bossard (see our earlier discussion p. 51) includes *family adequacy*, discussed in the previous section; *process*, illustrated best in this chapter by the anticipatory reactions of families to the impending crisis; and *content*, best exemplified by the hardships facing the families at the time of separation.

PROCESSES AFFECTING ADJUSTMENT TO CRISES

The material in this section is incomplete because the schedules were not specifically constructed to capture information concerning how families felt about induction before it happened, but the material found its way into the interviews often enough to make its use here worth while.

Those families made the most rapid adjustment to separation and to reunion in which the husband enlisted or complied with the draft with the wife's consent. However, families in which the husband enlisted without the wife's consent were also able to make a good final adjustment to separation, although their initial recovery was slow, and they also had good reunions. Families which accepted induction philosophically, realizing that there was a job to be done, or which worked through their emotions before the actual separation came, "crying it out" in advance, made a good adjustment both to separation and reunion. Planning ahead for the separation period by buying or building a home or moving in with parents also made for good adjustment both to separation and reunion. (Moving in with parents could make either a very good or very poor separation adjustment presumably depending on the nature of the wife's relationship with the parents.) Families which had been in conflict and were brought closer together by the prospect of separation made a good separation adjustment but did not have a good reunion. There were exceptions to this, but, on the whole, the separation in itself could not mend a damaged relationship. Similarly, families who regarded the separation as a good thing, an opportunity to "think things out," made a good adjustment to separation, usually in terms of excluding the husband, and did not have a good reunion. We conclude that those families will adjust best to separation and reunion which make some kind of preparation, either mental or physical or both, for the impending crisis. Also, war separation cannot of itself improve a marriage that is already in difficulties, even if the immediate effect on the marriage is good.

Content (Hardships). The families that made the most rapid adjustment to separation had considerably fewer hardships than other families, and the families that made a good but slow adjustment had slightly more than their share of hardships, except in the poor reunion group. The families that made only a fair adjustment to separation had by far the greatest share of hardships, which explains, perhaps, why they made only fair adjustments in spite of their high family adequacy scores. The group that made the poorest adjustment to separation had only slightly more than their share of hardships, so their failure to adjust would seem to be due to a combination of low family adequacy and hardships.

A distinction was made between family hardships that would be defined as such by the community in general, and hardships as defined by the family itself. Families that made a good, rapid adjustment to separation defined far fewer of their hardships as such than any other group, and families with good, slow adjustment defined fewer of their hardships as such than the fair and poor adjustment groups. Families with fair adjustment also did not define all their hardships as such, but came closer to it than the other two groups. The poor adjustment group frankly defined all their hardships as such.

The most important conclusion that emerges here is that family adequacy alone cannot be used as an index of adjustment to crises without also taking into consideration the number of hardships involved in the situation. However, one might also say that, within limits, family adequacy determines the extent to which hardships are defined as such. The families with high family adequacy and comparatively few hardships refrained from defining many of their hardships as such. Even when families with high family adequacy and many hardships were forced by the pressure of some of their hardships to recognize them as real difficulties, there was a tendency

to ignore other hardships they were experiencing. Only the families
with low family adequacy considered *all* their hardships to be real
troubles. To repeat, then, hardships have to be considered along with
family adequacy in determining adjustment to crises, but family adequacy also determines the extent to which hardships become real
troubles to a family.

PROCESSES OF ADJUSTMENT TO SEPARATION

On the assumption that the roller-coaster pattern fits the process of
adjustment to separation of these families, the findings are divided
into: disorganization, which includes the immediate reactions to
crisis of the wife; recovery, which includes the short-term efforts at
adjustment; achievement of reorganization, which includes the final
readjustment to the crisis.

Disorganization. Families that made a good adjustment to separation and reunion reacted to the immediate induction crisis in
ways that ranged from excitement, through feelings of unreality, to
calm. Indifference was felt by families that adjusted well to separation but not to reunion, and extreme loneliness, emotional upset, and
numbness was felt by families which adjusted poorly to separation
but well to reunion. A certain amount of emotional excitement, we
may conclude, is allowable at the moment of separation, but extreme
reactions do not augur well for final adjustment to separation. Indifference augurs well for adjustment to separation but hardly for
reunion.

Recovery. Families that made a good final adjustment found the
recovery period difficult but not impossible, were generally too busy
to mope, and had some help from friends and relatives. The families
who managed too well, the wife enjoying her new-found freedom,
did not in general have good reunions. Families that made a poor
final adjustment to separation worried a lot in this period. Some
wives had trouble managing the house and children, and several
made unsuccessful attempts to take jobs. All the families except

those in which husband and wife were estranged missed their men very much. However, the initial disorganization effects of the husband's departure wore off in a matter of months in all the cases except those that never did make a satisfactory adjustment to separation.

Achievement of Reorganization. The best adjustment to separation was made by those families who partially closed ranks and redistributed most of the husband's responsibilities among the remaining members; the husband was bound to the family through his affectional and companionable relationship with them, shared and maintained through their letters. Good adjustments were also made when the husband continued more completely his old role in the home, sharing in the decision making, providing that the family was not absolutely dependent on his decisions but shared the decision process with him in order to make him feel as much a part of the family as possible. Good adjustments were also made by families where there were grandparents who could step in and take over some of the husband's responsibilities and by families where children were given additional responsibilities in order to relieve the mother of her double load. It was rare for mothers in these families to take full-time employment outside the home.

The types of reorganization just discussed made good reunion adjustments possible. A type of reorganization which made a successful separation adjustment but led to poor reunion adjustment was the closing of ranks by mother and children. In these families the wife enjoyed having a free hand with the children, frequently had a full-time position outside the home which she enjoyed very much, and dreaded the husband's return. The children were an emotional outlet for the mother in both types of adjustment, and the mother actually was more independent in both areas of adjustment, whether she enjoyed her independence or not. The families which made a poor adjustment to separation did not close ranks at all but just existed in a dismembered state, throwing on the absent husband the full burden of decision making for the family (in contrast to the well-adjusted families which permitted the husband to continue to share in the family council in order to keep him feeling that he "belonged"). The children of these families were often badly adjusted too, and unable to reconcile themselves to "Life Without Father."

We conclude that the best reorganization of a temporarily dismembered family is a partial closing of ranks, with the father continuing an affectional and companionable relationship with the family through letters, and sharing in the family council if this is desired, and where the children relieved the mother of some of her added responsibilities. The wife may be expected to become somewhat more independent and may use the children as an affectional outlet to compensate for the loss of a husband to love. If, however, the wife enjoys freedom to the extent of closing ranks against the husband, the reorganization is not satisfactory in terms of future family life.

Nearly all the hypotheses regarding the process of adjustment to crisis have been confirmed as regards the adjustment to separation. The hardships of the individual family situations were clearly shown as helping to determine the type of adjustment made to separation. The roller-coaster pattern of disorganization, recovery, and reorganization was not universal, since some families made a calm and immediate readjustment to the crisis. An approximation of the roller-coaster pattern, however, was fairly general if we allow for some variations in the steepness of the up-and-down-grade slopes, as families were more or less disorganized by the induction and had more or less trouble in getting reorganized. The immediate and secondary reactions to the crisis were noticably different, the immediate reactions being generally of emotional distress, and the secondary reactions those of a determination to "get along" somehow. There was no evidence, however, that families which made a rapid adjustment to separation were less well adjusted finally than those families which made a slow adjustment. The importance of the continuation of the companionship relationship with the husband, but not the decision-making relationship, and the importance of help from relatives and children in carrying extra responsibilities was confirmed.

PROCESSES OF ADJUSTMENT TO REUNION

Disorganization. In the families that made a successful adjustment to reunion there was infrequently a period of immediate disorganization. Immediate reactions were primarily those of joy, which might be considered disorganizing in a nondestructive sense. Many husbands and wives stepped into a second honeymoon and went off somewhere with or without their children. Others just picked up family life where they had left off when the husband went into service. Those families which had been estranged before the separation and had gotten along well without the husband but were willing to try a reconciliation did not, with one or two exceptions, succeed in their reunion adjustment.

Recovery. The process of recovery presents a much more complex picture. Waller, in his discussion of disillusionment following the euphoria of the wedding and honeymoon, has presented the essential elements of the process of recovery that we have rediscovered in war reunion adjustments.[5] After the honeymoon glow dies down, problems frequently arise both in families that make a good final adjustment and in families that don't. Some families were actually able to resume family life as if it had never been interrupted (at least according to their testimony and what observations the interviewer could make). However, many had to make a conscious process out of redistributing the family roles after the husband returned, trying to remember to consult him about family problems, teaching the children to recognize his authority and to accept his discipline, and so on. Husbands were frequently subject to moods and blues, wives experienced a letdown as their men turned out to be human after

[5] Reuben Hill, *Waller's The Family: A Dynamic Interpretation* (New York: Dryden, in Press).

all, and many husbands and wives experienced a vague dissatisfaction that they often could not account for in any specific way. Housing conditions, job seeking, illness, and other troubles aggravated this dissatisfaction, of course. Wife and children found themselves competing for the husband's affection, or husband and children found themselves competing for the wife's affection. Wives rebelled against the continuing extra load of responsibility they had carried during the separation and sought a more dependent role, sometimes with the husband's approval, sometimes with his violent disapproval. Some families who had not had a very close relationship before the separation, however, discovered new values in family life and established a more coöperative relationship than they had before.

The kind of maladjustments that developed in the recovery process did not give any indication of what the final outcome of the struggle for adjustment would be. An exception to this was in those cases where the wife wished to continue in her new independent role and the husband wished her to return to the more dependent role she had before the separation; this situation rarely resulted in a good final reunion adjustment. Furthermore, if there was overt conflict or estrangement carried over from the early stages of "recovery," it was rare that a good reunion adjustment eventuated. One can only conclude that the determining factors in the question of how the family would finally emerge from its recovery period are the same as the factors determining adjustment to separation; namely, family adequacy and hardships. Housing conditions in particular were not helpful for the reunion adjustment, and some families that might otherwise have passed on to the reorganized state were still struggling in the recovery stage at the time the study was made, because of the pressure of housing hardships.

Achievement of Reorganization. Many families had not yet reached the stage of final reorganization at the time that the study was made. This was partly due to the fact that some husbands had been home only a few weeks at the time of the interview and partly due to external circumstances like lack of housing which were beyond the family's control. A certain number of families were still working toward reorganization or had experienced conflict, estrangement, or divorce. Half of all the families in the study, however, had settled down to their former pattern of family life at the time of the interview. Other families were completely adjusted except in regard to the children's acceptance of the father's discipline, and this problem was solving itself gradually. A number of families had an increased appreciation of their family life and some who had been indifferent to family life before were now much more coöperative in the home and shared more experiences together. These families just described were the ones who were judged to have made a good reunion adjustment.

In other families old arguments, troubles, and infidelities were being revived; new sources of conflict were emerging, competition for affection between family members was still keen, husband and wife could not agree on division of authority, or there were bitter arguments over what kind of job the husband should have, whether to buy a house or a car or just save, "and so on far, far into the night." Some of these families may make a good ultimate adjustment. We can only say that if they have a high family adequacy score and are not pressured by too many hardships, we predict that they will eventually attain a workable equilibrium. A few families have already filed for divorce and still others have come to tolerate a thoroughly unsatisfactory married life for the sake of the children, because the wives do not have the courage to break away or because they know they have been just as miserable apart as they now are together.

The reunion roller-coaster course of adjustment is a little different from the separation roller coaster, then, in that the initial reaction is usually one of intense joy, disorganizing perhaps, but not in the same sense that sorrow is. The drop comes when the honeymoon is over and the family must reorganize to meet the exigencies of daily life, but the drop is not a steep one and recovery is much quicker than the recovery from the separation crisis. This is probably due to the fact that the family is now not so much exploring uncharted fields (as in the attempt to get along without a husband) as it is attempting to reëstablish a way of life that in most cases was pretty well worked out before the husband left.

We return now to a question that was asked earlier in this chapter: What is the best type of adjustment to separation that a family can make to guarantee a good reunion adjustment? What processes ought a family to go through in order to achieve a good ultimate adjustment to the two-headed crisis of adjustment and reunion? The best answer that can be given from this study is that there is no one ideal process that results in a better adjustment than any other process. Several different types of adjustment to separation resulted in good reunions, and in order to be able to evaluate the types of adjustment we would have to be able to judge the quality of the kinds of reunion achieved. We can simply say that some families made "good" reunions and others did not. It is not possible to differentiate between good, better, and best.

If we look at the percentages of good reunions achieved by the different type-of-adjustment-to-separation groups, the picture is confusing indeed. The good, rapid adjustment to separation group had 71 percent good reunions, the good, slow group had 62 percent. This is not unexpected, nor is the record of 63 percent good reunions in the fair adjustment group, since we know that this group suffered from undue hardships.

The question immediately arises: Is the reunion adjustment made by the good, slow adjustment to separation groups as good as the reunion adjustment made by the good, rapid adjustment to separation group? We have already indicated that we cannot answer this question directly. However, it may be possible to answer the question indirectly. Ordinarily, a good adjustment to reunion means a return to the family patterns worked out before the separation. If

there is any change, it is in the direction of intensification of affectional relationships and habits of coöperation. Assuming, then, that
the reunion is a return to the family's previous equilibrium, we
might judge the quality of the reunion on the basis of the quality of
the family's previous adjustment. This brings us to the family adequacy types discussed in detail earlier in the chapter. These were
ranked, it may be recalled, in the order of their assumed adequacy to
the exigencies of family living. The most adequate type was the
democratic-adjustively integrated family. In all but two cases this
type of family was rated as having achieved a good reunion adjustment, which means that they returned to their previous high level of
adjustment. The democratic type was characterized by a good, rapid
adjustment to separation, with a minimum of dislocation of family
patterns. These families planned for the separation, were temporarily hard hit by the departure of the husband, but quickly
made up their minds to get along as well as they could. The resources they used to keep the family functioning well were partly
resources already available within the family circle, with the wife
and children taking more responsibility, and partly external resources, such as help from relatives. They kept in close touch with
the husband, but were not dependent on him for family decisions.

According to the hypotheses taken from the bereavement studies
that a period of mourning is helpful to ultimate adjustment, the
slow adjustment to separation should have been more adequate than
the rapid adjustment.[6] Admittedly, one aspect of the slow adjustment to separation made it appear to be a superior type of adjustment, and this was the fact that families with an equality of affectional focus made preponderantly good, slow adjustments to
separation. When this finding was discussed (p. 230), it was pointed
out that in families where such an equality of affectional focus
existed the immediate adjustment to life without one member was

[6] We make this test with due apologies to the specialists who have studied
bereavement. The two crises are probably not sufficiently comparable to expect confirmation, although they are both crises of dismemberment.

more difficult, but that such families were well equipped to meet crises in the long run. It seemed possible that families with equality of affectional focus would also display other characteristics of integration that would slow up the adjustment process but make a very stable final adjustment. No specific family type making this kind of adjustment emerged, however. Instead, we find affectional equality as a trait in the democratic-adjustively integrated families which made a good, *rapid* adjustment to separation, and the families with this trait making a good, slow adjustment are lost among the "unclassifiables." The case for good, rapid adjustment is overwhelming, with a preponderance of the traits of integration, adaptability, and good adjustment to previous crises falling in this type of adjustment to separation. The good, slow adjustment group not only has less integration and adaptability, but has an overwhelming record of poor adjustment to previous crises; in other words, this group has a lower adequacy record then the rapid adjustment group.

SUMMARY

This chapter has dealt with generalizations concerning adjustment to separation and reunion drawn from a careful analysis of the family histories collected for our study. The factors chosen for further analysis as possible determinants of the type of adjustment to separation and reunion, together with the techniques developed for recording these factors, have been described. Finally, the findings on the relative importance of each factor have been presented. Since the authors hoped to capture the process of adjustment to supplement the static picture of family organization, an analysis of the family situations at the time of the separation crisis and of the course of adjustment to both separation and reunion crises have been included.

CHOOSING FACTORS IMPORTANT TO FAMILY ADEQUACY

After a careful reading of the case histories, master cards were devised to summarize each case. Face-sheet information and ratings on social status and marital adjustment were recorded. Next was given a description of the course of adjustment to separation in five steps: (1) the pre-crisis situation (type of family control, adjustment to previous crises and ratings on integration and adaptability); (2) reactions to the impending crisis; (3) immediate reactions at the moment of crisis; (4) short-term adjustments or recovery; and (5) long-term readjustment or reorganization achievements. After an interval of introspection additional data were recorded on the types of roles performed by family members: (1) decision making, (2) maintaining and managing the household, (3) performing distinctly parental, "child-rearing" responsibilities, and (4) meeting the need of affection of family members.

Patterns of decision making were divided into six main family types: patriarchal, modified patriarchal, matriarchal, modified matriarchal, equalitarian adult-centered, and democratic. Diagrams were constructed which could give a picture of authority relationships between every member in a given family of each type. Patterns of household maintenance in each family were described by rating husband and wife on a nine-point scale on degree of complementing of roles and degree of individual responsibility assumed. Parental responsibility was similarly described by rating husband and wife on a nine-point scale on the degree to which parents fulfilled their roles both as disciplinarian-guide and as companion to their children. Affectional configurations for each family were described by diagrams indicating the strength of feeling of various family members for one another. Information on family roles was recorded in this fashion for each of the following three periods in family life: pre-separation period, separation period, and reunion period. This completed the information recorded on the master cards.

FACTORS IMPORTANT IN FAMILY ADEQUACY TO CRISIS

In patterns of decision making, the democratic type was confirmed as important in determining successful adjustment to separation and reunion. The equalitarian adult-centered families also adjusted well, but not as often as the modified patriarchy and modified matriarchy. This indicated that the process of *mutual consultation* might be more important than the seat of ultimate authority in the home.

A high degree of acceptance of responsibility for the maintenance of the home and physical care of family members on the part of both parents, combined with a coöperative relationship between parents, was more predictive of good adjustment to reunion than of adjustment to separation. Families with a coöperative relationship between parents, in which the husband took a little more responsibility than the wife, also made a good adjustment to separation and an even better adjustment to reunion.

A high degree of acceptance of parental responsibility on the part of both parents was moderately predictive of good adjustment to separation and still more predictive of good adjustment to reunion. The frequency of good adjustments in this group is not very much above the expected, so parental responsibility does not seem to be a factor of primary importance in determining adjustment to the crises.

Families in which all members had affectional relationships of more or less equal intensity made both a good adjustment to separation and to reunion. Families with affectional "cliques" made all kinds of adjustments both to separation and reunion but in general tended to make poor adjustments.

Families with any combination of moderately adaptable to very adaptable and moderately integrated to very integrated tended to make good adjustments to separation and reunion. Contrary to expectation, adaptability was of more importance in determining good adjustment both to separation and reunion than was integration.

Good marital adjustment was distinctly related to good adjustment to reunion, but less clearly related to separation adjustment. Many families with a poor marital adjustment made a good adjustment to separation by the closing-of-ranks technique, which was highly predictive of poor reunion.

The factor of good adjustment to previous crises was moderately significant for the adjustment to separation and very significant for the reunion adjustment. Families with a history of poor adjustment to previous crises, however, were not doomed to poor separation and reunion adjustments unless general family adequacy was also low.

There was no relationship between the number of children in the family and the type of adjustment made either to separation or reunion.

Above-average social status in the community seemed to be predictive of good adjustment to separation and reunion, but the authors were neither satisfied with the concept of social status as used in this study nor with the accuracy of its measurement.

The same factors are not always equally important for adjustment to separation and adjustment to reunion, and in some cases factors are important for only one or the other. However, when good separation adjustment is defined in terms of the entire family unit, the same factors are important both in separation and reunion. On the other hand, the factors which make for a good closed-ranks adjustment to separation do not make a good reunion.

To summarize the data a Family Adequacy Scale was constructed (see p. 237), using the factors shown to be important to separation and reunion adjustment. The differences between the average adequacy scores for each type of adjustment group indicated that. the scale was fairly successful in measuring family adequacy to crisis.

The above findings were checked and summarized in a second way by classifying the families into six family types ranging from democratic-adjustively integrated to anarchistic-nonadjustively integrated. The types were based on various combinations of the factors tested previously. Each family type made a distinctive adjustment to separation and reunion, with the adjustively integrated family making the best open-ranks adjustment to separation and the nonadjustively unintegrated families making a good but closed-ranks adjustment. In the reunion adjustment the adjustively integrated families did the best and the nonadjustively unintegrated families did the poorest.

FAMILY SITUATIONS

Assuming that the process of adjustment to crisis cannot be properly understood without a knowledge of the family situation upon which the crisis impinged, a study of these situations was made. This included an analysis of *family adequacy* (already undertaken in the previous section), of *process* (anticipatory reactions to crisis), and *content* (hardships facing family at time of separation).

It was found that those families adjusted best to separation and reunion which had made some kind of preparation, either mental or physical or both, for the impending crisis.

The number of hardships clearly helped to determine the type of adjustment made to separation, in that families with high adequacy and undue hardships made only fair adjustments to separation. However, it was also true that families with low adequacy and few hardships made even poorer adjustments to separation. It was concluded that family adequacy and hardships should both be taken into consideration in predicting adjustment to crises. It also seemed that, within broad limits, family adequacy determined the extent to which hardships were defined as such by the family.

ADJUSTMENT TO SEPARATION

On the assumption that the roller-coaster pattern fitted the process of adjustment to separation of these families, the findings were divided into disorganization, recovery, and achievement of reorganization.

A certain amount of emotional excitement in the period of disorganization immediately after the husband had left for service did not interfere with good final adjustment, but extreme reactions did not augur well for adjustment to separation. Indifference promised a good adjustment to separation but poor reunion.

Families that made a good final adjustment to separation found the recovery period difficult but not impossible, were generally too busy to mope, and had some help from friends and relatives. Families that managed too well—the wife *enjoying* her new-found freedom—did not in general have good reunions.

The best adjustment to separation was made by those families that partially closed ranks and redistributed most of the husband's responsibilities among the remaining members; the husband was bound to the family chiefly through his affectional and companionable relationship with them, continued through letters.

ADJUSTMENT TO REUNION

In families that made successful adjustment to reunion there was rarely a period of disorganization. Immediate reactions were those of joy, which might be considered disorganizing in a nondestructive sense.

A few families skipped the recovery period and resumed normal family living immediately. Most families experienced something of a letdown after the honeymoon was over and had to make a conscious process out of redistributing the family roles, trying to remember to consult the husband about family problems, teaching the children to recognize his authority and accept his discipline, and so on. Except for situations of severe conflict and situations where a wife was struggling to keep her separation-gained independence against her husband's wishes, the kind of maladjustments that developed in the recovery period did not give any indication of what the final adjustment would be. The exceptions mentioned ended in poor final adjustment.

Many families, because of the shortness of time that the husband had been home or because of undue hardships such as lack of housing, had not yet achieved a final reorganization. Half the families had settled down to their prewar ways of family living, however, and many more were in process of achieving this, with an increased appreciation of the meaning of family life. The fate of other families hung in the balance, with family adequacy battling against great hardships. Where family adequacy was low, good final adjustment seems doubtful.

The type of adjustment to separation that was most promising of good reunion was the good, rapid type. This did not confirm the bereavement findings that a slower adjustment was a more sure and lasting one, but, as has been pointed out, the nature of the materials gathered were probably not comparable for the two types of studies.

CHAPTER VIII

TEAMING THE STATISTICAL AND CASE STUDY METHODS

"WHAT method will you follow in collecting and analyzing your data—the statistical or the case study method?" was the question posed by the committee chairman of a group of researchers called by the National Council on Family Relations in 1945 to consider, among other problems, the project statement and preliminary schedules for the present study. The group was divided almost equally between the advocates of the competitive methodological schools. The discussion became quite warm when the author suggested that both methods might be yoked profitably to study the problems of families under stress. Agreement was not immediately forthcoming because the case study approach had had a monopoly in this area of research since the first studies of families in crisis were launched. There was good evidence that this method was admirably adapted to the exploratory tasks faced by the pioneer family researchers dealing with crises. Crises of impoverishment, bereavement, alienation, and the manifold critical troubles besetting families were thought to be difficult to capture by statistical methods.

The division of labor between the two methods, which we devised at this meeting, has been followed quite faithfully. The statistical method has been used to test definitively the hypotheses built up from previous studies of families in crisis and from studies of marriage·success in the new context of war separation and reunion. Wherever possible in the statistical end of the study, family behavior has been reduced to scales and inventories which can be

264

scored quantitatively. The rich use of the continuum for ranking families has characterized this method. The results are given in Chapters V and VI, and the limitations of the methodology are discussed in some detail in Appendix B.

The case study method has been assigned a broader area including both the definitive testing of hypotheses carried over from previous studies concerning families in crisis which do not lend themselves to statistical methods, and exploratory advances into the unknown crises of separation and reunion.

The case study method has been given full sway in the capturing and analysis of the many courses of adjustment, the processes of adaptation, and the shifting, changing nature of family life under stress of separation and reunion hardships. The results from this analysis are detailed particularly in Chapter IV and Chapter VII.

By agreement, Reuben Hill, who directed the statistical analysis, and Elise Boulding, who conducted the case study inquiry, have up to this point operated independently of one another in order that the findings from one method might not prejudice the generalizations obtained from the other approach. Conferences on methodology have been held but the discussion of results has been studiously avoided. The authors are now ready to bring their tabulation sheets, master cards, tables, and other research paraphernalia from the two methods together to do jointly what neither has been able to do alone. (See the methodological implications of this teamwork in Appendix B.)

We propose in this chapter to use the statistical method and the case study method in tandem on three byways: (1) the locating and explaining of the behavior of unpredictable families whose properties and characteristics should have enabled them to survive separation and reunion handily, but who did poorly; and the locating and explaining of the behavior of deviant families whose resources were woefully inadequate for life in a dynamic society, but who nevertheless managed to ride out these two crises of separation and reunion relatively unscathed; (2) the validating of inadequately standardized statistical scales, the checking of family types, and the checking of ratings of families derived from the statistical materials against the judgments reached for the same families by means of case study; and (3) the verification of findings wherever the two methods covered the same ground, comparing and accounting for differences wherever they crop up.

We hope to achieve by means of this analysis a partial test of the validity and reliability of our methodology, new insights into the variables at work as families adjust to crisis, and provocative leads for further research.

Identifying and Explaining Unpredictable Families

One of the glaring weaknesses of the statistical approach has been its inability to allow in its generalizations for the individual families, located at the tails of the distribution, which do not perform as expected. Only life insurance companies and marketing groups can afford to ignore the behavior of individual families in favor of classes of families. The life insurance executive can be satisfied if the actuarial tables predict correctly the proportions of a population which will die at given ages, or for given occupations, or for given risk groups. However, social workers, counselors, and other clinicians must make individual prognoses for families and individuals and, therefore, must ask of the researcher more detailed information about causal sequences in individual families. In predicting scholastic success, parole success, marriage success, and family success the value of the prediction is limited greatly if it cannot be applied to individuals successfully.

We are in the same situation with respect to our findings that the marriage prediction researchers find themselves. They know certain classes of attributes are frequently present in numbers among those couples who do well in marriage, but they are at a loss to explain why some couples with high scores do poorly in marriage.[1] We hope that we can, by joining case study with statistical analysis, add to our understanding of the average family and evolve a set of insights which will explain the individual variants which surround it. Moreover, we feel that additions to knowledge come sometimes through an intensive analysis of the behavior of the deviants in any study. In the field of family behavior the deviant may be just a representative of another successful family type too infrequently represented in the sample to count for anything but a deviant. Hypotheses based on these results can be tested in later studies and may eventually account for a larger and larger proportion of families until the behavior of practically all families makes sense.[2]

LOCATING THE DEVIANTS

The unpredictable families in this study are identified as those families who were exceptions to the rules and generalizations arrived at, based on the behavior of most families or the average families. We used data from both statistical and case study sources to locate our deviants. We will describe our identifying procedures briefly.

One group of unpredictables may be obtained from the statistical data by the simple procedure of noting all families whose adjustment to separation score and/or whose adjustment to reunion score exceeds or is below the average scores by more than one standard deviation for the statistical family type in which the family is lodged.[3] For example, Case No. 614 is one of eighteen families located in the

[1] See especially the discussion of five case studies of marital adjustment in E. W. Burgess and L. S. Cottrell, *Predicting Success or Failure in Marriage* (New York: Prentice-Hall, 1939), pp. 290–312.

[2] We have here another illustration of the interplay between research and theory reported by Robert Merton as the serendipity pattern, the phenomenon of the anomalous datum exerting pressure for initiating theory, "The Bearing of Empirical Research Upon the Development of Social Theory," *American Sociological Review* (October, 1948), pp. 506–509.

[3] The basic data from which we worked are found in Table 13 (pp. 164–165) in which the nine major statistical family types are portrayed.

Low Integration–Medium Adaptability statistical family type which you may remember was not an outstandingly successful family type in facing separation, the average score for adjustment to separation being only 3.63. Case No. 614 adjusted much better than this with a score of 4.50. The standard deviation of the distribution is 0.46 which, added to the average of the family type, gives an upper limit of 4.09, beyond which families would appear as deviants. Case No. 614 is clearly a deviant on this basis and some explanation is needed to account for such a good performance with such modest resources. Altogether, thirty-seven families were identified as deviants by this procedure; that is, scores for their separation and reunion adjustment were more than one standard deviation higher or lower than the average of the statistical family type in which they were lodged.

From the case study materials a variety of evidence was mulled over to locate deviants. A family adequacy score based on this evidence was constructed which included the type of family control, the most favorable combinations of adaptability and integration, the most favorable division of labor and responsibility in caring for children and managing the home, and the desired equality of and closeness of affection within the family circle. Families varied from zero to seven in the scores they could receive on family adequacy. All families had already been classified as having experienced one of the following types of adjustment to separation and reunion:

Ia. Good, rapid adjustment to separation, good reunion
Ib. Good, rapid adjustment to separation, poor reunion
IIa. Good, slow adjustment to separation, good reunion
IIb. Good, slow adjustment to separation, poor reunion
IIIa. Fair adjustment to separation, good reunion
IIIb. Fair adjustment to separation, poor reunion
IVa. Poor adjustment to separation, good reunion
IVb. Poor adjustment to separation, poor reunion

Deviant families by the case study method were those which had possessed high family adequacy scores before induction yet adjusted only moderately well or poorly to separation or to reunion, and conversely those families with low adequacy scores which adjusted well to separation and reunion. From her files, Mrs. Boulding located twenty-one families which she identified as unpredictable families.

Six families were branded by both the statistical and the case study methods as deviants, without question. Roughly half of the deviants remaining in the statistically produced list were also judged as nonconformists by Mrs. Boulding from her case study analysis, but not sufficiently so for her to include them as bonafide deviants. Of the deviants remaining on the Boulding list roughly three-fourths were found to be within a step or two of being included as deviants by the statistical analysis. For whatever it is worth, it is apparent that the two methods are sharpshooting at the same target, although the weapons are different.

AN ANALYSIS OF THE DEVIANT CASES

All the data within the statistical and case study files were pored over to bring understanding and illumination to bear on the deviant cases. The fruits of our intensive interviewing were tested in this analysis. The technique of the probing interview, mentioned elsewhere as necessary for discerning, proved its worth in providing us with pointed information to help explain deviant behavior among many families. In a few cases it was apparent that the crude statistical scale's classification of the family was faulty with respect to its adjustment to separation and sometimes to reunion—the tendency for the respondent to put "his best foot forward" showed in the statements he checked. There were occasional faulty ratings of adaptability and integration by interviewers. In a very few cases there was not enough relevant data in the files to explain satisfactorily the family's deviation from the expected.

We present below an analysis of six families which have been identified by both the statistical and case study data as deviants. When we have completed that analysis, we will present four selected cases from the lists of nonconformists made up separately by the two methods. For ease in reading, each history is constructed uniformly to contain the following information: (1) a brief thumbnail portrait of the family, (2) a brief history of the family's growth and development before induction, (3) the expected reactions of the family to separation and reunion based on data from (1) and (2), (4) the deviant's actual reactions to separation and reunion, and (5) explanations and hypotheses growing out of the analysis.

Case I. A Family Which Adjusted Well to Separation Despite Low Family Adequacy and Low Scores on Statistically Important Factors

Fred and Gretchen Glauser and Two Children

This is a family of low social and economic status and of meager educational attainments living in the mill and factory section of southern Iowa's Ottumwa. The family is surrounded by many helpful and interested kinfolk who, though poor unskilled workers, are willing to share and share alike. The family at the time of the interview is patriarchal with Gretchen playing an irresponsible rather than a subservient role. Nevertheless, the family is relatively more flexible than it is integrated. Fred and Gretchen are not well adjusted maritally as seen in occasional expressions of jealousy, bickering, and some stepping out on one another. The affectional ties are of a "loose noose" type for all family members. The Glausers are rated as having one of the lowest family adequacy scores of the entire sample.

Both Fred and Gretchen came from large families characterized by happy relationships among parents and siblings, and by marginal hand-to-mouth living. They met in their early teens and married at 19 and 15 respectively after a year's acquaintance. Gretchen accepted housewifely responsibilities reluctantly, would rather have worked outside the home, but Fred felt the wife's place was in the home. Conflicts have raged over this issue and Gretchen's love of parties. Her interests have continued to be adolescent despite her marriage. Two children, now four and two years respectively, were born and further complicated Gretchen's living arrangements. Both parents love the children, but take only incidental responsibility for their bringing up. In the pre-induction period Fred was dominant in most things and Gretchen gave in. He also paid for this privilege by assuming most of the responsibilities for the management of the home. His role as sole wage earner was badly hit early in their marriage when he was laid off at the plant for several weeks, though he was finally hired back. Gretchen went to work for her sister, caring for her children to keep an income coming in, and they recovered from that crisis satisfactorily.

From the low statistical scores on vital factors of marital adjustment and integration and low family adequacy components, we would have expected low to fair separation achievement and a closed-ranks type of adjustment to Fred's absence after induction. Gretchen's irresponsibility in caring for her home and children also argues for poor adjustment to separation. The one saving factor is the relatively adequate adaptability component (19.5), which, however, owes more to Fred's personal flexibility than to adaptability as a family. The previous successful experience with unemployment would also make for good separation and reunion. Adding all these scores and judgments together we would predict only a low to fair adjustment to separation.

Actually Gretchen and children made an excellent although expedient adjustment to separation. They moved rapidly and surely after Fred's induction to a mode of family life which was quite satisfactory to them. They joined the household of Fred's parents who in turn took over almost complete responsibility for the children, for managing the home, for providing meals and shelter. Fred's father assumed the father's role with the children most effectively. He escorted Gretchen to occasional parties. Gretchen was released to work spasmodically when her mother-in-law wasn't ill. She stepped out alone and also on occasional dates with former male friends, and became quite independent of Fred and the children. She wrote frequently to Fred at first, but gradually decreased the number of her letters. Fred learned of his wife's "gadding about" and argued about it in his letters. He maintained a regular correspondence even after he asked Gretchen to get a divorce if she planned to continue dating promiscuously. She complied with his wish for divorce with a minimum of recriminations, and to show there were no hard feelings she remained with Fred's parents until he returned home. Their correspondence continued on a somewhat less intense basis after the divorce. After

Fred had been home a few weeks they decided to remarry and are now living in their own quarters. Fred wrote on his questionnaire after returning from service, "I think servicemen should forget what things they had to go through while apart from their wives such as going out with other men and women—just forget they were apart and start where they left off, then everything will come out fine." The scale measuring adjustment to separation gives this family a high score, 4.60, and Mrs. Boulding classifies the family as Ia or good, rapid adjustment to separation with good reunion. Both measures show results which exceed the expected achievement for this family.

Explanations after the fact are to be distrusted, except in so far as they are used as hypotheses. In this instance a statistically unimportant resource, the availability and helpfulness of relatives, played a decisive part in adjusting the Glauser family to separation. The kinfolk had helped before induction, and were turned to as a natural refuge when Fred was called into service. Fred's superordination in managing the family finances and organization of the home routines was taken over by his mother. Fred's role of father-protector to the children was assumed by Fred's father. Gretchen also indicates she sometimes was escorted to a show or a social by her father-in-law, which would indicate a rather complete substitution for Fred by his father. Gretchen could hardly have had a better means of maintaining her little family in the face of separation than this cushion of in-laws. They were ready and willing to assume many of the father and husband roles Fred left dangling when he departed. There would probably be violent disagreement in some circles as to whether this family really made a good adjustment to separation in view of the nontraditional roles played by the wife and the divorce which took place during the separation. The family is not a model of conformity and the case is filled with contradictions, but it is our judgment based on our definition of adjustment to separation that the outcome for all members appears satisfactory, both for children, father, and mother. The reunion has to date worked to prove the permanence of the adjustment.

One hypothesis growing out of this case which might be tested in future studies of dismemberment involves the further searching for the family situations in which kinfolk and neighbors may be of most help. Statistically, the hypothesis that families who have helpful relatives will adjust best to the crisis of dismemberment due to war separation has been disproved within the present set of 135 families in Iowa, but the hypothesis will need sharpening and retesting before it can be rejected entirely. The new hypothesis might read: Those families in which the wife and mother is relatively irresponsible or excessively dependent and the father is dominant and responsible will succeed best in adjusting to separation if kinfolk or substitutes are accessible and willing to assume the father's managerial and decision-making roles during his absence.

CASE II. A Family Which Adjusted Poorly to Separation and Never Reunited Despite High Family Adequacy and High Scores on Statistically Important Factors

Alvin and Mary Harbison and Two Children

The Harbisons are a model family with two charming children, respected and well liked by the community and of high social and economic status. In the division of labor Mrs. Harbison ably carries an extra share of the family responsibilities because of the demands of her husband's medical practice.

Mary Harbison was the daughter of a Kansas farmer and met Alvin while she was doing secretarial work in the same city in which he began his practice. They had a casual friendship for several years which blossomed unexpectedly into love and marriage. Mary had been the child of her mother's old age in a fairly congenial family of seven children, and had learned to look after herself from an early age because of her mother's poor health. She contributed an affectionate and self-reliant nature to the marriage, and she and Alvin quickly worked out a satisfying coöperative relationship in the home. Their interests were family-centered, and they were unusually close to each other and to their children. They were not alike in temperament: Mary was outgoing and sociable while Alvin was withdrawn and introverted, but there was strong emotional interdependence and they rarely quarreled. Alvin's father was a well-loved member of the household.

The statistical scales for marital adjustment, adaptability, integration, and dynamic stability all rank this family in the highest quartile of the sample. The family adequacy score built for the identifying of deviants rates this family with a score of six out of a possible seven. The family would appear to be a very good risk in any crisis. One would predict a good adjustment to separation in terms of the wife carrying on to the best of her ability but continuing with the children a close companionship with her husband through letters. The reunion would probably be a recapturing of the honeymoon experience followed by a heightened appreciation of the joys of family living and a gradual settling down to the old family routines.

Things didn't happen that way. The separation adjustment started out on the predicted course with Mary managing pretty well at home, but living for his letters and writing long letters in return. Toward the end of Alvin's overseas service period, however, his letters became strangely impersonal and she worried about this. One letter came announcing his return to the United States and after that there were no letters at all. After three months of silence Mary wrote to the War Department and was informed that her husband had been discharged. By this time seriously disturbed, Mary telephoned her husband at the West Coast address given by the War Department and asked him why he didn't come home. He replied coldly that he didn't want to. Poor Mary took the next train out West to try and find out what had happened, and found that Alvin had "turned to stone," as she put it. He declared that he no longer had any interest in his family nor had any intention of returning to them, and was applying instead for a permanent army appointment. When Mary, heartbroken, was getting on the train to return to her children he suddenly seemed to relent and said that maybe his future would include her and the children after all, and promised to write to her immediately. A month later, at the time of the interview, she still had not heard from him and had given up all hope of ever getting him back. Mary met this new crisis bravely and was doing her best to continue as normal a family life as possible without her husband for the sake of the children. The news that Alvin was not coming back cracked the previous adjustment badly and the family became disorganized as following a desertion crisis.

What broke this family up? The case history gives only one tantalizing clue to account for the rejection of the family by the father, namely, his quiet introverted personality. We have consulted with a specialist who has had considerable experience in dealing with the personal problems of enlisted men who places an interesting interpretation upon the facts here presented. Alvin, who had been a pillar of the community had also maintained a very strict moral code, in service may well have shared with other servicemen sexually deviant experiences which have made him ashamed to face his family and his community. Being more sensitive than his associates to what he had done, he may have developed guilt feelings to the point of rejecting himself as unworthy of his family. The specialist regards Alvin's frozen indifference as a neurotic adjustment to acute guilt feelings from what may well have been a comparatively insignificant moral lapse. Any explanation is in the realm of conjecture. It should be pointed out that what makes this family a deviant is the deviant behavior of one member whose actions have thrown into confusion all the remaining members—heretofore well adjusted to separation and well prepared for reunion.

A hypothesis arising out of the present case that might be tested in later studies follows: When a family has a member with an inadequate personal adjustment, a crisis of dismemberment that deprives the maladjusted member of the family's resources may result in a deterioration of that individual which results in disorganization of the entire family unit.

Case III.   A Family Which Adjusted Well to Separation and Reunion Despite Low Family Adequacy and Low Scores on Statistically Important Factors

Howard and Sarah Brown and Three Children

The Browns are an atomistic and dissatisfied family, the product of the unfavorable social environment of the colored community of a large Iowa city. Mr. Brown neglects his family in order to do things that will gain him prestige in the white and colored communities, and Mrs. Brown runs the family as best she can, turning to her children both for help in the home and for the companionship Mr. Brown fails to give.

The family rates in the lowest quartile on the scales for marital adjustment, adaptability, and integration. Their rating on the family adequacy materials constructed from the case histories was only two out of a possible score of seven.

Sarah, an attractive colored girl, was one of five children in a "good-for-nothing drunkard's" family. At sixteen she met Howard Brown, a popular high-school boy two years her senior, at a social club. They went steady for five years while he worked as a porter and tried to find a better job so they could marry. When they finally married, Sarah took her new responsibilities very seriously, painfully aware of the deficiencies in her own parental home. Howard did not regard his family responsibilities with anything like equal seriousness, and Sarah soon discovered that he was more interested in gaining recognition in the community than in providing for his family. A self-centered man, he preferred unpaid community activities such as Scouting and YMCA work that brought him prestige to a paying job, and Sarah was compelled to work in order to support their growing family. What Howard really wanted was a college education and a law degree but this he could not afford, and Sarah had no patience with his compensating activities which kept him from helping her at home or adequately supporting the family. She turned to her three children for the affection and coöperation which Howard denied her in his preoccupation with the community, and came to enjoy the freedom and independence that her work gave her. At the time that Howard left for the service they had drifted apart, and though Sarah felt that she could live just as well without him she did not ask for a divorce because of the children.

The prediction for this family which the above history justifies would be a closed-ranks adjustment to separation on the part of the wife and children, little sharing of experiences through correspondence, and a widening of the rift between the husband and wife. There would probably be a reunion if Sarah still felt that the children should have their father, but it would be more an agreement to continue to live together than a happy reunion. She might, on the other hand, decide on a divorce.

The family actually made a good adjustment to separation without closing ranks. Howard took much more interest in his family than he had ever done before, wrote long letters full of longing for Sarah and the children, plans for the future, and interesting accounts of his exciting new life in New York City where he was stationed throughout his entire period of service. Sarah, too, found that she missed her husband and though she did a successful job of managing the home without him because of previous experience, she found herself also developing an interest in the community activities that he had liked so well so that she could feel closer to him.

Now that Howard has finally returned to his family his new attitude toward them is continuing and he spends much more time in the home being helpful to Sarah and playing with the children. Through the GI Bill of Rights he is fulfilling his old ambition to train for the legal profession, and the community activities that he is able to continue are now shared with Sarah. She doesn't really understand why he wants to become a lawyer nor does she comprehend his craving for prestige in the community, but she accepts his aspirations philosophically and has succeeded in becoming much more sociable as a person herself.

The real source of difficulty in this family before induction was a craving for public recognition on the part of the husband, so strong that it prevented him from satisfactorily performing the husband-father roles in his own family. He probably resented his family as an economic burden since it prevented him from fulfilling his most cherished ambition, to become a lawyer. While he was in the army he was suddenly plunged into a new social environment. He became a part of the sophisticated, intellectual inner circle at Harlem and achieved a social position that carried considerable prestige. It is possible that this unexpected fulfillment of long-felt desires in a new environment where his family was not present to nag at him and make him feel guilty set in motion a beneficent personal adjustment cycle which made him feel socially more adequate and therefore better able to cope, in imagination at least, with the family demands that had irritated him for so long. Instead of having to return from his cultural safaris to a disapproving family and hated chores, he was able to return to his bachelor quarters and sit down and share with his family through letters his new ideas, hopes, and ambitions for the future. His wife, accepting the fact that temporarily all the home responsibilities were hers to bear alone, responded warmly to this new sharing of ideas, and their relationship reached a new level of companionship and intimacy that had not been achieved since courtship days. When Howard was discharged he was able to retain his new feelings of security because he was able to study law and plan his entire future in terms of a new social status. His self-confidence made him more livable within the family and enabled him to accept and even enjoy the traditional role of the husband and father. Adjustment was also aided by the fact that his wife finally recognized and accepted his need for social status, even though she did not fully understand it. She was now coöperative with his plans and made a real effort herself to participate in community life.

This explanation of the deviant adjustment of the Browns is the best interpretation the writers could make on the basis of the information they had, but it cannot be considered definitive. It would be interesting to set this interpretation forth as a hypothesis, to be tested in a later study, as follows: When maladjustment or disorganization has occurred in a family as a result of the failure of the social environment to meet certain deep-seated needs of one or more individuals in the family, a change in the direction of a more favorable social environment for such an individual may set in motion a beneficent cycle which enables the individual to function more effectively in the family unit so that an improved state of adjustment is achieved.

CASE IV. A Family Which Adjusted Well to Separation Despite Low Family Adequacy and Low Scores on Statistically Important Factors

Paul and Grace Watson and Two Children

The Watsons are an unintegrated family in which there are plenty of quarrels. Paul and Grace have guarded their personal independence through several years of courtship and married life, and have only begun to show interdependence where the children are concerned.

Grace's mother was an Englishwoman of good education, and family plans had been made for Grace to go to England when she graduated from high school in order to complete her education and train in medicine. The war interfered with these plans, and since mother and daughter did not get along very well Grace married a boy she had been going with in high school in order to get away from home. Grace was quick-tempered and unstable and a spendthrift, so disagreements between Paul and her were frequent. She didn't care for housework so worked outside the home whenever possible. The children were cared for adequately, but Grace never felt very close to them. A warm, affectionate relationship existed, however, between Paul and the children. On the whole, the marital relationship has been a precarious one, and has been further endangered by "interfering in-laws."

The family scores on the statistical scales of marital adjustment, adaptability, and integration were moderately low, in the next to lowest quartile. The family adequacy rating was also moderately low, three out of a possible seven. In the light of the family's general inadequacy and the mother's irresponsibility, one would not expect the family to make a good adjustment to separation, either of the open- or closed-ranks type. Grace would probably resent the burden of looking after the children alone and might let the home deteriorate. When Paul returned from service the previous unsatisfactory family life would probably be resumed but with even more conflict. Paul would be justified in feeling that Grace had not done a good job with the children while he was gone and would insist that she had not carried her fair share of the burden of separation.

As it happened, Grace managed an excellent adjustment to separation. She very quickly tired of staying home alone and looking after her family, but it was her good fortune to find a very fine boarding home for the children so that she was freed of all responsibility for their supervision and could take a job which she said was necessary for "financial reasons." The children soon came to regard their boarding-house parents as their real parents and adjusted very well to their new environment. Grace visited them regularly and reported feeling badly because she could not make a home for them herself. This statement was chiefly a lip-service to society's standards because she could have managed to keep the children home inasmuch as her army allotment was almost as large as the total Watson income before separation. As Grace defined it she was no longer a household drudge: she had a good job, money to spend, and freedom to have "good times." Grace and Paul wrote to one another but the letters were not intimate, and each made his own new life. This arrangement is essentially new, an atomistic adjustment to separation as differentiated from the open- and closed-ranks types discussed previously. Each parent made his personal adjustment independently of everyone else, though the children remained interdependent. It must be rated a good adjustment because everyone's needs including the children's were well taken care of.

The reunion adjustment on the other hand fell into the expected pattern. The children resented being pulled out of their boarding home and kept wanting to go back to "mother and daddy," and Grace's adequacy as a mother had not increased. The whole family was crowded into the one room that Grace had been living in during the separation, and Paul resented her free spending which left the family without resources to buy a house. Grace was glad to have Paul back and was ready to return to family life, but Paul is not so sure of the future. He worries about supporting a spendthrift wife in these difficult times and wonders if it might not be a heavier burden than he can manage. The family's adjustment to separation is better than its adjustment to reunion.

The reason why this family adjusted so well to separation is hard to disentangle from the many subsidiary factors which supported the family's adaptations. The expedient use of commercial resources to care for the children characterizes Grace's resolution of her problem. She was able to buy on the market a secularized version of the resources ordinarily supplied only within the sanctity of the domestic kinship circle; that is, she was able to purchase from a boarding home food, shelter, parental affection and attention, and supervision for her children. This limited her responsibilities to the children to a purely financial relation and left her free to enjoy herself in her own way. Familistic-minded people will object strenuously to this secularized handling of a parent-child responsibility, but there is little evidence that irreparable harm was done. This adjustment is a secularized version of the adjustment made by the Glausers in Case I with a bought-and-paid-for boarding home replacing the more traditional parent substitutes, the close relatives.

A hypothesis growing out of the analysis of this case, phrased in more general language than the hypothesis in Case I, is as follows: A family which has inadequate internal resources can make a good adjustment to crisis if it can draw on the resources of another family or individual agency, whether it be on the basis of friendship, blood relationship, or simply a business relationship.

CASE V.   A Family Which Adjusted Well to Reunion after a Fair Adjustment to Separation Despite Low Family Adequacy and Low Scores on Statistically Important Factors

James and Sally Fessler and Two Children

At the time of the interview the Fesslers were a highly individuated, anarchistic family of moderate means who registered low on marital adjustment, family adaptability, family integration, and family adequacy. They are fun-loving, enjoy bowling, dancing, drinking, and conspicuous spending. The children were not planned for, indeed they had not been invited. Sally and the children were quite close, however, but Jim assumed little responsibility for them. Sally and Jim have been married for almost nine years and are now in their middle thirties.

Sally is a sexually inhibited girl of a small laboring-class family and dominating mother whom she has resented for years. James is a boy from the same neighborhood reared in a family of five girls. They met as teen-agers in school and went steady for six years, and although they postponed marriage, Jim moved into Sally's home to be near her. Sally's sex relations in marriage have not been enjoyable, the reasons for which she dates back to her repudiation of womanhood as a child and to a sordid sex experience with her uncle. The coming of babies has been a source of dismay to the husband. They threatened the couple's carefree life. Sally continued to share the partying until the baby was born, gradually dropping out of these activities afterward. During the late period of pregnancy James started stepping out for his sex satisfactions. After their daughter was born he resented her, and he tended to blame her for the fact that Sally couldn't continue the companionable tag-along roles of their courtship and early married years. They were seriously considering separation and divorce and agreed that James might improve the domestic situation by enlisting, which he did.

From the data given we might have expected a closed-ranks type of separation which would be fair or good depending on the provisions made for the care of the children and Sally's freedom to step out. We did anticipate that the reunion would be a repetition of the pre-induction conflicts, and have predicted eventual separation.

Actually, the war separation had some interesting results. Sally and her daughter were thrown closer together and became really fond of each other. Surprisingly, when James did return he was much more responsible. He took a job, turned his money over to Sally, and proved to be a good father to the children. The latter have gradually made a place for him although they still turn to Sally and to her father for many services James could provide. The daughter continues to resent giving up her place in Sally's bed to Jim. He has not discontinued drinking as a pastime and still spends freely, but he returns home to Sally at night instead of stepping out alone as he did before the separation. They are still living with Sally's parents though the relationships are not congenial. They have started to look for another place to live, however. Until James has been back a bit longer Sally reports she is not making a scene about the drinking, the free spending, or the cracks about her parents whom she doesn't care much for either. He is still irritable at times but is almost free of his erratic pre-induction tantrums. (As an aside of interest, Jim made appointments through his wife for interviews on the study three times and then retreated from them, because "I never talk about these things." All information had to be obtained through the wife.)

The scale for adjustment to separation and the judgment from the first reading of the case history rate this family as having attained a fair separation. Both measures also agree that there has been a good reunion. These judgments do not jibe with the more intensive analysis of the case made by both authors in teaming the case study and statistical method in this chapter. The conclusion that we have both reached is that the wife's checking of the scale measuring adjustments in her original reading appears too high. The fact of the matter is that the reunion adjustments are not yet complete and it is a matter of conjecture how well they will turn out. There are master symptoms of marital trouble ahead: the wife is not as yet frank and honest with her husband, the daughter is not yet completely reconciled, the relationships with the in-laws are strained, the husband still drinks although he is more settled and paternal in his relations with the children. The psychic honeymoon following reunion is nearing its end, and when it is over anything can happen!

CASE VI. A Family Which Adjusted Well to Separation Despite Low Family Adequacy and Low Scores on Statistically Important Factors

Allen and Claire Lockridge and Two Children

The Lockridges have reversed the traditional roles of wife-homemaker and husband-breadwinner. Claire Lockridge has always preferred a career to homemaking. As a matter of necessity Allen Lockridge has taken the major responsibility for managing the home and caring for the children. The division of labor has never been too happily settled, however, and the Lockridges are known as a couple which does not get along well together. Allen's whole life has been built around the family while Claire has more or less ignored both husband and children in favor of her position as personnel director of an industrial concern.

Claire was brought up as an only child by doting grandparents and entered marriage at eighteen, a willful, irresponsible, and flighty girl. Allen was several years older, a steady conscientious boy who had left the farm to work in the city. Claire had little interest in domesticity from the very beginning, but Allen painstakingly taught her to cook and care for the home. He tried to teach her to keep a budget, too, and wanted to leave all household decisions in her hands, but she was always very careless with the money and ignored the necessity for making decisions. When her grandmother came to live with them, Claire gladly dropped all her domestic responsibilities into grandmother's lap and went off to take a job. She was promoted regularly and occupied a responsible position in a large firm when Allen was inducted. She loved her work, but spent proportionately less and less time with her family, which grieved her husband very much. The grandmother became too feeble to carry the full burden of housekeeping for a family of five and handle the children too, so Allen helped out as much as he could evenings and Sundays, spent all his spare time with the children, and often got the family dinners besides. Allen, naturally an affectionate and dependent type of person, was deeply hurt by Claire's repudiation of the family, and his reproaches led to frequent quarrels. The children always sided with the father in the fights, so the family drifted further and further apart. When war production was booming, Claire and Allen worked different shifts and never saw each other at all. Claire found a congenial sophisticated social set that drank and spent money freely, and Allen turned for comfort to another group of friends and did some drinking on his own. The alienation processes were well along at the time of Allen's induction, and Claire frankly didn't care whether the marriage continued or not. Although Allen still loved her and longed to have her devote herself to the family, he felt that she would probably divorce him and departed for service depressed and discouraged.

The statistical scales ranked this family in the lowest quartile on marital adjustment, adaptability, and integration. The score for family adequacy was only two. The family is obviously not a good risk and separation adjustment does not promise to be successful even in terms of the closed-rank process because the children are aligned with the father against the mother, and the grandmother is not strong enough to take over the responsibility that the father had assumed. When the time for reunion comes, Claire might easily decide to chuck the whole thing and divorce her husband.

Again, the unexpected happened. Claire missed Allen very much after he left and went through agonies during the Battle of the Bulge, knowing he was in the front lines. Night after night she walked the floor unable to sleep for worry. She also discovered how difficult it was to run a home without a husband. Everything went wrong that first winter—the furnace went out on the coldest day of winter, the gas stove broke down and filled the house with gas one day, the sewer pipes developed a leak; she was kept on the run much of the time just looking after the physical side of family living which Allen had once managed so well. Claire had her pride and did not immediately confess these troubles to her husband although she did write him daily. Their letter-to-letter relationship became better than their face-to-face relations had been when he was home. Allen particularly wrote long, ardent love letters. Claire's discovery of how much her husband meant to her led her to spend more time with the children, and she began to take a personal interest in the housekeeping aspects of family life. Because she was an intelligent and capable woman, she did a good job of managing the home. Although the children missed their father at first, they soon became engrossed in school activities and made a rapid adjustment to his absence. Claire won their loyalty handily when she took the time to become acquainted with them.

Claire wanted to preserve the new close relationship with her husband that had developed during the separation. She realized that part of their earlier difficulties had come from her own driving desire for independence and felt that she was now willing to sacrifice some of that independence and give up her career for her home. She had some fears that if she did not make some such move they would fall back into the same old rut. Actually their reunion got off to a very auspicious start. Claire went to meet Allen at the hospital in which he had been convalescing from wounds received in battle, and he looked so wan and tired that she immediately lost any misgivings she might have had and felt nothing but love and sympathy for "her man."

After five months of reunion their adjustment is still good. Claire has stuck by her promise to stay home and look after the family and seems to be more aware of the needs of her husband and children. Allen is extremely appreciative of the new role his wife has taken, and although he still suffers from nervousness as a result of his war experience, he takes it out on the children, never on Claire. They still disagree some on finances and don't always agree on how to handle the children, but in general the family is very happy together. There are some indications of a reversion to the original roles in that Claire had already changed her plans of devoting herself to the home entirely to a modified plan of only staying home for a year or two and then going back to work. She is already beginning to feel somewhat restless in her new role.

The case materials are not adequate to explain the unexpectedly good adjustment to separation and reunion achieved by the Lockridges. We can put our finger on the immediate cause of the good adjustment—Mrs. Lockridge's changed attitudes toward her husband and family and a reversal of roles within the husband-wife relation. *Why* her attitudes changed we cannot say. Although the adjustment to reunion at present appears to be good, it may not be a permanent adjustment. There are already signs that Claire is dissatisfied with her new role as homemaker and will not be able to continue it indefinitely. If the need for a career and distaste for home life are deeply enough rooted in her personality, she cannot, with the best will in the world, repudiate the career roles she has enjoyed and embrace the domestic roles for which she has had neither preparation nor affinity.

Although the material given here does not really warrant the following hypothesis, it at least suggests it: An improved family adjustment precipitated by a crisis situation cannot be permanent if it does not take into account the deep-seated conflicting needs of family members that provoked the original maladjustments.

CASE VII.   Deviant as Judged by Case History Materials—A Family Which Adjusted only Fairly Well to Separation Although Possessed with High Family Adequacy and High Scores on Statistically Important Factors

Swen and Edna Swenson and Two Children

The Swensons have been exposed to more trials and hardships than any other family in the study. They are highly endowed affectionally, both husband and wife relationships and parent-children ties are good. Despite occasional quarrels they are well integrated and adaptable. Yet they live in squalor back of the roundhouse in the railroad yards. They have suffered sickness, unemployment, and have gone through the face-losing experience of applying for relief checks and county help for medical care. Edna at the time of the interview was emotionally flattened out and apathetic from worry and overwork. Swen, too, who before induction was away from home much of the time as itinerant truck driver, has had many long hours to think over the debts and obligations which were piling up against him. The children are sickly in appearance and to the interviewer acted tongue-tied in contrast with the noisy children in other homes. The children are regarded by visitors as mannerly because of their strangely quiet and deferent mien.

Edna was reared in a family of nine children. She married Swen, an easygoing, Danish-born itinerant laborer, at seventeen after two years of courtship. Her family disapproved of the marriage because they needed her wages from the sawmill and her housekeeping services at home. Against Swen's wishes she took a job as waitress after they were married, something they still disagree on. Swen, though easy to live with, was inclined to change jobs frequently, and the period between jobs was hard to finance. Edna resented this occupational mobility and Swen's affinity for his relatives who would occasionally drop in to board for an indefinite period. The Swensons never seemed to catch up financially even with Edna working and after the children came, Swen found it necessary to go to the county relief office to get help to pay for the medical care the children needed. At one time, all four family members were sick and their credit was so poor that no physician would come to see them until the relief office had given its approval. During this period of stress no church organization came to their aid and no social service agency learned of their plight. They were forced to take the pauper's oath to qualify for the badly needed medical care and food. Despite all this train of troubles there is no record that the family unity within the Swenson family was ever seriously threatened. They gave no hint that they have ever considered separation or divorce. "If I had the insurance, suicide might have been more helpful," commented Swen.

With these many evidences of high family adequacy, high adaptability, and high integration, combined with excellent marital adjustment, one would expect that the adjustment of the Swensons to separation would be good and that their adjustment to reunion would be excellent. It was not to be expected that Edna would make a closed-ranks adjustment, but that she and the children would adjust to Swen's absence by keeping his roles intact within the family, writing him and continuing his place in the circle.

Actually, we underestimated the impact of the hardships which the absence of Swen would bring to the Swensons. Edna reported that she was only half a parent, that the job of working and caring for the children was too much for her. She didn't sleep nights worrying about Swen who was overseas in the Normandy invasion. The physician decided her eldest daughter should be sent to Iowa City for a prolonged hospitalization for rheumatic fever, and Edna had no funds to visit her. Edna became anxiety ridden and depressive, beaten by the tasks facing her. On the positive side Swen and Edna wrote daily progress reports and although his advice was always too late to be acted upon, Edna always asked for it whenever issues arose. After he was wounded in Normandy Swen sent a photograph of himself to show that he had no limbs missing. Edna gave the children a daily account of what "daddy" was doing and the children talked of it in their play, reëxperiencing their daddy by living with him at camp. Swen remained overseas altogether fifteen months and was almost eighteen months without seeing his family. The adjustment to separation made by the family in his absence was judged to be only fair because of its effects on Edna and the children, and the deprivation which accompanied it.

Reunion, on the other hand, has proved most satisfying to this Job-like family. Swen's return was anticipated by the children. He paid a visit to the daughter in Iowa City on the way back and brought her home, too, a week later. Thanks to the wife's coaching and the children's love for him, he claimed he felt completely back in the harness as "father of the family" in a matter of days. He shifted from his old job of truck driving to work in the roundhouse which was a more permanent position, although it involves working nights and is awkward for sleeping. He yearns for a farm but the GI Bill won't help him. Plans are being made to remodel the house when the doctor bills are paid. Both hope for better days, but they have had so much adversity that they don't expect easy going ahead financially.

The explanation for this family's fair adjustment to separation probably lies in the number and severity of hardships experienced and the inadequacy of the wife and children to face crisis without the husband's presence and emotional support. Highly integrated families adjust better to reunion than to dismemberment because the family is accustomed to operate with all members present. Taken together, the poverty of economic resources, the lack of credit and margin, and the absence of kinfolk meant that this family's superb social-psychological resources were not enough when adversity hit. Perhaps the surprising thing is that this family which had been victimized before induction by sickness and impoverishment did as well in the face of separation as it did. Every family has its breaking point! The Swensons survived a pre-induction series of crisis well, rode out the separation intact social-psychologically although weakened physically, and have achieved a superb reunion adjustment. The determination to succeed as a family was never mentioned in the interview, but it is undoubtedly a significant factor in the success of this family. It was an unspoken assumption that nothing can break us up! In future studies the hypothesis should be tested that: Families that have been badly used by trial and circumstance but include in their definition of marriage the expressed or unexpressed assumption of permanence and successful persistence of the marriage relation succeed best in the face of crisis.

CASE VIII. Deviant as Judged by Statistical Scores—A Family Which Made only a Fair Adjustment to Separation Despite High Family Adequacy and Moderately High Scores on Statistically Important Factors

Harvey and Iris Brownell and Two Children

The Brownells are hard-working, God-fearing Baptists, an affectionate and closely integrated family that take all their pleasures in the home. Mrs. Brownell is a shy, timid woman for whom marriage has been a haven from an extremely unhappy parental home. As a young girl she was extremely shy, and when her mother remarried, her stepfather made it clear that she was an unwanted member of the new household. What little social poise she had was thereby struck a mortal blow. There were some of the elements of escape in her marriage to a grade-school sweetheart from the same working-class neighborhood after she finished high school. She has received from her husband the love and security she had always longed for. The Brownells were a tightly knit family and built all their plans around the two children. When Harvey was laid off during the depression just after their first child was born, it became necessary to live with his parents for a while. They did not adjust well to this new situation, and there was conflict between them for the first time. With his reëmployment, however, their earlier closely knit pattern of family life was resumed.

The statistical scores for the Brownells are moderately high on marital adjustment, adaptability, and integration. The family adequacy score is five. The family presents a picture of resources quite adequate to meet a separation and reunion crisis situation. We would expect from these resources that Iris would be able to manage the home and the children pretty well, although she would miss Harvey acutely and depend very much on his letters for strength and support. The reunion would be a joyous event for all concerned, and family life would probably be picked up where it had been left at the time of the separation.

Instead of buckling down to the job of keeping the family going while Harvey was away, however, Iris just let things go. She felt that she was just existing without her husband in the family circle and regarded her life until he should return simply as a very dull waiting period. Harvey's letters were her only source of excitement. She tried to give more attention to the children but found that they were no substitute at all for Harvey. They were living in a small temporary house that had been hurriedly put up before Harvey left for service so the family would have a place to live in his absence. Iris complained constantly about its inadequacies and about repairs that needed to be done, but made no attempt to do anything herself or get outside assistance. She was completely unable to keep her family going with their reduced income and so went into debt. There had been no reunion at the time of the interview, so no information is available about the actual reunion as compared to the expected. Even in view of the poor separation adjustment, however, it would still be possible for the family to make a good reunion adjustment and resume its previous way of life.

Why does this family, which seems to have all the ingredients for good adjustment, fail to adjust to a difficult situation? The answer seems to be that they don't know how to *use* the resources that they have—the family lacks *savoir-faire*. This is something that none of the scales used in the study were designed to measure, but as illustrated here it may be an important factor in adjustment to crisis. A family may be very closely knit and adaptable within the narrow limits of a familiar situation. The members may even have worked out a series of interchangeable roles which carries them through the ordinary exigencies of life, and yet not know how to put this pattern to use in a completely new situation. Families, in order to survive successfully in the rapidly changing world of today, must be able to use the resources they have in as many different ways as there are situations which they may be called upon to face. Some measurement of this factor certainly should be attempted—the capacity as a family to attack an unfamiliar problem, break it down into its components, work out a solution, and carry it out. The readiness to change roles, to face changed situations, and to use the consultative process in working out family solutions is approximated in our measurement of family adaptability, but the capacity as a family to solve the problem implied by the term savoir-faire is something different. A suggested hypothesis for future testing might be the following: Adequate resources are not alone sufficient to produce a good adjustment to crisis unless accompanied by savoir-faire, or the ability to utilize one's resources effectively.

Case IX. Deviant as Judged by Statistical Scores—A Family Which Adjusted Well to Separation Despite Low Scores on Statistically Important Factors

Donald and Margaret Coons and Three Children

The Coons are the kind of family that make up the solid core of every Midwestern community. Moderately integrated, with the husband and father dominant in the family and his wife willingly playing a complementary role, the family is a fairly self-sufficient unit, and parents and children have good times together.

Both Donald and Margaret were reared on farms, and went to high school together. Donald was already earning his own living in high school, having revolted against his father with whom he could not get along. Margaret left high school at the end of her junior year in order to marry him, well prepared as the middle child of eight brothers and sisters for the give and take of family living. There was little money during the depression years, but they both wanted children and settled down to having them as soon as possible. They were just beginning to get ahead financially when the war came, and Donald enlisted in the Seabees to prevent being drafted.

The family has low statistical scores on the scales for marital adjustment, adaptability, and integration. The family adequacy score indicates a much "sounder" family than the statistical scores, with a rating of five. Since the adequacy score captures many of the elements of family life which the statistical scores omit, it is not surprising that the adequacy rating is occasionally more accurate than the statistical scores, although the reverse is also sometimes true. According to the statistical scores, the family would not make a good adjustment to separation, but would either live in a state of suspension or become actively disorganized while the husband was gone. There would presumably be difficulty in fitting the husband back into the home when he returned, too.

Margaret had "cried it out" before Donald left, and although she missed him very much she settled down to do the best job she could for her family until he should return. Their income was cut almost in half but Margaret never mentioned this as a problem—she had had plenty of experience in doing without during the depression and simply made out with what she had. Donald had enjoyed being the dominant member of the family and she had become used to leaning on him for decisions and letting him handle the children's problems. Consequently, it was hard for her to do these things alone. But like most family routines they needed to be done, and she developed in the process a new-found independence and initiative. The children adjusted well to Margaret's assumption of authority. Letters between Donald and Margaret were full of family news. There was little worrying about or planning for the future because both felt that nothing much could be done until he returned. They would manage that problem when it arose as they had managed all their other problems in the past.

The reunion turned into a family honeymoon at home, with Donald sticking close to the family until he was satisfied that they were all back in the groove again. Margaret was delighted to resume her old role of dependence and relax a bit after the strain of her earlier responsibilities. Donald went into a new line of work which he found more congenial than his old job, and the family is functioning now as if there had never been a crisis.

Whether one accepts the statistical scores or the adequacy rating for this family, one contrast between this case and the preceding one stands out sharply. Though the Brownells had both high statistical scores and high family adequacy scores, they just didn't know how to use the resources they had. The Coons, with fewer resources, somehow had the techniques for squeezing through a tight spot— they had the savoir-faire that the Brownells lacked!

CASE X. Deviant as Judged by Case History Materials—A Family Which Adjusted Well to Separation and Reunion Despite Low Family Adequacy Scores

Fred and Alma Van Wagoner and One Child

The Van Wagoners at induction were regarded as immature by associates, interested primarily in dancing, partying, and youth-centered activities, despite the presence within their home of a fine five-year-old son. Their social status was lower class. Fred's wages were only $180.00

a month, but he has been adamantly set against Alma working. She has been closer to the child than Fred, and has assumed slightly more responsibility in the home operations. Fred has been particularly irresponsible in housekeeping and managerial tasks, and there has been serious disagreement on the handling of finances.

Fred and Alma married at eighteen after an eight-month's courtship. Both left school before graduating—Fred in the 9th grade. They spent his wages as a common laborer in a feed mill on dances, shows, and furniture. Early in the marriage Fred ran around with a "fast" bunch (by his wife's definition). Alma was an independent person and would often stalk off to dances by herself after a quarrel. While both were still reluctant to settle down Alma found she was pregnant. She had a hard time in childbirth and developed serious complications. Fred matured markedly in the emergency and treated her with consideration. She reported he spent all the time he could with her. Nevertheless, they remained an individualistic trio, husband, wife, and child, not too cooperative and not too well integrated as a family.

From the moderately high statistical scores on adaptability, integration, and marital adjustment, we would expect a fairly high adjustment to separation for the Van Wagoners, but the family adequacy ratings from the case study are low and the prediction from the case materials is for a fair or poor adjustment to separation and a poor reunion. It will be expected that the adjustment in separation will be a poor one of the closed-ranks type.

The actual adjustment was good, rapid, and quite satisfying from Alma's standpoint. Fred and Alma sold their belongings before Fred left and arranged for Alma to move in with Fred's family. Without so much as shifting gears, Fred's folks took over the grandchild and added him to their brood. Alma was freed to step out, to go partying, to work, to do many of the things Fred had objected to before his departure. Although he wrote that he worried about Alma stepping out on him, he made it no issue, and eventually she said, "I got it out of my system." She felt little desire to be dependent again, and expressed no sense of interdependence. Affectionally, Alma reported she felt indifferent toward Fred for six months before he returned, and then she began to get twinges of desire for him. Fred's love for her remained constant throughout the separation, he reported. There was never any talk of divorce or alienation in any of their letters; they were simply highly individuated, independent persons who were enjoying their vacation from one another. As reunion approached both showed interest in planning for future living quarters, and neither showed regret that their partying days were over. There was an uneventful reunion, a few difficulties in making over an abandoned filling station into an apartment, but Fred demonstrated his Navy-learned housekeeping skills in helping put up the curtains and in keeping the place shipshape. He was inclined to be pleasant but authoritative in dealing with Bud, the six-year-old, and there has been no problem of acceptance there. The impression is that both Fred and Alma have found themselves as parents at last and are prepared to grow in accepting family responsibilities instead of fighting them as they have in the past.

One is tempted in explaining the deviations of this family to ascribe to increasing maturity the major credit. The presence of in-laws contributed greatly, to be sure, but there were major growth changes too. Married young, Fred and Alma's developmental interests remained those of teen-agers, and their marriage reflected the adolescent's desire for new adventure, for variety of experience, and for good times. Fred obtained his fill of new experience in the Philippines and yearned for his job at the feed mill after a stint of four hours on and four hours off on a windy, cold deck on convoy duty. Alma too outgrew her adolescent yearnings for new experience and the freedom to come and go at will. Moreover, the in-laws adroitly managed to give her added responsibility as it became apparent that she could take it. She helped tend Fred's brothers and sisters who were about the same age as her son, and learned the role of mother under friendly supervision. The case worker interviewing this family closed the case with the statement, "I feel this couple gradually acquired adulthood during the separation, and each furlough contributed to their increasing maturity. In the reunion they have demonstrated ingenuity in the furniture they have made, the curtains they have fashioned from cheap material, and they are planning coöperatively as they never did before the separation. They are just beginning to find their own capabilities." Angell (1), in his study of impoverishment crises, has also referred to this internal growth within families which sometimes changes their capacity to handle new situations and which upsets the predictions made for these families before the growth took place.

Phrased as a hypothesis our explanation of the better-than-expected adjustments achieved by the Van Wagoners might read: Families tend to succeed better than expected in crisis in which one or both of the spouses has been delayed in maturing and/or is developmentally ripe for a maturational spurt which the crisis precipitates.

DISCUSSION OF RESULTS

We have just depicted ten unpredictable family careers in the face of crisis. On six of the deviant families discussed, both case study and statistical method agreed concerning the magnitude of deviation from the expected. The last four cases discussed were drawn from a pool of fifteen deviants identified by case study procedures and from a pool of thirty-one deviants identified by statistical procedures on which the two methods did not agree as to the magnitude of the deviation from the expected. These four cases were selected because the explanations of their deviations could be formulated into useful hypotheses which did not duplicate any of the other hypotheses obtained from the first six cases presented.

The experience of analyzing the family histories of our unpredictable families has been a heady one. One needs to be wary of explanations made after the fact, particularly when they are advanced as generalizations. In our case we are asking that these explanations be studied in future projects as hypotheses to see if they add purchase to the baffling problem of predicting the behavior of individual families from the generalizations which hold for most families.

In all but two cases (II and VI), the materials in the files provided new information which partially explained the deviations from the expected. The ten deviants analyzed are disproportionately made up of families which adjusted better to separation and/or reunion than expected. Only three families (Cases II, VII, and VIII) of the ten did less well than could have been predicted from their family adequacy and statistically important scores. In one of these cases (VII) the deviation would not have occurred had the scores for adjustment to separation been corrected for the number and severity of hardships incurred. In another of the three cases (II) the deviation could have been predicted had the bizarre behavior of the absent member been known. His personal inadequacy created a situation to which a family of high integration would have reacted precisely as this one did. This leaves only one case out of the ten in which a family of good resources was found incapable of meeting the crises of separation and reunion adjustively.

A second look at the family resources of the ten deviants analyzed shows that most of the deviants are drawn from poorly endowed families with respect to family adequacy and/or family adaptability, family integration, and good marital adjustment (Cases I, II, IV, V, VI, IX, and X). We confirm Angell (*1*) in his study of families responding to impoverishment in which he found that his most unpredictable cases were disproportionately in the families of low integration and low adaptability. They yielded to the crisis in a variety of ways, sometimes making interesting adaptations of which they did not appear capable. Because we are dealing with deviant families only, in this analysis we differ with Angell's findings in so far as our lowly endowed families all do better than we predicted, rather than less well than expected.

The analysis of the fifty-two deviant families, ten of which have been presented here, has been rewarding. We can conclude that the method is worthy of continued exploration. This is indeed an area in which the case study and the statistical method can be teamed profitably.

Validating Statistical Scales and Checking Family Types

The findings from the case study method and the findings from the statistical approach can stand on their own feet, and usually do without challenging one another. One of the unique features of this study is to bring them together to compare results from statistical scales with results from configurational judgments. Four variables have been central to the study: adjustment to separation, adjustment to reunion, family adaptability, and family integration. In the statistical section of the research these variables have been measured by means of scales prepared especially for the study of families in crisis. (For a detailed discussion, see the methodological note in Appendix B, pp. 368–383.) In the case study section of the research these four variables have been broken down into ordered types or classifications. (See Chapter IV, pp. 74–99, and Chapter VII, pp. 261–263, for details.) We propose to join the results of these two methods in this chapter to see how much agreement there is between the scores obtained by the statistical scales and the types obtained through the intuitive pigeonholing of families into ordered types, drawing primarily on the dynamic materials in the family history.

ADJUSTMENT TO SEPARATION

The statistical scale measuring adjustment to separation was checked by the wife and a score was given to the family based on the average of all the scores received for adjustment in five areas of family life: husband-wife relationships, father-child relationships, and child-father relationships; adequacy of reallocation of roles within the family occasioned by the husband's absence; satisfaction with the marriage now a redefinition is possible; relationships with in-laws, relatives, friends, and neighbors; and evidences of planning for the reunion. The pigeonholing of the family into a type of adjustment to separation by means of the case study method involved reading each family history to assess the dynamics of reality facing, the redistribution of roles so that needs of family members can be met, and the absence of emotional tension and threats to the family fabric as the adjustment is stabilized. Table 21 illustrates how closely the two methods agree in their ordering of 135 families. The extent of agreement is not phenomenal, but it could hardly be accounted

TABLE 21. Distribution of 135 Families by Type of Adjustment to Separation Cross-Classified by Their Scores on the Adjustment to Separation Scale

Adjustment to Separation Score (From statistical scale)	Type of Adjustment to Separation (Classified from case study materials)				
	Poor Adjustment	Fair Adjustment	Good, Slow Adjustment	Good, Rapid Adjustment	Total
4.5–4.9	0	1	0	5	6
4.0–4.4	3	1	11	26	41
3.5–3.9	2	13	16	28	59
3.0–3.4	3	5	7	9	24
1.0–2.9	0	2	0	3	5
Total	8	22	34	71	135
Average Adjustment to Separation Score	3.63	3.59	3.73	3.83	3.72

for by chance, probabilities being less than one in a hundred. It is quite possible that neither method of measurement is sufficiently precise to expect a larger confirmation that they are both measuring the same phenomenon. This is another step along our research trail where we would leave perfectionists behind.

ADJUSTMENT TO REUNION

The statistical scales measuring adjustment to reunion were checked by both husband and wife and an average of the two made the family score. The scale touched on husband-wife relationships, the division of labor within the home, the reallocation of roles, the father-child relationships, and the areas of conflict which are apt to crop up in reunion. The case study attempts at classifying reunion were unsuccessful in producing more than two types of adjustments: good adjustment to reunion and poor adjustment to reunion. Effective role reorganization was one clue to good adjustment. The re-opening of the family circle to absorb the father, renewal of husband-wife marital ties, and the growth and development of all family members were also items important in classifying families by type of adjustment to reunion. Table 22 indicates the extent of agreement between the two methods in ordering the classification of 114 families by type of reunion adjustment experienced. There is far greater correspondence between the two methods on reunion than on sepa-

TABLE 22. Distribution of 114 Families by Type of Adjustment to Reunion Cross-Classified by Their Scores on the Adjustment to Reunion Scale

Adjustment to Reunion Score (From statistical scale)	Type of Adjustment to Reunion (Classified from case study materials)		
	Poor Adjustment	Good Adjustment	Total
4.74–4.99	0	21	21
4.50–4.74	4	36	40
4.00–4.49	7	27	34
3.00–3.99	5	7	12
1.00–2.99	7	0	7
Total	23	91	114
Average Adjustment to Reunion Score	3.50	4.48	4.21

ration adjustment, but the agreement is probably insufficient to validate the scale. Even though the case study classifications are predicted nicely by the scale, there is evidence from other sections of the study that it should be sharpened and expanded before we can be sure it differentiates adequately between well-adjusted and poorly-adjusted families reunionwise. One might be justified from inspection of Table 22, however, in saying that the two methods of ordering families were shooting at the same target.

FAMILY ADAPTABILITY AND FAMILY INTEGRATION

In the statistical section of the study our 135 families were rated by interviewers on adaptability and integration by means of two scales developed by Cavan (10) for the restudy of Angell's (1) families by a Committee on Evaluation of Research of the Social Science Research Council.[4] Since two interviewers did most of the interviewing, the differences in judgment were kept at a minimum. In the case study section of the study Mrs. Boulding classified the families into

TABLE 23. Distribution of 135 Families Classified by Degree of Adaptability Cross-Classified by Their Scores on the Scale for Family Adaptability

Family Adaptability Score (From statistical scale)	Extent of Adaptability (Classified from case study materials)			
	Unadaptable	Moderately Adaptable	Very Adaptable	Total
19.4–25.0	1	20	17	38
16.5–19.3	7	37	12	56
9.0–16.4	13	27	1	41
Total	21	84	30	135
Average Adaptability Score	15.4	17.5	20.0	17.7

three constructed family types for adaptability (Unadaptable, Moderately Adaptable, and Very Adaptable) and into three types for integration (Unintegrated, Moderately Integrated, and Very Integrated) following carefully the definitions worked out by Angell (1). Mrs. Boulding made full use of the story of growth and development recorded in the family history in arriving at her family types. Table 23 and Table 24 show the extent of agreement between the statistical scores for families on adaptability and integration and the pigeonholing of families into empirical family types by case study analysis. The moderately adaptable type is most variable in the scores it receives on the statistical scale, and this is true of moderate integration too. There is more agreement on the families which are very adaptable or unadaptable, and very integrated or unintegrated.

[4] For a full discussion of the methods of measuring validity and reliability of these scales, see the Methodological Note, Appendix B, pp. 379–381. Copies of the scales appear in Appendix C, pp. 424–428.

There is a very low probability that the association is due to chance. The tables could probably be used, if we were so minded, to prove that the two methods have measured in this instance the same phenomena of adaptability and integration. This is an exploratory use of the findings from the two studies and the material probably does not warrant more involved statistical treatment.

TABLE 24. Distribution of 135 Families Classified by Degree of Integration Cross-Classified by Their Scores on the Scale for Family Integration

Family Integration Score (From statistical scale)	Extent of Integration (Classified from case study materials)			
	Unintegrated	Moderately Integrated	Very Integrated	Total
19.1–25.0	0	10	26	36
16.8–19.0	4	34	21	59
7.5–16.7	25	11	4	40
Total	29	55	51	135
Average Integration Score	13.5	17.7	19.3	17.4

We can carry the analysis one step further in Table 25 by comparing the statistical family types achieved by trisecting the distribution of scores on adaptability and integration and then cross-classifying families with the constructed family types built by combining these same attributes as patterns of family organization by the case approach. The nine possible combinations, abbreviated in the table, are readily comparable: High Integration–High Adaptability (HI-HA), High Integration–Moderate Adaptability (HI-MA), Moderate Integration–High Adaptability (MI-HA), Moderate Integration–Moderate Adaptability (MI-MA), High Integration–Low Adaptability (HI-LA), Moderate Integration–Low Adaptability (MI-LA), Low Integration–High Adaptability (LI-HA), Low Integration–Moderate Adaptability (LI-MA), Low Integration–Low Adaptability (LI-LA). When one considers the arbitrariness with

TABLE 25. Distribution of 135 Families by Statistical Family Types on Combinations of Integration and Adaptability Cross-Classified by Constructed Family Types Combined on the Same Factors by Case Study Methods

Statistical Family Types (Based on scales for adaptability and integration)	Constructed Family Types (Based on case study classifications)									Total	Number of Cases with More Than One Step Disagreement
	HI-HA	HI-MA	MI-HA	MI-MA	HI-LA	MI-LA	LI-HA	LI-MA	LI-LA		
HI-HA	5	5	2	1	0	0	0	0	0	13	None
HI-MA	4	5	1	5	1	0	0	0	0	16	None
MI-HA	5	6	4	5	0	1	0	0	1	22	Two
MI-MA	3	6	5	10	0	4	0	2	0	30	None
HI-LA	0	4	0	1	1	1	0	0	0	7	None
MI-LA	0	1	0	5	0	1	0	0	0	7	None
LI-HA	1	0	0	1	0	0	0	1	0	3	One
LI-MA	0	2	0	3	0	1	0	3	1	10	Two
LI-LA	0	1	1	5	0	10	0	0	10	27	Two
	18	30	13	36	2	18	0	6	12	135	Seven

which families were assigned a position in the statistical family types (for details see pp. 160–169), it is reassuring to discover the relatively close agreement they achieve with Mrs. Boulding's classification of the same families through the careful reading of the case histories. In only seven instances did Mrs. Boulding's intuitive classification of a family differ by more than one step in either direction from the statistically derived classifications. The statistical family types which gave trouble were Moderate Integration–High Adaptability, and the three combinations of adaptability which were linked with low integration, LI-HA, LI-MA, and LI-LA. Angell (*1*) found difficult the classifying and predicting of family combinations involving low integration and termed them amorphous and formless.[5]

From an analysis of Table 25 one might feel justified in discounting our original qualms about the method used to identify the statistical family types combining integration and adaptability. Certainly there is a close correspondence with the classifications achieved by the more time-consuming method of constructing types from the case histories. In this instance the statistical method may show some advantages over the more laborious case study method. In any event our results have encouraged us to move ahead with the standardization of the scales for adaptability and integration for use in future studies of family adjustment.

OTHER POSSIBLE COMPARISONS

Three other variables used both in the statistical and in the case study analysis which might be compared are. marital adjustment, social class status, and types of family control. In the statistical study

[5] It is interesting that both Angell working with families facing impoverishment and Boulding classifying families facing war separation found it impossible to locate any Low Integration–High Adaptability type families. It was possible to identify three such families by means of the statistical method, but there is some doubt concerning even these three. Mrs. Boulding disagrees with the classification of one of these famililes by more than two steps, claiming it is a combination of High Integration and High Adaptability rather than a LI-HA type.

scales were used by which families were scored along a continuum for both marital adjustment and social class status. The case study utilized interview data and narrations from the family history as the basis for categorizing families into ordered types. In the interest of economy of space this comparative analysis will not be carried out here.

Our attempts to compare types of family control broke down when we discovered that the two methods had not used the same definitions in setting up their family types. The statistical method utilized evidences of dominance-submission in the husband-wife relationship in four areas: in personal aggressiveness, in freedom allowed the wife to deviate from traditional social roles of wife and mother, in control of the purse strings, and in settling disagreements. The case study method included parent-child as well as husband-wife relationships and considered the processes of arriving at decisions in typing the family. We have, therefore, abandoned any attempt at a validation of the types of family control constructed by the two methods.

Verification of Findings from Two Methods Wherever They Are Comparable

The division of labor agreed upon for the two methods of study has resulted in relatively little overlapping of factors studied. Wherever the two methods did cover the same ground, however, we took care not to bias our results by conferring about findings during the period of tabulation and actual analysis. So far as we know, if the findings in these common areas support one another, the confirmation arises from the data and not from any collusion in that direction.[6]

The division of labor adhered to by the analysis using the two methods was such that there are no comparable findings concerning

[6] See the Methodological Note, Appendix B, for an account of the division of labor assigned for the two methods, pp. 394–396.

childhood experiences of spouses, courtship experiences, readiness for marriage at marriage, social and personal roles in marriage, or occupational make-up. Comparable findings are revealed concerning the relative importance of types of family organization, social class position, family size, experiences in separation and in reunion, and wife self-sufficiency, as they severally appear to affect family adjustment to war separation and peace reunion. We will discuss them in parallel columns with appropriate comments showing whether they verify or cast question upon the generalization reached.

TABLE 26.   A Comparison of Findings from Statistical and Case Study Analysis

Findings from Statistical Analysis	*Findings from Case Study Analysis*
Social Class Status: measured by statistical scale filled out by interviewers; moderately and positively related to separation adjustment but not to reunion adjustment	Social Class Status: assigned by analyst from interview data; lower-upper and upper-middle class most frequently adjusted to separation and to reunion
Family Size: negatively related to separation and to reunion adjustment	Family Size: no differences observed as between one-child families and multi-child families in adjustment to crisis
Types of Family Control: obtained through indices of husband-wife balance of power; randomly distributed so far as success in separation and reunion go	Types of Family Control: designated by husband-wife and parent-children relationships; democratic clearly superior, modified patriarchal and modified matriarchal excellent, equalitarian adult-centered less frequently good, and the pure patriarchal cases poor in adjustment to both separation and reunion
Marital Adjustment: obtained through scale; positively related to adjustment in both crises, by partial as well as simple correlation analysis	Marital Adjustment: designated by reading cases; more important for reunion than separation—good maritally adjusted did well in both crises, poorly endowed did next best, and fair adjustment were most vulnerable to separation and reunion crises

TABLE 26.   A Comparison of Findings from Statistical and
Case Study Analysis (*Continued*)

Findings from Statistical Analysis	*Findings from Case Study Analysis*
Family Adaptability: obtained through scale; positively related to adjustment to separation, but in partial correlation analysis unimportant as factor in reunion	Family Adaptability: constructed from same definitions as statistical scale; most important single factor for adjustment to both crises, and more important for reunion than separation
Family Integration: obtained through scale; highly related to adjustment to reunion, but in partial correlation analysis unimportant as factor in separation	Family Integration: constructed from same definitions as statistical scale; more important for reunion than separation adjustment success
Hardships of Separation: obtained by weighting number of hardships experienced in separation; negatively related to success in separation adjustment	Hardships of Separation: obtained by taking into account number and severity of hardships experienced as well as family's definition of hardships; negatively related to success in separation adjustment
Adequacy of Communication Between Husband and Family During Separation: obtained by rating content of letters; positively related to adjustment to both crises	Adequacy of Communication Between Husband and Family During Separation: obtained by taking into account gifts, letters, types of decisions achieved by correspondence; positively related to adjustment to both crises
Wife's Self-Sufficiency: obtained by weighting all evidences of self-reliance, independence, and scoring the wife; curvilinear association to good adjustment to separation and to reunion, showing moderate self-sufficiency better than either high or low self-dependence	Wife's Self-Sufficiency: wife's sense of independence or dependence not important unless wife gave evidence she was enjoying new independence, in which cases there was a good separation, but a poor reunion
Types of Affectional Outlet During Separation (Wife): important in determining separation but not reunion adjustment; best when affections were focused on combinations involving women or her children, poorest when any combination involving men appeared	Types of Affectional Outlet During Separation (Wife): important that outlet be children, no others appeared significant; important only for separation adjustment

TABLE 26.   A Comparison of Findings from Statistical and
Case Study Analysis (*Continued*)

Findings from Statistical Analysis	*Findings from Case Study Analysis*
Hardships of Reunion: obtained by weighting number of hardships experienced in reunion; highly important negatively in affecting adequacy of reunion adjustment	Hardships of Reunion: obtained by taking into account number and severity of hardships experienced as well as the family's definitions of the situation; an important factor in achieving good adjustment to reunion

DISCUSSION OF RESULTS

Out of a total of sixty-five factors studied by statistical methods and roughly forty items studied by the techniques of case study, we found eleven areas in which we had covered, sufficiently, precisely the same territory to warrant a comparison of findings. The burning question is: If we use different methods for classifying and pigeonholing families by types of adjustment to separation and reunion and different techniques for ranking families by their characteristics and properties, will we get corroborating or conflicting findings?

A review of the parallel columns in Table 26 shows us that there was a confirmation of generalizations reached in five out of eleven factors: Social Class Status, Family Integration, Hardships of Separation, Adequacy of Communication, and Hardships of Reunion. Partial mutual corroboration of findings was apparent in three of the remaining variables: Marital Adjustment, Family Adaptability, and Types of Affectional Outlet During Separation. In only three instances of covering the same areas were the findings clearly in conflict or not at least partially corroborated: Family Size, Types of Family Control, and Wife's Self-Sufficiency.

These corroborations are enheartening, indeed, and further support our conviction that case study and statistical methods can be teamed in the same study for mutual strengthening. The stability of our results will be given a further test in the next chapter where our findings will be compared with those of several other representative studies of families in crisis.

SUMMARY

This chapter has struggled with a difficult task—the rapprochement within one study of two competitive approaches to research, the statistical and the case study methods. The two have been permitted in the rest of the study to operate independently in the areas for which they are best designed, the statistical dealing with the statics and the case study with the dynamics of family organization and adjustment. In this chapter an attempt has been made to explore means for yoking the two methods for mutual advantage. Covering the same ground and dealing with some of the same data, but approaching them differently, the statistical and case analyses have been tested against one another.

One method of teaming the two approaches has been to locate by statistical devices and explain by means of case history delving, the deviant families and their unorthodox behavior when faced with crisis. Thirty-seven families were identified as unpredictable from the statistical records and twenty-one such families were segregated from the case study files. They were poorly equipped for crisis yet thrived—or were well equipped for crisis yet cracked up in the face of separation and reunion. The two methods agreed completely on the branding of six families as unpredictables, and were in close agreement on more than half of the other forty-six deviants. The six families on which there was complete agreement and four others selected as illustrative of the range of explanations for deviant conduct have been analyzed in this chapter. Most of the deviants were found to be lowly endowed families with respect to family adequacy and/or family adaptability, family integration, and marital adjustment achievements, who performed better than expected in the face of separation and reunion crises. Only three families who were highly endowed in these resources made lower-than-expected scores on adjustment to separation and reunion. A careful review of the case histories provided many provocative hunches which can be regarded as partial explanations of the deviant conduct of these families. One needs to be wary of all explanations made after the fact, particularly if they are advanced as generalizations. We are suggesting that these explanations be treated in future research projects as hypotheses to see if they do not add purchase on the baffling problem of predicting the behavior of individual families from the generalizations which have been made for most families. Phrased as hypotheses, these explanations are as follows:

1. Those families in which the wife and mother is relatively irresponsible or excessively dependent and the father is dominant and responsible will succeed best in adjusting to separation if kinfolk or substitutes are accessible and willing to assume the father's managerial and decision-making roles during his absence.

2. Closely related to the first hypothesis, but more general and less circumscribed, is the second hypothesis: A family which has inadequate internal resources can make a good adjustment to crisis if it can draw on the resources of other families or agencies, whether it be on the basis of friendship, blood relationship, or simply a business or client relationship.

3. When a key family member has an inadequate personal adjustment, a crisis of dismemberment that deprives the maladjusted member of the family's resources may result in his further deterioration and spread to produce disorganization of the entire family unit.

4. When maladjustment or disorganization has occurred in a family as a result of the failure of the social environment to meet certain deep-seated needs of one or more individuals in the family, a change in the direction of a more favorable social environment for those individuals may set in motion a beneficent cycle which enables them to function more effectively in the family unit so that

an improved level of adjustment is achieved by the entire family.

5. Families that have been badly used by trial and circumstance but include in their definition of marriage the expressed or unexpressed assumption of permanence and successful persistence of the marriage relation succeed best in the face of crisis.

6. Adequate resources are not by themselves sufficient to produce a good family adjustment to crisis unless accompanied by savoir-faire, the ability to utilize family resources effectively. Reversely, families meagerly endowed may nevertheless make expedient and successful adjustments to crisis by the "know-how" of problem solving, utilizing effectively the few resources at their disposal.

7. Families tend to succeed better than expected in crisis in which one or both of the spouses has been delayed in maturing and/or is developmentally ripe for a maturational spurt which the crisis precipitates.

A second mode of utilizing the strengths of the case study to offset the weaknesses of the statistical method is to use the former to validate results from statistical scales against the judgments from reading the family histories. Our crude nonstandardized scales for measuring adjustment to separation, adjustment to reunion, family adaptability, and family integration have been partially validated in this chapter by evidence of fairly close agreement with the judgments made concerning the separation, reunion, adaptability, and integration attainments of the same families from the case study analysis. All four scales were shown to be in substantial agreement with the ratings made from the case records. In order of correspondence family integration comes first, family adaptability second, adjustment to reunion third, and adjustment to separation last. The amount of agreement between the scores achieved by the statistical scales and the case study classifications may not be sufficient to validate the scales but they certainly indicate the two methods of ordering families are aiming at the same objective.

A variation of the attempt to validate statistical scales with ratings from an internal analysis of the case histories is a comparison made between the statistical family types achieved by trisecting the distribution of scores on adaptability and integration and then by cross-classifying families, with the constructed family types built by combining these same attributes as patterns of family organization by the case approach. In this instance nine statistical family types correspond, in name at least, with nine constructed family types involving combinations of adaptability and integration components. When all 135 families had been pigeonholed in their appropriate cells, it was found that the correspondence between the two methods of classification was very close. In only seven out of 135 families were there evidences of differences of judgment involving more than one step in any direction. Our results would argue for the further standardization of the scales for family integration and family adaptability and their use in future studies of family adjustment.

A third system of illustrating the complementary nature of the two methods is to compare findings wherever they are comparable and account, if possible, for any differences which crop up. The sixty-five factors studied statistically and the manifold areas probed by the case study overlapped on eleven different points. When the results in those common areas were examined, it was found that the findings from the two methods were mutually corroborated in five areas. When one takes into consideration the differences in approach and the distinctly unfriendly origins claimed by the two methods, the results of this analysis are encouraging for an approaching marriage of these two ways of doing research—the case study and the statistical approach.

CHAPTER IX

RETROSPECT AND SYNTHESIS

IN the eight chapters covered thus far we have presented in sequence: (1) the context of our study with respect both to other
pieces of research and to the universe of social situations facing families, (2) the make-up of the families which coöperated with us,
(3) the crises they experienced during the period of study, and (4)
the evidence that certain types of families have proved themselves
better equipped to meet crises than others differently endowed. We
have attempted in this broad survey also to share our research procedures wherever it seemed appropriate, but we have reserved discussion of the technical aspects of our methodology for a methodological note in Appendix B.

In quick overview, we have attempted to control some of the individual differences between families by selecting 135 families for the
study, all of whom are Iowa residents, of unbroken homes, containing at least one child over four years of age; all of whom have also
experienced the crisis of wartime separation, and most of whom have
also experienced the critical adjustments of reunion. We have followed carefully the histories of these 135 families faced with the
temporary loss of the husband and father through military service
as they reorganized and carried on without him, most families looking forward to his return and finally reuniting. For most of these
families separation was defined as a crisis, though not an insurmountable one, and reunion, according to their testimony, has been
an even more assimilable experience. Generalizations concerning
family success in meeting these crises have been based on both sta-

tistical and case study analyses of the characteristics, patterns, and modes of attacking problems and meeting difficulties which set off families who thrived under crisis from those who cracked under stress. A summary of findings from the statistical analysis is given in Chapter VI and the more dynamic generalizations from case study analysis are presented in Chapter VII. The primary task of this chapter is to capture the meanings behind these findings, and to indicate how they may be fitted into the general body of knowledge that has been accumulating about families in crisis from preceding studies. To that task we now turn.

HETEROGENEITY OF FAMILIES, CRISES AND ADJUSTMENT PATTERNS

VARIETY IN FAMILY MAKE-UP

Perhaps the most overpowering impression of our study is the tremendous variety in family organization, living conditions, family objectives, interpretations of what's important and what's not important in life, and ways of reacting to family-shattering crises. Families from all walks of life, impoverished and rich, immigrant families and "best families," city, town, and country—adjusted almost equally well in the face of trouble. It is hard to tell what it takes to be a "good" family today. Not only the research workers but the family members themselves in discussing the matter were conscious of shifts in family authority, in attitudes toward children, and in what's properly "man's work" and "woman's work," not to mention what are father's duties and mother's duties in child rearing. The majority of the families preferred to think of themselves as modern, that is, equalitarian in their family relationships; but in their practices only ten of 135 families could be designated as democratic families. More on that point can be found in Chapter VII.

DIFFERENCES IN CRISES EXPERIENCED

If this study makes no contribution other than to point out the variability of the crisis as it impinges on different families, it will have been justified. The bereavement, impoverishment, and divorce studies as well as Koos' (27) challenging analysis of family troubles do not take into account this high variability of the crisis from family to family. We found both the number and severity of hardships attendant upon separation and reunion were directly related to the adequacy of the family's later adjustment. A family which was forced to cut down its level of living, move to crowded quarters from comfortable quarters, adjust to living with relatives, and forced to have the wife go to work to support the family is not facing the same event of separation as the family which continues in the same home, with an assured income and the means of financing trips to visit the father. Chapter IV provides a colorful series of contrasts of this sort.

Two suggestions for taking into account the variability of crises have come out of the study: (1) A correction factor can be computed to deflate the adjustment scores of families who experienced few or no hardships and inflate the scores of families who experienced many hardships; (2) Future studies should be designed in such a way that the variation in the crisis is at a minimum within the sample; that is, select for study only families who have experienced the same crisis, taking into account the nature, the severity, and the number of hardships and deprivational experiences it entailed. For example, to get a more homogeneous type of crisis situation in a study of bereavement, only those families would be studied where there was adequate insurance to rule out economic pressures, and no families would be accepted where there were no young children under ten.

These corrections leave untouched the most important source of variation in the crisis—the definition the family makes of the situation. This can be dealt with only through case study analysis, by segregating families that define their experiences as crises from those which regard them as exigencies that all families must face.

The discovery in our case study analysis that families with superb resources for meeting crises made only fair adjustment to separation because of the number and severity of hardships which attended the separation points up this problem clearly. If the variation in severity of crisis is not taken into account, all generalizations made concerning the families which adjust well to crisis may be vitiated by the reminder that they apply, after all, only to those families which were so well situated or so fortunate as not to be faced with hardships of any consequence.[1]

VARIABLES IN ADJUSTMENT PATTERNS

In preparing the silhouettes of adjustment to separation and to reunion we have been impressed both by the variety and the similarity of adjustment patterns. In facing the separation crisis two kinds of good adjustment which involved distinctly different relationships with the absent husband and father were evident. One set of families made an excellent adjustment to separation by including the absent father in their thinking as they made decisions, writing him progress reports, and mentally keeping his place in the family circle intact. Other families made equally good adjustments to separation but excluded the father, closed ranks well, and enjoyed life without an interfering adult male in the household. Both family types did equally well in separation, but those who included the absent father met reunion without a murmur, while those who excluded him faced their most serious family crisis when he came home. The first family type might have been badly crushed had the father been killed in service and would have had a serious bereavement adjustment to make. The second type had already made its adjustment to the absence of the father and would have had minimal changes to make had he never returned. Is it enough to say that the adjustment pattern preferred would depend on the future the family faced?

When analyzed from the standpoint of speed of readjustment, it

[1] This is not precisely the case in the present study. When we corrected for number of hardships in our statistical analysis, the correction was small enough not to change the results significantly. See the behavior profiles in Table 13, pp. 164–165.

was apparent that there are two other modes of good adjustment to separation. One set of families made a good, rapid adjustment and another made a good, slow adjustment to crisis. There was some evidence that the good, slow adjustments involved families with more hardships, or families which had not previously met a serious crisis. The resources of the good, slow adjustment families were not quite as adequate as the more rapidly adjusting families. In future studies the implications of speed of adjustment should be probed. As in bereavement and in divorce, a period of mourning may serve a valuable purpose in preparing the family for a healthier permanent adjustment.

The silhouettes for both separation and reunion have been merged into profiles in summary tables in Chapter IV. Although the majority of families experienced a roller-coaster pattern of disorganization→recovery→achieved reorganization in the face of separation, the modal pattern for reunion follows a distinctly different course of adjustment and recovery. The reunion is anticipated much as the wedding was, by both husband and wife, and in this case the children, too, and the family builds up to a high-pitched emotional state of elation at the time of reunion which shows graphically on the profiles as a bump upward, rather than a dip downward. This reunion-induced state of elation is characterized by a joyful but disorganizing holiday atmosphere and by exaggerated illusions of family unity and compatability. There follows the "morning after" disillusioning eye-openers as to what family life is like, and only later when the necessity of getting jobs done presses into consciousness is there settling down to family routines.

A minority of families, who had closed ranks too well, experienced reunion with ambivalent feelings of joy and sorrow and their course of adjustment followed more closely the roller-coaster pattern of the separation period. The variety of reactions to both separation and reunion, however, reminds us that there is still much to be done to capture the adequacy of adjustment into one single score or profile for each family.

Compared with the simple, relatively uniform four profiles Koos (27) constructed to designate the range of adjustment patterns for his 62 families in New York City who experienced 109 troubles in three years, our modes of adjustment to separation and reunion are highly varied and heterogeneous. We owe to Koos a debt for indicating a method for graphically capturing the depths and plateaus of the adjustment process, and we have carried his method manifestly farther in the following ways: (1) all families don't start with the same degree of internal adjustment, (2) the slope of disorganization differs from family to family, (3) the angle of recovery and the time taken to achieve an equilibrium of reorganization differ for groups of families, and (4) the recovery upward is not regular or in a smooth line even when reorganization is successful.

Vulnerability to Hardships of Separation and Reunion and Family Adequacy

Koos (27) found crisis-proneness distributed disproportionately among his families whom he judged as below average in organization and found his trouble-proof families largely in the well-organized units. We confirm his finding in this study. We find that families with low family adequacy scores define as crisis producing, the separation and reunion hardships which they experience more frequently than do families better endowed. Many families with high family adequacy had experienced more actual hardships but were not inclined to define them as critical. We are approaching the day when "crisis-proneness" in families, like "accident-proneness" in individuals, will be diagnostically identifiable. It is closely related in this study to low family adequacy.

Social Time and Adjustment to Crises

A second major impression of our study is the role of *social time* in determining what will and what will not affect the family's recuperative capacity in the face of crisis. The child-rearing families in this study live almost exclusively in the social present tense. Items from the past must be socially relevant to receive weight in their conduct. Contrary to the claims of the orthodox Freudians, it is our impression from this study that childhood experiences of spouses are many light-years away from the day-to-day experiences of a husband and wife in their family of procreation Only those experiences which are closely linked with immediate family histories appear to bear on crisis-meeting adjustments in our study. Two sets of forces are particularly close in social time: (1) the family's adaptability skills and bonds of integration, and (2) the family situations in which the family is enmeshed at the time of the crisis and afterward. In contrast, items such as childhood happiness of spouses, happiness of parents' marriages, number of siblings in parental family, and even years of schooling, appear remote and distant measured in social time.

To test this impression there is needed some measure of the source for capacity to get along with others which Terman (*32*) has implied is directly involved in marriage aptitude. Both Terman and Burgess (*8*) found early childhood factors very important in predicting marriage success. It was something of a surprise to us to be unable to confirm their findings in predicting success in family adjustment to separation and reunion crises. Moreover, the kinds of courtship experiences, the length of acquaintance before marriage, and the length of engagement, which were important for success in marriage in these earlier studies, also appear remote in social time from the struggles of families facing wartime hardships. (See the condensation of these findings in Table 27 on p. 324.)

These findings light up somewhat the dark pall of doom cast by the marriage prediction studies, which assert that childhood happiness and happy parental marriages are prerequisites for a happy marriage. Our 270 spouses have been married almost ten years, average almost three children per family, and the majority of families have adjusted well both to separation and to reunion. Yet many of these families reported spouses with unhappy childhoods and unfavorable relationships with parents. This is not to deny the validity of the marriage prediction studies, but to point out the diminishing importance of spouses' childhood background as the marriage matures and becomes a family.

Success in dealing with family problems and in getting along with others is probably learned largely within the parental family of the spouses, but it can also be learned elsewhere in friend-friend relationships, or in the successful families of acquaintances, or even (horrors) through trial and error in the process of early marriage adjustment. That it has to be learned is admitted, for the art of living with others is not passed on in the germ plasm. In good families the know-how of dealing with others is absorbed as easily and simply as good table manners and acceptable speech forms. Our own findings do not explain where our families picked up these skills, if they did not learn them in the spouses' parental homes. After ten years of marriage most of the families have at least a rudimentary acquaintance with them, for families usually do not persist for ten years in America without developing these skills. Indeed, without them they would have broken up long since through annulment, divorce, or desertion.

The answer to the question of why certain items in the family history appear closer in social time than others is not found among our data. The author has demonstrated elsewhere that the family cumulates its patterns from past experiences and from the successes and failures of those experiences, and that the significant thing is not what were the childhood experiences of spouses, but how the family has benefitted from those experiences.[2] It is the translation into present family patterns of these experiences which determines their importance for crisis meeting. We pick up the translations better through marital adjustment measures, through measures of family adaptability and family integration, and through the patterns of

[2] Reuben Hill, *Waller's The Family: A Dynamic Interpretation* (New York: Dryden Press, in press).

meeting previous crises, than through a "play-back" of a spouse's childhood. It is as though we were looking back on life through the large end of a telescope; it is no wonder the experiences in childhood appear so remote. What we need is a microscope to disentangle from the patterns of the present family the transmuted childhood heritages of the spouses, a more difficult task but one which must be done before this question is adequately answered.

IMPORTANCE OF PREVIOUS HISTORY WITH CRISIS

Closely linked with the previous discussion is the confirmation in our study of Cavan's major finding (*11*) that previous experience with crisis gave excellent clues both as to the outcome of the family in the new crisis and as to the pattern of adjustment the family would follow. Angell (*1*) cites Cooley's concept of the "tentative method" as explanation of the way families develop a pattern of adjustment which is satisfying to them. The idea that social forms feel their way by a sort of trial-and-error process, developing those parts or attributes which seem to work and discarding those which do not, certainly applies to the families facing the crises of separation and reunion. For those families which had experienced any kind of separation crisis before, the use of the "tentative method" had already supplied them with certain workable patterns. Less similar crises—such as illness, impoverishment, and loss of loved ones—nevertheless, appeared to have tried and tested the families in such a way that they met the present crises with more confidence. Family life is a series of trying experiences, interlarded with relative peace and quiet. Family members learn on whom they can count, who will go tense and moody in times of trouble, and which members will predictably grow in stature under stress. The fighting front is formed with some members guarding and protecting others. Previous experience with crisis gives clues as to this form, and is an indication of the eventual outcome should there be another crisis.

To make the confirmation of Cavan's hypothesis conclusive, the reactions of the family to the crisis of separation were tested against the reactions to the crisis of reunion. The two patterns of adjustment were closely related. Indeed, no better preview of reunion adjustment could be found in the schedules than the patterns established in the separation itself. The hypothesis is conclusively confirmed!

FAMILY ADJUSTMENT AND MARITAL ADJUSTMENT

There is no hand-in-glove relationship between good marital adjustment and family adjustment to crisis. To be sure, an intact marital relationship is of tremendous importance, but the phenomenon of family adjustment is more demanding and the relationships more complicated than in a simple pair relationship. Few of the factors that have been thought important for good marital adjustment from the Burgess and Terman studies proved important in our study of family adjustment to crisis. Although the two realms are highly interrelated, there is no guarantee that pairs which have worked out a satisfactory marital relationship are competent to assume the responsibilities of parenthood with its challenging troubles and sicknesses, its jealousies and competitions, and its heavy obligations.

In designing future research projects the differences as well as the similarities of the two phenomena need to be recognized. We need, and do not as yet have, a good criterion of family success, although considerable exploration and testing of criteria for marriage success has been accomplished.

CONTENT OF FAMILY LIVING IMPORTANT

There is abundant evidence that American families are in transition from authoritarian forms of family living to more permissive forms, from large families to smaller units, from production-oriented families working as economic units to consumption-focused families concentrating on meeting the needs of family members. The families in this study reflect these changes in form, and on first meeting would appear to be still more traditional than developmental in form.

We found that the forms families presented to the eye did not give us handles on their capacity to meet crises. No single family form proved most invulnerable or most vulnerable to separation stresses; indeed, the tangible evidences of family form, such as family size, hierarchy of authority, division of duties and privileges, and so-called graciousness of family living seen in protocol and traditions, provided few clues to crisis-proneness.

It was not the form of the family, but its processes and substance of living that determined its success as a family. Many modified matriarchies and patriarchies used the consultative process freely in decision making and consequently did well in separation and reunion. Some families claimed to be equalitarian, at least the husband and wife shared in the running of the home, but the parents were really a united front against the children and although they provided the form, they lacked the substance of democratic family living.

When we were able to take our blinders off and see the content of family living beneath the form which showed to the world, we found the ingredients of family success in a wide variety of family organizations. These ingredients appear to be: the recognition of interdependence of all members upon one another, the satisfaction of playing one's roles in the family whatever they are, the sharing of home management duties among all members, the flexibility of the family when facing new situations, the adequacy of intra-family communication, and the opportunities for growth and development in the family milieu. These patterns of behavior may sometimes be found in the most unlikely and outwardly rigid family forms, a sure piece of evidence of families in transition. The most tender and affectionate relationships were sometimes found between father and children in families whose outward appearance was little different from that of the New England Puritan family of 200 years ago.

Specific Findings of Other Studies Corroborated

In Chapter II we reviewed briefly the major findings of studies preceding our own which had bearing on the adjustments of families in crisis. From these findings we composed hypotheses to be tested in the special context of war separation and reunion. Some of the hypotheses held up well, others did not. The results have been condensed into two tables, Table 27, p. 324 and Table 28, pp. 325–328. We have followed the outline of the natural history of the family so far as it has been feasible, as has been done in preceding chapters.

From Table 27 it is apparent that few of the factors which were found to be conducive to good marital adjustment in the marriage prediction studies by Burgess and Cottrell (8) and Terman (32) held up as forces in family adjustment to separation and reunion. Two of sixteen factors were corroborated as important for separation adjustment, and three were partially corroborated. None were corroborated as important for reunion adjustment and only two were partially corroborated, but not statistically significant. Neither the factors making for marriage aptitude nor the premarital factors of childhood history and family background appeared relevant to family behavior in a war-born crisis. This is further evidence of the point made earlier in the chapter that the factors making for good marital adjustment are not near enough in social time to be relevant factors for family adjustment to crises. Marital adjustment, moreover, operates at a simpler level of interaction than family adjustment, and probably requires less maturity of spouses.

The results summarized in Table 28 are more hopeful for building a stable body of generalizations concerning family adjustments. Of nine factors found conducive to good adjustment to crisis in other family studies, all are corroborated as important for separation adjustment success by either the statistical or the case study methods and only two are not corroborated by one or the other method as important for reunion adjustments. Both methods agree on the

TABLE 27. Corroboration (by Statistical and Case Study Methods) of Extent to Which Factors Found Conducive to Good Marital Adjustment also Proved Conducive to Good Family Adjustment in Separation and Reunion Situations

Factors Found Conducive to Good Marital Adjustment in Burgess and Cottrell Study (526 couples) and Terman Study (792 couples)	Outcome in This Study of 135 Families	
	Good Separation Adjustment	Good Reunion Adjustment
Childhood Experience of Spouses		
Wife's childhood happiness, positive association	Corroborated	Not corroborated
Happiness of wife's parents, positive association	Not corroborated	..
Happiness of husband's parents, positive association	..	..
Number of siblings (wife), positive association	..	..
Number of siblings (husband), positive association	..	
Courtship Experiences		
Place of first meeting (other than "pickup" or place of private or public recreation)	Not corroborated	Not corroborated
Readiness for Marriage at Marriage		
Age at marriage (wife), positive association	Not corroborated	Not corroborated
Age at marriage (husband), positive association	..	..
Years of schooling (wife), positive association	..	..
Inter-faith vs. in-faith marriage, (preferably in-faith)	..	..
Length of acquaintance before marriage, positive association		
Time and Marriage		
Years married, negative association	Partially corroborated, not significant	Not corroborated
Stability and Security		
Occupation of husband (teaching and large business, not salesmen, laborers, etc.)	Partially corroborated, classifications not identical	Partially corroborated, classifications not identical
Income (moderate rather than high or low)	Not corroborated	Not corroborated
Number of children, negative association	Corroborated	Partially corroborated, not significant
Residential mobility, negative association	Partially corroborated, not significant	Not corroborated

TABLE 28. Corroboration (by Statistical and Case Study Methods) of Extent to Which Generalizations Concerning Family Behavior in Crisis from Representative Studies Carry Over to Crises of Separation and Reunion

Generalizations Made	Source and Type of Crisis Studied	Outcome in This Study of 135 Families In Separation	In Reunion
The following factors are conducive to good adjustment to crisis:			
Family adaptability, positive association	Angell, impoverishment, 50 families	Corroborated by both methods	Not corroborated by statistical; corroborated by case study
Family integration, positive association	Same study	Not corroborated by statistical; corroborated by case study	Corroborated by both methods
Degree of affection among family members, positive association	Same Study	Corroborated by both methods	Corroborated by both methods
Flexibility in shifting roles, positive association	Same Study	Not corroborated by statistical; corroborated by case study	Not corroborated by either method
Marital adjustment, positive association	Burges and Cottrell, marital crises, 526 couples	Corroborated by both methods	Corroborated by both methods
Family types by affection giving (companionable home best)	Bossard and Boll, family situations (many studies)	Corroborated by statistical	Corroborated by statistical
Previous successful experience with crisis	Cavan and Ranck, impoverishment, 100 families	Corroborated by case study	Corroborated by case study
Family council type of family control	Mather, family adjustment, 200 families	Corroborated by case study; not corroborated by statistical	Corroborated by case study; not corroborated by statistical

TABLE 28. Corroboration (by Statistical and Case Study Methods) of Extent to Which Generalizations Concerning Family Behavior in Crisis from Representative Studies Carry Over to Crises of Separation and Reunion (*Continued*)

Generalizations Made	Source and Type of Crisis Studied	Outcome in This Study of 135 Families In Separation	Outcome in This Study of 135 Families In Reunion
Social participation of wife, positive association	Duvall, loneliness among 70 servicemen's wives	Corroborated by statistical	Not corroborated by statistical
Crisis-proneness, the tendency to define troubles as crises, is distributed disproportionately among families of low family adequacy.	Angell, impoverishment, 100 families Koos, variety of crippling troubles, 62 low-income families	Corroborated	Corroborated
The course of adjustment is a roller-coaster pattern of disorganization—recovery—readjustment.	Cavan and Ranck, impoverishment, 100 families Koos, variety of crippling troubles, 62 low-income families Eliot, and others, bereavement (several studies)	Corroborated as modal pattern, many variations	Not corroborated as modal pattern, few conform to pattern
Family reactions to crisis divide between short-time, immediate reactions and secondary, long-time adjustments.	Angell, impoverishment, 50 families Cavan and Ranck, impoverishment, 100 families Eliot and Fulcomer, bereavement, 75 families Waller, alienation and divorce, 38 families	Corroborated	Partially corroborated, but pattern differs from other crises studied

TABLE 28. Corroboration (by Statistical and Case Study Methods) of Extent to Which Generalizations Concerning Family Behavior in Crisis from Representative Studies Carry Over to Crises of Separation and Reunion (*Continued*)

Generalizations Made	Source and Type of Crisis Studied	Outcome in This Study of 135 Families In Separation	In Reunion
Demoralization following a crisis usually stems from incipient demoralization before the crisis.	Cavan and Ranck, impoverishment, 100 families. Koos, variety of crippling troubles, 62 low-income families	Corroborated	Corroborated
Adversity may increase family solidarity, or even heal old conflicts between spouses and siblings.	Cavan and Ranck, impoverishment, 100 families. Angell, impoverishment, 50 families Eliot and others, bereavement, (several studies) Koos, variety of troubles, 48 middle-class families	Partially corroborated, most conflicts remain	Partially corroborated, most conflicts remain
The length of time a family continues to be disorganized as a result of crisis is inversely related to its adequacy of organization.	Cavan and Ranck, impoverishment, 100 families. Koos, variety of troubles, 62 low-income families	Only partially corroborated because of variability of hardship factor	Corroborated
Unadaptable and unintegrated families are more likely to be unpredictable deviants.	Angell, impoverishment, 50 families	Corroborated	Corroborated
Families which make a quick and immediate recovery from crisis do not make as good a final adjustment as those which make a slower recovery (allowing for mourning process).	Eliot and Fulcomer, Bereavement, 75 families Waller, alienation and divorce, 38 families	Only partially corroborated	Not corroborated

TABLE 28. Corroboration (by Statistical and Case Study Methods) of Extent to Which Generalizations Concerning Family Behavior in Crisis from Representative Studies Carry Over to Crises of Separation and Reunion (*Continued*)

Generalizations Made	Source and Type of Crisis Studied	Outcome in This Study of 135 Families In Separation	In Reunion
The best recovery from a crisis of dismemberment is to close ranks and reallocate the roles and duties of the absent one to other members.	Same studies	Not corroborated	Not corroborated, makes for poor recovery
Foreknowledge and preparation for a critical event mitigates the hardships and improves the chances for recovery.	Eliot, and others, bereavement (several studies)	Corroborated	Corroborated

practical significance of six of the factors for separation and five of the factors for reunion success. We are now on sounder ground, partly because we are dealing with phenomena at the family level, rather than with individual or marriage pair attributes. Moreover, we are operating in the social time span of family living instead of stretching backward to the spouses' parental family experiences for explanations of their procreational family behavior.

Again in Table 28, of ten major generalizations concerning family behavior in crisis (to be differentiated from the factors, just mentioned, making for good adjustment) made from preceding studies, only one did not carry over into the new context of separation and two were only partially corroborated. The carry-over of these generalizations to reunion was less automatic because reunion was not really a crisis of dismemberment, but a crisis of accession or readmittance of a family member. In the reunion situation, three generalizations were not corroborated and one was only partially corroborated.

In Table 28 nine studies are cited and two of the generalizations are backed by four different studies. This brings research on family crises to a more mature stage of development. Studies by Bakké (2), Morgan (30), Komarovsky (25), and Sletto (31) on impoverishment, and by Becker (4) of bereavement could have been added to further substantiate the increasing applicability of these findings. Definitive studies testing the findings from past researches of family crisis can now be made with confidence because the dimensions and quality of the phenomena involved are much better known.

LIMITATIONS OF EXPLORATORY STUDIES

Lest we become too optimistic concerning our abilities to predict family behavior in crisis, the limitations of our present study should be mentioned. This has been a hybrid study, in that we have attempted to test definitively, so far as possible, findings from other studies of families in crisis in a new context, war separation and reunion (see Table 27 and Table 28). It has also been exploratory, in that we knew nothing about the crisis of separation before launching the study and relatively little about the processes of reunion, and were therefore forced to use open-end questions concerning the unknown areas we were exploring. This places a serious limitation on the study, as a reading of Chapter VII and Appendix B will indicate.

Because of this exploratory work, however, it should now be possible to make studies of the many types of peacetime separations which afflict families in our commonwealth, with a more clear-cut vision of the range of responses that family members will exhibit. We need badly a confirmation of the generic aspects of separation and reunion. Wherever family members are affectionally interdependent, one would expect many of the trials and tribulations of war separations to be repeated, whether the separation is due to hospitalization in an inaccessible sanitarium or mental hospital, imprisonment, or service in foreign countries for whatever reason. The trails have been blazed in this study for a more definitive testing of hypotheses concerning the types of families best equipped to meet separation crises and concerning the processes which enable families best to assimilate the absence of the amputated one.

In future studies of separation and reunion it will be advisable to collect materials in such a way that cases may be rated on combinations of factors. Taken singly, factors were rarely important. The forces of real weight were omnibus factors which combined a number of items into a single score, such as, family integration, family adaptability, marital adjustment, dynamic stability, hardships of separation, hardships of reunion, and so on. Considerable experimentation with combining single factors by means of composite scores and ratings should prove fruitful. In an exploratory study this is not as easily accomplished as in a definitive study where many of the variables are known in advance.

Future studies will need to take into account the finding of this study that high scores on factor complexes may not be as conducive to good adjustment as moderate combinations. The assumption that because there is a relationship between a complex of factors and the dependent variable the relation is linear is an unsound assumption, and can easily be checked. We found best adjustment scores among our families which were moderately integrated, moderately or highly adaptable, and moderately well adjusted or highly adjusted, maritally. High and low concentrations produced many deviants, whereas the moderately endowed were a more homogeneous as well as a more predictable group in their adjustments.

The limitations of our study, methodologically are given in considerable detail in the note in Appendix B, but this much warrants saying here: The statistical analysis has been helpful in providing a picture of poor risks in our population of families, but it offers few insights into why individual families do poorly or well. Our expectations of capturing through statistical analysis the interrelationships of family characteristics and family success in adjusting to crises have not been fulfilled. We are open to criticism of having attempted to explain a dynamic functional disequilibrium of family adjustment by correlating it with a series of static facts artificially immobilized in space and time. Statistical method has been said to furnish a means for treating factors which involve a multiplicity of causes. It appears to us to be valuable mainly because it enables us to treat phenomena scientifically while ignoring their causes, and to arrive at an unreal and costly finality in our thinking—unreal because it is not based upon an exhaustive treatment of causes, and costly because it has diverted us from searching for causes. It is probably a mistake to use the statistical method extensively in an exploratory study when the understanding of causal sequences is at a minimum. Indeed, the chief use of statistics as a method seems to be to prove something we already know, or to show that something we already know is not true. It serves us best in follow-up studies, or in repeated studies of the phenomena which have already been adequately probed by more depth-delving methods.

These criticisms are softened when statistical methods are joined with case study methods as we have done in Chapter VIII. Used jointly, the two methods offer promise of a complementary matching of strengths to cover the other's weaknesses. They have been used to preserve the functional system of attributes within families, to identify and explain the behavior of unpredictable families, and to act as a constant check and source of validation one on the other.[3]

SUMMARY

As we look back over this chapter which had as its task the delineation of meanings behind the findings, their significance and applications, we perceive a few highlights.

1. Many distinctly different family types were successful in riding out the dismemberment crisis of separation and the disillusioning crisis of reunion.
2. The crises experienced varied in severity and number of hardships for each family.
3. Crisis-proneness—the tendency to define hardships as crises—was disproportionately found among families of low family adequacy. Crisis-proneness, such as accident-proneness, may run in families.
4. There were many types of successful adjustment patterns to crisis, but for most families the course of adjustment to separation followed a roller-coaster profile of disorganization→recovery →readjustment.
5. Social time, not chronological time, determines the importance a given event or experience will have on family adjustment behavior, particularly among the child-rearing families of our study.
6. Families follow the "tentative method" identified by Cooley in achieving patterns for meeting family crises; therefore, previous

[3] For more detail on the complementary possibilities of statistics and case study, see Methodological Note, Appendix B, pp. 396–398.

history with crisis proves the best prediction of family behavior in a new crisis.

7. Family adjustment is removed in social time and in complexity of interaction from simple marriage pair adjustments, and few, if any, generalizations from factors making for marriage adjustments carry over to the family level.

8. Because the family is in transition in America, the family form masks rather than reveals the content of family living. Many different types of hierarchical control succeed in the face of crisis, but those which do succeed share the consultative process in decision making. Family forms may vary but it is the content of family living which counts.

9. The majority of the factors from ten studies found conducive to family adjustment in the face of impoverishment and bereavement crises were also conducive to good adjustment to separation and reunion. These factors, however, were predominantly drawn from third dimensional family living rather than individual or marriage pair sources.

10. The majority of generalizations from ten studies concerning the dynamics of family adjustment and recovery in the crises of impoverishment, bereavement, divorce, and other critical troubles, were confirmed as applying also to the war-born crisis situations of separation and reunion.

PART FOUR

The Social Costs of Family Crises

C H A P T E R X

IMPLICATIONS FOR NATIONAL
AND LOCAL POLICY

AS we close this narrative of the successes and failures of 135 Iowa families in meeting the crises of war separation and peace-arranged reunion, certain questions insistently recur: Are the families in the Corn Belt not fundamentally similar in their reactions to trouble to families in other sections of the country? Are not the troubles of parting and reuniting peacetime as well as wartime problems?[1] Are they not really American problems common to families in all walks of life? Proof can be marshaled to answer these questions affirmatively. We believe that it is high time national and local policy was shaped which places family life *first* not only in the national scheme of values but also in the investment of time, personnel, and programs devoted to the commonweal.

As our industrial society has provided the elements leading to family disintegration, so must we now provide (through appropriate social organizations) for the conservation of family resources. We

[1] A partial answer to the question of the relative frequency of wartime and peacetime separations may be obtained from the U. S. Bureau of the Census, Population Series, P-5, No. 10, p. 3. A survey made of marital status of the civilian population in the peacetime year of 1940 showed 1,534,514 families with the wife away from home, and 1,573,531 families with the husband absent. In 1944 roughly 3 million husbands were separated from their families for a variety of reasons, many due to employment away from home and the scarcity of housing for their families at places of industrial activity, whereas in the same year only 2,760,000 husbands were separated from their families by reason of service in the armed forces. In 1946 there were still roughly 2 million husbands and wives living apart. There can be no dodging the fact that separation and reunion are imminent disturbing hardships in the life cycle of millions of American families.

have shown that we prize the American family with our annual
Mother's Day, Father's Day, and National Family Week, but we
have also allowed families to be torn apart during the rest of the year
by forces as devastating to them as floods and wind erosion have
been to our land resources.

We have built our faith in the permanence of the American family
on certain assumptions which need to be challenged: (1) the central
assumption of individualism that persons and families can and
should be left to take care of themselves, the myth of "every tub on
on its own bottom"; (2) the assumption that people know what is
good for them, that they know where they need social organization
and can be counted upon to build it when needed; (3) the casual assumption of liberal capitalism, discredited though it has been, that
the integration of a population into a *society* can be left to chance;
and (4) the assumption on which much of organized social work
has been built, that the world is divided into two kinds of people,
those who can and those who cannot care for themselves, and that
minimum aids are needed only to shore up the latter.[2]

Our findings in this study and the consensus among other investigators of family life today cast doubt on the soundness of the four
assumptions listed above. These assumptions have formed the basis
for a set of laissez faire "do-nothing" local and national policies with
regard to American families. Families have been expected to shift
for themselves, feed, clothe, and supply medical care and educational

---

[2] Earl Koos first demonstrated the fallacies of these four assumptions in his study
of low-income families in New York City, *Families in Trouble* (New York: King's
Crown Press, 1946), pp. 122–123. In mitigation of social work's untenable position
in this matter, we should point out that professional people everywhere have concentrated on the chronically disorganized and their problems at the expense of
those who muddle through. In the schools we have paid more attention to laggards
than to average students, and in medicine research focuses on the pathological
syndrome rather than the common cold. The students and counselors of family
groups have likewise paid more attention to patching up chronically unhappy
families than to the understanding and treatment of the occasional crisis needs of
essentially sound families. Is this sound public policy?

training to their dependent members through periods of depression, war, and inflation, bearing all the risks and assuming very nearly all the burdens brought on by a fluctuating economy and a vacillating polity. Laissez faire has existed alongside increasing rates of family disorganization and personality disorder. The costs in personality distortions defy accurate computation.

In the pages which follow we shall deal in some detail with the implications, which have grown out of this study and related investigations, for national and local policies for family life. Hopefully, the suggestions we make will form the basis for policies for family life that will be less punitive and more kindly to families rearing children than the hands-off policies of national and local government of today.

The "Aloneness" of Families

We find families increasingly vulnerable as they are shorn of kin, neighbors, and friends. Centered as they are about the husband and wife and their one or two children, modern American families are highly mobile, precariously small, and poorly structured units to survive the stresses of life—death, unemployment, war separations, infidelity, desertion, and so on. Years ago family members could turn to the kinship group in time of need. But today we no longer have easy access, in times of war or in times of peace, to innumerable male relatives who can act as father substitutes in the absence of the father. As a result we find among the small families of the present study, and we suspect it would be found among all small families cut off from their kin, the phenomenon of "aloneness."

The goal of self-sufficiency, of families being capable of surviving by themselves, may have had some merit in pioneer days when the family groups were large and included several relatives besides the children. Today the myth of family self-sufficiency requires discrediting. To replace it we bring the concept of interdependence of families within communities. This concept will need to be implemented in our communities with appropriate organization, to be sure, if it is to have any meaning to people.

The families in the present study who adjusted least well and most slowly were frequently solitary families characterized by past mobility and transiency, or they were families whose relationships with relatives and neighbors had become tenuous. In either case these families lacked the nests of supporting families with which to share their troubles and were, therefore, forced to live *alone* in an enforced anonymity.

Alert communities will provide newly arrived families with a recognized status of newcomers and will make provision for their orientation into neighborhoods and special interest groups. Left to their own devices, crisis-stricken families in a new neighborhood withdraw into their narrow family circles and fester inwardly rather than risk being rebuffed.

It is noteworthy that those families which succeeded best in meeting the crisis of wartime made frequent mention of the accessibility of relatives, neighbors, and friends. They rarely mentioned, we are sad to report, the churches, the family agencies, or welfare groups which claim in their annual bid for contributions from the community that they provide services of this kind to families in trouble. Except for isolated references to the local Red Cross chapters and occasional mention of the local relief office, no evidence was given that social agencies were regarded as helpful to any of our families. To be sure, the families probably didn't ask for help, especially since it is still a *disgrace* in our society to be helped by anyone except kin. Churches, social welfare agencies, and guidance workers state that they have plenty to do without seeking people to serve. One minister exclaimed, "You can't blame the church if people don't come to tell us they need help. A pastor can only wait until folks bring their problems to him."

On shaping a community program which is family-centered, we

need to face the fact that many families which once counted for help and comfort on kin and neighbors have lost contact with them and now live in anonymity. We must recognize that their problems are often such that they do not know which, if any, social agency could or would help if asked. We need to reorganize our communities to meet families *at their own level of need* and to operate from that base in providing services. As we have seen the need among the families in this study, help might often have consisted simply of providing an opportunity to ventilate their anxieties, share their woes, and ask for reassuring, simple advice about problems occasioned by the absence of the husband and father. There are, at the present time, few agencies to which families willingly turn for help on the more superficial levels of life (27).

Unfortunately, there are only a few hundred family service agencies in the entire United States and marriage counseling services are limited to the metropolitan centers and to a few college campuses. For several years the professional services for nonindigent families in trouble must come from the family physician, the teacher, the minister, the family lawyer, and the occasional child welfare worker with the public welfare department. To these professionals we have these suggestions to make.

1. Professional services will make their greatest contribution if they are made with the total family context in mind. Particularly is this true in the case of crises of dismemberment and demoralization.
2. Families, like football teams, combat teams, and other collectivities, have a morale and *esprit de corps* to maintain if they are to be effective. Physicians have found that illnesses that yesterday were called psychosomatic are today regarded as products of family aggravations.

From case workers, social workers will need to become family group workers, serving the child's family *as a family* rather than serving the child solely as a personality. This involves becoming an artist in relationship therapy, keeping all the family relationships healthy.

Good football coaches point out that they must not only keep their men in good physical trim, and in good emotional fettle, but they must also foster the relationships among all team members if team morale is to be preserved.

Our research highlights the need of professional services which take into account these factors of family morale in future practice.

3. Families need to be kept intact and relatively self-sustaining.

Both war separations and peacetime separations render a net disservice to most families, although many ride them out successfully. Voluntary separations should not be undertaken without serious thought as to the consequences.

Employers should know that transferring employees to positions in distant communities where housing is to tight that taking the family along would be impossible are doing their employees a serious disservice.

If separation is forced upon the family, our study shows that it is much more easily assimilated if prepared for in advance. If this fact alone were widely known, the effects of separation because of employment, hospitalization, institutionalization, and even imprisonment might be greatly mitigated.

ADEQUATE INCOME NOT ENOUGH

Several studies (*1*, *27*, *11*) have offered evidence that families, whose economic well-being is marginal, are more vulnerable to crisis. Koos (*27*) eloquently portrays the marginality of living in such families:

As the investigator strips off the outer layers of low-income urban existence he becomes increasingly aware of its hand-to-mouth quality. Only the things that must be done managed to get done. There are no sheltered reservoirs within which man can store up his surplus thoughts, energies and products—and not surprisingly, because for people living under these conditions there are no surplus thoughts and energies and products. They need all of their energies and every cent they can earn in order to meet the day-by-day demands, and they know that their environment will make endless demands upon them whichever way they turn. Life under such conditions takes on a nip-and-tuck urgency that belies our culture's middle-class *ethos* of a reasoned calculation of one's future.

Individuals and whole families of individuals suffer from these pressures. Housewives lament that they can buy only for the next meal because there is no place in which to store additional foods. Wage earners know that every cent they make is mortgaged in advance simply to keep up with basic expenditures, and they curse and worry because they cannot save for a rainy day. Adolescent girls have no place in which to entertain the "boy friend" because home offers no opportunity for privacy. Only the youngest members of the family can dawdle and dream beyond life's immediacies, and they too, suffer indirectly.[3]

Koos has depicted the true function of income in a family context in this portrait of family living where income is critically inadequate. The picture is confirmed among the low-income families in the present study. We have been unable, however, to confirm the importance of adequate income statistically in adjustment to wa separation and reunion crises. We might have expected that adjustments to these crises would have improved with the addition of successive increments of income. Our expectations were rudely upset. Tested in every conceivable way, neither the number of dollars available to the family before induction, during the separation period, nor the dollars saved, nor the indebtedness incurred appeared statistically related to success in meeting the crises of dismemberment. By itself, adequate income is not enough to insure adjustment to crisis.

Careful examination of the case studies enables us to see the function of family income in a more family-centered context, as Koos did. Here we see inadequate income associated with hardships of separation, with sensitivity to hardship, and with worries about the

[3] *Ibid.*, pp. 24–25.

future. We see the process by which dollars of income are translated into family satisfactions. Income reaches the family as money, and the thrifty family transforms it through careful stewardship into services, goods, and satisfactions. The real secret of the relation between income and family adjustment to crisis, we think, lies in the process of transforming income into family satisfactions. The capacity to achieve this transformation probably varies more among our families than does the *amount* of income.

By implication we see that families need training in making maximum use of community services which have already been paid for through tax moneys. They need to discover the satisfactions which come as a by-product of working and playing together which can't be bought on the market with money. Family heads and younger members need training in buying and in distributing these goods, services, and satisfactions to all members. In sum, education needs to be provided to enable families to make the most of family income! Adequate income by itself is not enough.

We are disposed to support the current efforts to place wage floors beneath which no family incomes shall drop, and we see good and sufficient reasons to control inflation or in some way to keep family purchasing power stable. However, such measures would not be enough to assure family adjustment to dismemberment crises. American families are today more social-psychological units than economic entities, conforming at the family level to the rational operations of the economists' Economic Man. This means that the stability of the families of America depends less and less on economic factors and inheres more and more in the inter-personal relations of its members. More is needed than increasing the family's purchasing power, desirable and pleasant though that may be to contemplate.

To carry our findings concerning the unimportance of the strictly economic and the vital importance of the social-psychological factors into recommendations, we suggest that efforts for assuring the security of the family—economic support, health, nutrition, and housing

—should be studied in terms of the needs of the highly variable cultural structure of American families, and in terms of the striving for companionship which today characterizes the Holy Grail of marriage and family life.

MARRIAGE AND FAMILY LIFE WITHOUT ADEQUATE PREPARATION
TODAY'S PATTERN

We would have expected, if our educational system had taken into account the fact that its students were going to be family heads someday, that the better educated family heads would have fared better than those with less education. Had our schools prepared their students for family living, educated them for family living, it should have made a difference in their family adjustments to the crises of war separation and reunion. Moreover, we would like to place on our schools the responsibility of teaching students to profit from life's experiences and to improve upon the skills developed in school through practice and exposure to life's situations. Now, just what was the record for these Iowa families? Years of schooling made no difference and parents showed little tendency to profit from years of exposure to life's situations. For our families facing the crises of dismemberment, the resources and capacities which enabled them to adjust and achieve an equilibrium were unrelated to the amount of schooling of spouses or their years of experience in the school of parenthood. This is an indictment of our society and of its lack of realistic programs for family life.

We have operated in our society, apparently, on the theory that marriages are made in heaven and have disregarded the necessity for their operating on earth.[4] There has been a head-in-the-sand attitude that anyone could become a good parent who wanted to. Upon investigation we found that only ten of the 135 wives in the study mentioned any specific formal training in school for their tasks as mothers. The fathers were not queried as a group, but in Elder's in-

4 *Ibid.*, p. 126.

vestigation (*18*) most of the thirty-two Polk County fathers studied confessed to no formal training for parenthood. Aside from some factual information on sex given to a few of our youth and occasional courses offered to high-school girls in home economics, our society has done very little in the past generation to prepare individuals for carrying on in adequate fashion for the most fundamental function in society.

Happily the situation is changing.[5] Over 600 colleges and universities now make explicit provision for course work in marriage and the family and preparation for parenthood, and the movement is finally spreading to the country's high schools. Too few students are reached as yet, however, to make any appreciable difference in the general stream of family living. There is more emphasis upon domestic skills than upon family relationships and getting along creatively with family members. More is taught about the family in other times and places than about our own, here and now, more about what is wrong with families than about how to improve one's own relationships. Moreover, there is too much neglect of the masculine role in the home and of educating boys for it. It takes two to make a home, but the school curriculum rarely recognizes that fact. Worse still, the typical high-school and college curriculum ignores the fact that most people will live out their days in family groups. Most curricula are designed for celibates, taught by celibates, and are quite as sterile as celibacy from a family-life education point of view.

There are large implications from our study for educational policies and programs. Successful marriage and family life must cease to be merely a by-product of our educational system and become one of its major objectives. There is much which can be learned about successful family living through formal education. Teaching methods are being devised which are more appropriate to the new areas of

[5] Reuben Hill, "Plans for Strengthening Family Life." In *Family, Marriage and Parenthood*, ed. by Howard Becker and Reuben Hill (Boston: D. C. Heath & Company, 1948), pp. 700–796.

education where the "art of living" is held in focus. Exploration in playing a repertoire of family roles will replace lectures on the history of the early American family. Experiences in developing insight and understanding into one's own personality and into the make-up and needs of others will replace the highly biological orientation of lectures on the "facts of life." Rich experiences in coeducational committees will provide training in giving and taking between the sexes. These same committees are laboratories in communication, in daring to differ with others, in working through those differences by finding a consensus which is acceptable to all. Teacher-centered classes which have had their part in affirming the rightness of paternalism in family relations will be replaced by committee-operated classes which provide training in consultation and in the equalitarian acceptance of every class member for the contribution he has to make. Thus may we prepare our students for effective democratic family living.

More specifically, our study suggests that successful family living depends upon the use of the consultative process in decision making, and that democratic family forms are well prepared to carry out that process. Closely related to these two requisites are the presence of family adaptability and of patterns of moderate self-sufficiency in the wife. Schools cannot take lightly the discovery that education of young women for assuming initiative and responsibility within the husband-wife relationship must be matched with the education of young men to a complementary set of creative roles.

Our study implies that women and men need training in *pairing* their strengths by a dovetailing of their roles and talents. Our most self-dependent wives were less successful in separation and in reunion because they lacked the skill to use their competence and strengths coöperatively *with* their husbands and wasted much of their energies competitively *against* them. Their husbands, on the other hand, had not been trained to accept the idea of a wife working outside the home, or assuming community leadership, and often felt threatened in their own families by the wife's accomplishments. Training for *pairedness* is a challenge schools will be expected to meet.

To go beyond pair living into family living, we see implications for schools in the demands of family members for the skills of communication to cross the barriers which separate child from parent, child from child, and husband from wife. Education in the creative use of argument, quarrels, and possibly more pleasant prolonged discussions, the better to understand the needs of family members, constitutes a provocative new area of operation for the teachers of English and speech. Child care and training classes offer some experience in communication with little children, from the two-year-old to the kindergarten candidate. Baby-sitting experiences and a few home management practice houses offer experience with babies in the early months of life and will do much to relieve the anxieties of young people who regard infants as noncommunicative vegetables. Actually, babies can and do communicate many of their needs if we tune in on the correct wave length. The pediatricians are currently reminding us of this fact with their shift for infants to self-demand feedings and self-demand toilet patterns, and with their training of parents to watch the *cues of readiness* before launching new experiences for the growing infant. Much of communication is nonverbal, and the capacity of speaking "through the elbows" by means of gestures, and of interpreting attitudes and needs of others through this same medium may be effectively built into young people with careful training.

At the literate level we find among the Iowa families of our study a tremendous range in capacity to write letters. This was the sole medium for maintaining communication during the absence of the husband. Families closed ranks too completely because they couldn't maintain good letter-to-letter relationships, and their adjustments both to separation and to reunion suffered thereby.

Training in communication needs to be extended from public

speaking and courses in composition to rough-and-tumble family conversing, consulting, and to pouring out one's love in intra-family letters when separated. What profit it a man if he win honors in *public speaking* if his lines of communication within the family are poorly maintained. These communicative skills must be learned somewhere.

From the standpoint of national and local policy the schools are our hope for ordered change in the habits and skills of people. As the family apprenticeships in other areas have broken down, the schools have provided the necessary training for living in an industrial civilization. The apprentice system in training for marriage and parenthood is today manifestly inadequate. The current wreckage of broken homes and the daily parade of blighted personalities begging for psychiatric aid bear muted testimony. It is timely that the schools assume their full share in filling the gap in teaching family roles which have some chance of producing happy personalities. Every age group from nursery-school youngsters to grandparents may now be served by the public school system. Few new agencies are required to do the job. It remains to bring the problems of family living into our educational focus as we have recently done with the problems of earning a living.

We know that a variety of family types are capable of meeting a crisis, that we do not have to stamp out uniform models. Successful families, however, share the resources of good marital adjustment, family adaptability, and, to a lesser degree, family integration. Their communicative lines must be kept open through frank discussions and the use of the consultative process in arriving at family decisions. Alert educators will see the challenge to train young people, and they will seize the opportunity through adult education to reach young parents, to encourage the development of patterns of family organization which make for survival in the face of trouble. To date, few educators have attempted, even experimentally, to produce students competent to exercise family leadership in flexible family organizations of this sort. Here lies the challenge of family life education of tomorrow!

REGIONAL RESEARCH INSTITUTES NEEDED

In the foregoing recommendations to expand family life education facilities, we have placed heavy responsibilities on educators. Research is badly needed, however, to underpin these educational programs. Substantive materials from the researches in family life are needed if teaching is to go beyond reiteration of the mores and repetition of common-sense generalizations. New insights into successful family living will be opened up most effectively through research. The assumption of family life education and of marriage and family life counseling is that the patterns of marriage and family adjustment are no longer transmitted from the past to the present generation. The function of family life education and of marriage counseling is to disseminate and to make available the findings of research in biology, psychology, and sociology to families and to their members who feel the need of them in planning types of family life which will endure.

If we are to educate family people in the know-how of meeting the exigencies and crises of family living, research in this field must keep abreast of education. From the present study have come several suggestions for future research projects to build and tie together the things we know about families facing all kinds of crises. We list some of them here.

Needed Research in Family Crises and Family Adjustment

1. Basic to research in family adjustment is an adequate scale or inventory to measure adequacy of family adjustment.
    a. Criteria of family success will need to be blocked out and put into measurable form which will segregate successful from less successful families.
    b. Experimentation with combinations of criteria as Dunigan (*13*)

has done with his Scale for the Measurement of Dynamic Stability in Family Life is in order.

   c. New components in family adjustment which demand investigation are: (1) empathy patterns, (2) psychological *set*—the determination to succeed, (3) capacity to use well resources at hand, savior-faire, and (4) problem-solving capacity, to break problems down into components and achieve solutions.

2. Studies of the factors, types of family organization, and conditions of living which make for successful family adjustment are recommended which will be comparable to the investigations of marital adjustment and marital happiness.

   a. The present study uncovered the disquieting evidence that family adjustment to crises was different from early marriage adjustment in the resources which were important for success. Is it possible that success in courtship, success in early marriage, and success in later family living do in fact require different resources?

   b. Repeated studies are needed to show the similarities and differences between marriage situations and later family situations if we are to construct a family life education which is permanently helpful.

   c. Experimentation with silhouettes, profiles, and graphs which take the course of adjustment out of the welter of words into the world of graphic symbols may prove productive in studies of family adjustment.

3. Peacetime separations and reunions should be investigated to follow up the present study of wartime crises.

   a. One index of the number of separations occasioned by employment in other cities, by imprisonment, institutionalization, desertion, and pre-divorce separation shows 2 million households so affected in the peacetime years of 1940 and 1946. A study of the impact of these separations within peacetime dismembered families is badly needed.

4. Crises of *accession* should be investigated to add to our knowledge of families in crisis.

   a. Unwanted pregnancies, unwanted stepmother or stepfather or stepsibling, and unwelcome returnees create situations which produce crises in families, the impact of which demands study.

5. To complete the generic picture of families in crisis we need studies of crises of the *nouveau riche* to parallel crises of impoverishment, and crises of infidelity to parallel crises of alienation on grounds of temperamental incompatability.

6. To answer the controversial question of the ultimate effect of crises on families we need a definitive country-wide study of the effects of sharp changes in purchasing power on families of all walks of life.
   a. Following the Koos (27) method, all the troubles of these families might be recorded over a period of time and the phenomenon of crisis-proneness as well as the ultimate adequacy of adjustment to trouble noted.

7. Continued experimentation with methods of teaming case study and statistics is recommended.
   a. Knowledge and understanding about family life will not be extended by statistical studies alone, and will move slowly if we march only in case study tempo.
   b. Case grouping which does not do violence to the functional make-up of individual families offers hope for combining the two methods.

8. We recommend studies which develop correction factors to take into account the differential frequency and severity of hardships associated with so-called common crises and which also take into account the interpretations or meanings families make of the troubles they meet.
   a. Statistical correction factors may need to wait upon case grouping of families, but ultimately families will need to be scored and weighted in line with the impact of the crisis. Generalizations which ignore the variable impact of crisis on families will have limited validity.
   b. One method of eliminating much of the variability of the crisis is to select families, initially, for study which have faced similar crises, both in terms of the number and severity of the hardships and of the definitions they make of them, thus rendering relatively homogeneous the social situations they faced.

9. Family crisis research must also look to coöperative research ventures with specialists of many disciplines contributing if it is to add to the accuracy of its predictions.
   a. The factors included in the present study accounted for roughly only 16 percent of the variation in the adjustment to separation

scores and about 38 percent of the variation in the adjustment
to reunion scores.
b. We need to add factors and sharpen our measures if we are to
understand the phenomenon of family adjustment to crises even
tolerably well.

These nine suggestions for research are but illustrative of the
work ahead for family specialists concerned with families in crisis.
Many other studies are needed if we are to provide educators with
the materials for preparing people for crises. A new field of training
would follow, "family crisis education."

Yet these nine research suggestions, if properly carried out, will
require the time of almost every professional family researcher in
the country who is engaged even part-time in paid-for research.
Family research workers are patently too few in number to conduct
the many research studies critically needed by our society. Fortunately there are many professionally trained personnel engaged in
teaching and social service who could be drawn into research if
the money were available. If we made research in family life an
integral part of our local and national planning, research workers
could be trained in a few years to man the posts that would be
created.

Our study argues for the establishment of regional research
centers for the study of family life which can coöperatively employ
the services of sociologists, psychologists, home economists, phys-
iologists, economists, and psychiatrists to conduct studies both independently and collectively in the areas of pressing importance to
family life. Dr. Leonard S. Cottrell of Cornell University has suggested that we should base the next decade of family life research
on a thorough-going, systematic work, "What We Know About
the Family." "Research will be more highly productive," he writes,
"if we can achieve enough of a consensus in our definition of the
situation to enable us to make a concerted attack on identifying the

more important problems, and in so doing use a common frame of reference for our analyses and interpretations. If this were done by a substantial proportion of investigators within regional centers and again nationally through professional meetings, the results would be more likely to add up to something than if each of us selects our problems and hypotheses haphazardly as we do now."[6]

The wisdom of regional centers is apparent if we are to capture both the heterogeneity of our country's families regionally and their common human aspects. The regions we would include for family study involve distinct cultural areas: New England, Middle Atlantic, Southeast, Southwest, Middle West, Northwest, Rocky Mountain, and Pacific. Active research stations are now located in each of these areas with substantial subsidies for studying farm animals and food production. We propose that family research be added to the functions of these centers.

In making this request for regional research centers for the study of family life, we ask only that as much support be given financially and administratively to the study of the *farm family* that has been devoted to the *family farm* and its productive operations. We ask that as much support be allocated for the study of the strains and stresses of family life that is currently channeled into the study of bridge construction and safety belts.[7] If the great industrial concerns which have been organized to serve American families with labor-saving devices, sweet-smelling soaps, and recreational equipment for the home would set aside just a tenth of their research budgets for research into the real needs of these families, our re-

[6] Leonard S. Cottrell, Jr., "The Present Status and Future Orientation of Research on the Family," *American Sociological Review* (April, 1948), pp. 123–136.

[7] Recently a researcher in safety did propose to his administrator two studies: the one a study of the types of webbing most likely to withstand strain and exposure to be used in safety belts for window cleaners, the second for the study of the common observation that proneness to accidents runs in families and might be related in some way to aggravations within the home. The first project was allocated several thousand dollars, the second was rejected with the notation, "short of money this year, keep on file."

search centers would be handsomely financed. Billboards advertise the American family on wheels under the caption "The American Way of Life," yet millions are spent studying ways and means of improving the wheels and only pennies are allocated to study the families which ride on them.

Field research with representative families requires a staff of interviewers and involves costs of transportation, living costs of workers, and clerical expenses. It is more expensive than armchair research, but less expensive than most medical research and most research in the biological and physical sciences. To complete the projects recommended above will be costly, but they could be financed with a fraction of the money spent to bring out a new model car for the national market. If there are values inherent in family life (and the evidence is too well established to need repetition here), and our society neglects to preserve these values, we can only expect further family breakdown with increased social disorganization. Through research adequately supported and through family life education and marriage and family counseling, the necessary shoring up of the nation's family resources may take place. Money invested to keep families well is certain to be less than the costs of patching up broken families *ad infinitum!*

NEEDED: A LOCAL AND NATIONAL POLICY FOR FAMILY LIFE

We return at the close of this book to the issues raised in the preface. For too long, American families have been called upon to take up the slack in a poorly integrated social order. For too long, the family has been ignored in social planning, and the strains are telling. The modern family lives in a greater state of tension because it is the great burden carrier of the social order, the bottleneck through which all troubles pass. Moreover, the good family today is not only the focal point of frustrations and tensions but also the source of resolving frustrations and releasing tensions, the great rehabilitator of personalities bruised in the course of competitive daily living. In the opinion of Dr. William C. Menninger, President of the American Psychiatric Association, "much of the world's sickness is due to home sickness, which can be cured only by the home remedy of family love, understanding and coöperation."[8]

This great national resource of recuperative capacities, America's families, has been intermittently and callously ignored and ruthlessly exploited by thoughtless vested interests. National morale depends upon the maintenance of adequate families equipped to provide the love-in-action which sends men back to their jobs morning after morning with some zest for work, and which speeds children on to school prepared to make something of the day's tasks. Our great oil and timber resources are tangible and visible, and the inches of top soil which produce our agricultural products may be dramatized by soil conservationists, but nations and communities are not strong because of their natural resources. They are measured by their effectiveness in using those natural resources in attaining the objectives of the good life. This effectiveness is in turn directly related to the nation's families and their recuperative capacities. Through our families the basic satisfactions for which we toil are achieved and transmuted into good national morale and healthy happy personalities.

If the family is such a vital link in the chain of events, it is high time we shaped a set of national and local policies which will affirm its place in our way of life. The recent National Conference on Family Life, in the White House (May, 1948), made some promising beginnings in that direction.

A national policy for family life would attempt to discover and recognize the many obstacles, resistances, conflicts, and confusions, many of which are now unrecognized but are existent in the lives of men and women, which are currently operating to disrupt or undermine the family. Policy making would offer to those who con-

---

[8] William C. Menninger, "How's Your Family Living?" *Parents' Magazine* (October, 1947).

duct our national affairs—governmental workers, economists, especially our businessmen, and other organized professional people —a clearly stated formulation of where and how their practices and decisions are affecting family life. In the field of housing the sacredness of property and the right to make a profit would be faced with the sacredness of family life and the right to adequate shelter and protection from the elements.

Lawrence K. Frank to whom we are indebted for many of our ideas in this chapter has clearly differentiated between a national *policy* for family life and national *programs* of family betterment.

What do we mean by a policy? It should be distinguished from a plan or specific program, which is concerned with more or less specified activities for a determinate time period and usually on an actual or estimated budget. We have innumerable programs, of private and governmental organizations, addressed to the family, but no underlying policy to give the programs much needed direction and articulation. . . .

A policy is a formulation of long term goals and purposes and of the values and aspirations by which those goals and purposes are not only defined but are to be translated into activities and practices. Thus a policy is an affirmation, perhaps a reaffirmation, of what may be taken for granted or is implied, but what is frequently ignored or neglected or inadequately recognized in plans and programs and customary operations. Sometimes a policy serves to point out where these goals and purposes and these values are being blocked or sacrificed to various short term ends or convenience. . . .

A policy, therefore, might be likened to strategy, the broad, overall, long term conception which gives direction and purpose to the tactics of immediately daily operations and decisions.[9]

The need for a set of national and local policies for family life arises out of the breakdown of our social order as we have shifted from an agricultural society with its self-sufficing farm household and its large extended patriarchal family to an urban, highly inter-

---

[9] Lawrence K. Frank, "A National Policy for the Family," *Marriage and Family Living* (Winter, 1948), p. 1.

dependent society with its variety of family types and forms. Many of our procedures which touch families were established on the assumption that we are still primarily a rural people organized into self-sufficient households. We have drifted along as a nation assuming that the family could and would meet the changes of industrial living and urbanization. The growing discrepancies indicate clearly how urgent is the need for a national policy to guide the long overdue revision of our legal conceptions and procedures, our medical practices, our educational programs, our economic arrangements, indeed, almost every aspect of our national life.

Many of these practices are contradictory and confusing to families today. An aim of national policy would be to foster the articulation of diverse agencies and professions, of focusing many specialized and autonomous activities into a more coherent, internally consistent synthesis, without regimenting or dictating to anyone or any organization.[10]

As we review how a national policy of an unwritten nature has affected the families in the present study, it is interesting to see how many procedures have been adopted without study or investigation.

1. The National Selective Service followed a policy of deferring fathers from military service because of their dependents, until the man power reserves were nearly depleted. They did not even register women for military service.
   a. The policy operates on the assumption that unmarried women and mothers are more important to the domestic scene than are men and reciprocally that men are more important to the military services than women.
   b. The policy assumes that fathers are less important than unmarried women and than mothers in their family roles. "A father can be replaced in the family, but a mother can't!"
2. The military services made allotments to men in service in line with the number of their dependents, but made no pretense at paying fathers in service a wage commensurate with their wages in civilian life.
   a. This is the most widespread application of the policy of paying

[10] *Ibid.*, p. 2.

a family wage yet attempted in America, and assumes that society shares some responsibility for the costs of child rearing.

3. The military services made available maternity care and limited medical services to dependents of servicemen.

    a. These services, though limited, were offered on the assumption that expenses for medical care fall disproportionately on those families in the child-bearing and child-rearing stages of the family life cycle and some means of sharing the costs should be established.

4. Through local chapters of the American Red Cross, attempts at keeping the family ties intact and helping families with their day-to-day problems were followed. Fathers were discharged from the services if hardships became too acute.

    a. The assumption that wartime separations constitute hardships which may be mitigated and that good family morale is important to good soldier morale underlies this policy.

    b. No large-scale program to deal with the crises attendant upon peacetime dismemberment of families has yet been attempted.

5. The military services as a policy granted periodic furloughs and allowed visits from family members to camps within the states, to keep the family ties intact.

    a. The same assumptions listed in the policy mentioned immediately above underpin this program.

Most of the provisions for families listed above have been based upon an unwritten and nonexplicit national policy followed in wartime by the selective service and the armed services in their dealings with American families. Most of them proved helpful for the families we studied in Iowa. The policy, for example, of deferring fathers is sound, quite as sound as the policy of not drafting mothers. The allotments to families was undoubtedly a great stabilizer, although the influence of income was not a direct force in separation adjustment. The easing of the burdens of maternity costs through maternity and infant care provided by government grant proved a mitigator of hardship. The policy of the American Red Cross was humane in its effects wherever families were reached. Again, the practice of providing furloughs produced disturbances in the families when the men returned on furlough, but were ultimately beneficial on their adjustments as families to both separation and reunion. The return of the father on furlough provided a healthy check on the letter-to-letter relationships established and reëstablished communication for those families which had done poorly by letter. All in all, American families were more thoughtfully considered under a military policy constructed with the objective of winning a war than they have been under the confusion of no policy at all, which characterizes the United States in peacetime. A national policy making explicit the needs of families and their place in the national scheme is certainly long overdue.

From the present study we would contribute these generalizations for consideration in the formulation of national policy: Families should be kept intact and relatively self-sustaining. The hardships of separation and the jolts of reunion are disintegrating in their effects on many families. In the absence of the father it is difficult for the family to continue operating *as a family,* although most of the families in the study survived both separation and reunion in good physical condition. It was their social-psychological condition which was threatened by the fracture of their ranks. Children experience insecurity in the withdrawal of a major source of parental authority and are less amenable to guidance when they need it most. Many children experience affectional deprivations during this period which stimulate mothers to say with fervor, "You can't raise children without a father!" The father does manifestly serve more than a meal-ticket function, and that is the only one of his many services to the family that the military services were able to replace. To be effective as a family, two parents are needed during the child-rearing years.

The day of taking the American family for granted is drawing to a close. The critical situation in family life today cannot be denied. The evidence is apparent everywhere. We have added to it within the covers of this book. Tensions and insecurity threaten even the most stable homes. The situation has passed beyond the capacity of any single family to cope with these difficulties unaided. We must consider what we can do as a concerted effort to help all families, not as a sentimental movement but as a basic need for national stability and social order. The capacity of families to take up the slack in the social order is approaching an upper limit. Their tremendous resilience and recuperative strengths must be fostered and conserved. A national policy which deals with American families as a precious national resource in social organization appears forthcoming. It will receive the support of the findings of this study and the approval of the great majority of families rearing children today.

APPENDIX A

SELECTED BIBLIOGRAPHY

1. Angell, Robert C., *The Family Encounters the Depression* (New York: Charles Scribner's Sons, 1936).
2. Bakké, E. Wight, *The Unemployed Worker* (New Haven: Yale University Press, 1940).
3. Becker, Howard, "Interpretive Sociology and Constructive Typology." In *Twentieth Century Sociology,* ed. by Georges Gurvitch and Wilbert E. Moore (New York: The Philosophical Library, 1945).
4. Becker, Howard, "The Sorrow of Bereavement," *Journal of Abnormal and Social Psychology* (January–March, 1933), pp. 391–430.
5. Bossard, James H. S., *The Sociology of Child Development* (New York: Harper & Brothers, 1947).
6. Bossard, James H. S., and Boll, Eleanor S., *Family Situations* (Philadelphia: University of Pennsylvania Press, 1943).
7. Burgess, Ernest W., "The Family and Sociological Research," *Social Forces* (October, 1937), pp. 1–6.
8. Burgess, Ernest W., and Cottrell, Leonard S., Jr., *Predicting Success or Failure in Marriage* (New York: Prentice-Hall, Inc., 1939).
9. Burgess, Ernest W., and Locke, Harvey, *The Family: From Institution to Companionship* (New York: American Book Company, 1945).
10. Cavan, Ruth, *The Restudy of the Documents Analyzed by Angell in "The Family Encounters the Depression"* (New York: Committee on Appraisal of the Social Science Research Council, unpublished).
11. Cavan, Ruth, and Ranck, Katherine, *The Family and the Depression* (Chicago: University of Chicago Press, 1938).
12. Daniels, Jonathan, "What Makes a Marriage Tick," *McCall's* (May, 1947).
13. Dunigan, Lowell H., *A Scale for the Measurement of Dynamic Stability in Family Life* (M.S. Thesis, Iowa State College, Ames, Iowa, 1948, unpublished).

14. Duvall, Evelyn Millis, "Conceptions of Parenthood," *American Journal of Sociology* (November, 1946), pp. 193–203.
15. Duvall, Evelyn Millis, "Loneliness and the Serviceman's Wife," *Marriage and Family Living* (August, 1945), pp. 77–82.
16. Duvall, Evelyn Millis, and Hill, Reuben, *When You Marry* (Boston: D. C. Heath & Company, 1945).
17. Eels, Kenneth, *Refining and Testing the Validity of the Index of Status Characteristics* (Committee on Human Development, University of Chicago, Chicago, July, 1945, unpublished).
18. Elder, Rachell-Ann Lusher, *Traditional and Developmental Conceptions of Fatherhood* (M.S. Thesis, Iowa State College, Ames, Iowa, 1947, unpublished).
19. Eliot, Thomas D., "Bereavement: Inevitable But Not Insurmountable." In *Family, Marriage and Parenthood,* ed. by Howard Becker and Reuben Hill (Boston: D. C. Heath & Company, 1948).
20. Eliot, Thomas D., "Handling Family Strains and Shocks." In *Family, Marriage and Parenthood,* ed. by Howard Becker and Reuben Hill (Boston: D. C. Heath & Company, 1948).
21. Fulcomer, David M., *The Adjustive Behavior of Some Recently Bereaved Spouses* (Ph.D. Thesis, Northwestern University, Evanston, Illinois, 1942).
22. Hill, Reuben, "The Returning Father and His Family," *Marriage and Family Living* (May, 1945), pp. 31–34.
23. Kinsey, Alfred C., Pomeroy, Wardell B., and Martin, Clyde E., *Sexual Behavior in the Human Male* (Philadelphia: W. B. Saunders Company, 1948).
24. Kirkpatrick, Clifford, and Caplow, Theodore, "Emotional Trends in the Courtship Experience of College Students as Expressed by Graphs with Some Observations on Methodological Implications," *American Sociological Review* (October, 1945), pp. 619–626.
25. Komarovsky, Mirra, *The Unemployed Man and His Family* (New York: Dryden Press, 1940).
26. Koos, E. L., "Families in Crisis." In *The Dynamics of Family Interaction*, ed. by Evelyn M. Duvall and Reuben Hill (Washington: The National Conference on Family Life, 1948, mimeographed report).
27. Koos, E. L., *Families in Trouble* (New York: King's Crown Press, 1946).
28. Koos, E. L., *The Middle-Class Family and Its Problems* (New York: Columbia University Press, 1948).

29. Mather, W. S., "Defining Family Types on the Basis of Control," *The Family* (1935–1936), pp. 8–12.
30. Morgan, Winona L., *The Family Meets the Depression* (Minneapolis: University of Minnesota Press, 1939).
31. Rundquist, Edward A., and Sletto, Raymond F., *Personality and the Depression* (Minneapolis: University of Minnesota Press, 1936).
32. Terman, L. M., *Psychological Factors in Marital Happiness* (New York: McGraw-Hill Book Company, Inc., 1938).
33. Waller, Willard, *The Old Love and the New: Divorce and Readjustment* (New York: Liveright Publishing Corporation, 1930).
34. Williams, Edith Webb, *Factors Associated with Adjustment in Rural Marriage* (Ph.D. Thesis, Cornell University Library, Ithaca, New York, 1938).
35. Winch, Robert F., "Heuristic and Empirical Typologies: A Job for Factor Analysis," *American Sociological Review* (February, 1947), pp. 68–75.

APPENDIX B

APPLICATION OF THE SCIENTIFIC METHOD TO THE STUDY OF FAMILY CRISES

We especially welcome persons who are methodology-minded to a reading of this methodological note. It is the "tool shed in the back" to which we have referred in several chapters in the book. In it may be found a brief description of some of the many tools used in the study. Some of the tools in our tool shed are standard makes and can be found in any text on statistical research methods; others we have borrowed from the people who made them with the promise of contributing to their standardization; and a very few we have been forced to construct ourselves from the materials available. In general, we constructed no new tool when a reliable scale or test was already available. The context in which the study was launched was one of pressure and haste. The war was over in Europe and there was hope that Japan would soon capitulate. If we were to collect our data while the crises of separation and reunion still had meaning for the families we proposed to study, we would have to cut all corners possible. The crudity of some of the tools we fashioned ourselves is explained, if not justified, on the grounds of expediency—the project needed to be pushed off dead center, if it were to become a study at all!

The research procedure we designed required the following kinds of tools.

1. Tools[1] for selecting and identifying families that would be representative of a universe, the dimensions of which no agency had yet calculated: Iowa families made temporarily fatherless by induction or enlistment into the armed services.

2. Questionnaires, tests, scales, and interview forms with which to record with some precision and uniformity our observations of families under stress of separation and reunion.

3. Methods of sorting, tabulating, ordering, categorizing, and testing observations made and any derivative generalizations arrived at concern-

[1] Discussed on pp. 27–28.

368

ing causal interconnections of data to determine whether they are reliable or happen-chance.

4. Devices of exposition to make findings more graphic and understandable for the general reader.

Because it has already been necessary to present a general picture of methodology in the chapters of this book—namely, Chapter II (pp. 8-24), Chapter III (pp. 25-31), Chapter V (pp.103-110), and Chapter VI (pp. 157-168, 194-207)—we will be selective in our discussion of method in this note. Schedule construction, validating and pretesting, and problems in collecting the data will receive major attention. Tools for analyzing the observations made with special reference to the complementary nature of the statistical and case study techniques of analysis will also receive treatment.

Devices for Recording Observations of Family Behavior

In Chapter II are listed fourteen areas of behavior which a survey of the literature on families in crisis and of the situations facing our families indicated should be investigated in this study of families under stress. To accomplish this task four questionnaires were constructed—two for the husband and two for the wife—as well as an interview form containing the basic unknowns for the interviewer to probe with both husband and wife. In these schedules over 500 separate questions were posed. Conferences with other specialists conducting family studies were held in the hope of cutting down the number of items in the schedules, but each man added more ideas than he pared away. A pretest with thirty families in Story County, Iowa, and Cache County, Utah, showed the questionnaires were not too time consuming but substantiated the fact that the interviews were too long. The pretest did give us, however, confidence in our method and dispelled any fears that people wouldn't talk about the intimate matters contained in the schedules.

A division of labor between questionnaire and interview form was worked out, in which materials that could be easily checked—such as scales, tests, and inventories—were placed in the questionnaire. By and large, items involving rating of one's marriage, one's happiness in childhood, and other items regarded by Ellis as "ego-involving" were placed in the questionnaire where they could be filled out with a minimum of embarrassment.[2] All questions involving narration of any sort were

---

[2] Albert Ellis, "Questionnaire Versus Interview Methods in the Study of Human Love Relationships," *American Sociological Review* (October, 1947), pp. 541-553.

placed in the interview form where the possibilities of "concrete interviewing," as Lazarsfeld terms it, could be followed up.[3] The vivid case materials laying bare the depths of past and present family experiences and revealing how the interviewee now felt about them were elicited through the interview form by open-end questions. Where hypotheses were already precisely formulated and tentative answers known the questionnaire was indicated. Where the material went beyond the definitive, into the exploratory areas and closed categories requiring "yes" or "no" answers were beyond our ken to supply, the information was obviously best attained through interview. In the scales for rating family adaptability, family integration, social status, and type of affectional home life, the judgment of the interviewer was needed, and it was, therefore, included in the interview form. More on that point later.

With this much introduction we will proceed to a discussion of our observational devices. The questionnaires will first be described and their validity indicated as far as possible. Second, the scales used in the interview form will receive similar treatment. The section will be concluded with an evaluation of the data-collecting process, with special emphasis on the approach used in obtaining the interview, the interviewing process, and the results obtained.

Copies of all schedules used are found in Appendix C, pp. 399–434. The extensive interview form is called Family Adjustments in Wartime (Interviewer). The questionnaires are listed in order of size: Family Adjustments in Wartime (Wife); Family Adjustments in Wartime (Husband); Adjustments to Reunion (Wife); and Adjustments to Reunion (Husband). Wherever scores were ascribed to responses they are shown in the appropriate blanks.

FAMILY ADJUSTMENTS IN WARTIME (WIFE)

In this questionnaire is contained, in addition to pertinent background data solicited through "face-sheet" questions, a relatives' helpfulness score, a happiness score for wife's parents, wife's history of happiness score, the Burgess-Cottrell Marital Adjustment Form, a social participation scale, the Thurstones' short form for psychoneurotic inventory, and

---

[3] See Paul F. Lazarsfeld's points in the Introduction to Mirra Komarovsky's study (25) of the effect of unemployment upon the status of the father in a New York sample of fifty-nine families. By means of concrete interviewing, Komarovsky was able to "discern" the causality of single events, eliminating some and including others.

a scale for measuring the adjustments of family to separation by Reuben Hill.

The face-sheet information requires no special explanation and is straightforward and easily provided. It involves items 1 to 13, 17 to 18, 22, and 25.

The relatives' helpfulness score, item 14, was devised by the author by assigning weights to responses which showed increased intervention and investment on the part of in-laws in the stricken family.

Happiness score for wife's parents, item 19, and wife's history of happiness score, item 21, were adapted from Burgess and Cottrell (8) and appear self-explanatory.

The Burgess-Cottrell Marital Adjustment Form, covered by items 15, 20, 23, 24, 27, 28, 29, and 30, is now well recognized as a test for marital adjustment. Its validity and reliability are discussed in detail in Burgess and Cottrell (8) in their chapter, "Constructing an Index of Marital Adjustment," pp. 58–74. Parts of the test have also been used by Terman (32) in an exhaustive study of California marriages, and by Williams (34) in a study of rural couples in New York State. The validity of the marriage adjustment scale of Burgess and Cottrell was given a double test in that it was found to have a high correlation with ratings of happiness—"very happy," "happy," "average," "unhappy," "very unhappy"— reported by husbands and wives, and with the presence or lack of marital disorganization as indicated by divorce, separation, contemplation of divorce or separation, and no contemplation of divorce or separation.

The social participation score of wife during separation, item 26, was devised by Evelyn Duvall and Reuben Hill to provide data comparable with the University of Chicago study of servicemen's wives conducted by E. W. Burgess and by Evelyn Duvall (15). The activities listed were modified to include interests not present in the Chicago study but likely to be pursued by Iowa women. The weighting, although arbitrarily arrived at, differentiated clearly in the pretest of Story County, Iowa families between nonparticipants and active participants.

The Thurstones' brief psychoneurotic inventory called by them a "Personality Schedule" was borrowed, with its scores, from the Burgess marriage study schedule. Its use as an index of personality adequacy in studies of engagement and marriage success has received careful consideration from Robert F. Winch.[4] The original test consisted of forty-two questions

[4] Robert F. Winch, The Relation Between Neurotic Tendency and the Adjustment in Engagement (Master's Thesis, Chicago, University of Chicago Library, 1942, unpublished).

which have been reported by the Thurstones as differentiating most significantly between "high scoring" and "low scoring" subjects on neurotic tendency.[5]

The Adjustments of Family to Separation Scale, items 32 to 37, was constructed for the study by Reuben Hill after several weeks of interviewing and consultation with the families of servicemen and the field workers for Story County Red Cross. Thirty families representing all walks of life in Story County, Iowa, and Cache County, Utah, coöperated in the pretest, and many of its ambiguities were eliminated following the analysis of the pretest results. The revised scale was presented to specialists in family research called together by the National Council on Family Relations in August, 1945. With minor suggestions, these workers, all of whom were conducting studies of the effects of war on the family, approved the application of the scale to the hitherto unmeasured crisis of war separation.

The scale attempts to disperse along a continuum families that have adjusted well to separation from those that have done less well. We attempted to measure both functional adjustment—that is, how the family actually behaves outwardly and overtly in reacting to the father's absence—and attitudinal adjustment—that is, how members of the family (particularly the wife) feel about being separated, the inward content of family life seen in its attitudes, dreams, and fantasies. Five areas of family life were probed: husband-wife relationships, father-child relationships, and child-father relationships; adequacy of reallocation of roles within the family; satisfaction with the marriage now a redefinition is possible; relationships with inlaws, relatives, friends, and neighbors; and evidences of planning for the reunion. For each of those areas statements were provided which would indicate shades of functional or attitudinal adjustment to the crisis of separation.

The scores to be given the forty-nine statements in the scale were obtained from the combined judgments of four judges: Evelyn M. Duvall, Ph.D., University of Chicago; Bertha Whitson, M.S., Iowa State College; Elise Boulding, and Reuben Hill, associates on the project. The judges had access to a common definition of adjustment to separation: "Good adjustment to separation involves closing of ranks, shifting of responsibilities and activities of the father to other members, continuing the necessary family routines, maintaining husband-wife and father-child

[5] See L. L. and T. G. Thurstone, "A Neurotic Inventory," *Journal of Social Psychology,* Vol. 1, pp. 3–30.

relationships by correspondence and visits, utilizing the resources of friends, relatives and neighbors, and carrying on plans for the reunion."

Marking on a five-point scale from poor adjustment to excellent adjustment, the judges agreed unanimously on the appropriate score designation of thirty of the forty-nine statements. On seventeen of the remaining nineteen statements one judge differed by one point from the other three judges. The two statements in which there was a difference of two points were also statements where more than one judge was in disagreement. These were reworded in such a fashion that agreement was possible. The scores for the seventeen on which there was only one judge in disagreement were left as the majority had designated them.

The task of validation of the scale was difficult to accomplish, both because there was so little time left in which to design and launch the study if the data were to be gathered while the memories of the crisis and adjustments to separation were still fresh, and because there were few external criteria of good adjustment to separation against which to appraise the validity of our scale.

Professor John Cuber of Ohio State University nobly undertook the task of distributing our scale to twelve of the families in his study of Kent University graduates who had been married in wartime, separated by service, and were now parents.[6] Dr. Cuber had known many of these young people as undergraduates and had followed them through three years of marriage, and was, therefore, able to add his own evaluation of the adequacy of their functional adjustment to separation as an aid in validating our scale. Cuber marked his rating on the following five-point scale:

1	2	3	4	5
Broken Up	Poor Adj.	Average or only Fair Adj.	Satisfactory Adj.	Excellent Adj. —Thriving—

From the Cuber ratings and the average scores for adjustment to separation obtained for each family from their responses on the scale Adjustments of Family to Separation, we received evidence that we were measuring to a limited extent the same phenomenon. Cuber's ratings had a much higher dispersion than the scores obtained from the scale; his ratings varied from one to five whereas the scale as it turned out pro-

[6] For an interesting discussion of this study see Jonathan Daniels' article, "Marriage Is Like That," *McCall's* (October, 1946).

374   FAMILIES UNDER STRESS

vided scores which varied only from 2.10 to 3.85. The coefficient of correlation between the two sets of scores was low and not significant, $r = 0.34.$[7]

A further attempt at validation of the scale was made following the pretest of the questionnaires and interview form on twenty-one Story County families. The field worker for the American Red Cross, who was working directly with these same families, was asked to rate their adjustment to separation following the same procedure used by Dr. Cuber. Again the same pattern of greater dispersion among the field worker's ratings than in the average scores obtained from the scale was apparent. We think perhaps that both the field worker and Dr. Cuber judged the adequacy of adjustment to separation largely from the standpoint of functional or behavioral adjustment. The scale goes beyond the behavioral and attempts to pick up the "how do you feel about," attitudinal materials which might mitigate somewhat the more categorical functional judgments. The coefficient of correlation between the Red Cross field worker's ratings and the Adjustments of Family to Separation scores was low and not quite significant at the 5 percent level, $r = 0.37.$

Perfectionists would undoubtedly have had us drop the idea of continuing the study at this point, or would have had us use valuable time revising and reorganizing the scale in the hopes of obtaining something which would correspond more closely with some external criterion of adjustment to separation. The reader will judge whether we should have followed such a course. Our alternatives were not black and white in this instance but grayish. We chose to continue the study using the Adjustments of Family to Separation Scale for what it was worth, as the best available index of family adjustment we knew about. An eloquent defense might possibly be written following the theme that this is really the first study of family adjustment which has made any large-scale attempt to use inventories, scales, and tests, thereby going beyond the highly individualized and intuitive judgments which have characterized the pioneer family studies to date. The statistical section of the study, nevertheless, is little stronger than its scales and inventories. The Adjustments of Family to Separation Scale may be its weakest link. Adjustment to separation is, after all, one of the two major dependent variables in the study!

[7] With so few cases it would have been necessary to have a correlation of 0.58 to achieve the 5 percent level of significance.

FAMILY ADJUSTMENTS IN WARTIME (HUSBAND)

This questionnaire, found in Appendix C, pp. 409–412, was mailed by the wife to the husband, if he were still in service, and mailed by him to the project. The return from these questionnaires was very poor, only about 20 percent. The returns were excellent if the husband were home because he filled out the questionnaire before his interview with the interviewer. The husband's questionnaire was, however, a slender reed on which to depend because of the large number of men still in service, and therefore most of the indispensable background data were obtained from the wife's questionnaire.

The husband's questionnaire contains a minimum of face-sheet information, items 1 to 7, the happiness score of husband's parents, item 8, the Burgess-Cottrell Marital Adjustment Form, items 9 to 14 (modified to take into account the husband's absence from home), questions eliciting the aspects of family life he most missed, item 15, a series of statements indicating role of family in building or hurting morale, item 16, the substitutes he found for family life in service, item 17, and concludes with a request for his feelings about life away from his family, item 18. With the exception of the Burgess-Cottrell Marital Adjustment Form (already discussed pp. 371–372), all of these questions were designed by the authors to test hypotheses concerning the family life of servicemen while in service. They are largely self-explanatory.

ADJUSTMENTS TO REUNION (WIFE) AND ADJUSTMENTS TO REUNION (HUSBAND)

These two questionnaires are found in Appendix C, pp. 413–416, and, as will be seen, are identical except for gender and person. They were designed by Reuben Hill to provide a measure of the relative success attained in adjusting to reunion which would be roughly comparable to what the Adjustments of Family to Separation Scale did for separation adjustments. With fewer statements from which to choose, the scale, nevertheless, attempts to capture the functional and attitudinal adjustments to reunion which were identified as the sources of friction in the separation period. The scale touches on husband-wife relationships, the division of labor within the home, the reallocation of roles, the father-child relationships, and the areas of conflict which are likely to crop up in reunion. These several areas were stressed because preliminary interviews with reunited families and discussions with family specialists and Red Cross field workers highlighted them as sore spots.

The scores (along a five-point scale) assigned for each statement were arrived at from a consensus of judges following a definition of adjustment to reunion worked out beforehand: "Good adjustment to reunion involves opening the ranks to let the father back, realigning the power and authority, reworking the division of labor and responsibilities, sharing the home and family activities with the father, renewing the husband-wife intimacies and confidences, catching up on one another's friends, resuming the father-child ties, bringng balance between husband-wife and mother-child and father-child relationships, picking up the plans made during separation, reworking and finally putting them into action."

The judges found some of the elements of the above definition missing in the scale but agreed rather well on the scoring for each statement in the scale. The same four judges evaluated the scale that undertook the assigning of weights to the Adjustments of Family to Separation Scale already discussed. Of twenty statements all judges agreed on the scores that twelve statements should be given. Three of four judges were in complete agreement concerning the proper weights to be given the other eight statements. The final scores assigned followed the consensus of the judges and can be seen in the questionnaire blanks, pp. 413–416. The score for the family as a whole was obtained by averaging the scores from the wife's and the husband's questionnaires.

There was neither time nor talent for the validation of the adjustment to reunion scales. The scales were rushed into mimeographed form late in the project after V-J Day, to be used in conjunction with the adjustment to separation scales for those families where reunion had already occurred at the time the interview took place. Considering the haste with which these latter scales were devised, it is gratifying that they have proved as valuable as they have in setting off the well adjusted from the poorly adjusted in reunion. Independent case study analysis of the reunion narratives by Mrs. Elise Boulding supports the scores assigned families from the adjustment to reunion scales.

Section B of each questionnaire contains a means of graphically charting the affectional heights and depths experienced by husband and wife with respect to each other during the long period from induction through reunion. A separate analysis of these graphs (for a later publication) will be made to test in the war separation context the hypothesis advanced by

Kirkpatrick and Caplow (24) and tested by them on college students that love affairs mount and decline in intensity in identifiable patterns.

THE FAMILY HISTORY [FAMILY ADJUSTMENTS IN WARTIME (INTERVIEWER)]

This form constituted the framework of a two-hour interview with the wife and the husband (if he had returned from service) and can be seen in Appendix C, pp. 416–434. It is organized functionally starting with the family's present living arrangements, an excellent conversation opener, and proceeds from there to a discussion of the hardships of separation, how the families were managing without a father, and so on. The form constitutes a personal document designed and shaped to obtain intimate data with minimum discomfort to the interviewee. We had many questions at the time we constructed the schedules about the advisability of combining case narrative and statistical materials in one interview, and we circulated such a set of questions among twenty of our colleagues, doing similar research elsewhere, asking for any help they could give us.

Special Problems Which Torment Us

1. How defensible are open-end questions in a schedule with several interviewers conducting the interviews?
2. Is there a better way than by specific open-end questions to obtain information on role patterns, family organization, and areas of tension? Are diaries written in chronological order more rewarding?
3. Are any scales developed to measure family adjustment to temporary dismemberment or to reunion afterward? Is it sound to formulate scales as we have done and validate them against case narrative materials as we plan to do?
4. Is there any best way to insure return of the wife's schedule and sending of the husband's schedule with any assurance of its return?
5. What are the hazards of depending so completely on the wife's version of the family and its problems? Must we rule out collateral checkups because of the need for complete confidence of the interviewee in his own anonymity?
6. Has anyone had any success with diaries or running records kept by the family members themselves? Would they serve as helps in recording the later adjustments in the reunion period?

The answers which were returned were mostly jocular: "Don't know, try it and see" or "Never tried it" or "You know more about this than we do, tell us how you come out." It was in such a context of willingness to experiment that the interview form was launched.

The family history to be obtained by interview divides into three major sections: I. The Family Since Induction; II. Pre-Induction Marital and Family Patterns and Organizations; and III. Adjustments to Reunion. The first section consists almost entirely of open-end questions dealing with the hardships of the separation period. The second section stresses early childhood, courtship, and marriage experiences with similar open-end questions, but also includes rating scales and scoring devices for the interviewer to manipulate. The third section returns again to the exploratory type of questions probing the reactions to the reunion of husband, wife, and children.

I. The Family Since Induction. The introductory materials involve straightforward recording and probing to make sure that the evidence is at hand for "discerning" causes from coincidences. The first three subdivisions are of this sort: Living Arrangements of Family; Adjustments of Wife to Separation (affectionally and psychosomatically and changes in her roles as father and mother too); and Adjustments of Children to Separation, with the painful accompaniments of father-sickness, anxieties, and disciplinary problems. The materials under the heading Nature and Frequency of Family Interaction During the Husband's Period in Service lend themselves to counting the number of visits, furloughs, and letters, and also involve evaluating the content of letters. Some of this material can be handled statistically, as indices of Family Communication During Separation. The material referring to family income, savings, and indebtedness before induction and during separation, is also subject to statistical treatment and probably requires no further explanation. There are few, if any, methodological problems in this section of open-end questions and verbatim recording of answers. Speed writing and/or shorthand helped in recording.

II. Pre-Induction Marital and Family Patterns and Organization. This section of the interview demanded more than interviewing skill of the interviewer. Beginning with item B (Roles Formed in the Marriage), and continuing with item F (Adaptability Before Induction), item G (Integration Before Induction), item H (Affectional Home Type), and ending with item I (Status Characteristics), an understanding of the concepts used and the basic hypotheses of the study were most important, and the ability to make sharp relative judgments was most crucial. Untrained, unschooled interviewers could not be entrusted with such a task.[8] For example, on the basis of data obtained by indirect questioning the interviewer needed to judge such intricate items as the relative dominance-submission in the husband-wife relation, the social roles played by the wife in the marriage, the method of handling the family purse, the method of settling disagreements, and the operation of the principle of least interest within the marriage, i.e., to whom does the marriage mean the most?

The scales for adaptability and for integration are found under items F and G. They have been adapted for the present study from the scales prepared originally by Ruth Cavan (*10*) for the restudy of the Angell (*1*) cases by the Committee on Appraisal of the Social Science Research Council. Leading questions to open a discussion on which the interviewer could base a rating were supplied by the author, but the scores assigned to individual categories have been retained so that the data obtained would be comparable to the Angell data and standardization made possible.

Two other changes were made following the pretest as we perceived our inability to rate families under the Cavan categories. The item "Willingness to Shift Roles" was reworked from Cavan's original "Adaptability to Roles"[9] to give it both a functional and an attitudinal component. In the integration scale, the original items from Cavan's scale involving "Absence of Tensions" and "Degree of Solidarity" were combined into one item listed in our revised scale as "Degree to Which Solidarity is Present."

Lowell Dunigan (*13*) conceived the idea that a scale for dynamic stability could be constructed out of the Burgess-Cottrell Marital Adjustment Form, the integration scale and the adaptability scale. He noted the intercorrelations we reported in the table on page 198.

---

[8] Although it was not planned that over 80 percent of the families would be interviewed by Reuben Hill and Elise Boulding, that is how it turned out. All schedules were scanned carefully to eliminate instances of careless, or dishonest recording (see our previous discussion of the shrinkage of cases, pp. 28–30). Both Hill and Boulding collaborated in the study from its inception, and were, therefore, thoroughly aware of the implications of the scales used in this section of the study. For other interviewers, a Manual of Instructions for Interviewers contained careful definitions of all terms and examples.

[9] For a copy of Cavan's original scale in published form, see E. W. Burgess and Harvey Locke, *The Family: From Institution to Companionship,* (New York: American Book Company, 1945), pp. 781–784.

Marital adjustment and integration   0.58
Marital adjustment and adaptability   0.54
Adaptability and integration   0.47

The correlations, which are all significant, indicated to Dunigan that the three criteria were probably both interdependent and yet measured slightly different aspects of the same phenomenon—family adjustment. Dunigan chose to call this three-way measurement of family adjustment, a Scale for Dynamic Stability. Using our families as subjects, Dunigan proceeded to test the new scale for validity and reliability.

In the absence of an external criterion of dynamic stability in family life, the validity of each item was tested by the method of correlation with the total score. The assumption was made that items which had at least a moderate correlation with the total score were valid items in that they measured whatever it is the total score represents. We show the results of Dunigan's item analysis of integration and adaptability in the accompanying table.

Item Analysis of Integration and Adaptability

Item	Mean	Sigma	Correlation
Adaptability	17.64	2.78	
1. Values	3.46	1.02	.56
2. Control	3.56	.90	.41
3. Flexible roles	3.44	1.05	.23
4. Responsibility	3.61	.67	52
5. Previous crises	3.57	.92	57
Integration	17.39	3.08	
1. Affection	3.54	.62	59
2. Joint activities	3.44	1.11	.77
3. Coöperation	3.94	1 04	44
4. Morale	2.97	.61	19
5. Solidarity	3.47	1.08	.74
Marital adjustment	17.13	3.85	
Total score	52.17	7.99	

Dunigan's comments on his item analysis are quotable: "The assumption was made that all items having significant correlations with the total score were valid items for the purpose of this thesis. With 135 degrees of freedom all of the items tested had significant correlations with the total.

"The means of the items tested are all roughly equivalent except for item 3 under integration, which may have been consistently overrated by the interviewers, and item 4 under integration, which may have been consistently underrated by the interviewers. There is some possibility that the concept of "Morale" Item 4, under integration or the definition employed in the Manual of Instructions for Interviewers may have been loose or inappropriate.

"In any refined weighting of the items the relative size of the correlations may be an indication of how closely the items in question get at the central factor of dynamic stability, and the relative size of the sigmas may be an indication of the differentiating power of the items."[10]

Dunigan's tests for reliability were confined to the integration and adaptability criteria. He obtained his measures of reliability by dividing the items under the two criteria into odd and even items and computing the coefficient of correlation between the scores made on the respective group of items. The corrected correlation coefficient by the Spearman-Brown formula was 0.77 between the five odd and the five even items. This split half reliability coefficient of 0.77 satisfied Dunigan that the adaptability and integration components of his Scale for Dynamic Stability were reliable.

Bossard and Boll (6) are originators of the Affectional Home Type Continuum which we used as item H. This set of classifications of homes involves not so much scoring of families as pigeonholing them in the appropriate spot. An elaborate set of definitions worked out by the authors was incorporated, for the elucidation of interviewers, into the Manual of Instructions for Interviewers. In spite of these aids, the continuum gave trouble to interviewers. There was a noticeable lack of convincing data in the interview on which to base a rating. There was, moreover, a decided halo tendency which resulted in making most families "companionable."

The Index of Status Characteristics, item I, was adapted from Kenneth Eels' report (17) for the Committee on Human Development at the University of Chicago. In the final scoring no attempts were made to incorporate the information on "Status as Families" which proved particularly difficult to rate in strange communities. Happily, the Eels' formula involved only occupation, house type, source of income, and area lived in. To get the weighted total used in our calculations, the four

[10] Lowell Dunigan, *A Scale for the Measurement of Dynamic Stability in Family Life* (M. S. Thesis, Iowa State College, Ames, Iowa, 1948, unpublished), pp. 24–26.

ratings should be multiplied by the following weights: occupation (4), source of income (3), house type (3), and area lived in (2). If the ratings for a given family were 5, 5, 7, and 6 for occupation, source of income, house type, and area lived in, respectively, the weighted total would be secured as shown by the accompanying table.

Characteristic	Rating		Weight for Multiplication	Product
Occupation	5	×	4	20
Source of income	5	×	3	15
House type	7	×	3	21
Area lived in	6	×	2	12
Weighted total				68

The weighted total may be any number from 12 to 84 inclusive.

Using a conversion index developed by Eels (*17*), five social classes were identified from these weighted totals. The resulting breakdown of our 135 families and its effects on adjustment to separation and reunion scores is described in detail on pp. 33–34, as well as our reservations about the wisdom of applying the Eels' index to families drawn from several communities.

Methodologically, the method of segregating families by their status characteristics used in this study breaks down at the point of the interviewer's rating. Occupation and source of income were straightforward and easy to rate. House types were not difficult to rate, but in many instances did not represent the long-time status of the family. One of the most frequent hardships of the separation period was the location of housing—the moving to new locations—since substandard dwellings in some communities were as expensive to buy or rent as much more adequate dwellings in other communities. "Area lived in" was even more difficult to rate, and if other investigators were to repeat our ratings there would probably be less agreement on this rating than on the other three. The interviewer was often new to each community he entered, and found differing conceptions of the desirability of residential areas when he consulted with natives.

It is undoubtedly true that those who fashioned this tool for identifying status characteristics did not intend it to be used as we have used it. The need is great for a similar model standardized for the small towns of the Middle West which might include "personal appearance at home" and "educational and literary interests," such as Duvall (*14*) has worked out for Chicago families. The differences among communities might discourage the tool maker, but the project would most certainly receive our hearty support.

III. Adjustments to Reunion. No methodological problems are presented by this section which have not already been touched upon earlier. Three foci for interviews are indicated dealing in sequence with the wife's, the children's, and the husband's special adjustments to the reunion. The interview form is fashioned as nondirectively as possible to elicit the attitudes and feeling tones of the reunion period.

A factor which worried the interviewers at the time of the interviewing was the recency of the reunion. We feared that the responses of a number of families would be sweetened by the elation of the reunion honeymoon which still pervaded some homes. A series of follow-up interviews in Polk County enabled us to test this hypothesis in connection with the more intensive study of fathers by Elder (*18*), but limited finances made it impossible to correct for "honeymoon glow" with other families in the state. To be fair to the study, Elder, in her follow-up several months after the original interviews, did not find herself in serious disagreement with the description of reunion recorded by the original interviewer nor with the reunion adjustment scores.

THE VALUE OF PRETESTING

Now that we have taken the schedules apart piecemeal to indicate their methodological strengths and weaknesses, we owe it to the reader to point out that the greatest aid in refining the schedules and preparing them for use in the field came in the pretesting process. A "dress rehearsal," so to speak, of the entire study was held with thirty families chosen by the American Red Cross chapters of Story County, Iowa, and Cache County, Utah. We practiced our approach to the interview, our interpretation of the study, and had the family members fill out the questionnaires and submit to the interviews we expected our sample families in the larger study to experience. We tabulated the results, ran preliminary analyses, and presented a preliminary report, based on the analysis, to the Mid-west Sociological Society meetings for criticism. The dress rehearsal served us well, gave us confidence that the "no-man's land" we were invading in our study of war separation and reunion was fundamentally like other crisis areas and that we were justified in continuing our investigations with a bonafide sample of the population of our interest.

The families coöperated typically enough to simulate working conditions in the field; that is, some refused to coöperate, some had moved away, and some proved reluctant to share the family secrets with us until we had adequately interpreted the study. Specifically, we learned from the pretest that some of our so-called open-end questions could be answered with "yes" and "no" answers, giving us sparse rather than rich case narrative data. The questions were rewritten to correct for that deficiency using beginnings like "how did you handle that problem" or "what was your experience with this situation," etc. In a few instances the materials requested in the questionnaires were left blank, or incorrectly filled out. We paid a few return visits to families to find out why, if we couldn't see ourselves, and corrected the questions. From the pretest we understood for the first time the importance of keeping the interview free from census-enumerator-type questions which could be answered tersely and factually, because we found it established a special kind of relationship between interviewer and the interviewee. The latter took a familiar role of fact giving rather than attitude sharing. We, therefore, transferred all census-type questions which required numbers, checks, and closed categories to the questionnaires to be filled out by the wife and husband in advance of the interview.

If our experience is typical, we would say the mistakes, errors of judgment, blind spots uncovered, and ineptitude of research design which our own pretest laid bare, lead us to the conclusion that no exploratory or definitive study should be launched which has not first undergone a rigorous pretesting with a population similar to the one to be studied. Dress rehearsals pay off!

Problems Met in Collecting the Data

Reference has already been made to the shrinkage in the number of cases due to high mobility of families, reluctance to coöperate with the study, and inadequate interviewing (pp. 28–32). We are inclined to look askance at researchers who claim ready and easy coöperation with families in providing the intimate workings of their lives. The families whose addresses selective service had given us were closed systems, hospitable but suspicious of strangers, courteous but stand-offish. They had to be won to the study. Our pretest proved how difficult the task would be, and we provided for a full morning's instructions for all field workers of the Iowa Department of Social Welfare who were assigned to help us complete the interviewing. Furthermore, in the Manual of Instructions for Interviewers we included eight pages of suggestions dividing between the "Approach in Obtaining Interview" and "Conducting the Interview."

At the inception of the study it was thought that field workers of the Iowa Department of Social Welfare could successfully locate families, interpret the study to them, complete an interview, and write it up, so long as a college supervisor was on the ground to edit and check the interview results. In only five counties were workers sufficiently well trained, or sufficiently courageous to accept the assignment. In most counties the college supervisors soon learned they saved time by conducting the interviews themselves. The inhibitions which make the family members resistant to interviewing are also present in most interviewers —the sanctity of the home is thus protected from without as well as from within.[11]

APPROACH IN OBTAINING INTERVIEW

The approach that our interviewers used and usually found successful was informal and easy of manner, "I am Mrs. B. of Iowa State College. We are working on a study in which we need your coöperation. May I come in and explain it to you? It won't take more than five minutes." This invariably produced an invitation to come in and sit down and provided the opportunity to give an interpretation of the study. The interviewer would then proceed to explain the nature of the study by saying, "Our project is to find out the effect of war separations on Iowa families with children. We want to know what kinds of problems women have when their husbands are overseas. I guess you know all about that, don't you!" This would frequently bring a flash of rapport and the woman might launch into an immediate discussion of her problems. She was usually not encouraged to carry this very far, but far enough for the interviewer to be able to say, "Yes, that is just the kind of material we want for our study." The questionnaire would then be produced and the procedure for filling it out explained. Many women did not respond so easily and further explanation was necessary. The interviewer would tell how useful this material was going to be to the Red Cross and social

[11] See our earlier discussion of the family as a closed system, pp. 3–7. Dr. E. W. Burgess, dean of marriage researchers, states: "My own experience as well as observation of the success and failure of students seems to show that the inhibitions to personal revelations are not generally so much in the subject as in the inquirer." See E. W. Burgess, "Statistics and Case Studies as Methods of Sociological Research," *Sociology and Social Research,* Vol. 12, p. 118.

service agencies, with a hint that the results of this study might conceivably affect the government's draft policy in the future.

Two things had to be stressed considerably in order to "sell" the study. One was the fact that hundreds of other families in Iowa were answering the same questions—people usually found safety in numbers—and the other was that the information given was strictly confidential, that no one but the interviewer would ever know the interviewee's name and that in the report she would only be a number, along with hundreds of other women. It helped to point out that we were not so much interested in all the idiosyncracies of her particular family as we were in the total picture of how Iowa families reacted—that so many families had *this* type of problem and so many families had *that* type of problem. The impersonality of the study was stressed and the fact that other families had problems possibly just like theirs.

If, after this explanation, the wife gave a point-blank refusal to coöperate, it usually did little good to try to persuade her.[12] If she seemed doubtful, we sometimes made more explicit the public service families who coöperated were rendering and repeated the confidential nature of the information she would give.

After the wife had consented to coöperate with the project, the interviewer explained the contents of the questionnaire, made an appointment to pick it up when he came for his personal interview in two or three days' time. If the husband had returned from service, arrangements were also made to see him for interview and his questionnaire was left with a note of interpretation. Women were usually interviewed right after lunch when the smallest children were taking naps, and the men at night after work.

It was found important to establish a working relationship in the first

[12] Mrs. Boulding, writing her impressions of interviewing shortly after completing the Polk County phase of the project, provides unusual sensitivity to the process of acceptance or rejection of the study, "One senses from the beginning with some women that it is only a matter of time, that they will eventually accept the questionnaire. In other cases, however, there seems to be some kind of emotional reaction from the very start, fear, distrust, or perhaps even dislike on the part of the wife . . . and while in only one case in my entire experience was I not allowed inside the door to explain further, I soon got to feel from the woman's very first words if she was going to be the type who would eventually refuse. In several cases where I used every persuasive trick I knew and actually got a woman to accept a questionnaire, when I had already originally spotted her as a potential non-coöperator, it never failed to happen when I returned for the interview that she had thought it over some more and decided not to participate after all."

brief contact if the interviewer expected to get coöperation later. Getting the wife to talk about herself a little helped. The author's best interviews were with families with which he could identify readily and quickly, and his refusals were disproportionately drawn from people he found it difficult to warm up to. Because of this personal equation, there would probably be an advantage in a quick withdrawal whenever the interviewer senses a dislike for the person, allowing another interviewer to return later who may not share his antipathies. This was tried on only three occasions after field workers of the welfare department had been refused, and two of the three finally coöperated well with the study.

In the first contact it is necessary to establish what Koos (27) has called the nonauthoritative position of the interviewer. We had no authority to coerce the families to coöperate, many of whom had been interviewed by social welfare workers or had had contact with Red Cross workers, and they were disarmed to learn we were so dependent on their voluntary coöperation. The contrast provided by an individual who had no authority and who readily admitted that it was really none of his business (except that he too had experienced painful separations and was interested in what people did about them) overcame much of the reluctance which ordinarily deters those interviewed.

REFUSALS TO COÖPERATE WITH THE STUDY

Forty-one families refused to coöperate with the interviewers for almost as many reasons. Their real reasons were hard to get and the first excuses, "no time" or "come back next month" or "I'll have to think about it," masked deeper resistances. Each variety of resistance represents an obstacle for the researcher to overcome if he is to meet the valid criticism that his sample is biased in the direction of the most coöperative families. Paul Wallin has suggested that investigators who foresee a refusal change tactics and pick up minimum information of a face-sheet type that will so identify the family that it can be replaced with another family with the same background characteristics. Another use of the data on refusals is to construct a picture of the bias created in the sample by refusals, with the possibility of correcting for it statistically in the final results.[13]

Many of our refusals fell in the category of half promises to coöperate

[13] From a personal conversation with Paul Wallin. The point is elaborated in his thesis, *The Characteristics of Participants in a Social Psychological Study* (Ph.D. Thesis, Chicago, University of Chicago Libraries, 1942).

followed by broken appointments for interview and as a result we failed dismally in obtaining basic identifying data on them as suggested by Wallin. The reasons for refusal have been listed for whatever they are worth.

1. The sanctity of the house must be kept inviolate.

Most frequent refusals were from those families which felt their private affairs were their own, not to be shared with college research workers. One man added for emphasis that he believed everyone should handle his own personal problems. "If they can't they shouldn't get married in the first place!" He pooh-poohed the idea that pooling experiences would ever help anyone else, even if there was such a thing as family research.

2. Returned servicemen disliked being interviewed for whatever reason.

A sizable proportion of refusals came from the man of the house. He had been interviewed to "death" in the service, and he wasn't answering any more questions now that he was home. He was fed up on the army and the Veterans Administration and our arrival reminded him painfully of his difficulties—so we paid for his dislike of veterans' services.

3. Recently returned fathers resented the free and easy way their wives talked to salesmen, pollsters, and research interviewers and demonstrated their power in the family by slamming doors.

One husband agreed to coöperate at first, but he got into a quarrel with his wife after the interviewer had gone, and when the interviewer returned, the husband eavesdropped on the interview with the wife. He became incensed at the answers she was giving. She had stated she had become more self-reliant and independent in her husband's absence, that she was still playing the role of "father and mother too" to the child. He came out with blood in his eye and tore up the questionnaires and ordered the interviewer from the place. To his wife he said, "You're too smart for your own good talking like you are boss of the kids, and the house. When I am buried six feet under is soon enough to hold these postmortems on our family life." The interviewer, retreating, couldn't resist cracking to the wife as he closed the door, "It's a date!"

Getting the husband's coöperation has been one of the most difficult problems in collecting our data, not because of any particular sex-linked personality maladjustments but because of the man's greater adherence to the cultural taboos on discussion of family matters with an outsider. In some of the cases the wife refused to show her husband the questionnaire, although she would coöperate herself because she "just knew" he would be very angry if he found out she was answering such questions. In a number of cases where the wife coöperated, the husband refused to answer questions himself although he didn't forbid her doing so, and the most usual reason for his refusal would be that he didn't like to answer such personal questions, or didn't want to be bothered with such things. The real clue to the husband's refusals lies much more in the culture pattern than in the area of sex differences in personality make-up. Men just don't discuss most of the matters investigated by this study, either with their wives or friends; and although the outsider may have the advantage of the psychology of the stranger, whom he will never see again, the husband is loath to open up his concerns.

4. A minor source of refusals was due to the timidity and lack of conviction of untrained interviewers.

Field workers of the departments of social welfare encouraged refusals at times by their attitudes. Since they lived in the community and had to face these people daily in their work, they were much more sensitive to the reverberations which might follow revealing intimate facts about one's family life. They were sometimes not convincing in their first contacts, and walked out too soon and too willingly when a refusal seemed likely. This source of refusals can be minimized by more adequate selection and training of interviewers.

5. "I wouldn't want to do anything my husband would criticize me for!"

Some wives expressed their personal willingness to coöperate but were afraid of what the husband would say if he found out. When we exclaimed that of course we wanted the husband to fill out a questionnaire too, they showed real fear. They had been instructed by their husbands not to sign anything, not to buy anything, and not to agree to anything, and they weren't taking any chances with this business!

6. A few interviewees were too illiterate to read the schedules and too sensitive to allow the interviewer to do the writing for them.

In only three or four cases have families been too poorly educated to understand the questionnaires, or to dull to understand the questions in the interview. This speaks well for the literacy and understanding of Iowans. Most people showed familiarity with the idea of being interviewed.

7. A miscellaneous set of families wouldn't participate, but wouldn't explain why either.

The families which rebuffed us did not seem too different in outward appearance from those who coöperated freely with the study. They appeared to share an identifiable sense of insecurity which didn't allow them to accept strangers, or to "spill" to them readily. We have no evidence to indicate that they were more frequently unhappy or disorganized than families which did coöperate. Actually, we found a sizable proportion of the most chronically unhappy were looking for a chance to "spill" their troubles to a stranger and were happy to coöperate. We provided a means of ventilation. They certainly found emotional release through the interviewing process; moods were often given form and positive significance through the discussions. The families which did not share in the study probably had the same need to "spill," but lacked the capacity to talk out their "locked-upness" and to explore the deep, anxious pockets of concern which Koos (27) points out are to be found in most homes.

CONDUCTING THE INTERVIEW

Several problems arose in the conduct of the interview: the excessive number and depth of questions, the interference of family members, tendencies to whitewash the family's failures, and tendencies to ask the interviewer for advice and counsel.

The authors knew from the pretest that the interview was excessively long but they did not anticipate that the interviewer would tire out before the interviewee. The interviewee often appeared to be still enjoying the prolonged session long after the interviewer was ready to slow up.

Interviews were difficult to complete wherever relatives, visitors, or both husband and wife remained in the room. The wife would usually become tongue-tied in her husband's presence, although there were notable exceptions, as will be seen below. Mother-in-laws were hard to shake loose, and it was usually the better part of good wisdom to make another appointment. On the other hand, children usually proved to be helpful assets. Children added convincingly to the authenticity of the family context, playing with the interviewer's pencils, climbing on his lap, offering him candy, bringing him toys to admire, and breaking into the middle of the interview for attention. Insights were obtained that would otherwise have been missing. When children were present, the quality of the family relationships often appeared more clearly in the family drama of personalities within the room than from the parents' description of the intra-family relationships.

The matter of frankness during the interview was less of a problem than we had anticipated. All our evidence indicates that most people tell the truth in interviews of this sort. Sooner or later the interviewer can spot the window dressing if it occurs, although it is not frequent. One wife began the interview by presenting a very conventional picture of family life, and then when the interview was well along she suddenly said, "Well, I might as well tell you the truth about us, although I have never talked to anyone about this before." Another stopped in the middle of answering one of the more searching questions and said, "Do other wives really tell you the truth about their marriages?" On being reassured that many do, by means of an illustration from one of the more severely maladjusted homes, the wife broke down and told a quite different story. In most cases where families did have something to hide, careful, sympathetic questioning at a point in the interview usually brought out the true story.

One check on the false front was the husband, although he did disturb the interview in other instances. One gentle, soft-spoken pretty little wife was busy painting an idyllic picture of her married life when her husband, who had been working in the garden outside and could hear what she had said, stormed into the room and asked her what she meant by making up all those stories about how happy they were and how they did everything together. She knew perfectly well that she made life miserable for him by bossing the life out of him and never letting him have any money and that the less he was home, the better he liked it. The gentle little wife became transformed into a somewhat sharper-tongued shrew and husband and wife embarked on a battle royal right in the presence of the interviewer. The balance of the interview was conducted with the husband present and was most revealing of their true family life. Every time the wife tried to make things look better than they were, he contradicted her and at the end of the interview she was a somewhat crestfallen, although chastened, spouse.

One outcome of a good interview was the need for a relaxed period of visiting after the interview in which it was not unusual for the family to ask for advice and counsel. The interviewers refrained from assuming the role of counselor but did build on the rapport which had been established to obtain an invitation to return for follow-up interviews at a later stage in the reunion. We did frequently establish in the brief period of contact with the family the basis for a personal friendship, much as Koos (27) has reported. This is a far cry from the detachment recommended by most instructors in research interviewing, but a case can be made for it in a study of family crises. Koos justifies this intimate identification with the family eloquently in his closing paragraph of *Families in Trouble*: "If the interview is to yield anything beyond the most superficial observation, it cannot be carried on with the persons immersed in an icy apartness. Once having yielded this point, interviewing becomes a matter of candor in one's self and one's data. The demand for scientific objectivity in social science is responsible for this icy apartness, and makes such an approach less objective rather than more so, because it leaves out of account the fact that human beings have emotions, and that emotions are in many situations a part of the data. To use techniques that detract from the possibility of getting this type of data is to detract from the hoped-for objectivity."[14]

SUMMARY

In quick overview of the devices used for recording observations of families under stress, we identify as our chief tools the questionnaire, the personal document or family history, and the rating scale.

The questionnaire contained structured questions which could be answered by means of checks, simple numbers or census-type responses, and self-administering inventories and tests. In the questionnaire the subjects recorded their own observations of their family behavior before, during, and after the crisis. The chief problem in collecting the data was to convince the families of its importance and check on the completeness of the answers.

The personal document or family history contained provision through open-end questions for a narrative account of the natural history of the family up to the point of the contact with the project. It provided for a description of the processes of adjustment, the motivations which prompted behavior, and for the aspirations and goals of the family. The effectiveness of the personal document rests almost wholly on the adequacy of the *interview* which was the sole means we used of collecting the family history data. The chief problems of data collection through the interview involved: (1) the initial interpreting of the study, (2) establishing a working relationship with the family, (3) maintaining

[14] Earl L. Koos, *Families in Trouble* (New York: King's Crown Press, 1946), p. 134.

the balance between controlling and decontrolling the interview to encourage the coöperators to share with the interviewer that which they deemed significant in the family history, and (4) probing beyond the statement of sequences of events in an attempt to uncover the causal relations within the family history.

The rating scale in the hands of the interviewer involved the use of the interview to obtain the data on which to base a rating while not sharing with the family the judgment as to how they should be rated. Social status, affectional home type, type of family control, family adaptability, and family integration were all scored by means of interviewer ratings based on data provided by the family. The major problems of the rating scale involved the absence of convincing data on which to base a rating, and the inability of the interviewers to make sharp relative judgments free both from halo and from the tendency to hug the average.

Tools for Analyzing Observations Made

Two methods of analysis have been used in this study: the method of enumerative induction, represented by our statistical analysis; and the method of analytic induction, represented by our case study analysis.[15] From the method of enumerative induction we have obtained a picture of the classes in the population that are most vulnerable and those that are most invulnerable to the hardships which attend the crisis of separation. Certain types of childhood backgrounds of spouses, certain types of premarital experiences, social and personal roles in marriage, and certain classes of status, occupation, income, have been shown to be poorer risks in the face of crisis than others.

Not unlike the actuarial tables built by the life insurance companies which show certain occupations and overweight physical types to be poor insurance risks, the method of enumerative induction which we have used also produces information of an actuarial variety about family types which are most likely to crack when the going gets tough. The method rarely yields insight into *why* any given family does well in the face of crisis, or why another family of the same risk category does poorly. To answer that question the case study method, the method of analytic induction, is needed. If the present study has been well conceived, these

[15] See Robert Angell's discussion of these two methods in his methodological note, *The Family Encounters the Depression* (New York: Charles Scribner's Sons, 1936), p. 296.

two methods have been used where they can most appropriately serve the purposes for which they were designed.

METHODS FOR TABULATING DATA

A division of labor was agreed upon between the associates working on the project in which Reuben Hill would assume responsibility for tabulating, ordering, categorizing, and analyzing all data which lent themselves to statistical methods; and Elise Boulding would direct the distilling of everything worth while from the records which might contribute to an analysis by case study methods. It was agreed that Mrs. Boulding would make her case study analysis as independently as possible of the statistical study. When she had completed her section, a reconciliation of findings from the two methods would be attempted (see Chapter VIII). Where the two methods are complementary, in the identification and explanation of deviants and in the joining of the strengths of the enumerative and analytic foci, Boulding and Hill have joined forces to make a collaborative analysis. (See also Chapter VIII.)

In the statistical study we combed the questionnaires and extensive interview form for everything that could be counted or handled arithmetically. Many of the narrative answers to the open-end questions were transformed into closed categories that could be tabulated, but some of the materials proved too variable to so tabulate. All possible data were transferred from the schedules to fifty-four large tabulation sheets in the form in which they could be summed up for use in tables and cross-classification matrices. Enough selected materials were then transferred to fill most of the space on two eighty-column cards devised by the International Business Machines for electrical punching, sorting, and tabulation. In addition, at a later date we placed data on the most crucial variables in the study on small 3 x 5 cards for experimental hand sorting and speedy cross-classification.

In the case study Mrs. Boulding read twice all of the 135 family histories carefully before designing her master card. On the third reading she condensed the family history for each case on one card. On the same card were placed basic face-sheet data and Boulding-devised symbols for the inter-personal materials she considered most important: power relations, assumption of responsibility for home management, degree of parental responsibility, foci of affection, flexibility in roles, and integration. Mrs. Boulding also devised silhouettes of crisis—disorganization—reorganization—recovery for all families which have been sufficiently complete in capturing the depths and heights of family adjustment that that aspect of the family's history can be read from them at a glance and yet are so clear-cut that by means of overlays one can see emerging general *profiles* of adjustment for categories of cases. From a grouping and summing of her master cards containing the basic data, Mrs. Boulding has erected generalizations and tested hypotheses concerning families under stress—which had been impossible for us to make from our statistical materials. Her method of analysis is one of identifying interconnected patterns by grouping and regrouping families after having intuitively graded and classified families into a multiplicity of types. The variety of family organization and behavior is conserved thereby, although the precision of statistical significance-nonsignificance is never attained.

STATISTICAL METHODS OF ANALYSIS USED

The statistical study had the benefit of the consultant services of the Iowa State Statistical Laboratory. Under their general supervision the computational work was executed and checked. The procedure agreed upon for treating the data involved, first, placement into simple tables relating one factor at a time to the dependent variables, adjustment to separation, and adjustment to reunion (see Chapter V). Simple scatter diagrams were visualized from these tables and average adjustment to separation and to reunion scores were computed for all categories, on the basis of which tentative generalizations about the interrelationships of factors were reached. The goodness of fit in the scatter diagrams which showed most visual promise was tested by linear correlation where possible, and by curvilinear correlation in two instances. For the nonquantitative factors, the interrelationships with the dependent variables were tested by chi-square analysis and checked for statistical significance. This further shortened the list of factors which were regarded as important in determining separation and reunion adjustment success. Cross-classification matrices were erected at this point to test the effects of holding constant two or more interfering variables on the dependent variables (see Chapter VI). Finally, the most rigorous test of the study was applied in the running of partial and multiple correlation analysis with both dependent variables on eight factors which had satisfied the following three criteria: (1) the factors should be representative of all phases of family make-up and experience; (2) the factors should have demonstrated some significant relationship to separation and reunion adjustment when tested singly; and (3) the factors should be quantitative, so that they could be manipulated arithmetically. On the basis of these several statistical analyses, the tentative generalizations of the statistical study in the initial stages were modified and corrected.

We have made no marked methodological contributions to statistical methods in this study. We have let sleeping dogs lie, although someone with more talent than we bring should stir them up. No new statistical devices have been designed for this study. Moreover, those we have used have all been adequately standardized and the assumptions underlying their use have been sufficiently delineated in the statistical literature that they warrant no further attention in this note.

COMPLEMENTARY NATURE OF STATISTICAL AND CASE STUDY TECHNIQUES OF ANALYSIS

Our major contributions to method have come, not from the shaping of new scales of adjustment to separation and reunion, or from the further experimentation with other as-yet-nonstandardized tests and scales in a new context, although we regard both of these as real services to our discipline. No, our major methodological contribution has been made in the techniques we have improvised as a team for interweaving the case study and the statistical approaches to support mutually one another in the same piece of research.[16]

IDENTIFYING AND EXPLAINING THE UNPREDICTABLE FAMILIES

From the statistical analyses we have identified the characteristics of families which thrive under stress and those which have cracked under stress. To be more precise, we have statistically cornered the characteristics which are most often associated with the most obviously successful families. But, there are many families that are exceptions to the statistical finding, the unpredictable families at the tails of the distribution who are poorly equipped for crisis yet thrive, or who are well equipped for crisis yet crack up. By identifying these families and studying them intensively via the *case study* method, we have obtained a better picture of the real meaning of the characteristics we have said make families crisis-prone or crisis-invulnerable.

[16] We acknowledge, especially, our great debt to E. W. Burgess who first introduced the author to the possibilities of teaming case study and statistical methods. See his most recent treatment of the problem in "Research Methods in Sociology." In *Twentieth Century Sociology*, ed. by Georges Gurvitch and Wilbert E. Moore (New York: The Philosophical Library, 1945), pp. 20–41.

PRESERVING THE FUNCTIONAL SYSTEM OF ATTRIBUTES IN FAMILIES

Until the study was nearing completion, we did not realize the importance of always retaining the pattern of attributes within our units of observation. It has been only as we have attempted to read back our statistical findings into bonafide families for purposes of recommended action that we have appreciated the importance of keeping in view our unit of observation, the individual family. The presence of case study materials and the influence of the findings from case study analysis have sharpened that point. We have latterly experimented with scoring families on the basis of patterns of interrelated attributes which still preserve the functional system within a given family. We have attempted to do the "case grouping" that Salter[17] has recommended by dealing with patterns of attributes within the family as in our attempts with types of family control, wife's self-sufficiency pattern, hardships of separation and reunion, and so on. In this process of case grouping, statistical method and case study join together to identify the patterns, count them, note their parameters and their significance, and again join in any generalizations made from the analysis. During the entire process due attention must be paid to the internal construction of the families that make up the sample. This process, to date, has been ignored by all statistical studies using the family as the unit of observation that have come to our attention.

CASE STUDY POINTS UP NEW ITEMS FOR STATISTICAL ANALYSIS

Not the least of the products of our joint teaming of statistics and case study is the lifting of family processes and inter-personal relationships out of the welter of *words* into diagrams, silhouettes, profiles, and symbols. Mrs. Boulding has made a distinct contribution in her application of Kirkpatrick and Caplow's (24) and Koos' (27) use of graphic charts to her own problem of identifying the levels of family organization and disorganization over a specified period of time (from before the father was inducted until after the reunion). Her symbols for identifying affectional relations within the family may also lend themselves to later statistical elaboration.

VALIDATING STATISTICAL TYPES, SCALES, AND FINDINGS AGAINST CASE STUDY

Covering the same ground, and dealing with some of the same data but approaching them differently, the statistical and case analyses can be

[17] Leonard A. Salter, Jr., "Cross-Sectional and Case-Grouping Procedures in Research Analysis," *Journal of Farm Economics* (November, 1942), pp. 792–805.

tested against one another. The statistical, operating from the nomothetic or cross-sectional perspective method, and the case study, from an ideographic or dynamic historical focus, ought to complement one another. We have attempted to validate the two sets of findings against each other wherever they are at all comparable. The results from the crude statistical scales measuring adjustment to separation and adjustment to reunion are compared with the intuitive grading of separation and reunion adequacy by the case study method. Statistical family types achieved by trisecting the distribution of scores on adaptability and integration and then cross-classifying families are compared with the constructed family types built by combining these same attributes as patterns of family organization by the case approach. Generalizations concerning what makes for good adjustment to crisis can be directly compared, too.

By joining the two methods we have saved ourselves from the error of other students whose findings, as we read them, imply that high scores on all important attributes are important to success, only to find that there are no individuals with high scores on all the attributes in question. Further investigation proves that the best adjustment is found actually in families of many different combinations of attributes, and in our own study moderate amounts of the attributes appear more favorable than high concentrations.

Statistical findings alone are necessarily synthetic in that they usually refer to attributes which have been yanked loose from their family moorings and manipulated statistically. It becomes difficult to integrate them back into actual families, and when it is tried, we usually discover there are no *average* families with all the attributes the average family should have! Case study findings alone, on the other hand, provide a dispersion of differences which are overwhelming in their variety and are unconvincing to the scientist. Taken together, however, the two methods give promise of a productive symbiosis. They offer the hope of social science of capturing, measuring, analyzing, and implementing in a form suitable for appropriate purposive action both the statics of family background and status and the dynamics of family process and organization.

APPENDIX C

SCHEDULE FORMS USED IN THIS STUDY

I. FAMILY ADJUSTMENTS IN WARTIME (WIFE)

Schedule # . . . .

1. Length of time since husband entered service: No. of months . . . . . .
2. Marital status at induction of husband: married and living with family . . . . .; divorced . . . . .; separated . . . . . .

	Wife	Husband
3. Number of brothers and sisters	. . . . .	. . . . .
4. Present age (nearest birthday)	. . . . .	. . . . .
5. Age at marriage	. . . . .	. . . . .
6. Occupation at induction	. . . .	. . . .
7. Income at induction (monthly)	. . . . .	. . . . .
8. Highest grade completed in school	. . . . .	. . . . .
9. Religious affiliation (if none, write none)	. . . . .	. . . . .

10. Employment record of wife: number of jobs held from marriage to induction . . . . .; induction to present . . . . . . List types of jobs held:
. . . .
. . . .

11. Give sex, age, and first initial or name of children in the family by order of birth:

First Name or Initial	Age	Sex	First Name or Initial	Age	Sex
1.	. . . . .	. . . . .	4.	. . . . .	. . . . .
2.	. . . . .	. . . . .	5.	. . . . .	. . . . .
3.	. . . . .	. . . . .	6.	. . . . .	. . . . .

12. Number of changes of residence from time of marriage to husband's induction . . . . .; induction to present . . . . . .

13. Did you ever live for any length of time (check): with his parents ... ; with your parents ... ; or had either set of parents live with you ... ; or always lived separately from parents .....?

RELATIVES' HELPFULNESS SCORE (14)

14. Have you found parents or relatives helpful with husband gone? Check as many as apply: have received virtually no help .0. ; occasional care or entertainment of children, take them to games, for rides .1. ; care for children while wife ill or hospitalized ..1..; day care for children while wife works .3. ; have received free housing .3. ; board .3. ; outright financial help .3. .

MARITAL ADJUSTMENT ITEM (15)

15. What effect have your children had on your happiness? (check) have had no effect ..−3. ; added to it very much ..+1. ; considerably ..−1. ; somewhat ..−2.. ; a little ..−3. ; have decreased it a little ..−3. ; somewhat ..−3.. ; considerably ..−3. very much ..−3..

16. How large a family do you finally want to have? Put H for number husband wants, W for number you want. 1 .....; 2 .....; 3 .....; 4 or more ..... ; have more than we want now ......

17. Are your parents (check): both living .....; mother dead .... ; father dead ....?

18. Their marital status (check): married .....; separated .... · divorced ......

HAPPINESS SCORE FOR WIFE'S PARENTS (19)

19. How happy were your parents with their marriage? Write M for mother's rating: F for father's: extraordinarily happy ..+3. ; decidedly happy ..+1. ; somewhat happy ..−2.. ; average ..−3. ; somewhat unhappy ..−3. ; unhappy ..−3.. ; decidedly unhappy ..−3. ; extremely unhappy ..−3..

MARITAL ADJUSTMENT ITEM (20)

20. Everything considered, how happy has your own marriage been for you? (check) extraordinarily happy .+3.. ; decidedly happy ..+1.. ; happy ..−1.. ; somewhat happy ..−2. ; average

..—3..; somewhat unhappy ..—3..; unhappy ..—3.., decidedly unhappy ..—3..; extremely unhappy ..—3...

WIFE'S HAPPINESS SCORE (21)

21. How happy was your life in the following periods? Write *1* if very happy; *2* if happy; *3* if average; *4* if unhappy; *5* if very unhappy. *Be sure to rate each period*. Until twelve .....; twelve to fifteen .....; sixteen to twenty .....; the year before your marriage .....; 1st year of marriage .....; 2nd year .....; 3rd .....; indicate how happy you were while husband was in service .....; and since he returned from service ......

22. How long were you and your husband acquainted before your marriage? (check) under six months .....; six months to less than two years.....; two years to less than five years .....; five years to ten years .....; more than ten years ......

MARITAL ADJUSTMENT ITEMS (23, 24, 25)

23. (a) What is your attitude to your father-in-law? (check) like him very much ..+1..; considerably ..—1 ; somewhat ..—2..; dislike him somewhat ..—3..; considerably ..—3..; very much ..—3 .; or is he dead ..0..?
    (b) What is your attitude to your mother-in-law? (check) like her very much ..+1..; considerably ..—1..; somewhat ..—2..; dislike her somewhat ..—3..; considerably ..—3..; very much ..—3..; or is she dead ..0..?

24. Prior to induction into the service did you and your husband engage in outside interests together? (check) all of them ..+2..; most of them ..0..; some of them ..—1..; few of them ..—2..; none of them ..—2...

25. (a) What were your immediate reactions after seeing your husband leave for the service? (check as many as apply) feeling of extreme loneliness .....; felt numb .....; felt it was all a dream .....; wept for hours .....; became highly excited .....; returned to work or other routines unemotionally .....; was indifferent .....; was prepared, had cried it out before he left .....; was relieved, at last that's settled .....; other, describe ....
    (b) Were these reactions repeated when husband went overseas? (check) intensified .....; same intensity .....; less intense ......
    Comment ....

WIFE'S SOCIAL PARTICIPATION SCALE (26)

26. Since your husband entered the service which of the following activities have you engaged in and how frequently? (check)

	Rarely or Never	Monthly	Twice Month	Weekly	Daily	Check if Activity Increased, Decreased, or Same Since Husband Left.
A. Group Activities						+ = −
1. Volunteer war activities						
2. Attending movies						
3. Visiting with neighbors						
4. War wives' group activities						
5. Church						
6. Talking with women friends						
7. Seeing men friends						
8. Bridge and card groups						
9. Concerts and lectures						
10. Activities with other couples						
B. Home and Family Activities						
1. Walking with children						
2. Picnics and outings						
3. Reading						
4. Listening to radio						
5. Knitting and sewing						
6. Fixing up the house						
Weights[a]	0	1	2	5	10	

[a] Wife's Social Participation Score = Σ (item checked $\times$ weight)

MARITAL ADJUSTMENT ITEMS (27, 28, 29, 30)

27. Indicate your approximate agreement or disagreement with your husband on the following things as of the period immediately preceding induction. Do this for each item by putting a check in the column which shows extent of your agreement or disagreement.

Check One Column for Each Item Below	Always Agree	Almost Always Agree	Occa-sionally Dis-agree	Fre-quently Dis-agree	Almost Always Dis-agree	Always Dis-agree
Handling family finances						
Matters of recreation						
Religious matters						
Demonstration of affection						
Friends						
Sex relations						
Child care and discipline						
Table manners						
Matters of conventionality						
Philosophy of life						
Ways of dealing with husband's parents						
Ways of dealing with wife's parents						
Things that are funny						
Ambition and future plans						
Moral code						
Wife working						
Weights[a]	+2	+1	0	−1	−2	−3

[a] Extent of Agreement Score = Σ (checks × weights)

28. Do you ever regret your marriage? (check) frequently . . −2 . .; occasionally . . −2 . .; rarely . . −1 . .; never . . +2 . .

29. How satisfied, on the whole, are you with your marriage? (check) entirely satisfied . . +3 . .; very much satisfied . . +1 . .; satisfied . . −1 . .; somewhat satisfied . . −2; somewhat dissatisfied . . −3 . .; dissatisfied . . −3 . .; entirely dissatisfied . . −3 . .

30. Check the items in the following list which you enjoy in your marriage: companionship with partner . . 0.2 . .; mutual understanding . . 0.2 . .; fighting and making up . . 0.2 . .; same outside interests . . 0.2 . .; coöperation . . 0.2 . .; confidence . . 0.2 . .; frankness . . 0.2 . .; love . . 0.2 . .; children . . 0.2 . .; good sexual adjustment . . 0.2 . .;

health of partner ..0.2..; interesting work ..0.2..; good management of financial problems ..0.2..; enough money to spend ..0.2..; freedom ..0.2..

Total Marital Adjustment Score=Σ of scores obtained from items 15, 20, 23, 24, 27, 28, 29, and 30.

31. Please answer the following questions as honestly as you can. They represent our way of becoming acquainted with you. Put a cross (X) through your answer to each question. Try to answer by a Yes or No, if it is possible. If you are certain you can't do this, then cross out the question mark. Correct responses are marked. (*Psychoneurotic Score=Total wrong responses plus ?'s checked*)

Yes X̶No̶ ? Do you get stage fright?
X̶Yes̶ No ? Do you take responsibility for introducing people at a party?
Yes X̶No̶ ? Do you worry too long over humiliating experiences?
Yes X̶No̶ ? Do you often feel lonesome, even when you are with other people?
Yes X̶No̶ ? Do you consider yourself a rather nervous person?
Yes X̶No̶ ? Do ideas often run through your head so that you cannot sleep?
Yes X̶No̶ ? Are your feelings easily hurt?
X̶Yes̶ No ? Are you sometimes the leader at social affairs?
Yes X̶No̶ ? Are you frequently burdened by a sense of remorse?
Yes X̶No̶ ? Do you worry over possible misfortune?
X̶Yes̶ No ? Are you usually even-tempered and happy in your outlook on life?
Yes X̶No̶ ? Are you troubled with shyness?
Yes X̶No̶ ? Do you daydream frequently?
Yes X̶No̶ ? Have you ever had spells of dizziness (except during pregnancy)?
Yes X̶No̶ ? Do you get discouraged easily?
Yes X̶No̶ ? Do your interests change quickly?
X̶Yes̶ No ? Is it difficult to move you to tears?

Yes X̶No̶ ? Does it bother you to have people watch you at work even when you do it well?
X̶Yes̶ No ? Can you stand criticism without feeling hurt?

~~Yes~~ No ? Do you make friends easily and quickly?

Yes ~~No~~ ? Are you troubled with the idea that people are watching you on the street?

Yes ~~No~~ ? Have you ever been depressed because of low marks in school?

Yes ~~No~~ ? Does your mind often wander badly so that you lose track of what you are doing?

Yes ~~No~~ ? Are you touchy on various subjects?

Yes ~~No~~ ? Do you frequently feel grouchy?

~~Yes~~ No ? When you were in school did you feel at ease and self-confident when you recited in class?

Yes ~~No~~ ? Do you often feel just miserable?

Yes ~~No~~ ? Does some particular useless thought keep coming into your mind to bother you?

Yes ~~No~~ ? When you were in school did you hesitate to volunteer in a class recitation?

~~Yes~~ No ? Are you usually in good spirits?

Yes ~~No~~ ? Do you often experience periods of loneliness?

Yes ~~No~~ ? Do you often feel self-conscious in the presence of superiors?

Yes ~~No~~ ? Do you lack self-confidence?

~~Yes~~ No ? Do you find it easy to speak in public?

~~Yes~~ No ? Do you usually feel that you are well dressed and make a good appearance?

Yes ~~No~~ ? Do you feel that you must do a thing over several times before you leave it?

~~Yes~~ No ? If you see an accident are you quick to take an active part in giving help?

Yes ~~No~~ ? Are you troubled with feelings of inferiority?

~~Yes~~ No ? Is it easy for you to make up your mind and act on your decision?

Yes ~~No~~ ? Do you have ups and downs in mood without apparent cause?

~~Yes~~ No ? Are you in general self-confident about your abilities?

ADJUSTMENTS OF FAMILY TO SEPARATION SCALE (34, 35, 36, 37)

This last set of questions is to tell us something of the way you, your husband, and the children have reacted to the separation. It is especially important that you be frank in checking the statements which apply here.

32. Husband-wife relationships often take a beating in the face of prolonged separation. Which of the following statements appear to describe the situation in your case? (check)
Weights

..5.. (a) From my husband's letters and furloughs I have been able to understand all the changes the service has made in him.

..2.. (b) I long to be dependent again, to have someone who will make decisions for me as husband did.

..2.. (c) I hate to give up my job and go back to housekeeping.

..1.. (d) I feel as if I don't understand the language of the service, find his ideas hard to accept.

..5.. (e) His friends seem human and friendly and I want to meet them after the war.

..2.. (f) We worry about how it will be when he returns and whether we will seem strange to each other.

..3.. (g) My husband has changed and will be more difficult to live with when he returns.

..4.. (h) We are eager to get together and see our plans for after the war work out.

..4.. (i) The war has drawn us together and made us stronger—we now know nothing can break up our marriage.

..2.. (j) Sometimes I'm scared about having him come home—the problems of getting a job and raising a family with a returned veteran are bigger than most people realize.

..3.. (k) I don't want to become adjusted to life without my husband—it will be too hard to readjust when he returns.

..1.. (l) Everything would be all right if it weren't for the women men in the service meet, the prostitutes, the foreign women, and even the WACS—I don't trust them.

..2.. (m) I confidently expect my husband to return unchanged. He will be the man he was when I married him.

..1.. (n) I have lost the feeling of being married—of needing a husband.

33. Father-child relationships are hard to keep intact because the child's memory is so short and other men come to take the place of the father for him. Which of the following are true in your family?

(a) Check those which are true.

..4..   1. Father writes to children.

..3..   2. Father includes inquiries about children in his letters
to mother.

..2..   3. Father has lost touch with children, indicates his lack
of knowledge about their problems in his letters.

..2..   4. Father and children anticipate reunion with some
uncertainty, afraid they will be strangers.

..5..   5. Father has kept his family so well advised of his life
in the service, with photographs and stories, that
children understand him and the friends he has
made.

(b) In the space provided write in the first initial of each of the
children whose reactions conform with the statements below.

..1..   1. Child has forgotten his father completely.

..4..   2. Child talks about and asks about father regularly.

..2..   3. Father has become less important than grandfather,
uncle, or other relative in child's life.

..3..   4. Child brags about soldier father to his playmates,
makes up stories about him.

..2..   5. Child regards father as a photograph more than as a
real flesh-and-blood person.

34. The responsibility of being father and mother too is heavy to carry
and interferes with the normal mother-child relationships. Which of
the following statements correctly describe your reactions to the
job of rearing children with the father absent? (check)

..1..   (a) Feel the importance of the father in rearing children is
greatly overrated, I like being father and mother too.

..5..   (b) Feel that I have grown as a result of increased responsibilities.

..3..   (c) Thank goodness I have my children; then if anything happens to him, I'll have them to remember him by.

..1..   (d) Children are a burden anytime, and especially with the
husband absent.

..2..   (e) My children mean more to me than anything in the world.
Without them life would be meaningless.

..4..   (f) I guess I'm like any mother. I feel close to my children but
sometimes I could wring their little necks.

..5..   (g) I have enjoyed watching my children change and grow up bringing new problems every day.

..2..   (h) I often feel panicky when the children get sick or fall and hurt themselves for fear I may lose them too.

..5..   (i) I feel my job is to help the children and protect them no more than absolutely necessary so that they can grow up normally.

..2..   (j) I hate to see my baby (babies) grow up, they are so cuddly when they are young.

..2..   (k) The child(ren)'s demands irritate me so I think I'll scream sometimes.

..3..   (l) Kids shouldn't grow up without a father, it's hard to do the job alone.

..4..   (m) The war and the separation have brought our little family closer together because the children seem to understand me and I them, better than other families with fathers at home.

..1..   (n) If I had my way I would have entered the service myself and left my husband to take care of the children.

35. If I could press a button which would rearrange my life, I would (check): like to be single and free again ..1..; be married to same man and living with him, but without children to tie us down ..2..; stay as I am, child(ren) and all ..5..; have more children ..5..; be married to same man but have fewer children ..2..; other (please write in) ....

36. In the absence of the father, the wife and children often find help from in-laws, relatives, friends, neighbors. This is not possible for many families because they have been cut adrift in strange surroundings. How has it gone with you? (check)

(a) have more friends than before husband left ..5..; have many friends ..5..; have a few friends ..3..; have no close and intimate friends ..2..; have no people I can turn to as friends ..1..

(b) in-laws proved very helpful ..5..; in-laws both help and hinder our happiness ..3..; in-laws wish well but don't fit with our way of life ..2..; in-laws constant source of irritation and annoyance ..1..; in-laws have taken over all decisions and child discipline ..1..

(c) neighbors are warm and friendly ..5..; neighbors will help if a crisis occurs, but seem busy with own problems ..3..; neighbors mind their business, we mind ours ..2..; neighbors are nosey ..1..; we ignore the neighbors, don't even know their names ..1..

37. The theme of business, government, and communities these days is postwar planning. Families too indulge in their own postwar plans. How do your own plans go? (check)

..3.. (a) We haven't any plans yet but we're going to start on them.

..1.. (b) We have enough troubles right now without worrying about the future.

..4.. (c) We have been saving everything we can set aside for a home when this is all over.

..2.. (d) With my husband's salary cut off we have been running into debt during the war, it's hard to plan with debts hanging over you.

..5.. (e) We have discussed where we are going to live and what he is going to do for a living, and have a pretty good idea about how many children we are going to have, and that's planning.

.... (f) Other evidence of your family planning (write in) ....

$$\text{Total Adjustment to Separation Score} = \frac{\Sigma \text{ (items checked} \times \text{weights)}}{\text{Total number of items checked}}$$

Now that you have finished answering the questions will you please give us your honest estimate of how frankly you were able to answer the questions. (check) with complete frankness .....; a good deal .....; some .....; a little .....; none .....

Date filled out ....

II. FAMILY ADJUSTMENTS IN WARTIME (HUSBAND)

Schedule # ....

1. Present age (nearest birthday) ...... 2. Age at marriage ......
   3. Occupation at induction ....
4. Number of brothers and sisters 1 .....; 2 .....; 3 .....; 4 .....;
   5 .....; 6 or more .....

5. How large a family do you finally want to have? 1 .....; 2 .....; 3 .....; 4 or more.....

6. Are your parents: both living .....; mother dead .....; father dead .....?

7. Their marital status (check): married .....; separated .....; divorced .....

HAPPINESS SCORE FOR HUSBAND'S PARENTS (8)

8. How happy were your parents with their marriage? Write *M* for mother's rating; *F* for father's: extraordinarily happy ..+3..; decidedly happy ..+1..; happy ..−1..; somewhat happy ..−2..; average ..−3..; somewhat unhappy ..−3..; unhappy ..−3..; decidedly unhappy ..−3..; extremely unhappy ..−3..

MARITAL ADJUSTMENT ITEMS (9, 10, 11, 12, 13, 14)

9. Everything considered, how happy has your own marriage been for you? (check) extraordinarily happy ..+3..; decidedly happy ..+1..; happy ..−1..; somewhat happy ..−2..; average ..−3..; somewhat unhappy ..−3..; unhappy ..−3..; decidedly unhappy ..−3..; extremely unhappy ..−3..

10. Prior to induction into the service did you and your wife engage in outside interests together? (check) all of them ..+2..; most of them ..0..; some of them ..−1..; few of them ..−2..; none of them ..−2..

11. Did you ever regret your marriage? (check) frequently ..−2..; occasionally ..−2..; rarely ..−1..; never ..+2..

12. How satisfied, on the whole, are you with your marriage? (check) entirely satisfied ..+3..; very much satisfied ..+1..; satisfied ..−1..; somewhat satisfied ..−2..; somewhat dissatisfied ..−3..; dissatisfied ..−3..; entirely dissatisfied ..−3..

13. Check the items in the following list which you enjoy in your marriage: companionship with partner ..1/3..; mutual understanding ..1/3..; fighting and making up ..1/3..; same outside interests ..1/3..; health of partner ..1/3..; interesting work ..1/3..; good management of financial problems ..1/3..; enough money to spend ..1/3..; freedom ..1/3..

14. Indicate your approximate agreement or disagreement with your wife on the following things as of the period immediately preceding

your entrance into the service. Do this for each item by putting a check in the column which shows extent of your agreement or disagreement.

Check One Column for Each Item Below	Always Agree	Almost Always Agree	Occa- sionally Dis- agree	Fre- quently Dis- agree	Almost Always Dis- agree	Always Dis- agree
Handling family finances						
Matters of recreation						
Religious matters						
Demonstration of affection						
Friends						
Sex relations						
Child care and discipline						
Table manners						
Matter of conventionality						
Philosophy of life						
Ways of dealing with husband's parents						
Ways of dealing with wife's parents						
Things that are funny						
Ambition and future plans						
Moral code						
Wife working						
Weights[a]	+2	+1	0	−1	−2	−3

[a] Extent of Agreement Score = Σ (checks × weights)

15. What aspects of family life do you miss? (write *1*, if very much; *2*, if some; *3*, if hadn't noticed; *4*, if relieved to be free of) family table talk .....; providing for the family .....; stepping out with the wife .....; playing with your children .....; visits to your parents .....; tenderness of intimate life with wife .....; evening welcome from children .....; chores and fixing things at home .....; feeling of family dependent on you .....; family quarrels and brawls .....; sheer satisfaction of sex hungers .....; responsibility of making decisions for family .....; other things you miss (please write in and rate) ....

Total Marital Adjustment Score = Σ of scores obtained from items 9, 10, 11, 12, 13, and 14.

16. Has your family been a factor in improving or hurting your morale? (check those which apply in your case) worry about children growing up and not knowing me ..−1..; finances at home worry me ..−1..; wonder if wife is stepping out on me ..−1..; wife working gives me concern for afterward ..−1..; family gives me something to work for ..+1..; have someone who cares ..+1..; gives me someone to write to ..+1..; the one thing I dream about most ..+1..; makes me a better soldier than if I were a single man ..+1..; makes me wish I hadn't been drafted or hadn't enlisted ..−1..; ties me down, not as free when on leave ..−1..; family troubles at home get me down ..−1..; at least I have something to go back to ..+1..

17. Have you found anything in the army to substitute in part for the intimate response and affection of family life? (check) letters .....; religious services .....; close friendships with men in outfit .....; pinups .....; talking things out with the chaplain, Red Cross officers, etc. .....; U.S.O. and Red Cross Club parties .....; women .....; other substitutes (you can state best what they are) ....
....

18. Write a summary statement giving your personal reactions and adjustments to life away from your family—do you think there is such a thing as growing away from wife and lovèd ones, as some writers claim? Has home and family faded out and army life become the only reality? A frank statement from hundreds of men like you will help answer this puzzling question. Thank you. ....
....
....

19. Now that you have finished answering the questions will you please give us your honest estimate of how frankly you were able to answer them. (check) with complete frankness .....; a good deal .....; some .....; a little .....; none .....
Other comments you may wish to make about home and family problems of servicemen ....
....
....

Date filled out ....

III. ADJUSTMENTS TO REUNION (WIFE)

Schedule # . . . .

A. Place a check (√) before any of the following statements which represent your feelings about your reunion, your marriage, or your husband. Check as many or as few as describe your feelings and be sure to read all statements.

Weights

..5..   1. I feel at home with husband again as if we were old companions.

..5..   2. The void which existed all the time he was absent is filled now and I feel again like a complete person.

..1..   3. We are still strangers living in separate worlds—don't use the same terms—he's still an army (navy) man.

..3..   4. There are some things we don't talk about, particularly his war experiences; otherwise we converse freely enough.

..4..   5. I don't think anyone could possibly be happier than my husband and I are with one another.

..5..   6. I'm beginning to be able to predict my husband's reactions, his moods and joys again—now and again we burst out with the same expressions simultaneously.

..4..   7. We have quarrels and arguments about a few things but we both care more about the relationship than we do about winning the battle so we eventually kiss and make up.

..1..   8. If it weren't for fear of hurting my husband I would leave him.

..5..   9. Having him home has not so much brought problems as it has given me a new enthusiasm for life.

..2.. 10. The separation has changed our relationship for the worse—we can't start in where we left off at all.

..3.. 11. I run the house and kids and he runs his end of things, but we have terrific arguments if either interferes or does any back-seat driving.

..2.. 12. I find my friends mean more to me than my husband because they understand me.

..2.. 13. My husband has forgotten how to live in a family—wants order, discipline, and obedience.

..5.. 14. Our marriage is stronger now than ever because it's a tested relationship.

..2.. 15. My husband pays more attention to the children than to me.

..2.. 16. He forgets I've been on my own for some time and wants to boss me as he did when we were first married.

..3.. 17. It was easier managing the children with him gone—now they play us off against each other.

..4.. 18. I wouldn't call our reunion adjustments completely successful, but I'm pretty well content.

..4.. 19. As the time he has been back increases we have fewer conflicts.

..1.. 20. We are seriously considering separation and divorce.

B. Check in the appropriate boxes below those which best describe your feelings of belongingness and tenderness toward your husband during the recent events of V-J Day, your reunion and afterward.

	Entrance into Service	After 6 mos. in Service	V-J Day	Reunion Day	Month After Discharge
Felt extremely close to husband	☐	☐	☐	☐	☐
Felt close to husband	☐	☐	☐	☐	☐
Average good relations	☐	☐	☐	☐	☐
Felt indifferent to husband	☐	☐	☐	☐	☐
Felt no ties to to husband	☐	☐	☐	☐	☐

$$\text{Adjustment to Reunion Score (Wife)} = \frac{\Sigma \text{ (items checked} \times \text{weights)}}{\text{Number of items checked}}$$

IV. ADJUSTMENTS TO REUNION (HUSBAND)

Schedule # ....

A. Place a check ($\sqrt{}$) before any of the following statements which represent your feelings about your reunion, your marriage or your wife. Check as many or as few as describe your feelings and be sure to read all statements.

Weights

..5.. 1. I feel at home with wife again as if we were old companions.

..5.. 2. The void which existed while I was separated from my family is filled now and I feel again like a complete person.

..1.. 3. We are still strangers living in separate worlds—we don't use the same terms—my wife has no understanding of the things I've been through.

..3.. 4. There are some things we don't talk about, particularly my war experiences; otherwise we converse freely enough.

..4.. 5. I don't think anyone could possibly be happier than my wife and I are with one another.

..5.. 6. I'm beginning to be able to predict my wife's reactions, her moods and joys again—now and again we burst out with the same expression simultaneously.

..4.. 7. We have quarrels and arguments about a few things but we both care more about the relationship than we do about winning the battle so we eventually kiss and make up.

..1.. 8. If it weren't for fear of hurting my wife I would leave her.

..5.. 9. Being here with my wife and family has not so much caused problems as it has given me a new enthusiasm for life.

..2.. 10. The separation has changed our relationship for the worse—we can't start in where we left off at all.

..3.. 11. We have a division of labor worked out and are each supreme in our spheres but we have terrific arguments if either interferes in the other's sphere of activity.

..2.. 12. I find my friends mean more to me than my wife since I've been out because they understand me.

..2.. 13. One of our difficulties is that the housework is poorly organized and there's no order to the way things are run.

..5.. 14. Our marriage is stronger now than ever because it's a tested relationship.

..2.. 15. My wife pays more attention to the children than to me.

..3.. 16. My wife has been running the home for so long she forgets and tries to order me around, too.

..3.. 17. My wife spoils the children or is too inconsistent in her discipline—kids need a firm hand.

..4.. 18. I wouldn't call our reunion adjustments completely successful, but I'm pretty well content.

..4.. 19. As the time I have been back increases we have fewer conflicts.

..1.. 20. We are seriously considering separation and divorce.

..2.. 21. The children are a source of irritation to me.

B. Check in the appropriate boxes below those which best describe your feelings of belongingness and tenderness toward your wife during the recent events of V-J Day, discharge and reunion.

	Entrance into Service	After 6 mos. in Service	V-J Day	Reunion Day	Month After Discharge
Felt extremely close to wife	☐	☐	☐	☐	☐
Felt close to wife	☐	☐	☐	☐	☐
Average good relations	☐	☐	☐	☐	☐
Felt indifferent to wife	☐	☐	☐	☐	☐
Felt no ties to wife	☐	☐	☐	☐	☐

$$\text{Adjustment to Reunion Score (Husband)} = \frac{\Sigma\,(\text{items checked} \times \text{weights})}{\text{Number of items checked}}$$

V. FAMILY ADJUSTMENTS IN WARTIME (INTERVIEWER)

Schedule # .... Interviewer .... Date ....

I. THE FAMILY SINCE INDUCTION

A. Living Arrangements of Family

1. How did you come to select this place to live? ....
....

2. What are your sleeping arrangements? ....
....

3. What do you think of the practice of moving in with wife's parents or husband's parents? ....

B. Adjustments of Wife to Separation
   1. Affectional relations
      (a) What sort of understanding did you and your husband have before his induction concerning his relations with women and your relations with men? (be sure and get both) ....

      (b) How have you been getting along without your husband?

      (c) What affectional substitutes have you found for your husband? Where do affections center now?
         1. Increased satisfaction in friends of same sex? ....
         2. Do you love children more? ....
         3. Have you found male friends of your husband or other men friends a source of companionship? ....
         4. Have you found no satisfactory outlet? ....
   Comment ....

   2. Changing roles
      (a) Are you working? .... Do you enjoy it? .... If working, what are reasons for working? If not, what are reasons for not working? ....

      (b) Do you feel you are permanently more self-sufficient, better able to fend for yourself, to make your own decisions regarding social engagements, children, and spending money, or do you long to be dependent again? ....

      (c) Do you now feel capable of earning your own living if necessary? Yes ..... No .....; Comment, if yes, doing what? If not, why not? ....

   3. (a) Do you notice any increased symptoms of nervousness, increased smoking, trembling, sleeplessness, headaches, nervous indigestion, etc., which might be due to the strains of separation?

(b) *Interviewer* will include his own observations of symptoms of tension, malaise, personality conflict? ....

....

....

4. What has been your most difficult problem during the period of separation? Living arrangements, the children, loneliness, neighbors? ....

....

C. Adjustments of Children to Separation (use first initial for each sibling referred to)

1. Breaking the affectional relation with the father

    (a) How did each child react to the departure of the father, immediately and later on? ....

    ....

    ....

    (b) Any substitutes sought for father? (other men, uncles, grandfathers, teachers, shown more dependence than ever on mother, more independence) ....

    ....

2. Are children harder to control? Yes ..... No ...... In what ways? ....

....

3. What are your methods for handling unruly conduct, e.g. smashing a window, smearing mud on slip covers, hurting other children? ....

....

....

4. Is the father remembered as human by children, merely a photograph, or idealized? ....

....

5. What evidences of antagonism, anxiety, nervousness, and tension are present to show child is missing father?

    (a) Motor, gastro-intestinal, mental symptoms (describe) ......

    ....

    (b) Antagonism, resentment, disinterest, apathy (describe) .....

    ....

    (c) Concern about safety of father, talk of death, killing, bombing, displacement of tension on playmates (describe) ....

    ....

(d) Other symptoms (describe) ....
....
(e) Doesn't miss father ....

D. Nature and frequency of family interaction during the husband's period in service to date.
1. Number of furloughs home ...... Total days.....
2. Visits of wife and/or children to camps in U. S. ...... Total days .....
3. Wife living at camp with husband. Total months .....
4. Frequency of letter writing during period since induction.

First Six Months of Service   Last Six Months
(a) Wife (per month) ....
(b) Husband (per month) ....
(c) Children (per month) ....

Do Parties Enjoy More Writing and Receiving
Letters Last Six Months Than at First?
More ..... Same ..... Less .....
More ..... Same ..... Less .....
More ..... Same ..... Less .....

5. Do letters of wife follow any definite pattern? What do you write to your husband about? ....
....

6. What is pattern of husband's letters? Interviewer should examine excerpts if wife willing and describe briefly the topics discussed, the adequacy of communication. Is it hello-good-by or something more revealing of life in service and inner thoughts of man? ...
....
....

7. Do you frequently tuck in such items as the following? (check) cartoons .....; snapshots of yourself and children, friends, places visited .....; notes or drawings from children .....; clippings of the newspapers, events he would have enjoyed .....; samples of dress material you are using, locks of hair from children, homey mementos .....; presents .....; other ..... please state
....

8. What happened when husband returned on furlough? What did you do with your time and how did it seem to be back together

again? (Did you spend it mostly alone, with parents, with children, with former friends, with new friends; were alone little?)

. . . .
. . . .

9. Did furloughs help or hurt your adjustment to separation? (Follow this question with "how" or "what do you mean"?) Did you feel reassured or was there a note of uncertainty? . . . .

. . . .

10. What were reactions of children to the father during the furlough? . . . .

. . . .
. . . .

11. Compare the roles played by husband and wife and children during furlough with the pre-induction roles in the marriage (write up at end of interview). . . . .

. . . .
. . . .
. . . .
. . . .

12. In your letters, furloughs, and visits, have plans been discussed for when he gets back? . . . . . (If so, what do they include—added education for husband, husband takes old job, new job, plans to set up business for self, wife continues working, stops work, both work and save for house—elaborate, showing anxieties, hopes, anticipations.) . . . .

. . . .

13. What do you think will be your biggest problem of adjustment when he returns? . . . .

. . . .
. . . .

14. (a) Approximate income (monthly) six months before induction . . . . Approximate expenditure . . . .
    (b) Present income (monthly) (allotment plus whatever husband sends and wife's earning, if any) . . . .
    (c) Approximate savings up to induction . . . . Induction point to date . . . .
    (d) Indebtedness up to induction . . . . Induction to date . . . .

(e) Primary source of income at induction (wages, salary, fees, investments, inheritance) ....

II. PRE-INDUCTION MARITAL AND FAMILY PATTERNS AND ORGANIZATION

A. Roles Formed During Courtship
  1. How did you and your husband first meet? (Describe briefly the involvement process and the adequacy of the courtship and engagement.) ....
  ....
  ....
  2. How well did you get along with each other before marriage? Many people quarrel more before than after. Did you? ....
  ....

B. Roles Formed in the Marriage
  Out of the adjustments of the early years of marriage family members find roles which are more or less comfortable for them to play which help to preserve harmony in the family. Show the roles played by each member prior to husband's induction into the service.
  1. Dominance-submission in husband-wife relation (check). Who is most frequently the boss?
  ..... husband much stronger, assertive, dominant, leading, responsibility-assuming
  ..... husband somewhat stronger
  ..... husband and wife equal
  ..... husband somewhat weaker
  ..... husband much weaker, non-assertive, passive, dependent
  Explain basis for checking. ....
  ....
  2. Social role played by wife in marriage (check). Is she a:
  ..... partner (works outside the home and/or pools earning and/or is person in own right)
  ..... wife and mother (traditional role)
  ..... companion (exists to please and entertain husband, clothes horse, an ornament, wears clothing and jewelry as means of conspicuous consumption)
  ..... other, invalid, sister role, etc., state ....
  Explain basis for checking ....
  ....

422   FAMILIES UNDER STRESS

3. Method of handling the family purse. Who controls the purse strings?
..... Husband handles all money
..... wife has allowance
..... joint checking account, husband handles most bills
..... joint checking account, wife handles most bills
..... wife handles all money

4. Method of settling disagreements. When they arise, they usually result in:
..... husband giving in most of time
..... wife giving in most of time
..... arguing it out until we reach agreement
..... other, state ....
Explain the basis for checking ....
....

5. To whom does the marriage mean the most? (check) husband
..... wife ...... Comment ....

6. What evidence is there of exploitation in the marriage relationship? ....
....

C. What were the most bothersome problems the family was facing *just before induction* and how were they solving them? (child discipline, in-laws, health, housing, mounting expenses, job troubles, sex satisfactions, nervousness of any member, clashing temperaments, differences as to what's funny and what's important, drinking, petty personal habits, jealousy of other men or women, disagreement about number of children to have, religion, handling of money, etc.) ....
....
....
....

D. From the discussion in Paragraph C and answers to the questions below, construct a picture of the pre-induction personality pattern of the wife, as follows:

GUIDE TO INTERVIEWER ONLY!

(a) How would you describe the temperamental traits of your parents individually, with the following guide: depressive, cheerful, irritable, conscientious, indifferent, prudish, tolerant, optimistic, pessimistic, unfeeling, affectionate, understanding? (b) Did they encourage you in your plans? Did they praise and reward your accomplishments?

(c) Would you consider that you had come from a well-adjusted family? (d) Did their attitude foster any feeling of inferiority? (e) Did their attitude foster certain of your ideas about raising a family, about marriage? (f) Did you have any special attachment to father or mother? (g) Did you have any timidity before or antagonism toward either parent? If so, when and why did this come about? (h) Have you been on a frank or formal footing with your parents? (i) Have you been on friendly terms with your brothers and sisters? If not, on what grounds is there difficulty? Do you have an older brother or sister who has been especially friendly and a source of inspiration? (j) Do you feel you are emancipated from home and parents? (k) Along what lines do you still turn to the home for advice and decision?

---

1. Wife's parental family and its relationship to her personality development ....
    ....
    ....
    ....

GUIDE TO INTERVIEWER ONLY!

(a) Are you naturally cheerful or inclined to depression or worry, or is this variable with you? (b) Are you usually aware of what produces the changes or do they seem to come from a clear sky? (c) Are you optimistic or pessimistic? (d) Have you a good sense of humor? (e) Do you get sullen or sulk, or hold resentment? Can you be cheerful or gay at will? (f) How do you react to disappointment, to trouble, to competition? (g) Are you irritable, impatient, fault finding? If so, what situations bring out this aspect of you? (h) Are you easily frightened? Do you indulge in forebodings about the future? (i) Are your feelings easily hurt? (j) How do you react to success in others? Is it easy to congratulate them? (k) Under what circumstances do you work best—i.e., by schedule, impulse, under pressure, or how? (l) Have you always the energy you wish for, or does this fluctuate? (m) Can you make judgments easily or are you vacillating? (n) What circumstances bring out uneasiness or blushing? (o) Are you overconscientious, superstitious? (p) Do you have any specific acts, habits, or thoughts which are a source of worry, doubt, or remorse to you?

---

2. Wife's temperamental make-up at time of induction of husband
. . . .
. . . .

E. From the discussion in Paragraph C above and from other materials gathered during the interview summarize the pre-induction role patterns of husband, wife, and children (see instruction sheet).

1. Note continuity of roles from parental family, e.g., dominant or spoiled child or demanding or coöperative roles and way that affects the interdependence of spouses and the development of complementary role patterns—show the extent to which spouses are interdependent. . . . .
. . . .
. . . .

2. Show place of the children as solidifying or frustrating or divisive factors on husband-wife adjustments as they are added to the family. Note quality of husband-wife relationship and compare with father-child and mother-child ties. Note affectional services members render each other. . . . .
. . . .
. . . .

FAMILY ADAPTABILITY SCALE

F. Classify the family as to adaptability *before induction* using the following scale.

1. Degree of non-materialistic philosophy. Question: When your husband went into service, what were the sacrifices which you hated most to make?

Weights 5	4	3	2	1
. . . . . cul-	. . . . .	. . . . . af-	. . . . .	. . . . .
tural	same, but	fectional	physical	would
and/or	less	and physi-	standard	make any
affectional	extreme	cal aspects	of living	sacrifice
values		both ap-	more im-	to main-
highly		preciated	portant	tain
esteemed;		and val-	than cul-	physical
disregard		ued	tural	standard
for physi-				
cal stand-				
ard of				
living				

2. Pattern of family control and flow of authority. Question: How are decisions made which involve all members of the family?

Weights	5	4	3	2	1
	. . . .	. . . .	. . . . fa-	. . . .	. . . . no
	family council, demo- cratic home	parents equally important	ther the "head"	mother "head" or sibling	apparent leadership

3. Willingness to shift roles. Question: Are husband and wife able to shift or reverse the traditional roles of father and mother when occasion demands?

Weights	2½	1	½
	. . . . father helps with housework and dishes	. . . . father helps grudgingly and ap- pears ashamed	. . . . father never helps in house or cares for babies

Weights	2½	1	½
	. . . . father adapts or would adapt to wife working with- out chagrin	. . . . father allows wife to work but is ashamed	. . . . father insists woman's place is in the home, would starve first

Weights	5	2	1
	. . . . mother en- joys or would en- joy equally well wife and mother and working part- ner role	. . . . mother will work but feels it's wrong	. . . . mother insists husband should earn the money and wants no man messing up her kitchen

4. Degree of responsibility assumed in the family. Question: How eager are members of the family to assume responsibilities to help out in the family duties? (Use symbols F for father, M for mother, and S^1 for oldest sibling, S^2 for next and so on, score only those 12 years and older.) Cite examples . . . .
. . . .

Weights	5	4	3	2	1
	.....	..... ac-	.....	.....	.....
	grasps at	cepts even	reasonable	dislikes	very irre-
	added	when very	acceptance	responsi-	sponsible
	responsi-	difficult		bility,	
	bilities			inclined	
				to be irre-	
				sponsible	

5. Previous experience in meeting crises. Question: Have you in your married life ever encountered any of the following blows—death in the family, loss of job, infidelity, desertion, serious illness? How did you react as a family? Have you recovered from it? Describe

. . . .

. . . .

Weights	5	4	3	2	1
	..... has	.....	....had	.....	.....
	adapted	made	no previ-	crisis but	very
	well to	satisfac-	ous crisis	not very	poor ad-
	previous	tory ad-		good ad-	justment
	crisis and	justment		justment,	to crisis,
	felt the			or still in	never
	crisis had			process of	fully
	been of			adjust-	recovered
	ultimate			ment	
	value				

Total Family Adaptability Score = Σ (items checked $\times$ weights)

FAMILY INTEGRATION SCALE

G. Classify the family as to integration before induction on the following scale:

  1. Degree of Affection. How close are members of the family affectionally? (If data inadequate check with wife.)

Weights	5/4	4/4	3/4	2/4	1/4
father and	.... deeply	.... in love	.... aver-	.... imper-	.... es-
mother	and obviously	more than	age, congenial,	sonal relation	tranged or very
	in love	average	loyal		detached

Weights	$\frac{5}{4}$	$\frac{4}{4}$	$\frac{3}{4}$	$\frac{2}{4}$	$\frac{1}{4}$
mother and children	.... extremely close relations to all children	.... closer than average	.... average, good relations with all children	.... some friction, favoritism, or detachment	.... much friction or great detachment

Weights	$\frac{5}{4}$	$\frac{4}{4}$	$\frac{3}{4}$	$\frac{2}{4}$	$\frac{1}{4}$
father and children	.... extremely close relations to all children	.... closer than average	.... average, good relations with all children	.... some friction, favoritism, or detachment	.... much friction or great detachment

Weights	$\frac{5}{4}$	$\frac{4}{4}$	$\frac{3}{4}$	$\frac{2}{4}$	$\frac{1}{4}$
children with each other	.... all very closely bound together	.... above average affection	.... passing friction only, average	.... friction minor but continuous	.... great friction

2. Extent to which the family engaged in joint activities or discussion. Question: How frequently did you get out as a family to social activities?

Weights	5	4	3	2	1
Joint Activities	.... do everything together	.... do most things together	.... enough things done as a family to maintain unity	.... few family activities, many individual activities	.... almost none; most activities individual

3. Willingness to sacrifice to attain family objectives. Question: Do you have family objectives and goals which are so important that you subordinate your own individual desires to these goals? Describe ....

....

Weights	5	4	3	2	1
degree of coöperation for family goals	.... make extreme sacrifices for family; great amount of coöperation	.... sacrifices if crisis makes necessary	.... moderate sacrifices but also maintained own interests	.... reluctant to sacrifice or coöperate, few family objectives	.... refuse to sacrifice or coöperate, no family objectives

4. Degree of esprit de corps. Question: Do either or both of you impress your children with pride in the family tree, in the line you have come from, in your illustrious forebears? Put *H* in proper spot for husband and *W* for wife.

Weights	$\frac{5}{2}$	$\frac{4}{2}$	$\frac{3}{2}$	$\frac{2}{2}$	$\frac{1}{2}$
	.....	.....	.....	.....	.....
	extreme pride in family style of living, in ancestors	great family pride	"average" thinks family all right	accepts family but would like to make changes	dislikes style of family life, would like to forget origins

5. Degree to which solidarity is present. Question: How interdependent do you feel as a family, are you dependent on one another for happiness, is there a feeling of unity?

Weights	5	4	3	2	1
	. . . . .	. . . . .	. . . . .	. . . . .	. . . . .
	extreme feeling of unity	more than average unity	loose noose, average unity	some dissatis- faction	feeling of tension and desire to break away

Total Family Integration Score $= \Sigma$ (items checked $\times$ weights)

H. Classify family on the following continuum of affectional relationships as of the period immediately before induction (see instruction sheet for definitions):

Excess of Affection	Normal Affection	Discrimination in Affection
. . . . . the possessive home	. . . . . the compan- ionable home	. . . . . the divided home
. . . . . the oversolic- itous home		. . . . . the favored- child home
. . . . . the overin- dulgent home		. . . . . the "impar- tial" home
		. . . . . the favored- parent home

Inconsistency of Affection	Lack of Affection	Frank Rejection
. . . . . the bickering home	. . . . . the nagging home	. . . . . the home of the unwanted child
. . . . . the unreliable home	. . . . . the frigid home	. . . . . the home of the unwanted mate
	. . . . . the neglectful home	

Explain basis for checking . . . .

SOCIAL STATUS SCALE

I. Scale for rating of four status characteristics of family before induction. (Note house type while out on interview.) Check:

House Type

..1.. large houses in good condition

..2.. large houses in medium condition and medium sized

..3.. medium sized houses in medium condition and all remodeled houses

..4.. large houses in bad condition and medium sized houses in bad condition

..5.. small houses in good condition and all dwellings over stores

..6.. small houses in medium and bad condition

..7.. Houses of any size in very bad condition

Occupation

..1.. large professionals, large proprietors and managers

..2.. small professionals

..3.. clerks and kindred workers

..4.. skilled workers

..5.. small proprietors and managers, farmers

..6.. semiskilled workers

..7.. unskilled workers

..... other, state ....

Primary Source of Income

..1.. savings and investments, inherited

..2.. savings and investments, gained by earner

..3.. profits and fees

..4.. salary

..5.. wages

..6.. private relief

..7.. public relief and non-respectable income

Status as Families

..... old families, original settlers

..... well-to-do families but not natives

..... well-to-do immigrant families of low status nationality

..... respectable, but not socially known

..... known ne'er-do-wells, bottoms, no-goods

..... other, newcomers undefined status, etc., state

....

Area Lived In

..1.. exclusive part of town   ..4.. business sections
..2.. next best part of town,   ..5.. mill and factory sections
      new sections   ..6.. across the tracks, bottoms,
..3.. respectable sections, but   slums
      mixed types

J. Are you willing to continue coöperation with the project? Yes .....
No ..... Comment ....

K. Interviewer's summary of entire case (see instructions for content of
summary). ....
....
....
....
....

A. ADJUSTMENTS TO THE REUNION (WIFE)

1. What expectations did you have for your family when the husband
   came home? (Did you expect to return to a more dependent role,
   that of wife and mother, or did you hope things would be different
   because of your training in self-reliance during the separation?) ....
   ....
   ....

2. What were you most worried about in anticipating the reunion? ...
   ....

3. Under what circumstances did the reunion take place? (honeymoon
   together or entire family) ....
   ....

4. Would you arrange the reunion differently if you were to plan it over
   again? ....
   ....

5. Now that you are together again in what ways do you feel the service
   misfits or helps a man fit into family life? Does it make him more
   difficult to live with, hard to understand, or how would you put it?
   ....
   ....
   ....

6. Are you and the children as well prepared for total family living as
   you were before the separation? Yes ..... No ..... In what ways

did living with a husband and father prove difficult during the first weeks of reunion? ....

....

....

7. Have you experienced a period of disillusionment concerning family life with the father home? ....

....

8. Do you still play father and mother too to the children, making most of the decisions with regard to child discipline, finances, entertainment, as during the separation? ....

....

9. What problems are most frequently the subject for prolonged heated discussion (what to do for a living, where to live, children, wife working)? Do they differ from the things you quarreled about before he went into service? ....

....

....

....

10. How have you solved these problems of adjustment? ....

....

11. Specifically, how have you and husband helped the children to accept him? ....

....

....

12. Will you continue coöperation with this project to record the later adjustments to reunion? ....

13. Other comments on reunion adjustment ....

....

....

B. ADJUSTMENTS TO THE REUNION (CHILDREN)

—interview with wife/or husband—

1. What were expectations of each child in contemplating father's homecoming? ....

....

....

2. Describe the circumstances of the reunion from the children's per-

spective, indicating reticence, withdrawal, reservations, jealousy, if
any. . . . .
. . . .

3. In what roles is the father now acceptable to the children (put each
child's name in appropriate spot)?
. . . .   (a) entertainer, storyteller, playmate
. . . .   (b) fixer of broken toys, household equipment, etc.
. . . .   (c) source of loving, hugging
. . . .   (d) father confessor—person who can be told tales of
woe and secrets too
. . . .   (e) disciplinarian, taking over from mother
. . . .   (f) earner and supplier of good things
. . . .   (g) head of the house
. . . .   (h) mother's sweetheart
. . . .   (i) other . . . .
4. What things does father or mother do which are most likely to cause
friction and irritation? . . . .
. . . .
5. What progress, if any, in adjustment of children to father has oc-
curred since the reunion? . . . .
. . . .
. . . .
6. How do you account for the success or failure of the father to win
the children during first few weeks? . . . .
. . . .
. . . .
7. Other comments on children's reactions . . . .
. . . .
. . . .

C. ADJUSTMENTS TO THE REUNION (HUSBAND)

Conversation opener: What do you think of the country's drafting fa-
thers? . . . .
1. Length of period of separation: months . . . . . How long have you
been home with family? months . . . . .
2. (a) Hazards of military experience (for Air Forces: no. of missions
. . . . .; for Ground Forces: days in combat zone . . . . .; for
Navy: no. of combat stars . . . . .). Comment . . . .
. . . .

(b) Highest rank attained .... Assignments ....

....

(c) Reasons for discharge from the service ....

....

3. What sort of dreams did you use to have about home and family?

....

4. What hopes plans, anticipations did you have for the reunion? .....

....

5. What anxieties and fears did you experience in anticipating the homecoming? ....

....

6. Now that you are back with your family again, what evidence can you give for or against the assertion that life in the service misfits a man for family life? ....

....

    (a) Do children seem more irritating than before you went into service? ....

....

    (b) Are family routines less well organized than you remembered them? ....

....

    (c) Do you find yourself expecting orders to be obeyed quickly and without question by wife and children? ....

....

    (d) Are you as comfortable in your role as father in the family as you were in the service? ....

....

    (e) Do the responsibilities of family life seem burdensome? ......

....

    (f) Have your views about marriage and family life changed since returning? ....

....

    (g) Have the wife and children been able to replace the close ties, the feeling of belonging which men found in the service? .....

    (h) Do you find need for associations outside the family with other returned veterans? ....

....

7. Has living alone without the father made the family more difficult to live with? Is wife too independent, too self-sufficient? Do children

seem undisciplined? ....

....

8. How have you solved these problems of adjustment? ....

....

9. Specifically, how did you go about winning the children? ....

....

10. What are your immediate plans for yourself and family?
    (a) with respect to a job or further education? ....

....

    (b) with respect to wife working? ....

....

    (c) with respect to housing and living arrangements? ....

....

11. Will you be willing to coöperate with us in recording your adjust-
    ments and achievements in the later stages of the reunion? ....
12. Comments ....

....

....

....

INDEX

INDEX

437

442